Urban Girls Revisited

Urban Girls Revisited
Building Strengths

EDITED BY

Bonnie J. Ross Leadbeater and Niobe Way

New York University Press

NEW YORK AND LONDON

NEW YORK UNIVERSITY PRESS
New York and London
www.nyupress.org

Library of Congress Cataloging-in-Publication Data

Urban girls revisited: building strengths / edited by Bonnie J.
Ross Leadbeater and Niobe Way.
p. cm.
Includes bibliographical references and index.
ISBN-13: 978-0-8147-5212-8 (cloth : alk. paper)
ISBN-10: 0-8147-5212-8 (cloth : alk. paper)
ISBN-13: 978-0-8147-5213-5 (pbk. : alk. paper)
ISBN-10: 0-8147-5213-6 (pbk. : alk. paper)
1. Poor teenagers—United States. 2. Teenage girls—United
States. 3. Urban youth—United States. 4. Minority teenagers—
United States. I. Leadbeater, Bonnie J. Ross, 1950– II. Way,
Niobe, 1963–
HV1431.U734 2006
362.7—dc22
2006026373

New York University Press books are printed on acid-free paper,
and their binding materials are chosen for strength and durability.

Manufactured in the United States of America

c 10 9 8 7 6 5 4 3 2 1
p 10 9 8 7 6 5 4 3 2 1

To Emilie and Chiara

Contents

Acknowledgments

We would like to thank not only the many contributors who are represented in this volume but also the many others who supported us by considering contributions but could not fit this into their busy schedules. Research with urban girls is burgeoning, and the richness of this work inspires us all to keep the momentum going.

Also many, many, many thanks to Shelley Booth at the University of Victoria, who organized all the manuscripts and prepared them for the publisher with unfailing patience, commitment, and determination. Thanks also to Shelley's assistant, Jonathan Patterson, who helped to edit, format, and check each of the chapters and to Sarah Gersick, who proofed the entire manuscript.

Thanks also to Jennifer Hammer, our editor and champion at NYU Press and to Despina Papazoglou Gimbel, the managing editor at NYU Press. We could not accomplish this work without their support.

Preface

Niobe Way

In response to an absence of girls and women in psychological research, researchers began in the early 1980s, with Carol Gilligan and her students from the School of Education at Harvard University leading the way, to investigate the development of girls and women. This research highlighted girls' and young women's strengths and strategies of resistance to conventions of femininity and the ways in which cultural constructions of gender shape girls' and women's development (Brown & Gilligan, 1992; Jack, 1991; Gilligan, 1982; Taylor et al., 1995). The focus on the development and strengths of girls and women was radical in a field that had long been dominated by the study of boys and men and by a perspective that pathologized girls' and women's development. In the midst of this dramatic shift, psychological researchers also began to note other critical absences in the research on human development. Primary among these was a lack of developmental research on girls and women who were part of ethnic minority and/or poor and working-class communities. Although social science research was being conducted with Black and Latino girls and women from poor and working-class communities, the vast majority of these studies were problem oriented, focusing on issues such as teenage pregnancy, dropping out of school, and drug use.

By the mid-1990s, however, the situation began to change. A small but significant series of studies began to emerge that focused on the development and strengths of girls and women from ethnic minority and/or poor and working-class communities. In response to this work, Bonnie Leadbeater and I decided to edit a book together that showcased the best of these studies. We were interested in including work in this volume that revealed the ways in which *urban* girls and young women, in particular, challenged widespread stereotypes of them, created their own identities, and maintained healthy relationships in the midst of discrimination, poverty, and violence. We focused on urban girls and young women because urban contexts provide the setting for much racial and ethnic diversity and because urban girls and young women were particularly likely to be ignored or misrepresented by the media and by the research community. This was the decade when conservative pundits created the notion of the "welfare queen," and when urban youth, a phrase often confounded by the media and the scholarly community with Black youth, were routinely characterized as neglecting their education in favor of high-risk behavior. Our edited book *Urban Girls: Resisting Stereotypes, Creating Identities* constituted a sustained effort to bring together diverse scholars who were writing about and with urban girls and young women in ways that recognized their vulnerabilities as well as their strengths. It examined the development not only of Black urban girls but also of Latino and White urban girls. *Urban Girls* became a staple on the reading lists of many social science courses and was read widely in professional circles. It has informed, along with other books in this genre, programs and policies that seek to help foster girls' sense of agency and nurture their resilience.

Then, an odd thing happened. Just as we were gaining a more complex understanding of girls' and women's development and improving their lives in concrete ways, there occurred—in academia but swiftly thereafter in the culture at large—a dramatic shift back to a focus on the development of boys and young men. Books on this topic muscled their way into bookstore windows and talk shows (e.g., Gurian, 1998; Kindlon & Thomson, 1999; Pollack, 1998; Way & Chu, 2004). Popular magazines ran title stories on the damage wreaked on boys by current pedagogical and psychological experts. Social scientists and journalists began to refer to a "boy crisis" that had presumably been undiagnosed and left unchecked, largely because academics and psychologists had been overly concerned with helping girls. It was boys, many claimed, who were neglected by researchers and by policy makers. If the 1990s was considered "the decade of the girl" (see Ward, this volume), then the first decade of the twenty-first century became the decade back to the boy. Evidence of this shift included a daylong conference focused on the healthy development of boys and men in 2004 sponsored by the Ms Foundation for Girls and Women.

The reasons for this shift are complex and include, most likely, the fact that girls and young women started to do better than boys and men by various educational indicators, including college attendance (see López, 2003). The current interest in boys and men is altogether salutary, and the expansion of voice-centered research to include both genders has brought about important new insights. What has been lost, however, in the renewed interest in boys and men is an understanding of the ways in which girls and young women, particularly in urban contexts, continue to resist stereotypes, nurture their own identities and relationships, create safe spaces for themselves, and have the potential to bring or are in the midst of bringing about real social, educational, and political change within and outside of their communities.

When Jennifer Hammer, our editor at NYU Press, approached Bonnie and me to update and edit a second volume of *Urban Girls,* we welcomed the opportunity to supplement the existing volume with more current research. We were interested in bringing together work, even if it was relatively rare compared with that of the mid-1990s, that explored the ways in which urban girls are creating and sustaining positive changes in their lives. After contacting the contributors for *Urban Girls Revisited,* we discovered that despite the heavy emphasis on boys and young men in the popular press, there continues to be a group of researchers who focus on the vulnerabilities and strengths of urban girls and young women. However, the ground has shifted. The construct of "urban" is now more inclusive of girls from different communities in urban contexts (based on race, ethnicity, socioeconomic status, sexual orientation). The language of strength, resilience, and resistance has also changed toward greater emphasis on the context of development and on relationships rather than solely on the individual. And there is a greater focus on the implications for practice and policy.

The chapters in this book reveal the ways in which the language, context, and discussion about urban girls have changed and opened up many new avenues of research and possibilities for intervention. Although the chapters in this book rely on diverse methodologies and samples, the consistent message is that urban girls and young women continue to challenge harmful stereotypes, create their own positive identities, and nurture life sustaining relationships. However, they are not doing it alone. Family members, friends, partners, teachers, and mentors are critical interlocutors and participants in this process of development and change, and these relationships are sources of challenge, contradiction, and strength. This volume offers us a glimpse into the ways in which girls and young women from diverse urban communities are negotiating their relationships within and across various types of institutions (families, schools) and contexts of development and the ways these institutions and contexts both foster and challenge girls' abilities to thrive.

Urban Girls Revisited underscores the necessity of continuing to include urban girls in our conversations about human development and to focus on vulnerabilities *and* strengths of individual girls *and* their communities, and not simply on shortcomings or on individual girls, respectively. It also implicitly and explicitly calls for an expanded view of "urban" and a more contextualized and relational understanding of girls' development so that researchers do not rank according to importance—girls or boys, urban or suburban, the individual or the context—but understand how all these strands are worthy of study in their own right and also shaped by all other strands. Bonnie and I hope that this volume helps to bring "urban girls" back into focus so that our understanding of development in context and of strength and resilience is enhanced and our ability to create better futures for all girls and women is greatly improved.

References

Brown, L. M. & Gilligan. C. (1992). *Meeting at the crossroads: Women's psychology and girls' development.* Cambridge, MA: Harvard University Press.

Gilligan, C. (1982). *In a different voice: Psychological theory and women's development.* Cambridge, MA: Harvard University Press.

Gurian, M. (1998). *A fine young man: What parents, mentors, and educators can do to shape adolescent boys into exceptional men.* New York: Penguin Putnam.

Jack, D. C. (1991). *Silencing the self: Women and depression.* Cambridge, MA: Harvard University Press.

Kindlon, D. & Thompson, M. (1999). *Raising Cain: Protecting the emotional life of boys.* New York: Ballantine.

Lopez, N. (2003). *Hopeful girls, troubled boys: Race and gender disparity in urban education.* New York: Routledge.

Pollack, W.G. (1998). *Real boys: Rescuing our sons from the myths of boyhood.* New York: Random House.

Taylor, J. M., Gilligan, C., & Sullivan, A. M. (1995). *Between voice and silence: Women and girls, race, and relationship.* Cambridge, MA: Harvard University Press.

Way, N. & Chu, J. (2004). *Adolescent boys: Exploring diverse cultures of boyhood.* New York: NYU Press.

Urban Girls
Building Strengths, Creating Momentum

Bonnie J. Leadbeater

A decade has passed since our earlier volume *Urban Girls: Resisting Stereotypes, Creating Identities* was published by NYU Press in 1996. As one of the first books to showcase the lives of girls who were growing up in contexts of urban poverty, violence, and racism, the volume received a lot of attention. It was included in many courses over the years, and Niobe and I hoped that it helped to shape the ways that we understand girls' development and their relationships with peers, parents, and their communities. In my own courses on the psychology of women's development I heard from students who, often for the first time, saw their own stories and those of their friends reflected and explained in the materials they were asked to study. Many of the former articles remain at the cutting edge of research about urban girls, and this new volume builds on this foundation.

In *Urban Girls Revisited: Building Strengths*, we revisit the diversity of urban adolescent girls' development. We focus, in particular, on the sources of support and resilience that help girls to build foundations of personal strengths, interpersonal relationships, and commitments to their communities, as they become young adults. Urban girls *are* frequently marginalized by ethnic and racial discrimination, political neglect, poor education, poverty, parenting as adolescents, dating violence, and high-risk behaviors. However, despite their higher risks for maladaptive outcomes, the majority of girls who are "marked" by such stereotypes show remarkable strengths in the face of these adversities. In this new volume we ask, why and how? Girls living in adverse, inner-city circumstances often grow up fast, taking on multiple adult roles and responsibilities at young ages in contexts of minimal support (Leadbeater & Way, 2001). However, the social ideals of success for today's young women focus almost exclusively on postsecondary schooling, delayed parenting, and career aspirations, and again urban girls fall short in comparisons. However, these can overlook girls' successes as caretakers, businesswomen, or young parents.

Knowledge about girls' identity development in contexts of adversity is still scant. In large-scale studies of risk, urban girls who weather the adversities of their environments well by graduating from high school, living independently, and earning a living wage are captured at the high end of the risk profiles but are rarely the focus of research or policy attention. The continued focus on risk statistics fails to make explicit the motivations and supports that help urban girls become not only successful young adults but also full, participating citizens in their communities and in the labor market, or political processes that affect them. In addition, ethical issues surrounding research with vulnerable minority youth have often led to their exclusion and neglect in research that could benefit them. Innovative solutions to ethical issues (consent, risks for harm, focus group methods, confidentiality, etc.) are emerging in collaborations among researchers, parents, youth, and community leaders (see Leadbeater et al., 2006).

This volume, like its predecessor, brings together many different disciplinary perspectives and methodological approaches. In the chapters in this volume, the researchers variously use qualitative and quantitative, participant-action and participant-observer methods. Together these many viewpoints elucidate the unique paths that young women take to open up opportunities for themselves and to take advantage of opportunities that are available to them. It also joins together an interdisciplinary group of researchers from education, psychology, nursing, sociology, and ethnography who continue to illuminate the diversity of these young women's lives through their work.

Looking Through a Resilience Lens

Research on resilience or strength building has also come a long way in increasing our understanding of how contexts can support young women in their struggle against poverty, discrimination, stereotypes, and urban violence (e.g., Luthar & Cicchetti, 2000; Maton, Shellenbach, Leadbeater,

& Solarz, 2004; Peters, Leadbeater, & McMahon 2005). We use this perspective here to focus specifically on urban girls' development. This is not meant to suggest that we should ignore the contexts of risks, adversities, and problems of urban girls but that we also need to add a lens that focuses on understanding and promoting the positive development, health, and success of these girls.

Research on the concept of resilience has underscored the need for this paradigm shift in our research and policy approaches to understanding and alleviating the negative consequences of a wide range of social problems. This shift requires that we focus our attention on (a) the *diversity* of individual, family, and community responses to adverse circumstances rather than generalized population risks; (b) the *strengths, competencies, and resources* needed for dealing with adversities rather than the deficits, pathologies, and deviance that can result from them; (c) the *long-term pathways* or life-span trajectories that are affected by variations in response to adversities rather than the immediate outcomes; and (d) the *interrelations* among individual, family, and community levels of development rather than the characteristics of adapted individuals. All the chapters in *Urban Girls Revisited* demonstrate how these shifts in the focus of our research frameworks can benefit our understanding of urban girls' development.

As before, we include chapters that show the benefits of a wide variety of interdisciplinary approaches and research methods (quantitative, qualitative, and participatory action and ethnographic). Together these demonstrate how complementary methodologies reveal a more integrated and complex understanding of girls' development than is available through only one discipline or research methodology.

What's New in this Volume?

1. This is the only volume we know of that addresses urban girls' resilience in the context of serious social adversities that include dating and community violence, sexual exploitation, poverty, homelessness, racial and ethnic discrimination, and so on.
2. Strengths and resilience, we argue, are not only characteristics of individual girls but also are located in the contexts of support available to these young women and in the actions, relationships, programs, and policies that support their positive development.

3. New issues are raised in this book about how girls control their own destinies and relationships, how sexuality is not just explored but also brought under their control. Issues are also raised about how safe spaces create the contexts of their successes through many challenges, including not only parent support but also the support of communities from "other mothers," mentors, educators, and even posses. We also hear how young women leave safe spaces and use public spaces for political and social actions.

In this introduction, I address questions created, in part, by *Urban Girls: Resisting Stereotypes, Creating Identities:* What *does* "urban" mean? Why are we interested? I also anticipate a question that is raised by this volume: What are strengths, and how should we understand strengths and protective influences in the contexts of "urban" adversities? I refer to the complexity and diversity of answers that are detailed in chapters of this book and summarize the key messages about strength building that these chapters bring forth. I end with a brief description of how the book is organized and hopes for its use in inviting new researchers into this important field of study.

Urban Girls: Who Are They?

Census definitions of *urban* vary from year to year in the United States, but the term generally, and simplistically, denotes all cities and incorporated places with populations of 2,500 or more (U.S. Census Bureau, 1995, http://www.census.gov/population/censusdata/urdef.txt). In Canada, concerns about urban density also enter into the definition: Urban areas have minimum population concentrations of 1,000 and a population density of at least 400 per square kilometer, based on the previous census population counts (1996 Census Dictionary at www.statcan.ca/bsolc/english/bsolc?catno=92–351-UIE). Neither of these two definitions, however, really typifies the meanings that have gathered around *urban* that we refer to in *Urban Girls.* Rather, this terminology has generally been used to connote the risks for girls that are associated with living in urban cores with high rates of community violence, poverty, drugs, homelessness, inadequate housing, and low rates of resources related to health, education, and social capital.

Concerns about the dangers of urbanization for youth are long-standing. In his book *Rites of Passage: Adolescence in America 1790 to Present*

(1977), Joseph Kett provides early evidence of the view that urban environments challenge positive youth development. In the eighteenth century, secular pressures for vocations, education, and marriage and also innate sins of pride and sensuality made youth, generally boys, who left farms for the city particularly vulnerable to straying from the religious fold. In this context, religious institutions took on the responsibility for protecting youth from the secularizing effects of urbanization (Kett, 1977). The rise in cities of a delinquent, lower class youth culture further augmented the apparent need for character building among youth to ensure their restraint and to prevent the loss of middle-class youth (Kett, 1977). Threats to youth development that continued to be stimulated by declining influences of the church and increasing economic opportunities in cities were answered by the rise of secular counselors and policy regulations aimed at child saving and character building.

Kett (1977) illustrates the new values of these secular youth counselors and child savers, citing Foster's 1820 essay on character building: "Foster listed as a fundamental mark of decisive character, the possession of a 'strenuous will' to accompany decisions of thought. The ablest men move through life with an internal, invincible determination" (p. 105). By the early nineteenth century, economic forces and the need for an educated workforce were accompanied by changes in family roles: Only one breadwinner was needed. Moreover, women's "natural" role as nurturers of the moral culture that was now needed by children threatened by urban environments. As Kett (1977) says:

> Leaders of the urban and commercial sectors of American society insisted that business-like efficiency replace casual, ineffective, sporadic application of discipline in the rearing of the young. At the same time, changes in the social position of women in American society rendered the feminine influence a more portent and self-conscious force than ever before in the nurturing of children. (p. 112)

The belief and, indeed, the reality that dangers of the urban core present adversities for developing youth continues unabated. Fueled by the disappearance of work from inner cities (Wilson, 1987), urban concentrations of poor, minority underclass, welfare recipients, single-parent families, violence, drugs, and low levels of social organization mounted in the twentieth century. In the context of these urban economic challenges, having one breadwinner in a family is not adequate to pull families out of poverty. Women's roles also have again undergone extreme changes. Once again they are breadwinners, parents, educators, and protectors of their children, and at the same time, they remain responsible for their children's character development, control, and nurturance. Given these challenges, can there be little wonder that deficits in urban girls were seen as inevitable?

As Lerner, Phelps, Alberts, Forman, and Christiansen (this volume) point out, social science research in the twentieth century often fueled a deficit view of inner-city or urban youth, who on average showed higher risks and greater deficits than did samples of middle-class youth by falling short compared with the normative (and idealized) developmental achievements of higher-income, suburban, and even rural youth. Urban girls *are* at higher risk for unwanted pregnancies, delinquency, problem behaviors, depression, school dropout, welfare, and low-income jobs. However, we know that these problems are not all-pervasive and rarely apply to the majority of girls. Moreover, risks for problems are a function of the cumulative effects of the adversities that girls face. Indeed, research repeatedly demonstrates that the effects of adversities in family and community contexts add exponentially to the probable occurrence of a number of youth problems (Sameroff, 2000). Adversities can and do interact and mutually influence each other, leading to chronic problems or chains of negative events (Sandler, Ayers, Suter, Schultz, & Twohey-Jacobs, 2004. Adversities (and protective factors) can also fluctuate in frequency and duration for inner-city girls. Adversities also vary in their effects not only on individual needs and motivations but also on their competencies to carry out valued social roles. For example, adversities created by poor parental health can affect parental monitoring, support for school success, stability of family resources, and so forth.

Recent research efforts to understand the diversity of girls' development and the diversity of inner-city contexts and opportunities that lay the foundations for their development are beginning to replace the one-dimensional, deficit-based, limited, stereotypes of urban girls. Chapters in *Urban Girls: Resisting Stereotypes, Creating Identities* emphasized the diversity of young women's identity, relationship, sexual, and career development within the contexts of urban adversities and challenges of inner-city life. This new volume takes the next step by illuminating the personal, family, and community protective factors that support the development of urban adolescent girls and showing the diversity of the pathways they take in responding to available opportunities. With a strengths-based gaze, our attention is broadened beyond the challenges of fixing individuals' deficits and pathologies or punishing their deviance toward illuminating ways to support key protective processes and adaptive outcomes for individuals, families, and communities who are facing adverse circumstances (see Maton et al., 2004).

Where Are Strengths Located?

For urban adolescent girls, the language of strengths characterizes positive development along dimensions that, as Lerner et al. (this volume) point out, include many "Cs" such as competence, confidence, connection, character, caring, control, contributions, and capacities, and for some also include children and condoms. The language of strengths is expanded in chapters of this book. The research also examines the contexts that engage adults to support girls' positive development by, for example, creating safe spaces that afford opportunities for dialogue and personal growth, as well as public spaces that allow for the exposure of social injustices and engagement in political action. Adults' active involvement in caring, advocacy, mentoring, and education of urban girls also characterizes contexts that support positive development.

Since the late 1960s, researchers have investigated the competencies, resilience, resources, and protective processes that lead some individuals to thrive despite adverse life circumstances. The early research emphasized characteristics of individuals that allowed them to pull themselves up by their own bootstraps despite these adversities (Werner & Smith, 1992). This research exposed individual capacities (e.g., high intelligence, easy disposition), personality characteristics (e.g., internal locus of control, sociability and optimism), and achievements (being at grade level, having positive peer relationships) that appeared to compensate for inadequate resources, protect against risks, or help children to resist maladaptive behaviors in adverse circumstances.

However, an almost exclusive attention to individual stress resistance gave rise to outcries against resilience models. Researchers, policy analysts, and service providers rightly feared that emphasis on individuals' or even families' capacities to rise above adversity overlooked the contexts of these problems and perpetuated blaming victims of adverse circumstances for their own deficits or failures to pull themselves up. Even well-meaning efforts to provide services to "fix" or correct perceived individual deficits can negatively stereotype and stigmatize individuals who are subject to ongoing adversities. A singular focus on individuals' strengths and resilience also can deflect research attention, intervention efforts, and funding from community- and institutional-level interventions that could work to correct the adverse circumstances that threaten or overwhelm individual efforts.

More recently, researchers have begun to draw attention to the contextual factors that influence individual differences in responses to adversities and to the necessity of understanding positive development as context based, multidimensional, nonstatic, and process oriented (see reviews by Leadbeater, Shellenbach, Maton, & Dodgen, 2004). In their review of the research on the development of individual competence, Masten and Coatsworth (1998) define resilience as "manifested competence in the context of significant challenges to adaptation or development" (p. 205). They go on to define competence as a "pattern of effective adaptation in the environment either broadly defined in terms of reasonable success with major developmental tasks expected for a given age and gender *in the context of his or her culture, society and time* or more narrowly defined in terms of specific domains of achievement such as academics, peer acceptance, or athletics" (p. 206, emphasis added). In other words, understanding the effects of sociocultural and historical contexts on the development of individuals, families, and communities (e.g., changes in the face of racism, rates of divorce, roles for women, markets, and job opportunities) is essential for understanding and promoting individual competence.

Past research has also suggested that the development of competence in one domain may or may not be accompanied by competence in others. For example, poor, minority children's academic success may be accompanied by their internal struggles with psychological distress rather than good emotional health (Luthar, Doernberger, & Zigler 1999). Moreover, changes in children's competence are often preceded by critical changes in their environmental supports (Egeland, Carlson, & Sroufe, 1993). On the other hand, continued harmful exposure to adverse circumstances such as poverty, unstable housing, or domestic violence can overwhelm resources that support competence, as exemplified in a study of inner-city adolescent mothers' transitions to early adulthood (Leadbeater & Way, 2001). In the course of their life cycles, children, families, and communities develop new vulnerabilities and strengths, and these risk and protective processes, in turn, interact with children's competencies in dealing with subsequent challenges, opportunities, or threats to their well-being (see Taylor, Smith, & Taylor, this volume).

How children and youth develop, maintain, and express competence in contexts of adversity can also vary depending on their developmental stage, family resources and expectations, and environmental circumstances (Cicchetti & Garmezy, 1993; Masten & Coatsworth, 1998; Werner & Smith, 1992). An adolescent, for example, can have an awareness of the importance of planning for the future that a young child does not have. This developing cognition can enhance the adolescent's ability to resist negative behaviors or to maintain adaptive ones when he or she is exposed to delinquent peers. On the other hand, future-oriented youth from communities with high unemployment that offer few prospects for earning a living wage may be more likely to engage in illegal behaviors when exposed to delinquent peers, if they see this as a means for gaining status or resources that are otherwise inaccessible. The adolescent's cognitive gains interact with environmental risks and protective processes to determine his or her adaptive functioning.

Changes in risk and protective factors continue to challenge and support individual competencies across an individual's life span. Competencies are not acquired once and for all and forever. They are reworked in evolving life circumstances that offer new resources and new challenges, suggesting that we would be well advised to think of positive development as *processes* of building strengths and capacities for resilient adaptation rather than personal characteristics or community assets that are present or absent. A process-oriented definition is provided by Pianta and Walsh (1998) who argue, "Resilience is best perceived in terms of a process that involves multiple factors interacting over time, from which occasionally precipitates success in a particular developmental domain or function" (p. 411). The building and maintenance of competence is a function of protective processes that inevitably fluctuate across the life span not only of individuals but also of their families and communities.

Research has also begun to specify the mechanisms of protective processes that operate to support the positive development and maintenance of individual competence. Protective processes include experiences, events, and relationships that *operate* to (a) interrupt or reverse downward developmental trajectories, (b) diminish the causes or impact of stressful situations, (c) reduce the negative chain reactions that characterize pathogenic family or school situations, (d) promote the development and maintenance of self-efficacy, (e) create beliefs or loyalties that are incompatible with deviant behaviors, and (f) provide opportunities for positive education, vocational, and personal growth. Research has also exposed the thresholds where the individual and family processes that support resilient adaptation are overwhelmed and where development falters. Inner-city youth and their families require the same opportunities for health, education, and safety as those not facing urban adversities (Tolan, Sherrod, Gorman-Smith, & Henry, 2004). Identifying and promoting strengths of youth, themselves, in these communities may be one promising approach to relieving social problems in inner-city neighborhoods, but youth also need to be met with opportunities in their communities that take advantage of their emerging enthusiasm and strengths. Identity development is not merely an answer to the question, Who am I? It must also answer the question, but to a young person's community: Who will you recognize in me?

The chapters in this book expand our knowledge of the protective processes that sustain positive development and resilient adaptation among urban girls. We see protective processes that operate in urban environments over time to support their transitions to young adulthood. Girls build on their own successes in the age-salient developmental tasks of growing up—getting an education, career preparation, forming positive relationships, and maintaining mental health (Shaffer, Coffino, Boelcke-Stennes, & Masten). We also see protective processes in their engagement in community action and political activism (Lerner et al.; Torre, Fine, Alexander, & Genao). Protective processes are seen in contexts that extend responsibility for girls' positive development beyond individual families to communities of concerned adults who contribute to the development of girls as "other-mothers" and mentors who create safe spaces for girls' (and often boys') protection and development (see Banister & Leadbeater; López & Lechuga; and Rhodes, Davis, Prescott, & Spencer). Here we see, in action, what Tolan and his colleagues (2004) argue we must do to promote positive development in inner-city youth: "We must reconnect what we would do for all our children with what we would do for inner-city youths; policy must confirm that they are all our children" (p. 208). We see resilient process in the resistance to discrimination and stereotyping that develops through African American girls' protective and empowering relationships with their mothers (Ward; Costigan, Cauce, & Etchison). Protection for immigrant girls also comes in the subtle dance of identifying with and resisting culture-based demands and prohibitions (Lee; López & Lechuga). We see girls' strengths in their courage to stand up for their emerging sexuality and in their ability to gain control of risk for sexually transmitted diseases by using condoms (Denner & Coyle) and resist homophobia (Savin-Williams) and relationship violence (Banister & Leadbeater). Even in contexts of extreme adversity, we see strengths in efforts of street.youth to imagine the exit points that the future may present to them (Benoit, Jansson, & Anderson) and in the businesses created by women who are long-term residents of inner-city Detroit (Taylor, Smith, & Taylor). But the stories are complex and told from very different perspectives using different methodologies. These perspectives and meth ods reverberate (sometimes with dissonance) against each other. Together, they draw a more complete picture of the contributions of research to our understanding of the contexts of adversity that challenge urban girls' development and of girls' and women's responses to these challenges.

We have divided this book into five parts, in each of which the research focuses our attention on the diversity of urban girls' resiliencies and strengths. In part 1, Lerner et al. offer an overview of the elements of urban girls' positive development (conceptualized as the Five Cs: Competence, Confidence, Connection, Character, and Caring) and how these relate to girls' contributions to their communities through leadership, volunteer work, helping friends and families, and valuing engagement. We are also encouraged to look at within-group differences in outcomes as urban girls transition to early adulthood. In the chapter by Shaffer, Coffino, Boelcke-Stennes, and Masten, the value of universal theories about urban girls' emergence into adulthood are questioned. Understanding the challenges and opportunities that fuel differences in the success of different groups of urban girls also requires a renewed effort to understand the trajectories of their lives in the context of both childhood foundations and anticipated opportunities, across the life span.

Part 2 begins with a reprint of the article by Pastor, McCormick, and Fine and their adolescent coauthors Andolsen, Friedman, Richardson, Roach, and Tavarez. This chapter, "Makin' Homes: An Urban Girl Thing," speaks to the need for "contexts of plain talk and conversation, trust and solidarity among peers and even with a few adults, with a sense of connection and a democracy of shared differences." Chapters 4 to 7 demonstrate the several responses to this appeal and present case studies of safe spaces that have been created. These include living rooms created and staffed by "othermothers" and parents in urban schools (López & Lechuga). They also involve natural and assigned mentors (Rhodes, Davis, Prescott, & Spencer), as well as more formal mentoring programs with trained facilitators who take on specific challenges, including relationship violence

(Banister & Leadbeater) or increase the likelihood of achieving postsecondary school aspirations (Taylor, Veloria, & Verba). Joining together adults and peers with similar concerns, these safe spaces create opportunities for open dialogue, offer support, advocacy, and interventions, connect youth and adult cultures, and at times empower girls to resist adversities and work within systems that disadvantage them.

Part 3 directly addresses a thread that weaves through several other sections: How do parents of minority and immigrant youth facilitate the development of independence and autonomy in girls while maintaining respect for cultural and family values and protecting young women from the potential perils of inner-city life, including damaged reputations, unwanted pregnancies, school failure, and "Americanization"? Costigan, Cauce, and Etchison examine changes in and interactions among conflicts, autonomy, and warmth in the relations between African America adolescents and their mothers across a 2-year period when the girls are 13 to 15 years old. Girls' autonomy appears to be actively negotiated in these relationships through, sometimes intense, disagreements in the context of the warmth. Lee also outlines the struggles of one of the newest immigrant groups to the United States: Hmong refugees. For these families, traditional values for women (including early marriage and childbearing) that are brought from predominantly rural lifestyles in Laos face off with the economic realities of supporting a family in urban centers in the United States. Adolescent girls' roles and identities are unraveled and reshaped at the boundary between these two cultures.

Part 4 raises the question of how girls leave safe spaces and claim and act in public ones. In the participatory action research of Torre, Fine, Alexander, and Genao, girls use poetry performances as conduits for social critique and political action to raises the profile of social injustices inherent in racism and sexism. But these actions are about more than performance. Public spaces of critical inquiry, constituted by heterogeneous groups of minority and White adults and peers, enable social critique and action. Ward also describes the empowerment and social action that are fostered by a more personal resilience that is spawned from adult-youth relationships of truth telling—that read, name, oppose, and replace oppression caused by racial discrimination.

Part 5 redraws urban girls' stance toward their sexuality from their own perspective where they are neither confused nor victims. Rather, they are active in both exploring their sexuality and protecting their health. Tracy and Erkut's large-scale study using a national data set shows the protective value of sports for urban girls. Denner and Coyle show how girls from an alternative urban school setting make decisions about condom use that are embedded in personal beliefs and efficacy, relationship characteristics, and cultural considerations. Together these complex influences are weighed and balanced in their decisions about safe-sex choices. Savin-Williams's interviews with girls situate explorations of same-sex sexuality in a normative framework, showing that girls' sexual identity development is not linear, easily dichotomized as heterosexual or homosexual, or sudden in its appearance. Even here we see girls' identities building on childhood foundations and transforming in anticipation of adult roles. No longer portrayed as the passive victim, girls announce and find their sexuality through active curiosity and in romantic (rather than casual) relationships.

Part 6 addresses the question of what is resilient adaptation in contexts of extreme adversity. Indeed, can the term even apply for urban youth living on the street (Benoit, Jansson, and Anderson) or in high-poverty violent neighborhoods characterized by political and social neglect (Taylor, Smith, and Taylor)? In Benoit et al.'s chapter, disadvantages from multiple moves and childhood disruptions, as well as weak family and school support, compound, and girls' experiences in the street (residential instability, tenuous attachments to the labor force, education, and families) show considerable continuity with their childhood experiences. Aspirations to return to school or to make something of themselves as young adults are confronted by an extreme lack of resources as these girls concentrate on surviving day-to-day. Similarly, walking the fine line between legal and illegal activities appears to be what is left of the opportunities offered to the young adult businesswomen in an inner-city neighborhood of Detroit. However, through long-term trusting relationships with generations of families living in "the hood," Taylor and his colleagues expose the diversity of the paths to young adulthood that are actually taken by young women as they fight the odds with resiliency, hard work, networking, and an indelible will to survive and to protect their children.

There are many windows opened by the research described in these chapters that help us to understand the experiences of girls who grow up in disadvantaged urban settings. There are many more windows to be opened by future researchers. Hopefully, the next generation of research on urban girls will emerge from among the readers who can build on this important research by looking with clear eyes at the contexts that limit and facilitate young urban women's strengths.

REFERENCES

Cicchetti, D., & Garmezy, N. (1993). Prospects and promise in the study of resilience. *Development and Psychopathology, 5,* 497–502.

Egeland, B. R., Carlson, E., & Sroufe, L. A. (1993). Resilience as process. *Development and Psychopathology, 5,* 517–528.

Kett, J. (1977). *Rites of passage: Adolescence in America 1790 to present.* New York: Basic Books.

Leadbeater, B. J., Banister, E. Benoit, C. Jansson, M. Marshall, A. & Riecken, T. (Eds.) (2006). *Ethical issues in community-based research with children and youth.* Toronto, Ontario, Canada: University of Toronto Press.

Leadbeater, B., Shellenbach, C., Maton, K,. & Dodgen, D. (2004). Research and policy for building strengths: Processes and contexts of individual, family, and community development. In K. Maton, C. Shellenbach, B. Leadbeater, & A. Solarz (Eds.), *Investing in children, youth, families and communities: Strengths-based research and policy* (pp. 13–30). Washington, DC: American Psychological Foundation.

Leadbeater, B. J., & Way, N. (2001). *Growing up fast: Early adult transitions of inner-city adolescent mothers.* Mahwah, NJ: Erlbaum.

Luthar, S. S., & Cicchetti, D. (2000). The construct of resilience: Implications for interventions and social policies, *Development and Psychopathology, 12,* 857–885.

Luthar, S. S., Doernberger, C. H., & Zigler, E. (1999). Resilience is not a unidimensional construct: Insights from a prospective study of inner-city adolescents. *Development and Psychopathology, 5,* 703–717.

Masten, A. S., & Coatsworth, J. D. (1998). The development of competence in favorable and unfavorable environments: Lessons from research on successful children. *American Psychologist, 53,* 205–220.

Maton, K., Shellenbach, C., Leadbeater, B. J., & Solarz, A. (Eds.) (2004). *Investing in children, youth, families and communities: Strengths-based research and policy.* Washington, DC: American Psychological Association.

Peters, R., Leadbeater, B. J., & McMahon, R. (2005). *Resilience in children, families and communities: Linking context to intervention and policy.* New York: Kluwer Academic Press.

Pianta, R. C., & Walsh, D. J. (1998). Applying the construct of resilience in schools: Cautions from a developmental systems perspective. *School Psychology Review, 27,* 407–417.

Sameroff, A. J., & Fiese, B. H., (2000). Transactional regulation: The developmental ecology of early intervention. In J. P. Schonkoff & S. J. Meisels (Eds.), *Handbook of early childhood intervention* (2nd ed., pp. 135–160). New York: Cambridge University Press.

Sandler, I. N., Ayers, T. S., Suter, J. C., Schultz, A., & Twohey-Jacobs, J. (2004). Adversities, strengths and public policy. In K. Maton, C. Shellenbach, B. Leadbeater, & A. Solarz (Eds.), *Investing in children, youth, families and communities: Strengths-based research and policy* (pp. 31–49). Washington. DC: American Psychological Foundation.

Tolan, P., Sherrod, L., Gorman-Smith, D., & Henry, D. (2004). Building protection, support, and opportunity for inner-city children and youth and their families. In K. I. Maton, C. J. Shellenbach, B. J. Leadbeater & A. L. Solarz (Eds.), *Investing in children, youth, and families: Strengths-based research and policy.* Washington, DC: American Psychological Association.

Werner, E. E., & Smith, R. S. (1992). *Overcoming the odds. High-risk children from birth to adulthood.* Ithaca, NY: Cornell University Press.

Wilson, W. (1997). *When work disappears: The world of the new urban poor.* New York: Vintage.

Part I

Resituating Positive Development for Urban Adolescent Girls

The Many Faces of Urban Girls
Features of Positive Development in Early Adolescence

Richard M. Lerner, Erin Phelps, Amy Alberts, Yulika Forman, and Elise D. Christiansen

For much of its history, the study of individual (ontogenetic) development was framed by nomothetic models (e.g., classical stage theories) that sought to describe and explain the generic human being (Emmerich, 1968; Lerner, 2002; Overton, 2006). Within the context of these models, both individual and group differences—diversity—were of little interest, at best, or regarded as either error variance or evidence for problematic deviation from (deficits in) normative (and idealized) developmental change (Lerner, 2004a, 2004b, 2006). With European American samples typically regarded as the groups from which norms were derived—and, as well, with *male* samples often set as the reference group for "normality" within the European American population (e.g., Block, 1973; Broverman, Vogel, Broverman, Clarkson, & Rosenkrantz, 1972; Maccoby, 1998; Maccoby & Jacklin, 1974)—racial, ethnic, and gender variations from these nomothetic standards were regarded not just as differences (as interindividual differences in intraindividual change). They were interpreted as developmental deficits (e.g., see Lerner, 2004a).

This difference as deficit "lens" has been applied as well to youth developing within the urban centers of the United States (Taylor, 2003; Taylor, McNeil, Smith, & Taylor, in preparation). This association has occurred in part because youth from these areas are often children of color and/or they come from family backgrounds that were not ordinarily those involved in the research from which normative generalizations about developmental change were formulated (Lerner, 2004a; Spencer, 2006;

Way, 1998). This characterization of urban youth as generically "in deficit"—as being "problems to be managed" (Roth & Brooks-Gunn, 2003a,
2003b) because of differences between them and "normative" samples in
regard to ontogenetic characteristics associated with their race, ethnicity,
gender, family, or neighborhood characteristics—is incorrect for both
empirical and theoretical reasons.

Empirically, this characterization is an overgeneralization; it paints
urban youth in brush strokes that are far too broad. That is, as is true of all
young people, urban youth are diverse, varying in interests, abilities,
involvement with their communities, aspirations, and life paths (e.g.,
McLoyd, Aikens, & Burton, 2006; Spencer, 2006; Taylor, 2003; Way, 1998).
For instance, the opportunity advantages of high socioeconomic status
(SES) available to some European American urban youth do not protect
them from manifesting risk and problem behaviors stereotypically associated with low SES urban youth (Luthar & Latendresse, 2002); in turn, the
low SES of some urban youth of color does not mean that these young
people engage in risk/problem behaviors or do not achieve scholastically
or civically to degrees comparable to higher SES urban youth (Mincy,
1994). Moreover, research in life-course sociology (e.g., Elder & Shanahan,
2006), in life-span developmental psychology (e.g., Baltes, Lindenberger, &
Staudinger, 2006), and in developmental biology (Gottlieb, 2004; Gottlieb,
Wahlsten, & Lickliter, 2006; Suomi, 2004) attests to the presence of intra-
group (e.g., intracohort) variation that is at least as great as
intergroup/intercohort differences.

Nevertheless, this within-group diversity has largely remained a hidden
truth to many academics, policy makers, and even practitioners working
in urban youth-development programs, who may assume that all urban
youth may be characterized either as "at risk" or as already engaged in
problematic or health-compromising behaviors. In addition to being
empirically counterfactual, this view of urban youth sends a dispiriting
message to young people, one that conveys to them that little is expected
of them because their lives are inherently broken or, at best, in danger of
becoming broken.

Moreover, the deficit interpretation of urban youth as invariantly defi-
cient is problematic for theoretical reasons as well as for empirical ones.
The problems that do exist among some urban youth are neither
inevitable nor the sum total of the range of behaviors that do or can
exist among them. Derived from developmental systems theory, a positive youth development (PYD) perspective (Theokas & Lerner, in press)

stresses the plasticity of human development and regards this potential for systematic change as a ubiquitous strength of people during their adolescence. The potential for plasticity may be actualized to promote positive development among urban youth when young people are embedded in an ecology that possesses and makes available to them resources and supports that offer opportunities for sustained, positive adult-youth relations, skill-building experiences, and opportunities for participation in and leadership of valued community activities (Lerner, 2004c). Such supports exist even in those urban settings that many policy makers have abandoned as resource depleted or resource absent (e.g., Taylor, 2003; Taylor et al., in preparation).

Goals of the Present Chapter

If theory and research combine to indicate that characterizations about urban youth as invariantly in deficit, and as constituting a monolithic group, are overgeneralizations, then any view of urban youth that fails to differentiate between boys and girls is at least equally ill conceived and mistaken. As do urban youth in general, urban girls as a group may be expected to show interindividual differences and, as well, they may be expected to manifest a range of behaviors across positive and problematic developmental dimensions. Accordingly, the purpose of this chapter is to use the PYD perspective to discuss the developing characteristics of urban girls.

We illustrate our points about the diversity and strengths of urban girls by capitalizing on data from a large, national longitudinal study of youth, the 4-H Study of Positive Youth Development (Lerner et al., 2005, Jelicic, Bobek, Phelps, Lerner, & Lerner, 2006). We will draw on both quantitative and qualitative data from the second wave of this study (sixth graders) to discuss the facets of positive development of these early adolescent females and to identify some factors that may be involved in the promotion of PYD, the diminution of risk/problem behaviors, and the level of contributions that these young people make to their selves, families, and communities.

To begin this discussion it is useful to provide a brief overview of the PYD perspective. This orientation to adolescence allows us to understand why diversity is not equivalent to deficit, and why there is variation in the course of development of young women growing up in urban centers.

Features of the PYD Perspective

Beginning in the early 1990s, and burgeoning in the first half decade of the twenty-first century, a new vision and vocabulary for discussing young people have emerged. These innovations were framed by the developmental systems theories that were engaging the interest of developmental scientists (Lerner, 2002, 2006). The focus on plasticity within such theories led in turn to an interest in assessing the potential for change at diverse points across ontogeny, ones spanning from infancy through the 10th and 11th decades of life (Baltes et al., 2006). Moreover, these innovations were propelled by the increasingly more collaborative contributions of researchers focused on the second decade of life (e.g., Benson, Scales, Hamilton, & Sesma, 2006; Damon, 2004; Lerner, 2004c); practitioners in the field of youth development (e.g., Floyd & McKenna, 2003; Little, 1993; Pittman, Irby, & Ferber, 2001; Wheeler, 2003); and policy makers concerned with improving the life chances of diverse youth and their families (e.g., Cummings, 2003; Gore, 2003). These interests converged in the formulation of a set of ideas that enabled youth to be viewed as resources to be developed, and not as problems to be managed (Roth & Brooks-Gunn, 2003a, 2003b). These ideas may be discussed in regard to two key hypotheses.

Hypothesis 1. Youth-Context Alignment Promotes PYD

Based on the idea that the potential for systematic intraindividual change across life (i.e., for plasticity) represents a fundamental strength of human development, the hypothesis was generated that, if the strengths of youth are aligned with resources for healthy growth present in the key contexts of adolescent development—the home, the school, and the community— then enhancements in positive functioning at any one point in time (i.e., well-being; Bornstein, Davidson, Keyes, Moore, & the Center for Child Well-Being, 2003) may occur; in turn, the systematic promotion of positive development will occur across time (i.e., thriving; e.g., Dowling et al., 2004; Lerner, 2004a; Lerner et al., 2005).

A key subsidiary hypothesis to the notion of aligning individual strengths and contextual resources for healthy development is that there exist, across the key settings of youth development (i.e., families, schools, and communities), at least some supports for the promotion of PYD.

Termed *developmental assets* (Benson et al., 2006), these resources constitute the social and ecological "nutrients" for the growth of healthy youth
(Benson, 2003). Although there is some controversy about the nature,
measurement, and impact of developmental assets (Theokas & Lerner, in
press), there is broad agreement among researchers and practitioners in
the youth development field that the concept of developmental assets is
important for understanding what needs to be marshaled in homes, classrooms, and community-based programs to foster PYD.

In fact, a key impetus for the interest in the PYD perspective among
both researchers and youth program practitioners and, thus, a basis for
the collaborations that exist among members of these two communities, is
the interest that exists in ascertaining the nature of the resources for positive development that are present in youth programs, for example, in the
literally hundreds of thousands of after-school programs delivered either
by large, national organizations, such as 4-H, Boys and Girls Clubs, Boy
and Girl Scouts, Big Brothers and Big Sisters, YMCA, or Girls, Inc., or by
local organizations. There are data suggesting that, in fact, developmental
assets associated with youth programs, especially those that focus on
youth *development* (i.e., programs that adopt the ideas associated with the
PYD perspective; Roth & Brooks-Gunn, 2003b), are linked to PYD. In
addition, Roth and Brooks-Gunn (2003b) report that findings of evaluation research indicate that the latter programs are more likely than the former ones to be associated with the presence of key indicators of PYD.

This finding raises the question of what are in fact the indicators of
PYD. Addressing this question involves the second key hypothesis of the
PYD perspective.

Hypothesis 2. PYD Is Composed of Five Cs

Based both on the experiences of practitioners and on reviews of the adolescent development literature (Eccles & Gootman, 2002; Lerner, 2004a;
Roth & Brooks-Gunn, 2003b), "Five Cs"—Competence, Confidence, Connection, Character, and Caring—were hypothesized as a way of conceptualizing PYD (and of integrating all the separate indicators of it, such as
academic achievement or self-esteem). The Five Cs were linked to the positive outcomes of youth development programs reported by Roth and
Brooks-Gunn (2003b). In addition, they are prominent terms used by
practitioners, adolescents involved in youth development programs, and

TABLE 1.1
Working Definitions of the 5Cs of Positive Youth Development

C	Definition
Competence	Positive view of one's actions in domain-specific areas, including social, academic, cognitive, and vocational. Social competence pertains to interpersonal skills (e.g., conflict resolution). Cognitive competence pertains to cognitive abilities (e.g., decision making). School grades, attendance, and test scores are part of academic competence. Vocational competence involves work habits and career choice explorations.
Confidence	An internal sense of overall positive self-worth and self-efficacy; one's global self-regard, as opposed to domain-specific beliefs.
Connection	Positive bonds with people and institutions that are reflected in bidirectional exchanges between the individual and peers, family, school, and community in which both parties contribute to the relationship.
Character	Respect for societal and cultural rules, possession of standards for correct behaviors, a sense of right and wrong (morality), and integrity.
Caring	A sense of sympathy and empathy for others.

From Lerner et al. (2005); Roth & Brooks-Gunn (2003a, 2003b).

the parents of these adolescents in describing the characteristics of a "thriving youth" (King et al., 2005).

A hypothesis subsidiary to the postulation of the Five Cs as a means to operationalize PYD is that, when a young person manifests the Cs across time (when the youth is thriving), he or she will be on a life trajectory toward an "idealized adulthood" (Csikszentmihalyi & Rathunde, 1998; Rathunde & Csikszentmihalyi, 2006). Such adulthood is theoretically held to be marked by "contribution," often termed the "sixth C" of PYD. Contribution, within an ideal adult life, is marked by integrated and mutually reinforcing contributions to self (e.g., maintaining one's health and one's ability therefore to remain an active agent in one's own development) and to family, community, and the institutions of civil society (Lerner, 2004c). An adult engaging in such integrated contributions is a person manifesting adaptive developmental regulations (Brandtstädter, 1998, 1999, 2006).

In turn, within the youth development field, longitudinal research has begun to test the idea that the development of the Five Cs, as individual indicators of a thriving youth, and/or as first-order latent constructs that are indicators of a second-order PYD construct, predict conceptual and behavioral indicators of contribution that may be indicative of development toward an idealized adulthood (e.g., see Jelicic et al., 2006). Table 1.1 presents definitions of the Five Cs that are derived from the youth development literature (e.g., Lerner et al., 2005; Roth & Brooks-Gunn, 2003a, 2003b).

A second subsidiary hypothesis to the one postulating the Five Cs is that there should be an inverse relation within and across development between indicators of PYD and behaviors indicative of risk behaviors or internalizing and externalizing problems. Here, the idea—forwarded in particular by Pittman and her colleagues (e.g., Pittman et al., 2001) in regard to applications of developmental science to policies and programs—is that the best means to prevent problems associated with adolescent behavior and development (e.g., depression, aggression, drug use and abuse, or unsafe sexual behavior) is to promote positive development.

In sum, replacing the deficit view of adolescence, the PYD perspective sees *all* adolescents as having strengths (by virtue at least of their potential for change). The perspective suggests that increases in well-being and thriving are possible for all youth through aligning the strengths of young people with the developmental assets present in their social and physical ecology. An initial model of the development process linking mutually influential, person ←→ context relations, the development of the Five Cs (i.e., well-being, within time, and thriving across time), and the attainment in adulthood of an "idealized" status involving integrated contributions to self, family, community, and civil society was presented in Lerner (2004c) and Lerner et al. (2005). In essence, this model specified that on the basis of mutually influential relations between individual actions (involving self-regulatory behaviors) and positive growth-supporting features of the context (developmental assets), that is, through person ←→ context relations, the individual develops the cognitive, affective, and behavioral characteristics included within the PYD concept (see Table 1.1).

Further, as a result of this individual development, there emerges the "sixth C" of contribution (to the context that, in turn, supports the development of the person as an individual). The working definition of the outcome variable of Contribution is "Effecting positive changes in self, others, and community that involve both a behavioral (action) component and an ideological component (i.e., actions based on a commitment to moral and civic duty)" (see Alberts et al., 2006). In addition to the impact of PYD on Contribution, the model specifies that, as a result of the development of PYD, the individual's development is marked as well by the diminution of problem and risk behaviors. This model is shown in Figure 1.1.

FIGURE 1.1

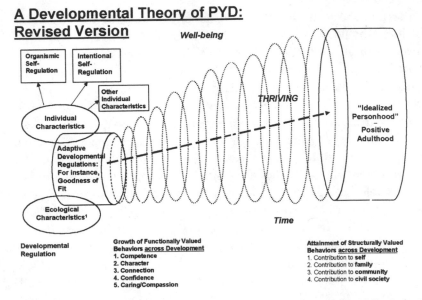

A Developmental Theory of PYD: Revised Version

1. Human resources; physical/institutional resources; collective activity; and accessibility in families, schools , and communities (Theokas, 2005).

Although still at a preliminary stage of progress, there is growing empirical evidence that the general concepts and main and subsidiary hypotheses of the PYD perspective find empirical support. Indeed, within this chapter we offer such support in regard to the positive functioning of urban girls within the early adolescent period, that is, in sixth grade. To provide this empirical evidence, we draw on data developed within the Institute for Applied Research in Youth Development—in the 4-H Study of Positive Youth Development (Lerner et al., 2005). In the following, we present the general characteristics of this study and then turn to the analyses of data specifically pertinent to urban girls.

The 4-H Study of Positive Youth Development

The 4-H Study of Positive Youth Development is a longitudinal investigation supported by a grant from the National 4-H Council. The 4-H Study was designed to test the theoretical model shown in Figure 1.1. It began in

2002–2003 by studying a national cohort of about 1,700 fifth-grade youth (from 13 states across all regions of the United States) and their parents (Lerner et al., 2005). At this writing, the study is in its fourth wave (2005–2006) and involves about 3,500 youth from 21 states and about 2,500 of their parents. Full details of the methodology of the 4-H Study have been presented in Lerner et al., 2005; Theokas & Lerner, in press; and Jelicic et al., 2006).

Framed by an instance of developmental systems theory, developmental contextualism (Lerner, 2002, 2004c), the 4-H Study is designed to follow youth across the second decade of life. The data set is being and will continue to be used to bring empirical evidence to bear on the two main hypotheses of the PYD perspective and, as well, on the subsidiary hypotheses associated with each of the two main hypotheses. The data set allows as well the appraisal of the use of the PYD perspective for understanding subsamples of youth within the larger 4-H Study. Accordingly, we describe here the link between the PYD perspective and a sample of urban girls within the data set from the second wave of the study, that is, grade 6. We turn here to a description of this sample of girls and of the quantitative and qualitative data we used to explore the link between the PYD perspective and the developing characteristics of these youth.

Assessing the Developing Characteristics of Urban Girls Within the 4-H Study

Lerner et al. (2005) and Jelicic et al. (2006) have described the overall characteristics of girls within the 4-H data set. Here, using both quantitative and qualitative data, we will examine whether the urban girls we discuss in this chapter differ from the overall sample of girls on measures of PYD, contribution, and risk. In turn, we will assess within-group characteristics of these urban girls. We will use quantitative and qualitative data available within the 4-H Study data set to assess whether there exist, across these approaches to understanding the participants, comparable views of the characteristics of the urban girls. Several questions will frame our analyses.

Key Questions

In confirmation of the second of the two hypotheses framing the study of PYD, initial research within the 4-H Study has established the empirical utility of operationalizing positive development through the "Five Cs," as first-order latent constructs, and through a score for PYD itself, as a second-order latent construct (Lerner et al., 2005). Also consistent with Hypothesis 2, this prior research has demonstrated the empirical utility of the indices of the "sixth C," Contribution, and of risk and problem behaviors that exist within our measurement model. For instance, within grade 5, there was a positive relation between scores for PYD and Contribution and an inverse relation between PYD scores and scores for risk/problem behaviors (Lerner et al., 2005). Moreover, Jelicic et al. (2006) demonstrated that grade 5 PYD scores are positively related to grade 6 Contribution scores and negatively related to grade 6 risk/problem behavior scores.

In all these findings, girls showed higher mean levels of PYD and Contribution than did boys, and the correlations among PYD, Contribution, and risk/problem behaviors were higher for girls than for boys. However, although these data were differentiated by SES and race/ethnicity, they were not disaggregated with respect to urban status. What we found in these earlier analyses was that all SES and race/ethnic groups had mean PYD scores reflective of good functioning and that PYD scores were higher for youth with higher SES. In addition, we found that European American and Latino youth had higher PYD scores than did African American youth.

Accordingly, in this chapter we ask whether urban girls within the 4-H Study sample show levels of PYD, Contribution, and risk/problem behaviors comparable to those of the nonurban sample of girls in the 4-H Study and if the links among these constructs found for the overall sample of girls (in Jelicic et al., 2006) are seen as well within the sample of urban girls. In addition, we include contextual variables that may be important to consider when focusing on urban girls in particular. Living in a mother-headed household may adversely affect development, while stability of living situations may provide greater access to programs and individuals that will promote PYD. Participation in out-of-school activities can offer opportunities for sustained, positive adult-youth relations, skill-building experiences that exist even in those urban settings that have often been dismissed as resource poor (Lerner, 2004c). Breadth of participation was found to be positively associated with PYD and Contribution (Balsano, Theokas, Lerner, Phelps, & Lerner, 2006) for the entire aggregated 4-H sample, and this relationship is evaluated here as well.

The 4-H Study data set includes several open-ended questions as well as items associated with quantitative scales (e.g., Alberts et al., 2006). The responses to the open-ended questions were coded to explore whether the characterization of urban girls afforded by the quantitative measures converged with characterizations derived from qualitative assessments. As detailed later, these open-ended questions pertain to young people's ideas about the characteristics that define a thriving adolescent, a youth who shows exemplary personal and social behavior, who is doing well in all walks of life; to young people's descriptions of the characteristics they would manifest if they were showing exemplary functioning; and to the characteristics of functioning they actually manifest.

Based on classic and contemporary theories about self-development in adolescence (e.g., Harter, 1998, 2006; McCandless, 1970), we reasoned that positive functioning should be reflected in girls' depictions of an exemplary other person (i.e., of an "idealized other"), of the exemplary "self," and of the actual self. Accordingly, we sought to describe the nature of the depictions provided by urban girls of idealized other, idealized self, and actual self and asked to what extent did the terms used to provide these three descriptions reflect constructs associated with the Five Cs and Contribution (see King et al., 2005). To explain how we addressed these questions asked of our quantitative and qualitative data, in the following section we describe features of the general methodology of the 4-H Study.

Methods

To understand the characteristics of positive development present among urban girls within the 4-H Study, we used data from the student questionnaire administered to adolescent participants in this investigation at Wave 2 (sixth grade). Additional information about the method can be found in Lerner et al. (2005), Theokas and Lerner (in press), and Jelicic et al. (2006).

Sample

At Wave 2, participants came from sites located in 18 states and varied by race, ethnicity, SES, religion, family structure, rural-urban location, and geographic region. Schools were chosen as the main method for collecting the sample. Assessment was conducted in 60 schools and in five after-school programs. Participants were 1,871 sixth-grade adolescents (43%

TABLE 1.2

Means, Standard Deviations, and Percentages of Demographic Characteristics and Outcome Variables for "Urban" and "Nonurban" Girls in the 4-H Study of PYD[****]

Demographic Characteristics	Urban Girls (n = 277)	Nonurban Girls (n = 799)
Mothers' education in years (mean, sd)	13.30 (2.94)	13.93 (2.35)[**]
Per capita family income in dollars	11,396.73 (9,293.17)	13,879.47(8,254.18)[**]
Race/ethnicity (%)		
African American	16.9%	4.9%[***]
Asian American	3.7%	2.3%
American Indian	6.0%	2.9%[*]
European American	27.3%	72.4%[***]
Latino/a American	36.7%	13.0%[***]
Multiracial	8.6%	3.6%[**]
Other	0.7%	0.9%
Single mother households (%)	13.0%	7.7%[**]
Time living in neighborhood (%)		
Less than 1 year	11.4%	8.9%
1 to 2 years	12.9%	10.8%
2 to 3 years	13.7%	9.3%[*]
3 to 4 years	5.5%	9.8%[*]
4 to 5 years	10.6%	9.6%
More than 5 years	45.9%	51.6%
Religious affiliation (%)		
Protestant	7.9%	25.4%[***]
Catholic	63.8%	33.1%[***]
Other religious affiliation	20.4%	29.8%[*]
Nonreligious	7.9%	11.6%
Geographic region (%)		
Northeast	22.1%	15.1%[**]
Southeast	15.9%	31.6%[***]
Northwest	13.0%	9.9%
Mid-Atlantic	0.0%	2.5%[**]
Midwest	12.7%	36.5%[***]
Southwest	36.2%	4.4%[***]
PYD (mean, sd; ranges 1–100)	75.24 (13.30)	76.19 (12.83)
Contribution (mean, sd; ranges 1–100)	46.34 (13.85)	46.58 (13.04)
Depression (mean, sd; ranges 1–52)	14.70 (9.76)	12.58 (9.54)[**]
Risk/problem behaviors (mean, sd; ranges 1–12)	1.08 (1.77)	0.95 (2.11)
Breadth of activity participation (count of activities, range 1–22)	2.61 (1.95)	2.91 (1.98)[*]

Key: [*]$p < .05$, [**]$p < .01$, [***]$p < .001$.
[****]Independent samples t-tests were computed for all continuous variable comparisons and chi-square analyses were conducted for all categorical variable comparisons.

males; mean age = 12.18 years, SD = .89 years; 57% females, mean age = 12.10 years, SD = .80 years) and 1,281 of their parents.

In order to look specifically at urban girls, we selected those who live in a large or midsize central city as defined by the 1990 census. The demographic characteristics of these "urban girls" are shown in Table 1.2, along with the characteristics of "nonurban" girls" in our sample.

The Student Questionnaire and the Parent Questionnaire

As mentioned earlier, the measurement model used in the larger 4-H Study of PYD was designed to provide indices that would test the developmental contextual, individual ←→ context model of the development of PYD. Accordingly, the student questionnaire (SQ) included measures pertinent to the Five Cs of PYD, problem behaviors, pubertal level of development, individual and ecological assets, developmental regulation, after-school activities, and demographics. The parent questionnaire (PQ) was composed of two types of items: (a) items about the parent or guardian and (b) items about the child. Information regarding the specific items included in both questionnaires can be found in Lerner et al. (2005). Within the SQ, youth responded to open-ended questions intended to appraise self-generated definitions of thriving in adolescence. More information about the measurement model used in the 4-H Study is presented in Lerner et al. (2005).

Procedures

At each research site, teachers or program staff gave each child an envelope to take home to his or her parent or guardian, containing a letter explaining the study, a consent form, a PQ, and a self-addressed envelope for returning the parent questionnaire and consent form. For those youth who received parental consent, data collection was conducted in either their school or after-school program by trained study staff or hired assistants for remote locations. The procedure began with reading the instructions for the SQ to the youth. Participants were instructed that they could skip any questions they did not wish to answer. Data collection took approximately 2 hours, which included one or two short breaks. Students who were unable to be surveyed at their school or 4-H site, either because they were absent during the day of testing or because the school superintendent did not allow testing to occur in the school, received a survey in the mail.

Measures

As noted previously, the 4-H Study assesses both positive characteristics of youth and, as well, risk/problem behaviors. In addition, assessments are made of the "sixth C," Contribution, of youth participation in after-school activities (which are hypothesized to serve as assets for PYD), and of several features of the context of youth.

The Five Cs and PYD

The Five Cs and PYD are measured using items from the Profiles of Student Life-Attitudes and Behaviors Survey (PSL-AB; Benson, Leffert, Scales, & Blyth, 1998); the Self-Perception Profile for Children (SPPC; Harter, 1983); the Peer Support Scale (Armsden & Greenberger, 1987; the Teen Assessment Project (TAP) Survey Question Bank (Small & Rodgers, 1995); and the Eisenberg Sympathy Scale (Eisenberg et al., 1996). PYD is constructed as the mean of the Five Cs. Detailed information regarding the measurement of each of the Cs is presented in the following.

CONFIDENCE

Confidence is constructed as the weighted mean of 12 items on the student questionnaire. Six of the items measure positive identity (Theokas et al., 2005) and come from the Search Institute's PSL-AB (Benson et al., 1998). The response format for these six items ranged from 1 = *strongly agree* to 5 = *strongly disagree*. An example of an item used to measure positive identity is "On the whole I like myself."

The remaining six items used to construct the confidence indicator form the self-worth scale from the Self-Perception Profile for Children (SPCC; Harter, 1983). Harter (1982) developed a structured alternative response format to assess perceived competence in a domain. Participants are asked to choose between two types of people. Once they have selected which person they are most like, they are asked to decide between it is "really true for me" or "sort of true for me." The items are counterbalanced so that half begin with a positive sentence, reflecting high competence, whereas half begin with a negative sentence, reflecting low competence. Each item is scored from 1 to 4, with 4 reflecting higher perceived competence. An example of an item used to assess self-worth is "Some kids don't like the way they are leading their lives BUT Other kids do like the way they are leading their lives."

COMPETENCE

Competence is constructed as the weighted mean of 17 items on the SQ. Twelve of the items used to measure competence come from the Self-Perception Profile for Children (Harter, 1983). Six of the items form the academic competence scale, and six of the items form the social competence scale. As mentioned earlier, the SPPC uses a structured alternative response format. An example of an item from the academic competence scale is "Some kids feel like they are *just as smart* as other kids their age BUT Other kids aren't so sure and *wonder* if they are as smart." An example of an item from the social competence scale is "Some kids have *a lot* of friends BUT Other kids *don't* have very many friends."

The remaining five items used to index competence come from the Search Institute's PSL-AB (Benson et al., 1998). Four of these items measure school engagement. Three of these items have a forced choice response to ascertain how often a respondent does something. The response format for these items ranged from 1 = *usually* to 3 = *never*. An example of an item measuring school engagement using this response format is "How often do you feel bored at school?" The fourth school engagement item "At school I try as hard as I can to do my best work" used a response format ranging from 1 = *strongly agree* to 5 = *strongly disagree*. The final item measuring competence, "What grades do you earn in school?" had a response format that ranged from 1 = *mostly As* to 8 = *mostly below Ds*.

CHARACTER

Eighteen items from the Search Institute's PSL-AB are used to measure character (Benson et al., 1998). These items measure interpersonal skills, valuing of diversity, personal values, and social conscience. The five items that measure personal values and the six items that measure social conscience use a forced choice response format and ask participants to rate how important each item is in their life. Response formats range from 1 = *not important* to 5 = *extremely important*. An example of an item measuring personal values is "Telling the truth, even when it's not easy," while an example of an item measuring social conscience is "Helping other people."

One of the items used to measure valuing of diversity, "Getting to know people who are of a different race than I am," uses the same response format as described earlier for measuring importance. The remaining three items used to measure valuing of diversity and the three items used to measure interpersonal skills ask participants to think about the people who know them well and how they think they would rate them on each of the items. The response format ranges from 1 = *not at all like me* to 5 = *very much like me*. An example of an item measuring valuing of diversity that uses this response format is "Knowing a lot about people of other races." An example of an item used to measure interpersonal skills is "Caring about other people's feelings."

CARING

Five items from the Eisenberg Sympathy Scale (ESS; Eisenberg et al., 1996) are used to measuring caring. The items measure the degree to which participants feel sorry for the distress of others (from 1 = *really like you* through 3 = *not like you*). High scores indicate low levels of sympathy. An example of an item from the ESS is "I feel sorry for people who don't have the things I have."

CONNECTION

To index connection, 22 of the items from the SQ are used. These items measure connection to family (six items), school (seven items), peers (four items), and community (five items). All the items measuring connection to family, connection to school, and connection to community come from the PSL-AB (response format ranging from 1 = *strongly agree* to 5 = *strongly disagree*). An example of an item measuring connection to family is "My parents give me help and support when I need it." An example of an item measuring connection to school is "I get a lot of encouragement at my school." An example of an item measuring connection to community is "Adults in my city or town make me feel important."

The items used to measure connection to peers come from the TAP Survey Question Bank (Small & Rodgers, 1995). These items, in which participants must decide how true a statement is for them, measure peer support (Armsden & Greenberger, 1987) (response format that ranges from 1 = *always true* to 5 = *almost never true or never true*). An example of an item is "My friends care about me."

CONTRIBUTION

Contribution is measured as a composite score of 12 items that are divided into four subsets. The first subset, called Leadership, is an item from the PSL-AB: "During the last 12 months, how many times have you been a leader in a group or organization?" (response format ranging from 1 = *never* to 5 = *five or more times*). The second subset, called Service, is derived by adding the responses of three items created for the study. For each item, participants are asked to indicate whether participation in a particular activity applies to them. An example of an item is "volunteer work." The third subset, called Helping, is a measure of the average of two items from the PSL-AB in which participants respond about the average amount of time they spend doing certain activities during an average week. The response choices range from 0 = *zero* to 5 = *11 or more hours*. One of the items is "Helping friends or neighbors."

Finally, a fourth subset is called Ideology, which is a scale that measures contribution ideology with four items from the TAP Survey Question Bank and two items that were created for this study (response scale ranging from 1 = *strongly agree* to 5 = *strongly disagree*). An example of an item is "It is important to me to contribute to my community and society." The two items that measure contribution ideology that were created for this study ask participants to think about their future and to assess their chances for doing certain things (response format ranges from 1 = *very low* to 5 = *very high*). An example of an item is "Be involved in community service."

Activity Participation Outside of School

Based on Eccles and Gootman (2002), a Youth Activity Survey was included in the SQ. Participation in after-school activities was assessed. Activities were grouped into four specific categories: youth development programs, sports, arts, and clubs. Youth development programs included the five major national youth-serving organizations with an expressed PYD mission (National 4-H, YMCA or YWCA, Boy Scouts and Girl Scouts, Boys and Girls Clubs, and Big Brothers and Big Sisters). Sports participation was assessed with two questions (sports and martial arts). Youth's participation in arts was assessed with five questions (school band, drama, dance, music, and arts/crafts), whereas two items were used to assess youth's participation in other after-school clubs (academic club and religious youth group). Youth reported if they participated in each of the activities, during the current school year or summer. In the present report, data from the responses to the activities survey were scored for breadth of participation, that is, the number of activities in which a youth reports being involved (out of a possible 15 different activities). Balsano et al. (2006) found that breadth of activity participation in grade 5 is positively related to PYD and Contribution in grade 6.

Depression

At Wave 2, depression is measured by the 20-item Center for Epidemiological Studies Depression Scale (CES-D; Radloff, 1977) Participants report how often they felt a particular way during the past week (response format ranging from 0 = *rarely or none of the time [less than 1 day]* to 3 = *most or all of the time [5–7 days]*). An example of an item is "I was bothered by things that usually don't bother me." Higher scores indicate higher levels of depressive symptoms.

Risk Behaviors

Risk behaviors are measured with scales of substance use and delinquency derived for this study from the PSL-AB and from the Monitoring the Future (2000) questionnaire. We asked participants to indicate whether they have done any of the following during the last 12 months (response format ranging from 1 = *never* to 4 = *regularly*). An example of an item is "Have you ever sniffed glues, sprays, or gases?" The four items used to measure delinquency ask respondents how many times during the last 12 months they have done something (response format ranging from 1 = *never* to 5 = *five or more times*). An example of an item is "How many times have you hit or beat up someone?"

Family Measures

Several features of the family and community context of the participants were measured. For the present analyses, the following indices were included.

FAMILY STRUCTURE

This information was obtained from the youth and indicates whether or not they live with one or more parents or guardians (excluding aunts and uncles, friends).

DURATION OF RESIDENCE IN A NEIGHBORHOOD

Youth responded to a question about how long they have lived in their current neighborhood (response alternatives ranging from 1 = *less than 1 year* to 6 = *more than 5 years*).

MOTHER'S EDUCATION

The adult who filled out the PQ was asked to indicate the youth's mother's highest level of education.

PER CAPITA INCOME

Annual household income was obtained from the PQ and divided by the number of people living in the household.

Open-Ended Items Used to Assess Exemplary Other, Idealized Self, and Actual Self

As noted earlier, the SQ includes several open-ended questions. Three of these questions were used to assess girls' conceptions of an exemplary, thriving youth (idealized other), of their own ideal characteristics (idealized self), and of their actual self. These questions were, respectively, as follows:

1. Everybody knows kids in their school or neighborhood that they think are doing well in all areas of their life. In your opinion, what is he or she like? What sort of things does he or she do?
2. Everybody also has an idea about how she or he would like to be. If you imagine yourself doing really well in all areas of your life, what would you be like? What sorts of things would you do?
3. Now, think about yourself and your life now. How would you describe how you are doing? What are you like? What sorts of things do you do?

The analysis aimed to address two questions. First, how do urban girls describe thriving? We were specifically interested in determining if the girls used the language consistent with the 5 Cs and contribution in their descriptions of thriving, and what other aspects of their lives urban girls emphasized as being important. Second, what can we learn about well-being of urban girls from their descriptions of themselves?

Two sets of codes were used to meet the research goals. The first set of codes was derived from the theoretical framework of Five Cs and the sixth C, contribution, in order to assess to what extent girls' descriptions of thriving utilize the language of PYD. This decision was based on recent work by King et al. (2005), who found that definitions of thriving by adults and youth were able to be organized according to the Five Cs of PYD. Additional codes were generated from the data through open coding (i.e., identification of concepts within the data; Strauss & Corbin, 1998) to capture descriptions of thriving that were outside of the framework provided by the terms linked to the Five Cs and contribution.

A preliminary codebook was developed by two raters based on the answers provided by 75 randomly selected participants. To determine intercoder reliability, each rater used this preliminary codebook to independently code an additional 75 randomly selected cases. There was a 91.26% agreement between the two raters and a high Cohen's kappa ($k =$ .92). Given this consistency, the remaining youth answers were coded by one of the two raters.

The second set of codes was developed to assess well-being of urban girls based on their descriptions of themselves in positive or negative terms. For a sample of 30 cases, there was a 97% agreement between the two raters and a Cohen's kappa of 0.873. Given this consistency, the remaining youth answers were coded by one of the two raters.

Results: The Many Faces of Urban Girls

The purpose of the analyses conducted for this chapter was to assess whether urban girls within the 4-H Study sample show levels of PYD, contribution, depression, and risk/problem behaviors comparable to the overall sample of girls in the 4-H Study and if the links among these constructs found for the overall sample of girls (in Jelicic et al., 2006) are seen as well within the sample of urban girls. We also assess whether within the sample of urban girls there is variation associated with SES, race/ethnicity, and geographic area of residence within the United States. Our expectation was urban girls would be comparable to the overall sample of girls in regard to the quantitative measures assessed in the present research.

In addition, in order to explore urban girls' views of thriving and of their own well-being, we coded responses to three open-ended questions that were aimed at assessing, respectively, young people's ideas about the characteristics that defined an exemplary, thriving youth (an "idealized other"); the characteristics they would manifest if they were showing exemplary functioning ("idealized self"); and the characteristics of functioning they actually manifest ("actual self").

Quantitative Findings: Urban Girls Manifest PYD

Table 1.2 shows means on demographic and outcome variables for urban and nonurban girls in the 4-H Study of PYD and indicates whether or not differences are significant. The sample of urban girls differs from nonurban girls in terms of race/ethnicity and religion (they are more likely to be African American and Latina than European American, and more likely to be Catholic than Protestant). In addition, looking at the geographic distribution of girls in our sample, there are more urban than nonurban girls in the southwestern United States and fewer urban than nonurban girls in the southeastern and midwestern United States. Finally, the urban girls have somewhat lower per capita family income, have mothers who are slightly less well educated, participate in slightly fewer activities, and have higher levels of depression than their nonurban counterparts. These differences are statistically significant but very small.

In order to determine whether or not urban girls within the 4-H Study exhibit the same patterns of relationships between background and contextual factors and PYD, contribution, and risk/problem behaviors found in analyses of the overall sample (in Jelicic et al., 2006), multiple regression analyses were conducted. The results are summarized in Table 1.3. SES is determined jointly by mother's education and per capita family income. To control for missing data due to missing PQ information, a variable was included in the analyses that indicated presence or absence of PQ (and therefore, SES) information.

First, the relationships between PYD and the combined effects of SES, living in a single mother family, duration of residence in a neighborhood, and activity participation were considered. The overall model is significant, accounting for 10.2% of the variance in PYD. In terms of the individ-

TABLE 1.3

Hierarchical Regression of PYD, Contribution, Depression, and Risk/Problem Behaviors on SES (Mother's Education, Per Capita Income, PQ Present?), Family Structure (Single Mother Household), Time in Neighborhood, Breadth of Activity Participation, and PYD for Urban Girls Sample (n = 277)

Behaviors	PYD	Contribution	Depression	Risk/Problem
Intercept	62.648***	-11.172	39.725***	4.568***
Mom's education	.040	.643	-.399	-.097
Income (in $1,000)	0.447*	0.029	-0.004	-0.012
PQ present?	.072	1.683	-1.108	-.049
Single mom	3.721	2.472	-2.112	.065
Time in neighborhood	.851	-.028	-.196	.005
Breadth of participation	.837	1.411**	.791*	.003
PYD	—	.577***	-.266***	-.028**
R^2	.102**	.403***	.160***	.080
df(Residual)	165	141	162	162

Key: *$p < .05$, **$p < .01$, ***$p < .001$.

ual predictors, family income was positively related to PYD, with other variables controlled, indicating that PYD is accounted for by higher family economic resources in the sample. Table 1.3 summarizes this analysis.

We then considered the effects of PYD, SES, living in a single mother family, duration of residence in a neighborhood, and activity participation on variables that capture positive outcomes (i.e., contribution) and indicate the existence of possible problems (i.e., depression and risk/problem behaviors). In order to do this, the outcome variables of contribution, depression, and risk/problem behaviors were regressed on PYD, SES, living in a single mother family, duration of residence in a neighborhood, and activity participation (see Table 1.3). These variables account for 40.3% of the variance in contribution scores ($p < .001$). Both breadth of after-school activity participation and PYD have significant coefficients ($p < .01$) when the other variables are controlled for. As breadth of participation and PYD increase, so too do adolescents' contribution scores. Any covariation between SES factors and contribution is mediated through PYD and activity participation for these urban girls. For depression, 16% of the variance is accounted for by the background variables, PYD, and breadth of participation. PYD has a significant negative relationship with depression, such that lower PYD predicts higher levels of depression. However, there is a significant and positive relationship between breadth of participation and depression in this sample. This may be evidence of what Elkind (1981) terms the "hurried child," that is, of a relation between a child's engagement with numerous extracurricular activities and the child's affect. Future, longitudinal analyses will be able to assess if there exist developmental patterns of covariation consonant with such a link.

Finally, as demonstrated in analyses of the entire 4-H Study sample, there is a negative relationship between PYD and risk/problem behaviors. For these sixth graders the incidence of risk/problem behaviors is very low and has low variance. Nevertheless, lower levels of PYD are significantly related to this variable when other background variables are controlled for, albeit the effect is small ($R^2 = .08$). Breadth of participation is not significant in this model.

Variation in Depictions of Idealized Other, Idealized Self, and Actual Self

The qualitative part of the data analysis aimed to answer two questions. First, what do urban girls write about when asked about thriving (or doing well)? We were specifically interested in determining if the girls used language consistent with the Five Cs of PYD in their descriptions of thriving, and any other attributes or activities the youth used to describe someone who is doing well. Second, what can we learn about well-being of urban girls from their descriptions of themselves?

To address the first question, we analyzed the girls' descriptions of an exemplary youth (or other), idealized self, and actual self. Of the 277 girls included in our sample, 239 participants provided codable descriptions of actual self, 247 participants offered codable responses to the idealized self question, and 229 participants wrote codable answers to the exemplary youth (or other) question. Answers such as "I don't know," nonsensical sentences, and sentences that did not contain information regarding thriving, such as "This friend wants to be older and she tries to act older but she's only twelve" were considered uncodable. However, there were only nine uncodable answers, all of which were in response to the questions about idealized self and idealized (exemplary) other.

Based on the final coding, we found that more than half of the girls used language consistent with the Five Cs and contribution when describing a thriving youth. One hundred forty-one (53.8%) girls used this language when describing an idealized other, 146 (55.7%) when describing idealized self, and 163 (62.2%) when describing actual self. Urban girls discussed competence mostly in relation to academic competence (such as getting good grades) and athletic competence, for example, "I am on the honor roll and I have great grades in all of my classes" and "I'm good at most sports except hockey." Girls wrote about connection mainly in relation to peers and family, for example, "I spend time with my family" and "My friends are great. They respect me and they are an important part of my life." Caring was expressed in multiple ways, including caring for friends, family, and animals, as in "I like to take care of my animals" and "I love everyone and myself." Urban girls discussed character as being good to others and doing the right thing: "I listen to my elders" and "I think of myself as a hard worker." Confidence was written about as being proud of oneself, for example, "I'm doing really well in school and I'm kind of proud of myself." Among the Five Cs, for all three items combined, respondents most often mentioned Competence (out of 277 girls, 152 mentioned Competence, 93 mentioned Connection, 88 mentioned Character, 30 mentioned Caring, and 11 mentioned Confidence).

The outcome of contribution was most often described by the girls as helping one's family or community. Sample statements include "I babysit and help people" and "I help out and organize school groups to keep kids in school."

At the same time, there were other concepts, not captured by the Five Cs and contribution framework, that were important for girls when they described thriving. These other concepts included (a) various activities, for example, sports and outdoor activities, arts and drama, hobbies, spending time with friends, and shopping; (b) descriptions of positive personal characteristics and behaviors, such as being spiritual and popular; (c) negative personal characteristics and behaviors, such as being lazy, bossy, and getting into trouble; (d) descriptions of positive and negative emotions, such as being happy or sad; (e) descriptions of positive and negative characteristics of contexts, such as family and neighborhood; and (f) descriptions of physical appearance. One hundred fifty-seven (59.93%) mentioned the concepts in these six thematic categories when describing an exemplary other youth, 153 (58.4%) used these concepts when describing the idealized self, and 192 (73.3%) used these concepts when describing the actual self. For all three items combined, the most often mentioned "non-C" themes were positive personal characteristics and outdoor activities/sports participation.

In essence, then, most of the answers to the open-ended questions included both language consistent with the Five Cs and contribution and, as well, descriptions of issues that are perhaps developmentally and personally important but are not considered as reflecting indicators of PYD. For example, the following description of an exemplary youth was coded as containing themes of competence and contribution, which are consistent with PYD framework and, as well, specific activities such as arts and drama: "She is a good friend to me. She helps me get through hard times. She dances a lot and does a lot of really great things. Her grades are doing well too." The following description of idealized self was coded for themes of Competence and Connection, which are consistent with PYD framework, and also for themes relating to positive personal characteristics: "I would want to have straight As I'll be smart, and my mom will be proud of me." The following example of a description of the actual self was coded for the PYD-related themes of Character and Connection, and for themes reflecting other types of activity: "I am responsible of my sister, respectful. I am liking school a lot, and my teacher because she teaches fun stuff. I like reading, I like seeing TV a lot."

We conclude that when sixth-grade urban girls are asked to describe thriving (or well-being) in their own words, more than half of them describe characteristics, activities, and contexts that are seen as contributing to positive youth development by using terms associated with the Five Cs and contribution. At the same time, additional themes are important to these girls that do not reflect indicators of PYD, at least as indexed by the Five Cs and contribution. King et al. (2005) reported comparable findings.

In order to address the second question—What can we learn about the well-being of urban girls from their self-descriptions?—we looked at the descriptions of actual selves that the girls offered. We found that most of the girls described themselves as doing well when answering the question about actual self, "Now, think about yourself and your life now. How would you describe how you are doing? What are you like? What sorts of things do you do?" Out of 236 cases that contained responses, we were able to code 221 in order to assess whether or not the girls view themselves in a positive light. Fourteen answers were deemed uncodable for this purpose. Some uncodable data were nonsensical sentences, such as "I am in the middle I like to hang out with my friends." Answers were also deemed uncodable if they provided descriptive information that could not be evaluated for positive or negative content, such as "I wear glasses. I always tie my hair the same way every day." In addition, uncodable data included answers that did not pertain to the question, such as "I would be nice and better looking, and I will be a tennis player."

One hundred seventy-one girls (61.7%) provided descriptions of themselves and their environment only in positive terms. Among those answers, we saw a range of responses from very upbeat to more subtle descriptions. The following self-descriptions are the examples of the more positive end of the positive spectrum: "I am doing incredible in my life. I have a wonderful and supportive family and I have great friends. I help other people with chores and I enjoy life," and "My life is great. I'm having fun and I have a lot of friends. I'm in volleyball, and in drama." Less positive and more neutral answers included responses such as "I'm doing ok. I'm just a regular pre-teen. I do nine sports each year!" and "Well, I would describe me doing ok, not great, not bad, just fine and ok."

Forty-one respondents (14.8%) used both positive and negative terms when describing themselves. Examples of these descriptions include such answers as "I am a good friend. I am good to people. I am nice but I can be mean sometimes. Be good to people, be generous," and "I am not so good. Me and my stepfather don't talk at all, when we do we always argue. I'm good, respectful, nice, and get into lots of fights with brothers and sister. I like just to be with my friends and spend most of my time with family."

When respondents described themselves in both negative and positive ways, it was often explained in terms of more than one reason. Sometimes, as in the examples just mentioned, the girls talked about difficulties in their relationships with their family members. Other girls mentioned family issues: "At times I feel very lonely. Not having a father around, and [some]times I'm happy. I like reading and drawing." Yet others, while describing themselves in a positive way, described their life as generally difficult: "I try to work hard in school. I try to help around the house as much as I can. Right now my life is hard and sad."

Additional negative issues mentioned by the girls included difficulties with school, being teased or disliked by peers, concerns about physical appearance, and awareness of negative personal characteristics such as bossiness and laziness. While more negative, it may be that these respondents are more reflective and insightful, or have higher standards for themselves than girls who talk about themselves only in positive terms.

Only nine girls (3.2%) described themselves exclusively in negative terms. Examples include such answers as "I think my life right now is like a four-way to nowhere, which means confusing. I'm like really confused right now"; "Everybody hates me. I am always hated and depressed"; and "I'm not doing so well. When mother got pregnant she stop[ped] working. We didn't catch up on our bills and I need clothes." These self-descriptions suggested that some girls (albeit only a few in this sample) are struggling with growing up and managing relationships with peers and family.

In sum, based on these analyses, we found that most of the urban girls in our sample view themselves as doing well. This result is consistent with the quantitative findings of high levels of PYD, moderate levels of contribution already by sixth grade, and low levels of depression and risk/problem behaviors in this sample of urban girls.

Conclusions and Implications

We believe our findings tell a useful and provocative story about urban girls during a portion of their early adolescence (i.e., their sixth-grade year). As is true of all girls we are assessing within the 4-H Study, urban girls are doing well, at least as indexed by their reports on quantitative items linked to the Five Cs of PYD and contribution and, as well, as evidenced by qualitative coding of their statements on the open-ended questions we posed to them. Despite the presence of some variation between our samples of urban and nonurban girls and within the sample of urban girls, the overall view one can derive from the present findings is that in early adolescence the probability is that urban girls have the cognitive, affective, and behavioral characteristics that are indicative of healthy, positive development (Eccles & Gootman, 2002; Lerner, 2004c; Roth & Brooks-Gunn, 2003b).

While these results thus lend further support to the strength-based conception of adolescence and, as such, speak against the use of the deficit model of urban youth (or youth in general), at the same time the findings we have reported suggest that the Five Cs model of PYD indicators is a necessary but also an incomplete frame for depicting the dimensions along which urban girls may thrive. As found also by King et al. (2005), our qualitative findings suggest that there exist concepts associated with positive development that are not captured by the current set of quantitative indicators of the PYD concept. While a preponderant portion of our qualitative data triangulated with our quantitative findings to indicate the usefulness of the quantitative operationalization of PYS through the Five Cs and contribution, the qualitative data revealed that a half dozen additional themes were reflected in the girls' conceptions of thriving in others and in themselves.

A key implication of these qualitative findings is that future research must expand the operationalizations used to index PYD. Clearly, the quantitative indicators of PYD associated with the Five Cs and contribution may capture a great deal of the variance in describing PYD among youth in general and in regard to urban girls in particular. In the study of the person, we know that there are features of structure and function that are shared by all individuals, and these quantitative indices may provide suitable appraisals of these nomothetic features of behavior and development. However, people also possess characteristics that are shared by others in a particular group they are in (i.e., they possess group differential characteristics); further, each individual may possess characteristics unique to her, that is, there may by idiographic characteristics (Emmerich, 1968; Lerner, 2002). The qualitative data we have reviewed suggest that urban girls, as a group, may possess differential features of their behavior and development. In addition, these data suggest that there may be important idiographic features of development as well (e.g., in regard to our findings that there is a small group of girls who are struggling in regard to their senses of self and/or that there may be, for some girls, an association between out-of-school activities and affect that reflect the "hurried child syndrome").

In short, then, the richness of the qualitative analyses confirms the utility of the quantitative approaches being taken to studying PYD and to testing the development systems ideas about the utility of a strength-based approach to youth development (Theokas & Lerner, in press). At the same time, these analyses suggest that these quantitative approaches need to be expanded to identify and, through applications of research to policies and programs, support the varied and important ways that urban girls travel across their adolescence toward a positive and productive life.

Note

The preparation of this chapter was supported in part by a grant from the National 4-H Council.

References

Alberts, A. E., Christiansen, E. D., Chase, P., Naudeau, S., Phelps, E., & Lerner, R. M. (2006). *Qualitative and quantitative assessments of thriving and contribution in early adolescence: Findings from the 4-H Study of Positive Youth Development.* Unpublished manuscript. Institute for Applied Research in Youth Development. Medford, MA: Tufts University.

Armsden, G., & Greenberger, M. (1987). The inventory of parent and peer attachment: Individual differences and their relationship to psychological well-being in adolescence. *Journal of Youth and Adolescence, 16,* 427–452.

Balsano, A., Theokas, C., Lerner, J. V., Phelps, E., & Lerner, R. M. (2006). *Participation heterogeneity and change in early adolescent after-school activities: Implications for positive youth development.* Unpublished manuscript. Institute for Applied Research in Youth Development. Medford, MA: Tufts University.

Baltes, P. B., Lindenberger, U., & Staudinger, U. M. (2006). Lifespan theory in developmental psychology. In W. Damon & R. M. Lerner (Series Eds.) & R. M. Lerner (Vol. Ed.), *Handbook of child psychology: Vol. 1. Theoretical models of human development* (6th ed., pp. 569–664). Hoboken, NJ: Wiley.

Benson, P. L. (2003). Developmental assets and asset-building community: Conceptual and empirical foundations. In R. M. Lerner & P. L. Benson (Eds.), *Developmental assets and asset-building communities: Implications for research, policy, and practice* (pp. 19–43). New York: Kluwer Academic/Plenum.

Benson, P. L., Leffert, N., Scales, P. C., & Blyth, D. A. (1998). Beyond the "village" rhetoric: Creating healthy communities for children and adolescents. *Applied Developmental Science, 2,* 138–159.

Benson, P. L., Scales, P. C., Hamilton, S. F., & Sesma, A., Jr. (2006). Positive youth development: Theory, research and applications. In W. Damon & R. M. Lerner (Series Eds.) & R. M. Lerner (Vol. Ed.), *Handbook of child psychology: Vol. 1. Theoretical models of human development* (6th ed., pp. 894–941). Hoboken, NJ: Wiley.

Block, J. H. (1973). Conceptions of sex roles: Some cross-cultural and longitudinal perspectives. *American Psychologist, 28,* 512–526.

Bornstein, M. H., Davidson, L., Keyes, C. M., Moore, K., & the Center for Child Well-Being. (Eds.). (2003). *Well-being: Positive development across the life course.* Mahwah, NJ: Erlbaum.

Brandtstädter, J. (1998). Action perspectives on human development. In W. Damon (Series Ed.) & R. M. Lerner (Vol. Ed.), *Handbook of child psychology: Vol. 1. Theoretical models of human development* (5th ed., pp. 807–863). New York: Wiley.

Brandtstädter, J. (1999). The self in action and development: Cultural, biosocial, and ontogenetic bases of intentional self-development. In J. Brandtstädter & R. M. Lerner (Eds.), *Action and self-development: Theory and research through the life-span* (pp. 37–65). Thousand Oaks, CA: Sage.

Brandtstädter, J. (2006). Action perspectives on human development. In W. Damon & R. M. Lerner (Series Eds.) & R. M. Lerner (Vol. Ed.), *Handbook of child psychology: Vol. 1. Theoretical models of human development* (6th ed.). Hoboken, NJ: Wiley.

Broverman, I. K., Vogel, S. R., Broverman, D. M., Clarkson, F. E., & Rosenkrantz, P. S. (1972). Sex-role stereotypes: A current appraisal. *Journal of Social Issues, 28,* 59–78.

Csikszentmihalyi, M., & Rathunde, K. (1998). The development of the person: An experiential perspective on the ontogenesis of psychological complexity. In W. Damon (Series Ed.) & R. M. Lerner (Vol. Ed.), *Handbook of child psychology: Vol. 1. Theoretical models of human development* (5th ed., pp. 635–684). New York: Wiley.

Cummings, E. (2003). Foreword. In D. Wertlieb, F. Jacobs, & R. M. Lerner (Eds.), *Handbook of applied developmental science: Promoting positive child, adolescent, and family development through research, policies, and programs: Vol. 3. Promoting positive youth and family development: Community systems, citizenship, and civil society* (pp. ix–xi). Thousand Oaks, CA: Sage.

Damon, W. (2004). What is positive youth development? *Annals of the American Academy of Political and Social Science, 591,* 13–24.

Dowling, E., Gestsdottir, S., Anderson, P., von Eye, A., Almerigi, J., & Lerner, R. M. (2004). Structural relations among spirituality, religiosity, and thriving in adolescence. *Applied Developmental Science, 8,* 7–16.

Eccles, J. S., & Gootman, J. A. (Eds.). (2002). Community programs to promote youth development/Committee on Community-Level Programs for Youth. Washington DC: National Academy Press.

Eisenberg, N., Fabes, R. A., Murphy, B. C., Karbon, M., Smith, M., & Maszk, P. (1996). The relations of children's dispositional empathy-related responding to their emotionality, regulation, and social functioning. *Developmental Psychology, 32,* 195–209.

Elder, G. H., Jr., & Shanahan, M. J. (2006). The life course and human development. In W. Damon & R. M. Lerner (Series Eds.) & R. M. Lerner (Vol. Ed.), *Handbook of child psychology: Vol. 1. Theoretical models of human development* (6th ed., pp. 665–715). Hoboken, NJ: Wiley.

Elkind, D. (1981). *The hurried child.* Reading, MA: Addison-Wesley.

Emmerich, W. (1968). Personality development and concepts of structure. *Child Development, 39,* 671–690.

Floyd, D. T., & McKenna, L. (2003). National youth serving organizations in the United States: Contributions to civil society. In R. M. Lerner, F. Jacobs, & D. Wertlieb (Eds.), *Handbook of applied developmental science: Promoting positive child, adolescent, and family development through research, policies, and programs: Vol. 3. Promoting positive youth and family development: Community systems, citizenship, and civil society* (pp. 11–26). Thousand Oaks, CA: Sage.

Gore, A. (2003). Foreword. In R. M. Lerner & P. L. Benson (Eds.), *Developmental assets and asset-building communities: Implications for research, policy, and practice* (pp. xi–xii). Norwell, MA: Kluwer.

Gottlieb, G. (2004). Normally occurring environmental and behavioral influences on gene activity. In C. Garcia Coll, E. Bearer, & R. M. Lerner (Eds.), *Nature and nurture: The complex interplay of genetic and environmental influences on human behavior and development* (pp. 85–106). Mahwah, NJ: Erlbaum.

Gottlieb, G., Wahlsten, D., & Lickliter, R. (2006). The significance of biology for human development: A developmental psychobiological systems view. In W. Damon & R. M. Lerner (Series Eds.) & R. M. Lerner (Vol. Ed.), *Handbook of child psychology: Vol. 1. Theoretical models of human development* (6th ed., pp. 210–257). Hoboken, NJ: Wiley.

Harter, S. (1982). The Perceived Competence Scale for Children. *Child Development, 53,* 87–98.

Harter, S. (1983). *Supplementary description of the Self-Perception Profile for Children: Revision of the Perceived Competence Scale for Children.* Unpublished manuscript, University of Denver.

Harter, S. (1998). The development of self-representations. In W. Damon (Series Ed.) & N. Eisenberg (Vol. Ed.), *Handbook of child psychology: Vol. 3, Social emotional, and personality development* (5th ed., pp. 553–617). New York: Wiley.

Harter, S. (2006). The self. In W. Damon & R. M. Lerner (Series Eds.) & N. Eisenberg (Vol. Ed.), *Handbook of child psychology: Vol. 3. Social, emotional, and personality development* (6th ed., pp. 505–570). Hoboken, NJ: Wiley.

Jelicic, H., Bobek, D., Phelps, E., Lerner, R. M., & Lerner, J. V. (2006). *Using positive youth development to predict positive and negative outcomes in early adolescence: Findings from the first two waves of the 4-H Study of Positive Youth Development.* Unpublished manuscript. Institute for Applied Research in Youth Development. Medford, MA: Tufts University.

King, P. E., Dowling, E. M., Mueller, R. A., White, K., Schultz, W., Osborn, P., et al. (2005). Thriving in adolescence: The voices of youth-serving practitioners, parents, and early and late adolescents. *Journal of Early Adolescence, 25,* 94–112.

Lerner, R. M. (2002). *Concepts and theories of human development* (3rd ed.). Mahwah, NJ: Erlbaum.

Lerner, R. M. (2004a). Diversity in individual ←→ context relations as the basis for positive development across the life span: A developmental systems perspective for theory, research, and application. *Research in Human Development, 1,* 327–346.

Lerner, R. M. (2004b). Genes and the promotion of positive human development: Hereditarian versus developmental systems perspectives. In C. Garcia Coll, E. Bearer, & R. M. Lerner (Eds.), *Nature and nurture: The complex interplay of genetic and environmental influences on human behavior and development* (pp. 1–33). Mahwah, NJ: Erlbaum.

Lerner, R. M. (2004c). *Liberty: Thriving and civic engagement among American youth.* Thousand Oaks, CA: Sage.

Lerner, R. M. (2006). Developmental science, developmental systems, and contemporary theories of human development. In W. Damon & R. M. Lerner (Series Eds.) & R. M. Lerner (Vol. Ed.), *Handbook of child psychology: Vol. 1. Theoretical models of human development* (6th ed., 1–17). Hoboken, NJ: Wiley.

Lerner, R. M. (2005, September). *Promoting positive youth development: Theoretical and empirical bases.* White paper prepared for the Workshop on the Science of Adolescent Health and Development, National Research Council/Institute of Medicine. Washington, DC: National Academies of Science.

Lerner, R. M., Lerner, J. V., Almerigi, J., Theokas, C., Phelps, E., Gestsdottir, S., et al. (2005). Positive youth development, participation in community youth development programs, and community contributions of fifth grade adolescents: Findings from the first wave of the 4-H Study of Positive Youth Development. *Journal of Early Adolescence, 25,* 17–71.

Little, R. R. (1993, October). *What's working for today's youth: The issues, the programs, and the learnings.* Paper presented at the Institute for Children, Youth, and Families Fellows' Colloquium, Michigan State University.

Luthar, S. S., & Latendresse, S. J. (2002). Adolescent risk: The costs of affluence. *New Directions for Youth Development, 95,* 101–121.

Maccoby, E. (1998). *The two sexes: Growing up apart, coming together.* Cambridge, MA: Harvard University Press.

Maccoby. E., & Jacklin. C.N. (1974). *The psychology of sex differences.* Stanford, CA: Stanford University Press.

McCandless, R. R. (1970). *Adolescents.* Hinsdale, IL: Dryden.

McLoyd, V. C. (1998). Children in poverty: Development, public policy, and practice. In W. Damon (Series Ed.) & I. Sigel & K. A. Renninger (Vol. Eds.), *Handbook of child psychology: Vol. 4. Child psychology in practice* (5th ed., pp. 135–208). New York: Wiley.

McLoyd, V. C., Aikens, N. L., & Burton, L. M. (2006). Childhood poverty, policy, and practice. In W. Damon & R. M. Lerner (Series Eds.) & K. A. Renninger & I. E. Sigel (Vol. Eds.), *Handbook of child psychology: Vol. 4. child psychology and practice* (6th ed., pp. 700–775). Hoboken, NJ: Wiley.

Mincy, R. B. (1994). *Nurturing young Black males.* Washington, DC: Urban Institute Press.

Monitoring the Future. (2000). *National survey on drug use, 1975–2000.* Bethesda, MD: National Institute on Drug Abuse.

Overton, W. F. (2006). Developmental psychology: Philosophy, concepts, methodology. In W. Damon & R. M. Lerner (Series Eds.) & R. M. Lerner (Ed.), *Handbook of child psychology: Vol. 1. Theoretical models of human development* (6th ed.). Hoboken, NJ: Wiley.

Pittman, K., Irby, M., & Ferber, T. (2001). Unfinished business: Further reflections on a decade of promoting youth development. In P. L. Benson & K. J. Pittman (Eds.), *Trends in youth development: Visions, realities and challenges* (pp. 4–50). Norwell, MA: Kluwer.

Radloff, L. S. (1977). The CES-D scale: A self-report depression scale for research in the general population. *Applied Psychological Measurement, 1,* 385–401.

Rathunde, K., & Csikszentmihalyi, M. (2006). The developing person: An experiential perspective. In W. Damon & R. M. Lerner (Series Eds.) & R. M. Lerner (Vol. Ed.), *Handbook of child psychology: Vol. 1. Theoretical models of human development* (6th ed., pp. 465–515). Hoboken, NJ: Wiley.

Roth, J. L., & Brooks-Gunn, J. (2003a). What exactly is a youth development program? Answers from research and practice. *Applied Developmental Science, 7,* 94–111.

Roth, J. L., & Brooks-Gunn, J. (2003b). What is a youth development program? Identification and defining principles. In R. M. Lerner, F. Jacobs, & D. Wertlieb (Eds.), *Handbook of applied developmental science: Promoting positive child, adolescent, and family development through research, policies, and programs: Vol. 2. Enhancing the life chances of youth and families: Public service systems and public policy perspectives* (pp. 197–223). Thousand Oaks, CA: Sage.

Small, S. A., & Rodgers, K. B. (1995). Teen Assessment Project (TAP) Survey Question Bank. Madison, WI: University of Wisconsin–Madison.

Spencer, M. B. (2006). Phenomenological Variant of Ecological Systems Theory (PVEST): A human development synthesis applicable to diverse individuals and groups. In W. Damon & R. M. Lerner (Series Eds.) & R. M. Lerner (Vol. Ed.), *Handbook of child psychology: Vol. 1. Theoretical models of human development* (6th ed.). Hoboken, NJ: Wiley.

Strauss, A., & Corbin, J. (1998). *Basics of qualitative research: Techniques and procedures for developing grounded theory* (2nd ed.). Thousand Oaks, CA: Sage.

Suomi, S. J. (2004). How gene-environment interactions influence emotional development in rhesus monkeys. In C. Garcia-Coll, E. L. Bearer, & R. M. Lerner (Eds.), *Nature and nurture: The complex interplay of genetic and environmental influences on human behavior and development* (pp. 35–51). Mahwah, NJ: Erlbaum.

Taylor, C. (2003). Youth gangs and community violence. In R. M. Lerner, F. Jacobs, & D. Wertlieb (Eds.), *Handbook of applied developmental science: Promoting positive child, adolescent, and family development through research, policies, and programs: Vol. 2. Enhancing the life chances of youth and families: Public service systems and public policy perspectives* (pp. 65–80). Thousand Oaks, CA: Sage.

Taylor, C., McNeil, R., Smith, P. R., & Taylor, V. A. (in preparation). *Growing up urban: Positively Affecting Urban Youth—A Model.* East Lansing: Michigan State University.

Theokas, C., Almerigi, J. B., Lerner, R. M., Dowling, E. M., Benson, P. L., Scales, P. C., et al. (2005). Conceptualizing and modeling individual and ecological asset components of thriving in early adolescence. *Journal of Early Adolescence, 25,* 113–143.

Theokas, C. & Lerner, R. M. (in press). Observed ecological assets in families, schools, and neighborhoods: Conceptualization, measurement and relations with positive and negative developmental outcomes. *Applied Developmental Science, 10*(2).

Way, N. (1998). *Everyday courage: The lives and stories of urban adolescents.* New York: NYU Press.

Wheeler, W. (2003). Youth leadership for development: Civic activism as a component of youth development programming and a strategy for strengthening civil society. In R. M. Lerner, F. Jacobs, & D. Wertlieb (Eds.), *Handbook of applied developmental science: Promoting positive child, adolescent, and family development through research, policies, and programs: Vol. 2. Enhancing the life chances of youth and families: Public service systems and public policy perspectives* (pp. 491–505). Thousand Oaks, CA: Sage.

From Urban Girls to Resilient Women

Studying Adaptation Across Development in the Context of Adversity

Anne Shaffer, Brianna Coffino, Kristen Boelcke-Stennes, and Ann S. Masten

The chapters in this volume draw our attention to many issues in the lives of urban girls in contemporary society, most notably to the variety and intensity of the stresses and challenges that these girls encounter in their daily lives. Yet many girls and young women continue to do well, and even thrive, under conditions regularly identified as perilous or stressful. In such cases, people are described as "resilient," suggesting that they have the capacity to succeed in the face of adversity. Many striking stories of resilience have been told and reported in legends and ancient tales, movies and television shows, books and newspapers. For example, a recent television movie, *Homeless to Harvard: The Liz Murray Story,* featured the true story of a young woman who was left homeless and alone at the age of 15 when her mother died as a result AIDS and drug addiction. Liz went on to win a scholarship to Harvard, to study film at Columbia University, and to write a book about her life. Such compelling stories of resilience have long captured human imagination and inspired hope in other people.

Although the phenomenon of resilience is not new, the systematic study of resilience did not begin until around 1970 (Luthar, in press; Masten & Powell, 2003). What researchers have learned in recent years has been somewhat surprising. Resilience is not especially rare, nor does it require superhuman powers or extreme good luck; it seems to grow out of "ordinary magic," the common protections, resources, and opportunities available in many individuals, families, neighborhoods, and cultures around the world (Masten, 2001). In this chapter, we present an overview of how researchers currently conceptualize risk and adversity, as well as competence and resilience in development. In addition, we describe findings from a 20-year longitudinal study of resilience in an urban sample, highlighting what we have learned from the girls (now women) who have participated in this research. Finally, we point out key issues for further discussion, and controversial topics that continue to raise questions in the field of resilience research.

Project Competence is one of the programs whose researchers have tried to understand resilience over an extended period of time in the development of individuals (see Masten & Powell, 2003, for an overview of this project). In this chapter, we highlight some of the theory, methods, and findings of this study that are relevant to the development of resilience in the lives of the girls and women who have participated for more than 20 years. In the concluding section, we raise some of the controversial issues that complicate and enrich the study of resilience in development, in the spirit of spurring further thought and discussion of this research field. First, we begin by defining key concepts, which provide the background for our studies of resilience in Project Competence.

Resilience

In order for research to move beyond case accounts and stories of resilience, the concept of resilience must be defined and operationalized. Broadly speaking, *resilience* refers to the general phenomenon of doing well despite exposure to significant threats to development. A comprehensive study of resilience therefore requires specification on two points: first, identification of the threat to development, and, second, a judgment about adaptational success (Masten & Coatsworth, 1998). Therefore, it is important to define and measure positive adaptation and also the risks or adversities that people have encountered. A person who is doing well but has not experienced any unusual or significant adversity might be considered competent or adaptive or well-adjusted, but he or she would not yet meet the criteria for resilience. If the same person encounters some kind of major hazards and continues to do well or recovers and goes on with life, then he or she would begin to meet the definition of resilience. It is also possible for an individual to meet the criteria for resilience at one time in life and yet experience later difficulties. Thus, resilience is not a static concept but a dynamic one; lives through time are always changing. In fact, it is interesting to study when resilience emerges and whether it endures through time and transitions. Some girls show resilience early in life and continue to develop well, with minor bumps in the road to adult adjustment. Other girls stumble in adolescence and never recover, and still others are late bloomers, who get on a positive road later, as they leave girlhood behind.

Competence

Defining resilience requires measuring how well individuals are doing. There are different ways to define "doing well" in life and various indicators of positive functioning; these depend both on the developmental criterion of interest and on the theoretical orientation of the investigator (Luthar, Cicchetti, & Becker, 2000). These include the presence of certain behaviors (e.g., academic success, positive peer relationships, community involvement), as well as the absence of other behaviors (e.g., drug use, violent behavior, truancy; Masten & Reed, 2003). Developmental scientists often define and judge how well a child is doing in terms of their progress or success in age-salient tasks, which are the benchmarks of psychosocial development in a given culture and time in history (Havighurst, 1972; Masten & Coatsworth, 1998). Some are universal across all human cultures, such as learning to talk as a young child, while others vary across history and culture, such as learning to read or doing well in school. In some cultures, developmental tasks may vary by gender, so that girls are expected to learn traditional dance or handiwork but boys are not. Across all cultures, developmental tasks vary by age. For example, getting along with peers has developmental importance by the early school years, but close friendships become more salient as children grow older, and the domain of romantic relationships emerges as a developmental task later in adolescence and young adulthood. As girls grow older, what is expected of them increases in complexity and responsibility, requiring more cognitive capacity, strength, skills, or the maturity that comes with puberty or rites of passage in a culture. Over historical time, the salience of particular developmental tasks may wax and wane, so that skill in farming, for example, becomes less important and the ability to read well becomes more important.

Competence arises from complex interactions between the child and her environment. As children grow up, the contexts in which they must function will change, and the challenges they must negotiate to demonstrate competence will differ (Masten & Coatsworth, 1998). Negotiating the transition to secondary schooling at the same time that a girl is adjusting to the many changes that accompany puberty is a common challenge; if a girl is also dealing with divorce or death in the family at the same time, it can become very difficult to stay on track with school, social life, and family obligations.

In Project Competence, studies have focused on competence in major developmental tasks in our studies of resilience (e.g., Garmezy, Masten, & Tellegen, 1984; Roisman, Masten, Coatsworth, & Tellegen, 2004). Some definitions of doing well in life also consider how a person is feeling on the inside, in terms of psychological well-being or happiness (Luthar, in press). It might also be reasonable to include additional domains of physical or mental health in defining or measuring positive adjustment when one studies resilience (Masten & Coatsworth, 1998). Therefore, it is important when judgments about resilience are made for research that the criteria for judging positive outcomes be clearly indicated. In any case, in order to capture the full range of human functioning, it is necessary to assess competence in multiple and diverse domains. Although there is agreement on many of the domains of life that must be included in the assessment of competence, some differences of opinion persist (Luthar et al., 2000). Similarly, there can be within-individual heterogeneity of adaptation or functioning; for example, some people are highly accomplished in certain spheres and wholly unfit in others. Researchers who are interested in defining and identifying competence in multiple domains must carefully consider all these issues.

Risk Factors and Adversity

Negative life experiences have been conceptualized and measured as risk factors for adversity. Risk factors are established predictors of negative outcomes, such as poverty, single parenthood, or premature birth, which means that the chances of certain problematic outcomes are higher among people with the risk factor. But risk factors are predictive of problems for large groups of people, not necessarily in individuals, and certainly no person's life is completely risk-free. Thus a girl can be a member of a "high-risk group" for learning problems (e.g., defined by having multiple risk factors for such problems) and never have any academic problems at all.

While the nature or intensity of the individual risks may vary, the aggregation of multiple risk factors leads to an increased likelihood of poor functioning. The co-occurrence of multiple risk factors (i.e., cumulative risk) has been a robust predictor of maladaptation (Sameroff, 2000). High cumulative risk can refer to the co-occurrence of multiple risk factors at the same time or to the piling up of risk factors over a more extended period (Masten & Reed, 2003). Notably, many risk factors tend to naturally co-occur and therefore are difficult to disentangle. For example, features of poverty include both community-level risk factors (e.g., neighborhood violence, underresourced schools) and individual- or family-level risk factors (e.g., marginalized cultural groups, substance abuse, divorce).

Adversity is a special kind of risk factor, referring to negative life experiences that are directly observed or measured rather than inferred via the presence of certain risk factors. In Project Competence, we have measured negative life events or adversity actually experienced by individuals instead of relying solely on the measurement of risk factors. (As an example that distinguishes between risk factors and adversity, living in Kansas is a risk factor for experiencing tornadoes, but a tornado destroying your home is a traumatic adversity.) Although there are differences in the meaning and measurement of risk factors and measured adversity (Obradović, Masten, & Shaffer, 2005), the terms are often used interchangeably in the literature.

Resources/Assets/Protective Factors

In the study of resilience, it is also important to identify *what makes a difference* in the lives of people who have succeeded despite risk or adversity. Investigators have identified positive attributes of individuals or their relationships and contexts that predict better adaptation. Some of these predict good outcomes at all levels of risk; they often are described as *assets* or *resources*. Having good cognitive abilities or a good sense of humor or having good parents is associated with better social adjustment in many studies, regardless of whether people experience risk or adversity. However, some predictors appear to be important or more important only under difficult circumstances; these are called *protective factors*. Some factors work both ways. Good cognitive abilities and effective parenting predict better academic achievement across all levels of adversity; however, under hazardous rearing conditions, such as dangerous neighborhoods, these advantages appear to play a particularly important role in adaptation and development (Masten & Coatsworth, 1998; Masten, 2001).

Collectively, assets, resources, and protective factors may diminish, nullify, or counteract the consequences of adverse life experiences. It is probably the overall balance of risk factors to resources, assets, and protective factors that results in adaptation or maladaptation, rather than the effects of any single asset or protective factor (Werner, 2000). Additionally, both risk and protective factors are defined in terms of their relation to the developmental outcome of interest. Some factors may be related to positive adaptation under certain circumstances, while in other situations, they may predict negative functioning (Masten & Coatsworth, 1998). For instance, extreme shyness may reduce risk-taking behavior in adolescence, but it may interfere with social skill development in childhood.

Description of the Study

As noted earlier, Project Competence is an example of a longitudinal study that has extensively examined the phenomenon of resilience in a sample of urban participants who have been followed from middle childhood through early adulthood. Although both boys and girls were recruited for participation in this study, only the girls are included in the participants and data we present in this chapter. An introduction to the study design and methods is provided here; more detailed information on study methods and procedure can be found elsewhere (Masten et al., 1999; Masten et al., in press; Roisman et al., 2004).

Participants

In 1977 and 1978, the children who would eventually participate in the Project Competence longitudinal study were 8 to 12 years old, in third through sixth grades at two urban schools in Minneapolis. Parents of children in these grades were invited to participate in a cross-sectional study of competence and life events, which involved extensive multiple sources of information (parents, teachers, self, peers, school records), multiple methods (interviews, tests, questionnaires, etc.), and many hours of data collection for each participant family. Of the 205 original participants and their families who decided to join the longitudinal study, 114 were girls. This cohort was a normative school sample, in that all the families of children in the third to sixth grade were invited to join. The socioeconomic status among the girls' families ranged from 7 to 92.3 (reflecting a range from unskilled labor or public assistance to professionals of high prestige) on the 100-point Duncan Socio-Economic Index (Hauser & Featherman, 1977), with a sample mean 40.23 (the level of skilled labor or clerical positions). The ethnic and racial diversity of the girls was very similar to that of the Minneapolis public schools at the time (74% Caucasian, 17% African American, 6% American Indian, 2% Hispanic, and 1% Asian).

This study became a longitudinal study when the original cohort was followed up after 7 (Time 2), 10 (Time 3), and 20 (Time 4) years. At the adolescent assessment (Time 2), the girls were 14 to 17 years old; at the emerging adulthood assessment (Time 3), the girls were 19 to 23 years old; and at the young adulthood assessment (Time 4), the young women were 28 to 34 years of age. Retention of the whole cohort has been excellent, with approximately 90% of the original cohort who are still living participating in the 20-year follow-up. Of the 114 original young women, 108 participated in the 20-year follow-up (95%), as well as most of their parents who were still living. Two young women could not be located. Much of the data collected during the study is described in the following.[1]

Measurement of Competence Domains

For the childhood assessment at Time 1, three major domains of competence were assessed: *academic achievement, social competence,* and *conduct.* These domains, as well as the emerging domains of *romantic competence* and *job competence,* were assessed in adolescence and the transition to adulthood (Times 2 and 3). The young adult follow-up around age 30 (Time 4) included assessments of all previous competence domains and the new developmentally salient domain of *parenting competence* for those participants who were parents. (Although a portion of the cohort had become parents at the time of the adolescent assessments, parenting was not considered an age-salient developmental task until adulthood. By Time 4, the majority of the young women participating in the study had become parents [$n = 74$].) The selection of domains of interest and the criteria used to measure success in these domains were guided by developmental task theory and the limited available developmental literature on competence and adaptation in development (see Masten, Burt, & Coatsworth, in press; Masten & Coatsworth, 1998; and Masten & Powell, 2003, for the history of these ideas and measures).

Measurement of Adversity

Information on life history was ascertained from questionnaires, detailed interviews, and multiple informants. To judge the overall adversity of a given period of a child's life (between competence assessments, for example), we included all the acute and chronic events that were independent of the child's own behavior, excluding events like breaking up with a boyfriend or getting arrested, that can be quite stressful but are likely influenced by a child's own behavior and therefore would be confounded with our measures of competence. Life events, which were included in analyses, included those originating in the physical self (e.g., hospitalized due to illness), family (e.g., family violence, divorce, incarceration of a sibling), or community (e.g., death of a friend, tornado). Based on this information, the overall level of psychosocial adversity experienced was rated for each interval before and between major assessments, on a 7-point scale (1 = no or very little adversity, 5 = severe adversity, 7 = catastrophic adversity). Independent ratings were obtained from multiple judges, with very high agreement (see Gest, Reed, & Masten, 1999; Masten et al., 1999, for more details). For the classification of resilience (high adversity, good competence) described in the following, high adversity was defined as a score of 5 (severe) or higher through two periods of time, from birth through Time 1 and from Time 1 to 2.

Measurement of Potential Resources, Protective Factors, and Subjective Well-Being

PARENTING QUALITY IN CHILDHOOD AND ADOLESCENCE

Composite scores of the quality of parenting experienced by each girl were created based on ratings of the parent-child relationship from the perspective of the child, parent, interviewers, and clinical judges. In childhood, high scores on this composite (high parenting quality) reflect a combination of high structure and rules, warmth and closeness, and high expectations for their child's achievement and prosocial behavior. In emerging adulthood, the measurement of parenting focused on closeness because structure and discipline were no longer age-appropriate indicators of parenting quality.

MEASURES OF PSYCHOLOGICAL WELL-BEING IN LATE ADOLESCENCE AND EARLY ADULTHOOD

Several aspects of psychological adjustment, including measures of *self-worth, psychological distress,* and *positive and negative affectivity,* were measured at multiple time points during the course of the study. An individual's general feelings about herself were assessed during emerging adulthood (Time 3) and again in young adulthood (Time 4) using a self-worth scale based on the Harter Self-Perception Scale (Harter, 1985; Masten, Neeman, & Andenas, 1994). Symptoms of current psychological distress were indexed by the Global Symptom Index (GSI) from the Symptom Checklist 90-Revised (SCL90-R; Derogatis, 1977, 1982) in emerging adulthood (Time 3) and with the Young Adult Self-Report checklist (YASR; Achenbach, 1997) in early adulthood (Time 4). Mean levels of total symptoms for this cohort were comparable to standardized norms, indicating that this sample was normative with regard to reports of distress. Two general trait personality dimensions, positive and negative affectivity, were assessed by the Multidimensional Personality Questionnaire (MPQ; Tellegen, 1982, 1985) in emerging adulthood and young adulthood at the Time 3 and 4 assessments.

Selected Findings

Over time, the members of the Project Competence research team have studied resilience in the longitudinal study in different ways. In this chapter, we highlight one of the person-focused approaches, in which we have classified people according to their history of competence in multiple domains at the time and also the level of adversity they have experienced earlier in life. In this approach, our goal has been to compare people who we define as resilient at a given time (OK on three major domains of competence and also high in lifetime adversity prior to the Time 2 assessment) with peers who have the same level of competence but low adversity (competent) or the same level of adversity and low competence (maladaptive group). Here, we present the results of these types of analyses with a particular focus on the female participants in the study.

Diagnosing Resilience

In emerging adulthood (Time 3) and early adulthood (Time 4), the girls and young women were classified into groups based on overall patterns of adaptive functioning in age-salient developmental tasks, as well as their exposure to chronic adversity in childhood and adolescence. These classifications ultimately enabled "diagnoses" of individuals as either competent, resilient, or maladaptive.

In late adolescence, three levels of competence groups were formed (low, mixed, and OK) based on patterns of success in academic achievement, social competence, and conduct. Girls classified as OK ($n = 58$) were judged to be performing competently in all three of the salient domains of competence, as evidenced by competence ratings within a half standard deviation (SD) of the sample mean or better. (Since competence was conceptualized as doing "OK," rather than doing very well, the cutoff score actually falls below the group mean, in order to include the average range or above.) Those individuals classified as low ($n = 25$ girls) fell below average on two or more major criteria of competence. The mixed group ($n = 26$) did not meet the criteria as either "low" or "OK."

In young adulthood, more domains of competence and a variety of adaptive life choices are available (work versus advanced education, parenting versus working, and many combinations). Developmental task domains included academic attainment, social competence, conduct, romantic competence, work competence, and parenting competence (when applicable). Women classified as "OK" ($n = 79$) were judged to be performing competently in four or more competence domains (including parenting, which was considered a mandatory domain of competence for those who were parents) as evidenced by competence ratings within .5 SD of the sample mean or better. Those individuals classified as "low" ($n = 12$) were performing below average in at least three domains of competence, and the middle/mixed group ($n = 17$) did not meet the criteria for either "low" or "OK."

Adversity levels were classified as low, middle/mixed, or high using the adversity ratings spanning pre–Time 1 and Time 1 to 2. To be classified as high adversity ($n = 57$), an individual had to have experienced adversity rated as 5 or higher (severe to catastrophic) across the two time periods of childhood and early adolescence. Low adversity was defined as experiencing little or no adversity in both time points. Those who did not

TABLE 2.1
Participant Classifications at Times 3 and 4.

	OK Competence	Low Competence
Low Adversity	COMPETENT	VULNERABLE
	Time 3 $n = 19$	Time 3 $n = 2$
	Time 4 $n = 27$	Time 4 $n = 2$
High Adversity	RESILIENT	MALADAPTIVE
	Time 3 $n = 26$	Time 3 $n = 17$
	Time 4 $n = 33$	Time 4 $n = 7$

experience consistently high or consistently low levels of adversity fell into the mixed/middle group.

Only the "extreme" groups were considered for person-centered analyses (i.e., those with mixed or ambiguous scores on either competence or adversity ratings were excluded), and diagnoses were made according to the classification shown in Table 2.1 Although the table includes a cell for the vulnerable group (low competence and low adversity), there are too few participants in the category for further analysis ($n = 2$). This "empty cell" is interesting and observed in other studies, suggesting that this is not a common pattern (see Masten et al., 1999). Table 2.1 also shows the number of participants who were classified in each category at both Time 3 and Time 4.

CHARACTERISTICS OF RESILIENT, COMPETENT, AND MALADAPTIVE INDIVIDUALS IN EMERGING ADULTHOOD

A number of group comparisons were conducted in order to analyze the various differences among the groups at Time 3. By definition, both the resilient and the competent individuals were doing significantly better than the maladaptive individuals in all developmentally salient domains of competence (conduct, social, academic) at the Time 3 assessment, although the resilient and competent groups were not significantly different from each other. As reported elsewhere (Masten et al., 1999), specific factors such as average or better intellectual functioning and good parenting quality were significantly more common among both the competent and the resilient young women, and appeared to serve as protective factors for those participants who maintained positive adaptation despite exposure to severe and chronic adversity.

A series of further analyses were conducted to compare the groups identified in late adolescence; the results of these analyses of variance are presented in Table 2.2. Notably, in addition to the concurrent differences

TABLE 2.2
Analyses of Variance Among Groups Classified at Time 3 (Late Adolescence).

	df	F*	Post hoc comparisons[1]
Time 3 Domains			
Academic	2, 61	48.205	C, R > M
Social	2, 61	33.790	C, R > M
Conduct	2, 61	32.781	C, R > M
Work	2, 58	NS	—
Romantic	2, 58	NS	—
Self-worth	2, 58	9.775	C, R > M
Positive affectivity	2, 57	5.274	R > C, M
Negative affectivity	2, 57	7.018	M > R, C
Global symptom index	2, 57	NS	—
Earlier Domains			
T1 Academic	2, 61	6.256	C, R > M
T1 Social	2, 61	4.517	C > M
T1 Conduct	2, 61	15.434	C > R > M
T2 Academic	2, 55	13.288	C, R > M
T2 Social	2, 55	4.257	C, R > M
T2 Conduct	2, 55	17.579	C > R > M

*All reported F values are significant at p < .05. NS = nonsignificant.
[1]C = Competent, R = Resilient, M = Maladaptive. Groups separated by commas are not significantly different using LSD post hoc analyses.

in domains of competence assessed at Time 3, the resilient and competent young women also showed evidence of better overall adaptation than the maladaptive participants in most of the domains of competence that had been measured at baseline (middle childhood) and the first follow-up (early adolescence). These findings represent a strong example of developmental continuity, such that a person's adaptational outcomes are often the product of long-standing developmental history. Interestingly, the groups do not differ significantly in their functioning in domains of competence that are not yet developmentally salient (e.g., Roisman et al., 2004); for example, while emerging adults who are doing well are typically more competent in terms of academic functioning, a highly relevant domain for girls of this age who are still completing their schooling, they do not show evidence of significantly better functioning in terms of work or job competence, a domain that is still emerging at this age.

Beyond competent functioning in various domains, which are largely measured via external behavior, there are also significant group differences in terms of *internal* adaptation, as measured via various indices of wellbeing. These analyses of group differences are also presented in Table 2.2. As these results show, girls who were classified as competent or resilient in emerging adulthood reported better overall self-worth and higher positive emotionality than the maladaptive girls. Interestingly, the resilient girls demonstrated the highest scores on a measure of positive emotionality, even more than the competent individuals. In contrast, the maladaptive group had significantly higher scores of negative emotionality than the competent or resilient groups, suggesting that these young women were more stress reactive and likely to become upset in the face of adverse events. However, comparisons of overall distress (using the Global Symptom Index of the SCL-90-R; Derogatis, 1977, 1982) and well-being did not differ significantly among groups at the time of the emerging adulthood assessment. Now that we have assessed outcomes for many of these young women 10 years later, we also have learned that competence and resilience tend to endure. If we compare how the three groups that were diagnosed at Time 3 are doing in adulthood, the competent and resilient groups are doing well in many areas, whereas the maladaptive group has much worse outcomes by comparison. In the next section, we discuss the results obtained when we rediagnose all the girls based on their competence in adulthood.

CHARACTERISTICS OF RESILIENT, COMPETENT, AND MALADAPTIVE INDIVIDUALS IN EARLY ADULTHOOD

The girls were reclassified in adulthood based on assessments of competence in the age-salient developmental tasks in early adulthood. The same criteria were used for defining early adversity as in previous analyses. Again, and by definition, individuals in the competent and resilient groups showed significantly better functioning in all age-salient domains of competence, as compared with those participants in the maladaptive group (see Table 2.3). Group differences on internal measures of adaptation were also examined at early adulthood. At Time 4, the young women who were classified as either competent or resilient demonstrated higher scores than maladaptive individuals in terms of their self-ratings of well-being, positive affectivity, and self-worth. In addition, the resilient and competent women reported lower scores than did maladaptive women in terms of negative affectivity and internalizing problems. Thus, the competent and resilient young women appeared to be consistently better off, on the inside (well-being, symptoms, prone to more positive and less negative emotion) as well as the outside (competence).

It is also clear that some young women turn their lives in a new direction, because there are girls who were classified as "maladaptive" in adolescence who have moved into the resilient category. These dramatic

TABLE 2.3
Analyses of Variance Among Groups Classified at Time 4 (Early Adulthood)

	df	F*	Post Hoc Comparisons[1]
Time 4 Domains			
Academic	2, 68	14.626	C, R > M
Social	2, 68	6.238	C, R > M
Conduct	2, 68	25.080	C > R > M
Work	2, 68	13.139	C, R > M
Romantic	2, 68	4.783	C, R > M
Parenting	2, 46	54.831	C, R > M
Self-worth	2, 66	17.877	C, R > M
Positive affectivity	2, 63	5.867	C, R > M
Negative affectivity	2, 63	13.899	C, R > M
Internalizing symptoms	2, 65	9.543	C, R > M

*All reported F values are significant at $p < .05$. NS = nonsignificant.
[1]C = Competent, R = Resilient, M = Maladaptive. Groups separated by commas are not significantly different using LSD post hoc analyses.

turnarounds are small in number but provocative when considering whether the transition to adulthood offers a window of opportunity to shift one's life in a much better direction. Looking back, there were hints that the maladaptive youth who would become resilient were already showing signs of higher motivation to achieve in the future, greater plan-fulness, and more adult support, even before the changes in competence occurred (Masten et al., 1999).

In summary, these data highlight that resilience is indeed an observable phenomenon in the lives of these urban girls and women. Patterns of adaptation across different levels of exposure to adversity reveal that positive functioning in the context of stressful life experiences is not only possible but also *predictable* from past behavior, and the presence of environmental resources and protective factors. Furthermore, external manifestations of competence are often accompanied by internal feelings of well-being, though certainly not all the time.

Our findings for urban girls in this study are very consistent with findings found in other research on resilience, including data obtained across both genders in the current sample and for rural youth in Iowa (Elder & Conger, 2000), Hawaiian youth from Kauai (Werner and Smith, 1992), and a host of other studies in the United States and other countries (Luthar, 2003, in press; Masten, 2001; Masten & Powell, 2003). Similar protective factors turn up across diverse studies, which suggests that there may be some fundamentally important protective processes at work when we observe resilience (Masten, 2001). But many questions regarding resilience remain. There are also many topics of debate that stir up controversy. Several of these issues are discussed in the following section, with the goal of spurring further thought and future research into these complex phenomena.

Issues for Discussion

As we have already noted, the type of research undertaken by Project Competence and related studies requires serious consideration of various decisions regarding how researchers define and operationalize concepts and terms of interest. The dilemmas explored here include how to define adversity, how to define competence, and how to identify appropriate competence domains.

How to Define Adversity

As noted previously in this chapter, the definition of resilience requires definitions of two distinct elements: adequate adaptive behavior and adversity. In order to measure adversity in large groups of people, we must make generalizations about the adversity of experiences, across very different life situations and knowing that each person may perceive events differently. Certainly, not everyone reacts to adversity in the same way, even when the adverse events themselves appear quite similar. However, despite this variability of experience, the ability to conduct empirical work requires the operationalization of adversity based on relatively objective criteria (e.g., tallying how many life events from a list have occurred over the past year, based on common events that usually cause significant stress, problems, or hardship). Yet we know that events like death, divorce, substance abuse, or physical maltreatment, while they are all risk factors for a host of negative outcomes, can vary tremendously in their severity and negative impact from one individual to another.

Some investigators also argue that stress is in the eye of the beholder; it must be perceived and experienced by the individual person as stressful. Investigators who take this point of view often include the perceived stressfulness of life experiences in their measures of adversity. The difficulty that arises in these studies is separating the adversity from the coping and adaptation processes we are trying to understand. In Project Competence, we chose to define adversity objectively and then try to study processes related to perception and adaptation; for example, we have found that perceived stress is highly related to symptoms of distress and also to individual differences in personality.

How to Define Competence

Challenges also occur in operationalizing competence. Often, the functioning of a normative, or reference, group is used to define what it means to be doing "OK." But is it reasonable to create competence standards that are based on the functioning of individuals who have never experienced adversity, or does this create the expectation that an individual who has experienced significant adversity should nevertheless be expected to attain a level of functioning comparable to those who have lived less stressful lives? The establishment of "cutoffs" for defining competent functioning is at the very core of resilience research, and these are decisions that must be made carefully.

Another aspect that must be considered is the context in which the child lives, including cultural factors. Differing values or expectations can certainly affect decisions about competence criteria (Masten & Coatsworth, 1998). Similar issues also arise in considering how to define global competence across multiple domains of functioning, as is described in the following.

Multiple Domains of Competence

Researchers often choose to focus on multiple domains of competence (e.g., academic, conduct, or social) in describing overall adaptation (Luthar, Cicchetti, & Becker, 2000), which affords the opportunity to conduct more expansive investigations of developmental outcomes. However, the inclusion of multiple domains also can lead to a larger question for studies of global adaptation: Is there a number of specific domains of competence in which a person must be functioning well in order to be considered competent overall? Might there be a hierarchical nature among domains such that adequate functioning in certain domains is mandatory in order to be considered generally competent? In Project Competence, this question has been dealt with using both methods, as noted earlier: At earlier time points, a participant must have been doing well in most, but not all, competence domains in order to be judged as "OK," while in adulthood, the domain of parenting competence was considered a mandatory aspect of overall competent functioning.

Other reasons for discriminating among multiple domains of competence include intraindividual variability in functioning. An individual may have certain domains in which she functions less well, perhaps due to developmental reasons or personal vulnerabilities. Alternatively, a person may make a conscious choice to focus on, or de-emphasize, particular domains. For example, if a person prefers not to enter into romantic relationships so that she can concentrate on a career, should she be evaluated differently than others in the domain of romantic functioning? Should she be considered to be less romantically competent than her peers? Obviously, by limiting research definitions to observable actions and behaviors, empirical standardization can be achieved, but perhaps at the expense of deeper explanations of competent functioning.

Conclusions

These examples of issues debated by investigators who study resilience serve to underscore a basic tension between conducting research that is methodologically rigorous and quantitative in nature and pursuing investigations that are more individually focused and oriented toward qualitative methods. Hopefully, the notable potential to integrate these methods (Sullivan, 1998) can be utilized by future investigations of the development of resilience. One of the most striking observations that has resulted from the studies of these urban girls is how many different paths these girls have followed to resilience. The women who have participated in this study have endured diverse experiences, drawing on multiple resources and protections. Many have relied on their relationships with family members and friends, and some have had mentors who came into their lives at just the right time. Spirituality and religious faith have been important for some women; others have found a path by means of talents for school or music or leadership. Some girls turned their lives around following the development of a positive romantic relationship or birth of a child; still others have found professional success that has bolstered their overall adaptation. Transitions to adulthood appear to offer new opportunities for positive development and resilience. The study of naturally occurring resilience has already informed efforts to intervene in the lives of children and adolescents who are at risk for maladaptive development, but there is much work still ahead.

By understanding risk and resilience and the processes by which girls overcome adversity to become successful young women, resilience investigators
aim to learn better strategies of prevention and intervention to promote
competence, reduce risk, and protect development.

NOTES

The research reported in this chapter would not have been possible without the
long-term support of the participants and their families, the contributions of
many graduate and undergraduate students who helped collect and analyze the
data, and the agencies that provided grant support over the past 25 years. Project
Competence has been supported by the William T. Grant Foundation, the
National Institute of Mental Health, the National Science Foundation, and the
University of Minnesota, through grants to Norman Garmezy, Ann S. Masten,
and Auke Tellegen.

1. Additional data not included in this chapter were collected at each time
point (for further details, see Masten et al., 1999; Masten et al., in press; Roisman
et al., 2004).

REFERENCES

Achenbach, T. M. (1997). *Manual for the Young Adult Self-Report and Young Adult Behavior Checklist.* Burlington: University of Vermont, Department of Psychiatry.

Derogatis, L. R. (1977). SCL-90-R administration, scoring and procedures manual. Baltimore: Clinical Psychometric Research.

Derogatis, L. R. (1982). Adolescent norms for the SCL-90R. Baltimore: Clinical Psychometric Research.

Elder, G. H., & Conger, R. D. (2000). *Children of the land: Adversity and success in rural America.* Chicago: University of Chicago Press.

Garmezy, N., Masten, A. S., & Tellegen, A. (1984). The study of stress and competence in children: A building block for developmental psychology. *Child Development, 55,* 97–111.

Gest, S. D., Reed, M. G. J., & Masten, A. S. (1999). Measuring developmental changes in exposure to adversity: A life chart and rating scale approach. *Development and Psychopathology, 11,* 171–192.

Harter, S. (1985). Competence as a dimension of self-evaluation: Toward a comprehensive model of self-worth. In R. L. Leahy (Ed.), *The development of the self* (pp. 55–121). New York: Academic Press.

Hauser, R. M., & Featherman, D. L. (1977). The measurement of occupation in social surveys. In R. M. Hauser & D. L. Featherman (Eds.), *The process of stratification: Trends and Analysis* (pp. 51–80). New York: Academic Press.

Havighurst, R. J. (1972). *Developmental tasks and education* (3rd ed.). New York: McKay.

Luthar, S. S. (Ed.). (2003). *Resilience and vulnerability: Adaptation in the context of childhood adversities.* New York: Cambridge University Press.

Luthar, S. S. (in press). Resilience in development: A synthesis of research across five decades. In D. Cicchetti & D. J. Cohen (Eds.), *Developmental psychopathology: Risk, disorder, and adaptation* (2nd ed., Vol. 3). New York: Wiley.

Luthar, S. S., Cicchetti, D., & Becker, B. (2000). The construct of resilience: A critical evaluation and guidelines for future work. *Child Development, 71,* 543–562.

Masten, A. S. (2001). Ordinary magic: Resilience processes in development. *American Psychologist, 56,* 227–238.

Masten, A. S., Burt, K., & Coatsworth, J. D. (in press). Competence and psychopathology in development. In D. Cicchetti & D. Cohen (Eds.), *Developmental psychopathology* (2nd ed.). New York: Wiley.

Masten, A. S., & Coatsworth, J. D. (1998). The development of competence in favorable and unfavorable environments: Lessons from research on successful children. *American Psychologist, 53,* 205–220.

Masten, A. S., Hubbard, J., Gest, S. D., Tellegen, A., Garmezy, N., & Ramirez, M. (1999). Adaptation in the context of adversity: Pathways to resilience and maladaptation from childhood to late adolescence. *Development and Psychopathology, 11,* 143–169.

Masten, A. S., Neemann, J., & Andenas, S. (1994). Life events and adjustment in adolescents: The significance of event independence, desirability, and chronicity. *Journal of Research on Adolescence, 4,* 71–97.

Masten, A. S., & Powell, J. L. (2003). A resilience framework for research, policy, and practice. In S. S. Luthar (Ed.), *Resilience and vulnerability: Adaptation in the context of childhood adversities* (pp. 1–25). New York: Cambridge University Press.

Masten, A. S., & Reed, M.-G. J. (2003). Resilience in development. In C. R. Snyder & S. J. Lopez (Eds.), *Handbook of positive psychology* (pp. 74–88). London: Oxford University Press.

Masten, A. S., Roisman, G. I., Long, J. D., Burt, K. B., Obradovic, J., Riley, J. R., et al. (in press). Developmental cascades: Linking academic achievement, externalizing and internalizing symptoms over 20 years. *Developmental Psychology.*

Obradović, J., Masten, A. S., & Shaffer, A. (2005, April). *Sorting out the significance of risks, adversity, and resources in childhood for success in adulthood.* Paper presented at the Society for Research in Child Development, Atlanta, GA.

Roisman, G. I., Masten, A. S., Coatsworth, J. D., & Tellegen, A. (2004). Salient and emerging developmental tasks in the transition to adulthood. *Child Development, 75,* 1–11.

Sameroff, A. J. (2000). Dialectical processes in developmental psychopathology. In A. J. Sameroff, M. Lewis & S. M. Miller (Eds.), *Handbook of developmental psychopathology* (2nd ed., pp. 23–40). New York: Kluwer Academic/Plenum.

Sullivan, M. L. (1998). Integrating qualitative and quantitative methods in the study of developmental psychopathology in context. *Development and Psychopathology, 10,* 377–393.

Tellegen, A. (1982). Brief manual for the Differential Personality Questionnaire. Minneapolis: Unpublished manuscript, University of Minnesota.

Tellegen, A. (1985). Structures of mood and personality and their relevance to assessing anxiety, with an emphasis on self-report. In A. H. Tuma & J. D. Maser (Eds.), *Anxiety and anxiety disorders* (pp. 681–716). Hillsdale, NJ: Erlbaum.

Werner, E. E. (2000). Protective factors and individual resilience. In J. P. Shonkoff & S. J. Meisels (Eds.), *Handbook of early childhood intervention* (2nd ed, pp. 115–132). New York: Cambridge University Press.

Werner, E. E., & Smith, R. S. (1992). *Overcoming the odds: High-risk children from birth to adulthood.* Ithaca, NY: Cornell University Press.

Part II

Safe Spaces Revisited

3

Makin' Homes
An Urban Girl Thing

Jennifer Pastor, Jennifer McCormick, and Michelle
Fine with Ruth Andolsen, Nora Friedman, Nikki
Richardson, Tanzania Roach, and Marina Tavarez

This chapter grows out of our collective work, which crosses the
boundaries typically constructed by researchers. We actively cross generations, colors, classes, and ideologies by writing this chapter with the
young women listed above.[1] This work is driven by the belief that we
and they are the best narrators of our lives. The title draws from the
fact that home is a theme that constantly surfaces in the lives of adolescent girls, and throughout this chapter we rely upon an old-fash-
ioned and rich metaphor—that of homemaking. If we stay loyal to the
nostalgic notion of home (Martin & Mohanty, 1986) as a safe space,
where one can weave whole cloth from the fragments of social critique and sweet dreams—a home few have known but most still
search for—we can say that these young women are searching for such
a place.

   We do not limit home to traditional definitions, because homeplaces
can be defined broadly to include comforting, safe spaces in institutions
such as schools or in social groups such as clubs, social movements, or
gangs. Listening to young women's critiques of schooling, domestic
spaces, gender relations, racial hierarchies, and social violence, we have
learned that homeplaces, so broadly defined, can also become constricting
places from which they often try to break free. This can have profound
and ironic consequences in young women's lives and for their emerging
identities as women.

All of us write together toward a four-part, shared argument: First, urban girls of many colors cannot simply pursue autonomy, freedom, and independence as Erikson (1968) theorizes. The challenges of racism, sexism, classism, and cultural hegemony profoundly interfere. Second, this interference does not necessarily result in deficits for many urban girls, as for the African American women bell hooks (1990) writes about, because these challenges help girls learn how to develop critical consciousness. We theorize that this development becomes part of a successful coping strategy. Third, this critical consciousness allows urban girls of color to know that there is much that is wrong with the world and that they cannot hide or "go underground" within white-dominated, class-based institutions as Gilligan (1991) has so aptly demonstrated white middle-class girls can do. Urban girls of color must learn how to assert themselves within white, often male-dominated institutions, because they know that these institutions are often not designed to protect them or promote their interests. We maintain as our fourth and last belief that this critical consciousness can manifest itself in various individual behaviors and styles, but within these behaviors a troubling theme emerges. Unfortunately, urban girls of many colors do not seek each other out for collective action, which might address the inequities of which they are so critically conscious. There are few experiences in their lives to prepare them to work collectively, especially given their legacy of growing up in the Reagan-Bush years, marked as they were by an affirmation of socialization through gender and traditional notions of feminine behavior, which do not include collective action.

Yet urban girls are unstoppable in their desires to preserve and develop their personal integrity. We have found that they construct individualistic strategies for accommodating to the contradictory needs and desires of family, friends, and school, while resisting the offensive boundaries that are constructed against them because of their race, gender, class, or culture. We write with deep respect for the work that they do as they pursue their own identities.

Methods

Our collective work draws from the young women's narratives, from girl's and women's group discussions, and from ethnographic observations of sites where the young women attended school. The work derives from two qualitative research projects, an ethnographic documentation project at an alternative public middle school (Jennifer Pastor), and a poetry workshop conducted within a traditional comprehensive high school (Jennifer McCormick). The young women who took part in the girl's and women's discussion groups, and with whom we wrote this chapter, were recruited from these two sites.

Description of Ethnographic Sites

The middle school is located in a working-class neighborhood of New York City that has a large Latino immigrant population. It is a small school with about 120 students and is committed to creating a safe, nurturing, and intellectually stimulating environment for its students.

The high school is also located in a working-class neighborhood of New York City and has a large Afro-Caribbean population. It is a comprehensive high school with roughly 2,000 students.

Participants

Three adolescent girls from the middle school (Ruth, Nora, and Marina), two adolescent girls from the high school (Nikki and Tanzania), and three adult women (Jennifer, Jennifer, and Michelle) participated in the discussion groups. The girls were approached by the researchers at each site and invited to participate in the discussion groups taking place during the summer of 1993. The ethnic-racial composition of the girls included one Jewish American, one European–Latina American, one Dominican Latina, one African American, and one Caribbean–African American. The ethnic-racial composition of the adult women was Puerto Rican American, European American, and Jewish American.

Procedures

For 2 years Jennifer Pastor made weekly visits to the middle school in order to observe and talk to students, staff, and parents. She recorded field notes, conducted interviews and focus group discussions, and was a participant observer in other activities. Jennifer McCormick tutored students and conducted poetry workshops over a 2-year period. Conversations with numerous students were recorded or reconstructed from field notes.

The summer discussions were held at the City University of New York Graduate Center, a central location that was easily reached by all participants using public transportation. A total of seven discussions took place. Discussions tended to last about 2 hours and were taped and transcribed. The content of the discussions varied at each session, but focused on issues of gender and race politics in the lives of girls and women. The researchers often introduced current newspaper articles, videotapes, and published essays to the group in order to stimulate conversations, but conversations were not limited to these materials.

In this chapter we focus primarily on the five girls who participated in the summer discussion groups. We also draw from field notes taken at the school sites, from interviews and conversations with other girls at each school, and from poetry written by the two high school girls.

Social Individuality, Collective Identity, and Homemaking

As other feminist researchers of identity have done, we question the Eriksonian (1968) model, which states that successful identity achievers are those who have weathered an identity crisis and have resolved such a crisis by acquiring independence and autonomy. Previous work has argued that the Eriksonian model is problematic because girls and women develop "in relationship" (Miller, 1976; Rotheram-Borus, Dopkins, Sabate, & Lightfoot, 1996). However, Lykes (1989) expands the notion of self-in-relation by calling attention to cross-cultural and cross-contextual variations in adult-child attachment processes. Lykes (1985) presents "social individuality" as a contrasting notion to autonomous individualism. According to Lykes, despite the fact that women's lives are nested inside power inequities, women have developed a keen ability to find spaces for resistance. Recognizing and making sense of social injustice and oppression is a fundamental part of social individuality.

Social individuality can arise from an awareness of racism. Robinson and Ward (1991) studied how a small group of African American adolescent girls attending an exclusive private school resist an individualism that views the self as disconnected from others. Similar processes within communities of color help individuals to preserve their cultural connectedness as a buffer against the isolation that could result from an overreliance on individualism, especially given the legacy of racism that dominates American culture (Phinney, 1989). The African American writer bell hooks provides a historical example of social individuality. In "Homeplace: A Site of Resistance," hooks (1990) describes how African American women in the pre–civil rights era became resisters of white racist supremacy within the contexts of their own homes. By nurturing their own families in the belly of white racist oppression, by creating spaces where family members could connect with each other and reaffirm their sense of collective pride and spirit, African American women helped build a revolution within their communities. According to hooks, the stable homeplaces that these women nurtured gave African Americans a strong base from which to organize politically during the 1960s.

Social individuality is also informed by experiences of sexism. Both mainstream culture and "native sub-cultures" (Torres, 1991) keep girls and women controlled and dependent throughout adolescence and often into adulthood (Klein, 1992). Peers, family, school, religion, and social services work in concert to keep girls bound, presumably "protected" from boys and men who would abuse patriarchal privilege if girls were "free" (Fine, Genovese, Ingersoll, Macpherson, & Roberts, 1994). Yet, girls and women do resist oppressive gender structures and have done so for decades. Women often begin a lifetime of resistance as social individuals working to influence the interactions that take place in their homes, schools, and communities. The sense of agency that results from resisting oppressive structures influences who we are as women—our identity—and this identity formation process begins in our youth. The adolescent coauthors of this chapter illuminate how their identities are shaped by resistance at home, at school, and beyond. This developing sense of agency is the beginning of a process of building their own homeplaces, places where they can be connected with others in ways that they desire.

Oppression in the 1990s had many forms. In urban landscapes dotted with drugs, violence, and deteriorating schools, both public and private spaces can be particularly dangerous for young women. The young women of this chapter demonstrate how they engage in social individuality within this landscape and how they attempt to create their own homeplaces. However, because social individuality is an individual-based resistance process, it may not be an optimal way to address injustice within schools and communities. In those cases where major reforms are needed, more collective action may be necessary to bring about change. Later in the chapter we demonstrate how collective identity can be achieved in the lives of urban girls and how this affects their ability to create their own homeplaces.

In Search of Safe Spaces

Resistance and Accommodation

We introduce a young feminist in the making. Marina is a lively 14-year-old Dominican from New York City who has been in New York since about the age of 5. Marina would not agree that the identity crisis of adolescent girls is resolved by independence and autonomy. In Marina's words, the trajectory for women is clear: "First you are owned by your father, and then you are owned by your husband." Yet her homeplace has been a site of resistance, but not against the forces of racism "out there." Instead, her homeplace has been a site for resisting the sexism "in here," within her home, where boys and men are privileged in the family. When Jennifer Pastor asked Marina about the space between her present home and her future home, Marina explained: "Well I'm already engaged. I want to finish school and prepare for a career, but I'm going to marry my fiancé and hopefully things will work out. If it doesn't work out, I guess we'll have to get divorced, but you can make a difference in your own home and the way you are with your children." Marina's early engagement is not surprising in Dominican culture, where such engagements are taken as a sign of a young man's serious intentions and respect for the girl and her family. In this sense, Marina is accommodating to the demands of her culture. Yet there are tones of resistance in her answer. She wants to have a career, and she wants to raise her children differently from the way she is currently being raised. Marina began to recognize her own process of resistance when she wrote 6 months later:

> I know that by saying this [getting married] I am going against my strong beliefs about feminist liberation. Eventually I'll probably change my mind about marrying so young. I guess at this point my greatest goal is going to a good university and becoming a psychiatrist. I would like to be able to help young women struggling against the grain of society like I am.

Marina's dramatic change of heart seemed surprising until she explained how she had been exposed to feminist ideals through a teacher whom she admired in her new high school. Marina had also begun to reevaluate some of the relationships in her life.

Anyon (1982) introduced "resistance and accommodation" to describe how girls and women find themselves accommodating to even those gendered, raced, and classed structures that they may abhor. Many girls and women find themselves caught in cycles of resistance and accommodation where they learn that *options for resistance more often than not reproduce the very oppressive cultures they think they are resisting* (Bordo, 1993; Fine & Zane, 1989; Thorne, 1993).

Homesteading

Stories narrated by young women display powerfully how they make sense of the worlds they have inherited. In each of these cases you will hear critique, resistance, and accommodation, a yearning for a safe homespace, and yet little sense that life could be very different.

Ana (pseudonym) was a quiet, reserved sixth-grade Latina. She was being repeatedly harassed by an eighth-grade African American boy known for abusing students and undermining teachers. Jennifer Pastor learned of Ana's situation during a visit to the middle school and recorded in her field notes:

> A small group of girls surrounded Ana as she walked along crying. The girls attempted to comfort her. I asked one of them what happened. "Thomas hit her again" was the reply. I followed the group until I was able to get near Ana and talk to her privately about her dilemma. She told me that Thomas kept beating her and described how, on different occasions, her arms had been yanked up behind her back, and how her head had been knocked against a school locker. Feeling enraged, I asked Ana if she wanted me to talk to Thomas. She emphatically said no. I asked her if she wanted me to talk to the director. Shaking her head sadly, she said, "No, it won't do any good."

Jennifer Pastor decided to handle this situation by confiding in a teacher who she felt was strong enough to help her solve Ana's problem. The teacher, an African American woman, listened intently and said, "I will speak with Thomas and tell him that his behavior must stop immediately or else he'll have to deal with me." The teacher then went on to describe how Thomas had terrorized another girl until she (the teacher) forced him to stop.

What was striking about these events was that girls and women in the school found themselves solving the problem of male violence quietly, covertly, and without making any public fuss. Ana believed that if she "told," Thomas's behavior would only worsen. Ana's friends felt helpless to provide anything but comfort after the fact. As a participant observer, Jennifer Pastor tried to respect Ana's wishes regarding the handling of the problem, but as she went underground with another woman of color to solve Ana's dilemma, she realized that this was another example of women and girls creating havens for one another without rocking the boat or changing the status quo. By not attempting to change the school, we had accommodated a structure where violence could take place, leaving potential violators wide latitude for abuse—and for getting away with it.

But not all girls or women are easily subject to continued abuse. Marina, the fourteen-year-old participant, is not a quiet, shy Latina. She is assertive and opinionated and loves to wear her "tight little jeans." She can receive compliments on her appearance with cool poise and charm. She can also defend her space on the street from aggressive men who dare to get "too personal" by ridiculing their sexist behavior and reframing it as "stupidity." Marina does not live in fear of being victimized. Yet, by wearing the confidence of her sexuality publicly, Marina is also struggling with a culturally prescribed contradiction for Latinas—encouraging young women to be sexually appealing and yet expecting them to remain sexually "pure." Thus, Marina's resistance to the gendered control of her sexuality displays an ironic accommodation to her culture.

Like Marina, many young women invent homes that cross the boundaries of culture, generation, and immigrant status. They not only cross borders, but they *knit bridges* for self and others (Moraga & Anzaldua, 1981; Torres, 1991). But these bridges can be woven with conflicting desires and the sense of being pulled in two.

Ruth, a participant in our discussion groups, is a 13-year-old who understands and embodies this pull. Born to white, middle-class parents in New York City and raised by a Puerto Rican babysitter, Ruth has grown up knitting more bridges with the Latin American community than she has with white, Anglo culture. In an interview with Jennifer Pastor, she explained: "I grew up in the same building I'm living in now, but across the street is not the same neighborhood. It turns into a whole different attitude and everything. That's where my babysitter lived and she used to let us stay on the street in the summer." This street, and all of the people connected with it, were Ruth's gateway into a different culture. The conflict for Ruth is that Latin culture becomes her homeplace, while she resists the Anglo culture of her parents. To do otherwise, she would "lose" language, values, friends, activities, and her sense of identity, which is Latina. Yet she cannot escape that which is Anglo. Her home does not "feel like" the homes of her friends: "It's hard because my friends' parents do things differently than mine do. So sometimes I wish that my parents were different so that I can be *myself* and accept what they're saying." Ruth hovers at the margins, but feels pressure from all sides:

> Girlfriends are fine. But like, with boys and stuff—they're scared of my parents! They don't even want to meet my parents, and I feel pressure from my parents. They want to meet my boyfriends, or anybody I'm with. They say I don't want to introduce them, but the reality is my friends think that most white people don't like their daughters going out with black guys or Spanish guys. I don't know. They just think my parents will flip or something, and in that sense it's hard for me.

Unable to imagine transforming European American culture, Ruth attaches to the culture she believes defines her childhood. Connections to biological family are sometimes tense, but so are her connections to boys who view her as different. Knitting bridges across treacherous waters, young women can swim in ways that feel quite alone.

A different kind of homespace is carved by Nikki, an African American 16-year-old who attends the comprehensive high school. Nikki chose to become involved in a poetry workshop at her school. Good-humored and passionately poetic, Nikki attends a high school that is systematically failing to provide her with opportunities for intellectual engagement or academic advancement. Poetry gives her a voice in this academic darkness. She reflects on, and writes about, a search for a home:[2]

> There is no place left to go
> There was no place left to go.
> She ran away from home.
> She went everywhere.
> She went to her boyfriend's house,

He told her to leave.
He couldn't keep her.
She went to family members' houses,
But there was no one home.
She's walking up and down the street.
She was scared and nervous.
A man came to her, he was talking to her
and trying to rub up against her.
She ran away from him.
there was no place to go.
She heard voices,
there was no place to go.
She walked to the nearest park,
She saw a bench.
She laid down,
and went to sleep,
and when she awakened,
she was home,
because there was no place left to go.

Nikki brings to life the pain, alienation, and loss that a girl can feel when she loses her connection to home without having found a new homeplace. Whether home is thought of as a geographic, concrete structure or as an emotional space inside the self, adolescent girls search for a home. As sites where homeplaces can be developed, what do urban secondary schools have to offer them in their life work?

On Surveillance

Typically, public schools, especially large, comprehensive high schools of the sort where Nikki and Tanzania are assigned, have been most unlikely sites for makin' homes. Trying to imagine this institution as a cozy site for making sense of social critique, for trying on ways of being gendered and raced, for imagining "what could be" becomes difficult when surveillance begins the school day. Jennifer McCormick observed: "Lines stretch in two directions outside of a side entrance. Students hide their faces inside hooded jackets. Sleeves cover their fists. I ask one solemn faced girl why she waits. 'We are allowed in at the beginning of second period.' Metal detectors are positioned like sentinels directly inside the doorway."

Surveillance induces students to wait in the cold until they are allowed into school. It causes them to tolerate public humiliation. It criminalizes them.

McCormick: Were you ever scanned?

Tanzania: Yeah, I hate it.

McCormick: Why did you hate it?

Tanzania: I have to put myself down. I have to put my hands out (she places her hands on the table in front of us, fingers are stretched apart). I don't feel right. I feel out of my element.

McCormick: What do you have to do?

Tanzania: I have to stand straight for a few minutes, legs apart, my hands out stretched in front of me. I have to take my bracelets off, take everything out of my pockets. It's very uncomfortable. I feel embarrassed amongst everybody else. It's not a productive way to start off school.

As subjects in an institution of subjugation, young women and men are both "subject to someone else by control and dependence, and tied to [their] own identity by a conscience or self-knowledge" (Foucault, 1982, p. 212). Jennifer McCormick watched this self-knowledge emerge in a group of young women as they explored their own complexities through poetry and wondered how public school space enabled or impeded these explorations. She wondered how girls could negotiate identities that are richly cultural and personally safe inside an institution that, as Foucault writes, brands adolescents as violent. McCormick observed:

Once inside, electronic surveillance, hall passes and police radios fix movement. To enter the cafeteria, teens slide coded identification cards into a machine. A white man surrounded by African American guards oversees the operation. He yells orders. "You need a card. . . . Can't come in." Newly arrived students stare in bewildered confusion. Inside the cafeteria, doors are bolted shut. Boys play ping pong in an area of the room not cluttered with lunch tables and food. They are ringed by uniformed guards.

Rudolph Giuliani, New York's mayor in 1993, says he wants to create "safety zones" by assigning police officers inside schools where "security is inadequate" and funding is atrocious and inequitable (*New York Times*,

November 11, 1993). This mix of concern and control is not new (Donald, 1992). School hallways have long been viewed as "out of control," but now they are spaces that must be patrolled by police. Rather than seeking educational responses to this trouble, we witness what Vergara (1994) calls the "bunkering of the poor."

This bunkering of the poor profoundly impacts how public policy becomes implemented, with effects that often undermine poor and working-class youth even further. For example, Michelle Fine (1991) and the American Association of University Women (1992) argue that placing the private lives of children and adolescents beyond school walls compromises a young person's education. When schools integrate young women's "public" and "private" lives, they may help young women commit to their education. However, we have seen these "solutions" pervert when implemented in schools serving poor children. When the private lives of poor adolescents become spectacles, public institutions may further brand those they "serve" and their families as deviant or immoral.

Adolescent girls are aware of this institutional surveillance and branding. Their desire to discuss personal issues diminishes radically when they believe that their "personal" stories will be turned against them, when their lives feel invaded but not engaged. If a poor or working-class student of color finds her way to a counselor's office, she may feel pried open, with little respect for her privacy: "Do you like your baby's father? . . . How long have you been without lights? Where does your child sleep?" One young mother complained that on numerous occasions her social worker "comes up too fast" (becomes personal too quickly). Her response was to remain silent. Within this context, silence is not an indication of passivity; it is a form of resistance and a means of protection. Tanya (a pseudonym), a young writer from the poetry workshop, describes an experience of intended help as one of surveillance:

> I think counselors should ask what you want. Sometimes you don't want something to happen in a certain way but they do what they have to do. My friend . . . had an incident with her mother. Her mother has a lot of kids. She is single. She has eight kids. My friend felt neglected. She was not getting attention or nothing like that, so she went to her guidance counselor thinking maybe her guidance counselor could talk to her mother and tell her how she feels because sometimes you don't feel right to tell your mother this, but the guidance counselors reported it to B.C.W. (Bureau of Child Welfare). That was the last thing my friend wanted.

When this girl's search for a safe place to talk met the institution's desire and responsibility to report and protect, both desires were undermined. Many of the girls of color in our discussion groups live ever ready to question and resist such help, which they experience, rightly or not, as prying, overdetermined conclusions that await them at school, silencing or appropriating their narratives to fit what the state has allocated "for" them. In such contexts, occasions where young women should be able to talk freely are subverted by "helpful" intrusion.

Surveillance comes in many guises; yet, in its face many young urban women resist. Tanzania presents a strong example of this. Even when we first broached the notion of writing a collaborative essay about her school and her community, Tanzania bristled: "I don't understand why we black teenagers are constantly being questioned about our neighborhood and the school we attend. What do they think is happening? Why are we constantly badgered? What do you want to find out? Do you want to confirm your own agenda? What information are you trying to get from me?" The voices of the young women in our group reflect an awareness of individual and group needs. Tanzania, for example, speaks of the differences between her community and the images that the white world projects in the media about her community: "I find it amusing that when one talks about city adolescents, we often see black or Spanish children. . . . If I were from another country, I would think that for some reason only black children in American schools are sexually abusive to one another. Should I be getting this message from the media?" Tanzania's awareness is unique, however, because it translates into the belief that she can protect others:

> I was afraid something might happen at school, and you'd hear about it on the five o'clock news. I didn't see anyone standing up to any teacher, any corrupt teacher, any corrupt person in that school. I didn't see any one making a nuisance of themselves like I was. I was making a nuisance of myself to get the greater good out of these teachers. It wasn't fair to us that we have to get the second best. Why can't we get the best? Why?

Tanzania's tireless protection of herself and her peers leaves little room for vulnerability or sweet dreams. Her school is a place where she has learned to cultivate resistance against surveillance and oppression. This resistance extends into an understanding of gender politics as well. During a group discussion about a newspaper article on a series of gang rapes in New York

City pools, Tanzania acknowledges that tensions of gender fracture her peers:

> These rituals, as they are now called, sugarcoat the fact that these damn boys think sexual harassment is something that only "adults" have to deal with. They've committed a sexual assault against someone and it's time they were penalized rather than praised, as they often are. They have to stop hiding behind the belief that boys will be boys. And I would like to ask this much: When the hell can girls be girls? No matter what "girl thing" that may be?

As female adolescents living in New York City, Tanzania and the other young women of our discussion group are highly aware of the sexual violence that pervades women's lives. They were able to critique and connect the oppression in both racism and sexism. In her poem "Don't Hurt Me Anymore," Tanzania writes:

> Don't follow me
> like a rapist stalks his prey
> Don't quiet the words I have to say
> like a rapist covers the mouth of his victim
> to hold back what she must say
> Don't rip savagely apart my dreams
> as a rapist rips the clothes off his victim
> don't throw me down when I try to get up
> like a rapist throws his victim down
> when she tries to escape
> Don't beat me when I struggle to learn and survive
> Don't pin my thoughts down
> like a rapist pins the arms of his victim
> on the cold concrete
> Don't heave your hateful thoughts down on me
> like a rapist heaves his body down on his victim
> Don't thrust anymore of your sick ideas into my head
> like a rapist thrusts his body into his screaming victim
> don't force me to say what you want
> like a rapist forces his victim
> to perform debasing sexual acts
> Don't leave me crying without a shred of confidence

to go on
without a shred of dignity to continue living
Don't make me second guess myself
when I know I have the right to speak
You've left me with the hate I never asked for
Rapist. Racist. They look almost the same.
Rapist. Racist. They are the same.

Tanzania's poetry displays an uncanny ability to *deconstruct,* critically, the messages floating in the culture about gender, race, sexuality, and class.

In our discussions with our young coauthors, we have found that they often engage in deconstructing what they see and feel around them. They question the meanings of people's actions; maneuver creatively within spaces they create (and the crevices that society allows them); and resist, while accommodating to, social prescriptions for girls. These deconstructions—seeing and analyzing *the discrepancies between what they are told they can achieve and what they witness as possible in their social contexts*—can be very unsettling, particularly so because they critique elegantly but often alone, without trust in social institutions, without a shared identity with other women, and without any sense that individual analysis could incite broad-based social transformation.

Nikki worries about tensions within her community that fracture relationships among peers—tensions such as those fostered by an individualistic focus on designer clothes and jewelry: "I would love to remove all the name brands that kids wear. They cause too much competition." She realizes the ironies of her community feeding the designer industry: "Look at the Ralph Lauren ad. You don't see a lot of black people playing polo. You see white people playing polo." Yet Nikki and her peers defend their individual spaces in the hallways of school, which have become unsafe territories due to unmitigated competition and escalating violence. They resist with talk; they refuse the role of passive victim. According to Nikki: "Girls talk more of their business in the hallway than they do at home. They speak loudly in the hallway." And some girls, eager agents within these unsafe territories, carry razors and knives, sometimes for protection and sometimes to "disfigure" other girls. In random school raids for weapons, young women are as likely as young men to be found "holding." But these individualistic strategies cannot change the ongoing oppression of surveillance sanctioned by police and the state, nor can it transcend harassment from young men, misogyny from (and toward) other young women, or low expectations from teachers. These young women, like the rest of us, yearn to know—is there possibility for transformation? Will young women ever be allowed the chance to create their own homeplaces that are respected and valued?

Schools, Surveillance, and Possibilities for Young Women of Many Colors

We now ask how contemporary public schools could be designed to nurture a sense of homeplace that allows for growth, critique, and possibility for young women of many colors. Many large, anonymous high schools are an unmitigated educational disaster that should be laid to rest (Fine, 1994). Is it oxymoronic to expect these institutions of inequity and surveillance to melt their borders and barbed wire long enough to allow young women to nestle inside, to roll around with their critical contradictions and their confusions and breed a sense of "what could be"?

As we see it, there are several problems with the ways schools are currently designed, with respect to the kinds of concerns young women are narrating. These schools provoke and then pathologize critique, thus making an independent negative contribution to the intellectual, emotional, and cultural curtailment of young urban women. First, as described earlier, the schools most likely to be attended by urban girls of color are designed as sites of intrusive surveillance or "fortification" (Vergara, 1994). These schools, costumed as prisons, educate young women and men to distrust and to understand that they are not to be trusted. Second, these schools (and sometimes families and peers) are organized in ways that discourage young women's pursuit of academically rigorous work and sanction male harassment of women's bodies and minds (Stein, 1993). This happens across race, class, and ethnicity. Third, we have growing evidence to suggest that, notwithstanding Fine's early writings on silencing and Freire's writings (1985) on liberatory education, simply learning about social oppression can be problematic for young women (and men) of poverty or color, if they cannot imagine that their oppressive conditions can be interrupted and transformed. If young people see pervasive social inequity and its adverse consequences, but they cannot imagine transformation, such information may simply fold into a heap of hopelessness, cynicism, or alienation (Miller, in press). Critical insights without opportunities for students to reconstruct a world rich in the wonders of race, culture, gender, and social justice may wound a sense of possibility. Indeed, we may be witnessing a generation of young women and men who know well, in heads and hearts, the horrors of race, class, and gender subordination, without being able to organize, or make it better. Collective protests and activism seem like a nostalgic memory of parents and grandparents.

Evidence for the latter point comes from a study conducted by Jennifer Pastor (1993) of "possible selves" (Markus & Nurius, 1989) envisioned by African American, Caribbean American, and Latino eighth graders in an inner-city junior high school in New York. A group of 136 students were asked to project themselves forward and list their "possible" occupational selves. Pastor correlated these responses with measures of their perceptions of racism and of limited economic opportunities. Greater awareness of racism and limited economic opportunities were significantly correlated with lower-prestige occupational aspirations. As with Fine's data on high school dropouts, it appears to be the case that students of color with sophisticated social consciousness of race and class relations may also have the most depressed sense of what is possible for themselves (see also McLoyd & Jozefowicz, 1996).

Although the direction of causality could not be established in either Pastor's (1993) or Fine's (1991) study, the results serve as a caution to educators who have embraced the ideals of multicultural and feminist curricula and are enthusiastic about teaching students of color about race and gender relations historically and currently. *While we are distressed by these findings, we should not be understood as retreating from multicultural and feminist educational ideals.* To the contrary, we are deepening our commitments to such education with the understanding that activism must also be learned. Without engaging an activist pedagogy that educates students of color in the history and politics of *successfully fighting conditions of injustice,* well-meaning educators may risk exposing students to a sense of disempowerment.

Girl's and women's groups can provide insular homeplaces where young women can begin to learn how to transform their isolated analyses and make the "personal political" with profound opportunities for development. Our experience, matched by that of a growing number of feminist educators of many colors who are bringing groups of girls together, is that the young women of the next generation are "hungry for an us" (Fine & Macpherson, 1995). They are searching for ways to trust and connect with other girls and women. They are at the same time thrilled to carve out spaces for "girl talk" and frightened by the prospect. They become hopeful and excited when they realize they can create their own homeplaces.

We might try to imagine, then, what could (and does) happen inside schools and communities that engage young women (separately and with young men) in social critique and in activist experiences of social transformation? There are a growing number of feminist spaces, created between adult and adolescent women of many colors, from which we can breathe some sense of hope.

Recent writings by Linda Powell (1994) may help us picture such classrooms and schools. In an essay on Family Group, Powell describes how an urban high school is designed so that every student enjoys an adult confidant for all her years in high school, and every willing adult in the building has a critical mass of 10 to 15 students for whom she or he is responsible over time. Family Group, according to Powell, challenges the social defenses that constrict but also construct typical urban school culture. This process allows for community building and the possibility of erecting homeplaces for both teachers and students.

A variation on Family Group was crafted by Diane Waff (1994), an African American teacher-researcher in Philadelphia who set up a mentor group for her students. The creation of this group was an attempt to reinvent schooling as a safe homeplace for the poor and working-class Latina and African American young women in her class. Marked with the label "special education" for too many years, these young women carry stories and scars of racism, sexism, and classism in their bodies and minds. Waff created a mentor group and witnessed a remarkable shift: "As soon as the girls realized that someone was really listening to them, they were empowered to see themselves as people who mattered. They knew they had the chance to have a direct impact on their lives. They became more vocal about everything" (p. 201). The space Waff created became the home that bell hooks talked about—the place where young women shared secrets, connected stories, made political sense out of personal misery, and organized in resistance.

If Family Group and Waff's girls' group represent emotional, intellectual, and political interventions within school life, there is also evidence that empowering education can also come from outside school. An example of this is Youth Force, an organization designed for, by, and about urban youth. Youth Force works to organize groups of young activists in New York City and testifies to the strength of democratic, activist education from the streets.

In an interview conducted by Nikki, Tanzania, and Jennifer McCormick with members of Youth Force, we hear a coalition of youth activists who critique and organize for collective change resulting in their own empowerment:

> Wubnesh: Youth Force was started 5 years ago by a woman and about 12 young people who were living in different welfare hotels in the midtown Manhattan area.
>
> Cindia: [The purpose of the organization] is to school young people to the fact that they are not powerless, that they should be heard and seen, and to also remind them, or even let them know, that young people were always on the front lines when it came to organizing . . . so to encourage them that they can make a difference.
>
> Wubnesh: And to give them resources that are not usually accessible and also to help them access public officials and policymakers who set policy around youth issues. So *we try to act as a group of young people* who represent the masses of young people who, quote unquote, fall between the cracks or who society has dismissed as underprivileged, disadvantaged, high risk. . . .
>
> McCormick: How do you maintain cohesion?
>
> Cindia: I think that a lot comes from maybe the struggles we face here. *Either we stay together and we move forward, or we decide to separate and everybody goes down.* To keep us moving forward we have to tolerate and learn how to deal with one another.

Critique and possibility braid in the biography of Youth Force, Family Group, Waff's classroom, the collective of activist adolescent women of color in the South Bronx who call themselves "Sistahs!" and groups of young women proliferating across the country. Young women of many colors are hungry for spaces in which to talk and dressing rooms for trying on (and discarding) ways to be women: white, African American, Latina, Asian American, straight, lesbian, bisexual, celibate . . .

Within contexts of plain talk and conversation, trust and solidarity among peers and even a few adults, with a sense of connection and a democracy of shared differences, the onetime "deficits" of young women shine as strengths; their histories of oppression and victimization are reread as struggles and victories; their biographies of loss are reconstructed as archives of collective resilience. Peers link arms to create safe spaces/homeplaces. Fragile individualities can grow into stronger collectivities. Critique within community can be voiced and worked through. Knowing all too well Nikki's poetic plea for a place to go, these young women (and men) are creating such places. Do we not, as adult women and men, have an obligation to help them reinvent and create their own homeplaces?

NOTES

Jennifer Pastor and Michelle Fine are grateful to the Bruner Foundation for its support of portions of this research.

1. Our collaborative work with the girls includes reading, questioning, and editing earlier versions of this chapter. We did not print anything that they did not approve of.

2. This poem was written in the context of a project done in Nikki Richardson's high school that was a collaborative program between the Poetry Exchange and the School Partnership Program of New York University.

REFERENCES

American Association of University Women. (1992). *The AAUW report: How schools shortchange girls.* Washington, DC: American Association of University Women Educational Foundation and National Educational Association.

Anyon, J. (1982). Intersections of gender and class: Accommodation and resistance by working-class and affluent females to contradictory sex-role ideologies. In L. Barton & S. Walker (Eds.), *Gender, class, and education* (pp. 19–37). London: Falmer Press.

Bordo, S. (1993). "Material girl": The effacements of postmodern culture. In S. Fisher & K. Davis (Eds.), *Negotiating at the margins: The gendered discourses of power and resistance* (pp. 295–315). New Brunswick, NJ: Rutgers University Press.

Donald, J. (1992). *Sentimental education: Schooling, popular culture, and the regulation of liberty.* London: Verso.

Erikson, E. H. (1968). *Identity: Youth and crisis.* New York: Norton.

Fine, M. (1991). *Framing dropouts: Notes on the politics of an urban high school.* Albany: State University of New York Press.

Fine, M. (1994). Chartering urban reform. In M. Fine (Ed.), *Chartering urban reform: Reflections on urban high schools in the midst of change* (pp. 5–30). New York: Teachers College Press.

Fine, M., Genovese, T., Ingersoll, S., Macpherson, P., & Roberts, R. (1994). White li(v)es: Looking for a discourse of male accountability. In M. Lykes, A. Banuazizi, & R. Liem (Eds.), *Unmasking social inequalities: Victims and resistance.* Philadelphia: Temple University Press.

Fine, M., & Macpherson, P. (1995). Hungry for an us. *Feminism and Psychology, 5,* 181–200.

Fine, M., & Zane, N. (1989) Bein' wrapped too tight: When low-income women drop out of high school. In L. Weis, E. Farrar, & H. G. Petrie (Eds.), *Dropouts from school: Issues, dilemmas, and solutions* (pp. 25–53). Albany: State University of New York Press.

Foucault, M. (1982). The subject and power. In H. Dreyfus & P. Rabinow (Eds.), *Michel Foucault: Beyond structuralism and hermeneutics* (pp. 208–226). Chicago: University of Chicago Press.

Freire, P. (1985). *The politics of education.* South Hadley, MA: Bergin and Garvey Press.

Gilligan, C. (1991). Women's psychological development: Implications for psychotherapy. In C. Gilligan, A. Rogers, & D. Tolman (Eds.), *Women, girls, and psychotherapy: Reframing resistance* (pp. 5–31). New York: Haworth.

hooks, b. (1990). *Yearning: Race, gender, and cultural politics.* Boston: South End Press.

Klein, S. S. (1992). Sex equity and sexuality in education: Breaking the barriers. In S. S. Klein (Ed.), *Sex equity and sexuality in education.* Albany, NY: New York: State University of New York Press.

Lykes, M. B. (1985). Gender and individualistic versus collectivistic bases for notions about the self. *Journal of Personality, 53*(3), 56-83.

Lykes, M. B. (1989). The caring self: Social experiences of power and powerlessness. In M. Brabeck (Ed.), *Who cares? Theory, research, and educational implications of the ethic of care* (pp. 164–179). New York: Praeger.

Markus, H., & P. Nurius. (1989). Possible selves. *American Psychologist, 41,* 954-969.

Martin, B., & Mohanty, C. T. (1986). Feminist politics: What's home got to do with it? In T. de Lauretis (Ed.), *Feminist studies, critical studies* (pp. 191–212). Bloomington: Indiana University Press.

McLoyd, V. C., & Jozefowicz, D. M. (1996). Sizing up the future: Predictors of African American adolescent females' expectancies about their economic fortunes and family life courses. In B. Leadbeater & N. Way (Eds.), *Urban girls: Resisting stereotypes, creating identities* (pp. 355–379). New York: New York University Press.

Miller, F. S. (in press). Living in chaos: Social adaption responses of African American adolescents. In J. C. S. Fray & J. King (Eds.), *Psychosocial and physiological dimensions of black child development.* Boston: Erlbaum.

Miller, J. B. (1976). *Toward a new psychology of women.* Boston: Beacon Press.

Moraga, C., & Anzaldua, G. (Eds.) (1981). *This bridge called my back: Writings by radical women of color.* Watertown, MA: Persephone Press.

Pastor, J. (1993). *Possible selves and academic achievement among inner-city students of color.* Master's thesis, City University of New York.

Phinney, J. S. (1989). Stages of ethnic identity development in minority group adolescents. *Journal of Early Adolescence, 9*(1–2), 34–49.

Powell, L. (1994). Family group and social defenses. In M. Fine (Ed.), *Chartering urban school reform: Reflections on urban public high schools in the midst of change.* New York: Teachers College Press.

Robinson, T., & Ward, J. (1991). "A belief in self far greater than anyone's disbelief": Cultivating healthy resistance among African American female adolescents. In C. Gilligan, A. G. Rogers, & D. L. Tolman (Eds.). *Women, girls, and psychotherapy: Reframing resistance* (pp. 87–103). Binghamton, NY: Harrington Park Press.

Rotheram-Borus, M. J., Dopkins, S., Sabate, N., & Lightfoot, M. (1996). Personal and ethnic identity, values, and self-esteem among Black and Latino adolescent girls. In B. Leadbeater & N. Way (Eds.), *Urban girls: Resisting stereotypes, creating identities* (pp. 35–52). New York: New York University Press.

Stein, N. (1993). It happens here too: Sexual harassment and child sexual abuse in elementary and secondary schools. In S. Biklin & D. Pollard (Eds.) *Gender and education* (pp. 191–203) Chicago: University of Chicago Press.

Thorne, B. (1993). *Gender play: Girls and boys in school.* New Brunswick, NJ: Rutgers University Press.

Torres, L. (1991). The construction of the self in U.S. Latina autobiographies. In C. Mohanty, A. Russo, & L. Torres (Eds.), *Third world women and the politics of feminism* (pp. 271–287). Bloomington: Indiana University Press.

Vergara, C. J. (1994, January 31). The bunkering of the poor. *Nation,* p. 121.

Waff, D. R. (1994). Girl talk: Creating community through social exchange. In M. Fine (Ed.), *Chartering urban school reform: Reflections on urban public high schools in the midst of change* (pp. 192–203). New York: Teachers College Press.

"They Are Like a Friend"

Othermothers Creating Empowering, School-Based Community Living Rooms in Latina and Latino Middle Schools

Nancy López and Chalane E. Lechuga

How does school context shape the resilience of racially stigmatized youth, Latinas in particular? How can parental involvement be conceptualized to specifically support the education of Latina and Latino communities? This chapter examines the experiences of Latina middle school youth and mothers who participated in school-based, parent-run community living rooms (*salas comunitarias*). Drawing from resiliency theory, we underscore the importance of school context in the education of Latinas and Latinos. We found that community living rooms provide a culturally empowering safe space, particularly for Latina girls, who described them as their second home. Latina middle school students spoke about the parent volunteers, mostly mothers, as friends and confidants with whom they enjoyed mutual trust and respect.

In this chapter we describe three school-based, parent-run community living rooms that served different purposes and grew and thrived in different school contexts. The community living rooms each aimed to be an empowering homespace that nurtured the resilience of Latina and Latino students and their families. Clinton Middle School, the most overcrowded school, presented the most difficult school context for Latina students and their parents who attempted to create the *salas comunitarias*. The *sala comunitaria* at Irving Middle School provided individualized tutoring, counseling, and mentoring. Huerta Middle School was the school context that was most receptive to refashioning parental involvement and Latina and Latino education. Each of these school case studies illustrates the importance of creating empowering homespaces for Latinas and Latinos in any school context.

Before providing snapshots of each school, we give a brief review of our anchoring theoretical frameworks, as well as the larger socioeconomic and political backdrop for the study. We then provide portraits of the schools, highlighting the experiences of the women and girls who participated in the community living rooms. Finally, we end with a discussion of how schools can begin to create homespaces as a way of nurturing resilience of Latina and Latino students, families, and their communities.

Contextualizing Resilience and Empowerment

Resilience theory calls attention to the need to understand how youth from racially stigmatized communities succeed against the backdrop of multiple intersecting adversities that include oppression vis-à-vis race, class, gender, and ethnic discrimination (Taylor, 1994; Garza, Reyes, & Trueba, 2004). While resilience has been seen traditionally as an individual-level trait that depends on a nurturing family and individual agency, the concept has been expanded to include other social supports that foster resilience, including teachers, peers, and schools (Leadbeater & Way, 1996; Pastor, McCormick, & Fine, 1996; Freiberg, 1994; Rigsby, 1994). Here we are interested in how school contexts can support young women in their struggle against poverty, discrimination, stereotypes, and urban violence.

How can we operationalize race? Racial formation theory, which is at the foundation of this research, defines race as an ubiquitous socially constructed and historically variable process that represents

> social conflicts and interests by referring to different types of human bodies. Although the concept of race invokes biologically-based human characteristics (so-called "phenotypes"), selection of these particular human features for purposes of human signification is always and necessarily a social and historical process. . . . there is no biological basis for distinguishing among human groups along the lines of race (Omi & Winant, 1994, p. 54).

Race can be understood as sociohistorical processes that have created, circulated, represented, and enacted racial categories in social structures and racial meaning systems. These processes occur both at the microlevel of individual lived experience, identity, cognition, and face-to-face inter-actions and at the macrolevel of collective identities, public discourses, representation in the mass media, social movements, state regulations, rules, social relations and organization, and state institutions, such as schools. Racial formation is the synthesis of multiple racial projects—definitions, interpretations, and representations of racial dynamics and attempts to redistribute resources along racial lines. This social construc-tionist understanding of race contrasts sharply with essentialist approaches, which assume that race is an innate biological trait (Murray & Hernstein, 1994). According to genetic essentialists, all people placed in a racial category are assumed to possess some innate and unchanging biological trait.

We join theoretical perspectives on racial formation with descriptions of the empowering roles of other mothers (Collins, 2000) and the need for "homespace" (Pastor et al., 1996) to understand the function of the community living rooms. A central premise of our research is that schools are a central social institution where oppression related to race, class, gender, and disability is either challenged or reproduced (Fine, 2004; Hehir, 2002; López, 2003; Staiger, 2005; Lewis, 2003; Lee, 2005; Wang & Gordon, 1994; Flores-Gonzales, 2002; Omi & Winant, 1994). In particular, we focus on the racial formation process in community living rooms and the larger school context and unravel how racial meanings, practices, and common sense are created, circulated, enforced, and con-tested in the school context.

To understand the role of the women who participated in the *salas comunitarias,* we also draw on Collins (2000, p. 178), who describes the role community "othermothers" play in nurturing the resiliency of their own families and the entire African American community and also describes the distinction between blood mothers and othermothers. She sees community othermothers, who feel responsible for their own chil-dren and also invest in the futures of the children of the entire commu-nity, as key to the empowerment of oppressed communities. Finally, we borrow Pastor et al.'s (1996, p. 15) conceptualization of homespace as "comforting, safe spaces in institutions such as schools or in social groups such as clubs or social movements," to describe the safe haven that school-based community living rooms provide for urban Latina girls in the Southwest.

Critical Ethnographic Case Studies

To uncover the narratives and meanings participants gave to their experiences in school-based community living rooms at three public middle schools in our study, we chose a qualitative research design (Brown, 2005). Critical ethnographic research methods are premised on the notion that all research is political. We take the position as advocates for oppressed groups by detailing the oppression and resistance of said groups (Collins, 2000; Brown, 2005; Garza et al., 2004; Fine, 1991; Lewis, 2003; Staiger, 2005; López, 2003; Valenzuela, 1999; Torre & Fine, this volume; Ybarra & López, 2004; Hunter, 2002). The names of the city, public school district, individual schools, programs, and participants have been changed to protect their anonymity.

Funded by private foundations dedicated to expanding educational opportunity programs and social change, community living rooms fall under the umbrella program called Puentes (Bridges). Puentes is part of a national network of state-based programs designed to increase the number of Latinos and Latinas graduating from high school and pursuing higher education across the United States. Among the programs included in the seven states where Puentes operates are Chicano and Chicana studies classes, Amigos (an individual mentoring program that follows a cohort from middle school through high school graduation), extra offerings of classes required for graduation, and the parent-run community living rooms. The main objective of the community living rooms is to provide emotional, social, and academic support to students and their families. Exclusively unpaid parents and other community volunteers staff them. Although community living rooms target Latino communities and include bilingual Spanish and English signs, paperwork, and cultural representations, they are open to all students and parents, regardless of ethnic, racial, or socioeconomic status background. The open-door policy of the community living rooms means that everyone is eligible for their services.

In 2001 the Santiago school district was chosen as a site for Puentes programs because it is located in a major southwestern city where one in two public school students is Latino or Latina, but the educational outcomes of Latino and Latina students are disturbingly low: Only 44% of Latina and Latino students graduated from high school in 2003, and although a third of entering undergraduates at the local public university are Latinas or Latinos, only a quarter of them are degree recipients. Community living rooms were initially available in the high schools; in 2003 another private foundation sponsored community living rooms in the middle schools. Subsequently, the state legislature funded nearly two dozen community living rooms throughout the state, spanning elementary to high schools. The school district assumes in-kind support and maintenance of the *salas comunitarias*. The community living rooms are generally open Monday through Friday during regular school hours (9:00 A.M. to 4:00 P.M.). Students generally access the community living rooms during their free periods, such as lunch. Our evaluation of community living rooms in three public middle schools took place between the fall of 2004 and spring 2005, when they were in their second year of operation in the middle schools.

Methodology

Using qualitative methodology and ethnography, we conducted participant observation and informal conversations with school staff, including principals and administrative staff, and collected field notes and observations. We also conducted semistructured interviews with program participants. During our participant observation, we randomly asked students in the community living rooms to participate in our study. We conducted interviews with those students who had signed consent forms from parents authorizing their participation in the program. Our interview protocol included questions that explored how parents and students got involved in the community living rooms, specific issues and activities they participated in, and the successes and challenges they faced at school. We interviewed a total of 36 participants: 9 parent volunteers, 2 college student volunteers, and 25 middle school students.[1]

All the participants in the study were Latina or Latino, with the exception of one school principal. All the parent volunteers were women with the exception of one man at Huerta Middle School. Fifteen of the participants preferred to speak in Spanish. López, a Dominican woman who was born and raised in New York City, who is in her mid-30s and who is most often racialized as Black, conducted all the Spanish interviews, as well as all the interviews at Huerta and Clinton Middle Schools. Lechuga, a Chicana graduate student in her mid-20s, who was born and raised in Denver, Colorado, and is most often racialized as Latina or Native American, conducted most of the interviews at Irving Middle School. Interviews, which lasted from 15 minutes to an hour, were audiotaped and videotaped and transcribed. Spanish interviews were translated into English. We analyzed transcripts and field notes for themes that related to parent and student experiences, as well as the school context.

The City of Santiago: Urban Sprawl Southwest Style

The urban context of our study is the city of Santiago, New Mexico. Santiago is a large city of 448,607 people in a predominantly rural state where Latinos and Latinas constitute the largest minority group (43%), followed by Native Americans (10%; U.S. Census Bureau, 2000). Due in large part to unprecedented urban sprawl, the geographic boundaries of the city have tripled over the last four decades. High property taxes and ongoing gentrification of low-income historic Latino and Latina neighborhoods have displaced many families to the outskirts of the city. The overwhelming majority of Latinos and Latinas are U.S.-born, and they trace their ancestry to colonial Spain in the Southwest. Most of the older generation identify as Spanish American. The younger generation identifies as Hispanic but does not necessarily feel any affinity toward the growing mostly working-class Mexican immigrant population that is moving into Santiago.

The major industries in Santiago include the military and related science and technology fields, health, education, and the arts, as well as abundant low-wage service sector work in tourism, retail, manufacturing, and construction. Although the per capita income of the city is just below the national average ($20,000 vs. $21,000), an examination of the 2000 census reveals notable disparities in income, with per capita income by census tract ranging from $8,000 to $50,000. One in five families with children under the age of 5 lives below the poverty line.

Half of the students in the Santiago public school district of more than 88,000 identify themselves as Hispanic. Of the remaining students, more than a third identify themselves as White, the rest as Native American, Black, Asian, or other. Fifty-six percent of students in the school district live in poverty, as indicated by eligibility for free or reduced-price lunch. Although at the aggregate level, the Santiago school district appears quite diverse, racial and socioeconomic segregation is palatable at the school level (Kozol, 2005). Huerta, Irving, and Clinton Middle Schools had a student population that was overwhelmingly Latino and Latina (80% to 90%) and low income. The majority of students (75% to 94%) qualified for free or reduced-price school lunch. The per capita income in the census tracts where these schools were located was also among the lowest in the city. The district-wide statistics also indicate a racially and ethnically stratified school personnel. Whereas nearly three-quarters of the middle and secondary school teachers in the district identify as white, close to two thirds of the teacher's aides identify as Hispanic. Similarly, the majority of teachers at the schools in our study identify as white (60% to 70%); only 24% to 40% of the teachers identify as Hispanic. Now we take a tour of each of these middle schools.

Resisting Controlling Images at Clinton Middle School

Clinton Middle School is located in one of the most congested and sprawling sections in the outskirts of Santiago. Over the last several decades massive housing developments have sprouted in this part of the city, creating considerable traffic congestion and school overcrowding. Clinton Middle School includes about a dozen trailer classrooms that are located behind the main building. Unlike Irving and Huerta schools, there was a visible security concern at Clinton, with security guards patrolling the hallways. A police car is regularly stationed at the entrance of the school. Students, mostly Latino boys, who face in-house suspension are forced to wear orange vests and line up against the wall when going to lunch. At many overcrowded public schools, security guards and police officers have been instituted to manage the overcrowding problem, creating a prisonlike atmosphere (Pastor et al., 1996; López, 2003).

In November 2005, López called Clinton Middle School and asked to be transferred to the *sala comunitaria,* but the receptionist seemed uninformed about whether the community living room had a phone. I then decided to visit the main office, but to my disappointment it seemed that few staff knew where the community living room was located. Finally, one staff person indicated that it was located in the trailer classrooms. As I made my way outside the main building to the "barracks," I was left guessing which trailer classroom housed the community living room. I asked a random student walking through the trailer complex if he knew about the community living room, and he pointed to the main building. I mentioned that it had been moved to the barracks, and he directed me to a trailer classroom that was locked and dark. There were no signs indicating that this was the community living room or its hours of operation. Frustrated, I went back to the front office, and the receptionist remembered that it was not open on Fridays. I wondered how parents and students who may not speak English fluently would have felt after this ordeal.

After several abortive attempts to connect with the parent volunteers, I called back after the Christmas holiday break and learned that the community living room had been temporarily closed because the parents who had been volunteering at this school had problems with the administration. Although I never had an opportunity to speak with the parent volunteers who left this community living room, my interview with school staff suggested that a misunderstanding about what it meant to be a parent volunteer at a community center was part of the problem. The school principal described the first group of parents, mostly mothers who volunteered at this *sala comunitaria,* as unprofessional. The principal thought the role of the parents volunteering at the community living room was to help school administrators make photocopies and phone calls. The principal also complained that the volunteers brought their babies to the community living room and were just hanging out talking.

I later learned that there had been many problems with the community living room's original location near administrative offices in the main building because the room was too small to accommodate the number of students who sought its services. Consequently, when students came for the biweekly *lonches* (Spanglish for lunch), they were often left lining up outside the door, and the staff in the adjacent offices complained frequently about the level of noise generated by students. Although the current location in barracks was an improvement in terms of having a larger space, it was still quite inadequate. In its former life, this trailer classroom had been a kindergarten classroom, equipped with pint-size bathrooms, sinks, and furnishings.

After the first cohort of parent volunteers left, Señora Cecilia, a veteran parent organizer from Huerta Middle School, restarted the community living room in January 2005. By February, there were five parent volunteers. On a cold winter morning, Señora Cecilia arranged to have me meet with some of the students who came to the community living room on a regular basis. Among the themes that peppered students' narratives at Clinton Middle School was the issue of *respeto* (respect) and *falta de respeto* (lack of respect) and a sense that their culture, language, and heritage were denigrated by *some* of the teachers and staff at the school (Valenzuela, 1999). Isolda, an eighth grader, echoed the sentiments of many students who repeatedly said that they felt more comfortable in the community living room than in their classrooms: "The people in here are nice. They treat us good. They don't treat us bad. You can do your homework and get help here with your homework The parent volunteers help us with our homework. I wish we could take it as an elective." Although Clinton Middle School officially had a bilingual program, its mission to educate a predominantly Spanish-speaking immigrant population was not readily apparent from my interactions with administration or my assessment of the cultural representations that were visible as one walks down the hallways.

Oneida, a seventh grader at Clinton, who spoke English fluently but preferred to speak in Spanish, reiterated Isolda's sentiments. I probed further by asking what was happening in the classroom that made students feel disrespected:

> There is a teacher who doesn't respect us. He makes some jokes that are disrespectful. The other day he was on the computer and he was looking at the image of a woman's *tracero* [behind]. (Gasps from parent volunteers.) Here, they treat us well and they help us a lot. I wish we had a class so we could come here for a full period.

Collins defines "controlling images" as hegemonic ideological justifications for the exploitation and subordination of Black women (2000, p. 85). Schools, the news media, and government agencies are key sites where controlling images are circulated, enacted, and resisted. The "mamasita" stereotype of Latinas as sexually available and promiscuous women is a controlling image that Latinas encounter throughout their lives (López, 2003). What is important here is that Isolda and her peers did not accept the controlling image of themselves as sexual objects and exhibited resilience by seeking the safe refuge of the nurturing, safe space provided by the *sala comunitaria* in their middle school. In the community living rooms young Latinas resisted damaging stereotypes and re-created their identities by speaking Spanish and seeking companionship in ways that nurtured their resilience in school.

Latina girls also learned the valuable lesson of resistance and empowerment through the actions of the mothers who volunteered in the community living room. Upon learning about Oneida's negative experiences in the classroom, the parent volunteers immediately met with the principal, and they were assured that the teacher had been reprimanded. However, when I queried the principal about this incident, it was dismissed as "poor judgment" on the teacher's part. It did not appear that the principal had envisioned the possibility of creating a larger school-level discussion about multiple oppressions, such as racism, sexism, ableism, homophobia, and classism (Bettie, 2003). In spite of the administration's lukewarm response to racist and sexist incidents, the presence of the community living rooms provided community othermothers with a safe haven in which to continue advocating on behalf of students and their families. They tirelessly reminded the school administration to announce the presence of the community living rooms to students and repeatedly told the ubiquitous hallway security personnel that *all* students were welcome in the *salas comunitarias*, even those who had been labeled troublemakers. In due course the resiliency of Latina and Latino students and their families was enhanced.

Community othermothers were keenly aware of the substandard education that Latinas and Latinos were exposed to, and they worked actively to empower their children and the community. Señora Beatriz, a U.S.-born Latina woman who had been laid off from a telemarketing job the previous year, started volunteering at the community living rooms at her daughter's high school. When she learned of the problems at Clinton, Señora Beatriz volunteered to help the school restart the program; she described her motivation for helping our youth: "I have goals for these kids. I paint a picture for them and these parents paint that picture for them. They tell them this is what can happen and they treat them personable, something that they don't get in the classroom." Othermothers were key agents in creating these oases of support and nurturing, particularly in school contexts that are problematic for Latinos and Latinas. Señora Cecilia reflected: "When they [students] come here, they come here with full confidence that we respect them and that's when they start opening up and talking to us about their problems. That's why I like them to come here during lunch, I like that we learned about some inappropriate behavior from teachers." During the 2003–2004 academic year the community living room had 172 active students; this may be an underestimate, however, because many students who come do not have parental consent forms on file. Although parent volunteers sometimes get referrals from teachers who recommend that students access the services available at the *salas comuni-tarias,* most of the students come out of their own will. Parent volunteers also recruit students who have had troubles with the administration and serve as mediators between parents, students, teachers, and the school administration.

Señora Beatriz, who relishes the opportunity to circulate among the other community living rooms in the school district, articulated her counterhegemonic ideology about who can be considered experts in the education of Latina and Latino communities:

> Parents should be recognized for their community experiences. . . . if you put an educated person next to a community service person who has the same years of work, the community person has more experience. . . . They need to value the community experience that parents have. The parents need to be respected and recognized. It's not the education the parents have but all the experience that they contributed to the community.

Señora Beatriz's critique of the exclusion of parent voices, particularly those from low-income and racially stigmatized communities, from the formulation of educational reform policies illustrates the agency and resistance of social actors in any oppressive situation. It is important to note that while Señora Beatriz spoke about the importance of valuing the experiential knowledge that parents bring to addressing educational disparities among Latinas and Latinos, she is committed to promoting education to all "her children" by stressing that they should not settle for a bachelor's degree but should continue on for a master's degree.

Collins (2000, p. 183) credits the resiliency of women-centered networks with the resiliency of the African American community. In these woman-centered homespaces, mothers and students generated oppositional knowledge, "a type of knowledge developed by, for, and/or in defense of an oppressed group's interest" (Collins, 2000, p. 299), which in turn fosters their empowerment. Othermothers, particularly those who have had their own experiences with the school system, provide children with oppositional knowledge that propels youth to reject the negative expectations others may have set for them. This function is particularly important in schools like Clinton, where there was little, if any, meaningful effort to incorporate the culture, language, and community input of the students and their families in the running of the school.

Individualized Attention at Irving Middle School

Irving Middle School is nestled in one of the oldest Hispanic settlements in Santiago. This is one of the last areas of the city that maintains some of its agricultural past. Although Irving is a bilingual school that offers classes in English as a second language to all students who qualify, the physical appearance of the school does not portray its bilingual or bicultural focus. When Lechuga calls the office, the message is not bilingual, and signage to the community living rooms is nonexistent. Irving's community living room, now in its second year, provides services to 60 "active" students (with parent consent), as well as 40 to 45 "inactive" students (those without consent). In contrast to Clinton Middle School, which is overcrowded, Irving is underutilized, and the school district is planning to bus some students there from overcrowded schools. Señora Gloria, a parent volunteer whose first language was English, explains:

> About half of the active students are Mexican immigrants whose primary language is Spanish, while the other half are Native New Mexicans of Mexican American descent whose primary language is English. Most students come from working-class families. These demographics reflect those of the surrounding neighborhood, which predominately consists of working-class Hispanics.

Irving's community living room is open Monday through Friday during school hours. During the 2003–2004 school year, lunch was available Monday through Thursday. Currently, lunch is available only on Tuesday and Thursday, but students can use the community living room any day during their lunch period. With teacher permission, students may also access it during their homeroom period.

Irving Middle School participates in a reading enhancement program, whereby students are tested for appropriate reading level and are required to read books at their level until they reach the appropriate level. Testing is computerized. Irving Middle School dedicates the 35-minute homeroom period to this reading program. Students are allowed to work on their reading at the community living room and students often work with Señora Gloria. The *sala comunitaria* at Irving Middle School offers a wide range of services, but perhaps the most common service was coordinating individualized personal services for students who were struggling with coursework. Tanya, a sixth grader, spoke appreciatively of the *sala comuni-taria:* "In the classroom there's a lot of talking in there. Everywhere you look there's lots of talking. In here you can concentrate better. Over there they rush into doing stuff. Here you can take all the time you want." When Tanya was struggling with math, Señora Gloria intervened on her behalf and offered academic support. Together, Tanya, her parent, her teacher, and Señora Gloria agreed that Tanya could go to the community living rooms during math period once the teacher had completed the in-class lesson. This would allow Tanya the ability to concentrate on completing homework assignments. Tanya was then also required to submit a weekly progress report to Señora Gloria and to her mother. Over time, Tanya increased her grade by two letter grades. This is one example in which the entire community worked together to enhance student achievement. This type of intervention provided the individualized attention many students, particularly Latinas from low-income backgrounds, need in order to do well in school.

Mothers who volunteer at the community living rooms were also challenging the artificial divide between public and private spheres of students' lives. Señora Paola explains how the social, physical, emotional, and academic needs of students are addressed in the community living rooms: "We refer the students to social workers, and even if they have problems getting to school, we help them get to school." Señora Paola described instances in which mothers who volunteer at the *salas* provide rides for students who lack transportation and also participated in following up on students who were missing class by going to their homes and finding out what was happening. In this way, community living rooms address not only academic needs but also real material needs such as food and transportation. Holistic programs that address the academic, social, cultural, and individual needs of Latina and Latino students may indeed provide the missing link for connecting low-income youth who are racial minorities or English language learners with college aspirations and career possibilities (Fine, 1991; López, 2000; Valenzuela, 1999).

Community living rooms also provide a forum where even parents who do not speak English fluently can be valued for their skills. Formerly a bookkeeper in Mexico, Señora Paola, who speaks mostly Spanish, loves helping students with their math homework. While she enjoys tutoring students, it is the sense of friendship and community that is practiced in the community living rooms that keeps Señora Paola anchored in her commitment. As she explains:

I really like the companionship there is here. I like to be close to the students who come so that I can help them. We feel very happy here because
there is convivencia [camaraderie] here. . . . This is a program where we
improve communication between Hispanic students and teachers so that
things could be better. For example, there was a student who had a problem
because she was ill and the teachers didn't understand why she had not been
to class, so we went with her to the teacher with proof that she had been ill,
so we mediate between students and teachers.

Frequent misunderstandings between Spanish-dominant students and
teachers were often mentioned by students who were explaining why they
came to the community living room. Yesenia, an eighth grader, lamented
that some of her teachers were not supportive of Latina and Latino identity and culture: "I wish that there were more teachers who wouldn't treat
us bad. I wish that there were more teachers who understood students
who speak Spanish. There are some teachers who see that we are Mexicans
and they treat us differently."

The cultural and language gulf between students and teachers sometimes creates a hostile environment for racially stigmatized youth. In my
study of the race and gender gap in education, I also witnessed teachers
publicly reprimand students for speaking Spanish in a New York City public
high school that had a majority of Dominican students (López, 2003).
Although the United States has no official language, "English-only" is a de
facto rule at many urban public schools with Latino populations. In
November 2005, Zach Rubio, a U.S.-born student whose parents were born
in Mexico, was suspended from his public high school in Kansas City,
Kansas, because he spoke Spanish in the hallways of his school. Upon learning about this injustice, Zach's father spoke with the superintendent, and
the suspension was reversed. It remains to be seen, however, if this incident
will spark a national dialogue about the racial stigma placed on Spanish
speakers, particularly those who are dark skinned and low income.

As mothers visited community living rooms across the city and state,
they formed women- and student-centered networks that were the base of
empowerment. During the first year of the installation of the *sala comunitaria* at Irving, a group of parents and students organized to publicly voice
grievances against the principal, who they described as racist toward Latinas and Latinos. Eventually the principal was replaced. The women-centered networks and oppositional knowledge that were generated by the
mothers who ran the community living rooms were a powerful example

to girls of women's interest and engagement in political and school reform. Señora Rosalie was highly critical of government spending priorities: "To me it doesn't make sense why there is so much money, millions and millions of dollars for war. It's better to support our youth who are our future." Señora Rosalie spoke with pride about her daughter as a young activist. Alissa was part of a group of Puentes students who went to speak to the governor about the need to support programs that provide resources to low-income Latino and Latina communities.

Community living rooms may be one of the few spaces where immigrant Latinos and Latinas interact with the pre-annexation Mexican-descended population that has resided in this area for generations. This was true for the parents who volunteered at Irving. Senora Gloria, who understands some Spanish, identifies as a New Mexican Hispanic and traces her family roots to colonial Spain in the Southwest; however, the majority of the mothers who volunteer at the community living room migrated from Mexico recently. Although they each had quite distinct Latino and Latina identities, Spanish and English fluency, and experiences, in the community living room they shared a social, physical, and cultural space where they were able to engage in meaningful interactions and collaborations and bring distinct expertise to the task of educating Latino and Latina youth. This level of intergenerational and cultural exchange may facilitate the empowerment of a Latino community that is sometimes fragmented along racial, class, generational, and language borders. Ochoa's (2004) study of the relationships among first-, second-, and third-generation Mexican Americans in Southern California found that schools were powerful social spaces where Latina and Latino parents became neighbors by generating oppositional knowledge, organizing to oppose elimination of bilingual programs, and expanding educational opportunities for their children. In due course, parents were no longer simply advocating for their own children. They were fighting on behalf of all the children, paving the way for the empowerment of the entire community (Collins, 2000, p. 189).

Girls Feeling at Home at Huerta Middle School

Huerta Middle School is located in a quiet, residential, working-class neighborhood near one of the oldest parts of the city. It offers multiple bilingual programs and is focused on leadership and international studies. As you enter the front doors of the school, bright and colorful bilingual signs greet you, "*Bienvenidos*/Welcome." The hallways exude warmth and invite visitors to explore the many multicultural murals that camouflage brick walls. Many bilingual signs and arrows point to the central location of the community living room. A well-maintained bilingual bulletin board alerts passersby to multiple community activities that are taking place. As López walks past the main office to the *sala comunitaria*, I notice a flyer inviting students to a forum on the future of the Chicano Studies Program at the public university. Bilingual messages are heard over the intercom and when one calls the school. Student aides who greet visitors in the front office speak flawless English and Spanish. As a Latina woman, when I walk down the hallways, I feel that my culture and language are respected and validated and that they are an integral and legitimate part of the school context.

On a brisk December morning, although it was not yet 9:00 A.M., parents were already hard at work preparing today's *lonches*. Two days a week a warm meal is offered to students who come to the community living rooms. About 150 students are actively enrolled in the community living room, but countless others drop in periodically to enjoy a warm meal and a smile from the parents who volunteer there. Señora Elena, Señora Cecilia, and Señora Dolores were busy chatting in Spanish. They had adorned the room with holiday decorations and Christmas trees. The spacious room was equipped with stoves and microwaves and half a dozen round tables and chairs where students typically sit, eat, and talk during their lunch breaks or other free period. The other side of the room had couches, worktables and computers for homework, and free spaces for those who want to read and relax.

In anticipation of the heavy flow of students, beginning around 11:00 A.M., Señora Elena opened institutional-sized cans of nacho cheese and poured them into huge steel pots, while Señora Dolores and Señora Cecilia prepared the tortilla chips and jalapeño sauce. The mothers who volunteered at Huerta Middle School were primarily Spanish-dominant, Mexican immigrants. Most also worked in the low-level service industries. I queried Señora Cecilia in Spanish about how she got involved in the community living rooms, and she replied:

> I'll tell you a little of my story. I was one of the mothers who was afraid to go to school. I used to think that I could only go to school if they called me or if I had a meeting, but I had a problem with my son. He would cut school; he had bad grades. I left my job to see what was going on with my son, but they (security guards) started investigating me at the entrance of the school to

find out why I was going to school so often. They started to ask me for ID so I went directly to the principal to talk and I told him. Then he told me that I could come in the school and that was what they wanted—that we come in. Then I met the parents at the community living rooms and they told me that I could come in as a volunteer and so I helped my son and I am really happy because right now he is doing well and started his first year in high school. I am really proud of him. He's already graduated [this middle school] but I decided to stay here helping other students. If I had not gotten involved who knows what could have happened with my son.

Señora Cecilia's story about being initially intimidated is typical of how parents, particularly low-income and non-English-speaking parents, feel intimidated about entering the school (Fine, 1991). Parents at Huerta described their relationship with the principal as a partnership. Parents prided themselves on having a direct line of communication with the school administrators. The community living rooms serve as a bridge between parents and school officials so that parents now have a physical, social, and cultural space where they belong and feel welcomed. This paves the way for them to work on the behalf of all the children in the community.

Señora Cecilia works evenings doing *limpieza* (maintenance) at an office; however, she remains active in the community living rooms because she is committed to helping other youth and their families. Señora Cecilia reflected on the unique challenges facing children who are English language learners:

Many kids who come from Mexico and still don't know the language are placed with a teacher who does not understand Spanish, so that is where the problem begins for them. If they don't understand, they won't do their homework. They do not understand the class and that's when they give them the "F" and send them to detention. The students don't say that they don't understand. I don't know if it's because they are afraid. When there are problems with the students and teachers, we go and speak to the teacher and more than anything we have the principal's support. We talk directly with the teacher and discuss what we can do about it.

Although schools are prohibited from asking about the immigrant status of students and their parents, the principal at Huerta estimates that about half of the students are immigrant or the children of immigrants, mostly from Mexico.

One reason that many Latino and Latina parents are not able to spend much time in their children's schools is that they have restrictive work schedules or jobs that do not easily permit them time off. Just before she rushed off to work as a cook at a fast-food restaurant, I queried Señora Dolores about how she got involved with the community living room. She answered:

> I have always been involved since my daughters were in elementary school. I had problems with my daughter and they helped me and she's much better now. She didn't want to go to school. She had problems with her teacher and now she's doing much better. I tell the mothers that I know to come but some of them are afraid because they do not speak English. I had my daughters in a school that was English only but I still tried to understand them. Even though I don't speak English, I understand some things. *This is a place that supports people like us, Hispanics.*

For Señora Dolores, juggling work and remaining actively involved in her children's schooling is a challenge, as it is for other low-income immigrant parents. Señora Dolores lamented that she wished she did not have to work so many hours so that she could spend more time volunteering at the community living rooms. Although she worries about how much longer she can continue volunteering, Señora Dolores remains committed: "More than anything if one is interested in one's kids you have to follow them wherever they go. I have my job, but I come here right before and right after." Because the parent volunteers spoke Spanish, came from similar class backgrounds, and understood and respected Señora Dolores's struggles as a working mother, the community living room created a sense of connection between her and other parents that sustained her involvement. She, in turn, was committed to bringing other parents who felt alienated. Parental involvement is often touted as the panacea for low student achievement; however, few schools are prepared to meaningfully engage low-income, immigrant, and non-college-educated parents in their schools. Community living rooms are a step toward providing a space where the needs of low-income immigrant and working-class parents take center stage, thereby enhancing the resilience of parents, students, and the entire community.

Roaming from table to table at lunch, López randomly asked students about whether they had parental consent forms on file, and about half of students said that they were formally considered active. The other half were not officially registered with the program, but they regularly came by to the community living rooms for food, company, and guidance without having to meet any formal eligibility requirements. Unlike other educational opportunity programs that have either income eligibility requirements or grade point average requirements, community living rooms are open to anyone. This has meant that everyone feels welcome, without the stigma or resentment that can be associated with exclusive programs.

Girls and boys alike expressed warmth, mutual respect, and admiration for the parents who volunteered at the *salas comunitarias*. One key difference between the boys' and girls' narratives, however, was that girls described the mothers who volunteered at the community living rooms as friends in whom they could confide. Cecilia, an eighth grader at Huerta Middle School, beamed as she spoke appreciatively about the community living rooms: "What I like about the community living rooms is that you can come here and talk to the parent volunteers like a friend and they can help you out. If we tell them that someone is bothering us, then they will go and look for that person and find out what's going on before it becomes a big problem." The counseling that parent volunteers performed prevented potential fights among students. Mediating conflicts, miscommunications, and disagreements among students, and between students and their teachers and administrators, was a very important role of the parent volunteers at Huerta. Neyda, a seventh grader, explained that the community living rooms provided a safe space that in many respects was a home away from home:

> Sometimes there are people who want to cause you problems and when you come here you can avoid the problems, especially in the lunchroom. This is also an important place for people who are poor and don't have anything to eat and don't like the cafeteria food. It helps you because you don't feel embarrassed talking to the parent volunteers. They are like family; they treat you not like teachers but like a friend.

The parent volunteers exhibited a commanding presence among students and treated them with admiration and respect. Señora Cecilia commented that the girls often treated her as their confidant and shared their feelings about problems with boys, their grades, and intergenerational conflicts with parents, particularly their fathers.

As intergenerational spaces, community living rooms serve as learning communities that nurture young women and parents (Freiberg, 1994, p. 158). Anneris, a sixth grader at Huerta Middle School, said she loved coming to the community living rooms: "It's kind of like you're free. You get to speak any language you want, because in class you have to speak one language, like Spanish or English, but here you get to speak whatever you want." Community living rooms function as safe spaces were Latinas can just be themselves, even if that means speaking English, Spanish, Spanglish, or any combination thereof. Just as women-centered networks have nurtured the survival of the African American community, Latina *convivencia* in community living rooms nurtures the resilience of young Latinas and Latinos.

Parents, and particularly the mothers who volunteer at the community living rooms, play an important role in facilitating the resiliency and resistance of Latinas by validating their class backgrounds, language, culture, and identities. In an ethnography of a Texas urban school, Valenzuela (1999) describes the difference between aesthetic and authentic caring. Aesthetic caring as practiced in most schools is based on an abstract commitment to discipline, rules, and order that individualizes student achievement and ignores the larger structural origins of school failure. In contrast, authentic caring is based on reciprocal relationships between students and adults who value biculturalism and bilingualism and who work to engage students rather than to further alienate them from their schools. If schools adopted authentic caring strategies, alternatives to traditional disciplinary actions such as suspension would send a clear message: "We love and respect you, and we want you to succeed," rather than, "You are a failure; we are here to discipline and punish you. If you do not conform to our rules and regulations, we do not have to deal with you." The presence of parent volunteers who come with fresh ideas for dealing with old and nagging problems has already made a significant impact in student retention and academic achievement by democratizing the voices and decision-making power in the administration of schools.

Creating School Contexts That Foster Resilience

Our study began by asking how the school context shapes the resilience of racially stigmatized youth, Latinas in particular, and how parental involvement can enhance the resilience of Latina and Latino communities. Our program evaluation of a Latina- and Latino-focused dropout prevention program in three public middle schools in the Southwest contributes to the literature on resiliency by examining the experiences of girls and othermothers who participated in the parent-run school-based *salas comuni-tarias.* We found that community living rooms provided a culturally empowering homespace for Latina girls, who described them as their second home. Latina middle school students spoke about the parents, mostly mothers, as friends and confidants—othermothers—with whom they enjoyed mutual trust and respect. Othermothers are the embodiment of authentic caring (Valenzuela, 1999). In many cases the mothers who volunteered at these schools served as natural mentors (Rhodes & Davis, 1996; Rhodes, Davis, Prescott, & Spencer, this volume). Most important, the mothers who volunteered at these community living rooms provided young Latinas with a powerful example of resistance for liberation, "naming and addressing the oppressions in their lives" (Robinson & Ward, 1991; cited in Erkut, Fields, Sing, & Max, 2002, p. 506). The presence of a physical safe space where Latinas can enjoy the camaraderie of othermothers allowed them the possibility of addressing sexism, racism, and classism through liberatory and transformative resistance that can eventually work toward empowering the entire community (Galvan, 2001; Ward 2002; Ward, this volume). These lessons enhance the resilience of Latinas and the entire Latina/o community.

The findings from our study suggest the school context can help to foster the resilience of Latina and Latino students and their parents, families, and communities (Flores-Gonzales, 2002). This may require creating new forms of culturally sensitive ways of enhancing parental involvement and culturally relevant homespaces that address the race, gender, class, language, and cultural realities of Latina and Latino students and their families. What made community living rooms particularly empowering for students was that they were not stigmatized as an at-risk program. Instead, they were premised on the notion that Latino parents and communities had a legitimate place in the school and that they had the skills and knowledge to help young people. By redefining traditional notions of parental involvement, community living rooms literally provide a physical and emotional safe haven and homespace for students and their families. We are living in a time of heightened xenophobia, particularly toward dark-skinned immigrants. Affirmative-action programs have been eliminated in many institutions. Armed civilian border patrols who seek to apprehend undocumented workers crossing the U.S.-Mexican border are being organized by Minutemen founder Jim Gilchrist and his supporters. Congress proposes to deny citizenship to U.S.-born children of undocumented immigrants. Against this backdrop of discrimination, it is particularly important to provide spaces were Latina and Latino voices can be part of the decision-making processes at schools. These sources of support can be the building blocks of resilience for youth preparing to enter adulthood as agents of social change for the betterment of their communities.

Discussion Questions

1. How does school context matter in enhancing the resilience of Latinas? How can schools address the social, academic, and emotional needs of preadolescent Latinas?
2. How can parental involvement be reconceptualized to better address the needs of low-income and/or immigrant parents?
3. How can schools deal with racist, sexist, homophobic incidents in schools?
4. Discuss how your own institution creates resilience.
5. What relationships exist between your university, place of work and the larger community?
6. Consider how race, gender, class, and sexuality affect resilience.
7. Discuss how urban Latinas and Latinos in the Southwest may be different from the Latino and Latina community in your hometown and state.
8. How can community living rooms be instituted in your local public schools? How can they be enhanced?

NOTES

Nancy López and Chalane Lechuga are grateful to the Center for Southwest Hispanic Research Institute at the University of New Mexico for its support of portions of this research.

1. This chapter is based on the analysis of semistructured interviews with female participants: 17 middle school students, 8 volunteers, 1 principal, and 1 college student volunteer.

REFERENCES

Bettie, J. (2003). *Women without class: Girls, race and identity.* Berkeley: University of California Press.

Brown, K. (2005). "C'mon, tell me. . . . Does school ethnography *really* matter?" *Educational Researcher, 34*(9), 29–34.

Collins, P. H. (2000). *Black feminist thought: Knowledge, consciousness, and the politics of empowerment* (2nd ed.). New York: Routledge.

Erkut, S., Fields, J., Sing, R., & Max, F. (2002). Diversity in girls' experiences: Feeling good about who you are. In *The Jossey-Bass reader on gender in education* (pp. 497–509). San Francisco: Wiley.

Fine, M. (1991). *Framing dropouts: Notes on the politics of an urban public high school.* Albany: State University of New York Press.

Fine, M. (2004). Witnessing Whiteness/gathering intelligence. In M. Fine, L. Weis, L. Powell Pruitt, & A. Burns (Eds.), *Off-White: Readings on power privilege, and resistance* (2nd ed., pp. 245–256). New York: Routledge.

Flores-Gonzales, N. (2002). *School kids, street kids: Identity and development in Latino students.* New York: Teachers College Press.

Freiberg, H. J. (1994). Understanding resilience: Implications for inner-city schools and their near and far communities. In M. Wang & E. Gordon (Eds.), *Educational resilience in inner-city America: Challenges and prospects* (pp. 151–165). Hillsdale, NJ: Erlbaum.

Galvan, R. T. (2001). Portraits of *mujeres desjuiciadas:* Womanist pedagogies of the everyday, the mundane and the ordinary. *Qualitative Studies in Education, 14,* 603–621.

Garza, E., Reyes, P. & Trueba, E. (2004). *Resiliency and success: Migrant children in the US.* Boulder, CO: Paradigm Publishers.

Hehir, T. (2002). Eliminating ableism. *Harvard Educational Review, 72, Spring,* 1–32.

Hunter, M. (2002). Rethinking epistemology, methodology, and racism: Or, is White sociology really dead? *Race and Society, 5,* 119–138.

Kozol, J. (2005). The shame of the nation: *The restoration of apartheid schooling in America.* New York: Random House.

Leadbeater, B. & Way, N. (Eds.). (1996). Urban girls: Resisting stereotypes, creating identities. New York: New York University Press.

Lee, S. (2005). *Up against Whiteness: Race, school, and immigrant youth.* New York: Teachers College Press.

Lewis, A. (2003). *Race in the schoolyard: Negotiating the color line in classrooms and communities.* Piscataway, NJ: Rutgers University Press.

López, N. (2000). The missing link: Latinos and educational opportunity programs. *Equity and Excellence, 33*(3), 48–53.

López, N. (2003). *Hopeful girls, troubled boys: Race and gender disparity in urban education.* New York: Routledge.

Murray, C., & Hernstein, R. (1994). *The bell curve: Intelligence and class structure in American life.* Glencoe, IL: Free Press.

Ochoa, G.(2004). *Becoming neighbors in a Mexican American community: Power, conflict, and solidarity.* Austin: University of Texas Press.

Omi, M., & Winant, H. (1994). *Racial formation in the United States: From 1960s to 1990s.* New York: Routledge.

Pastor, J., McCormick, J., & Fine, M. (1996). Makin' homes: An urban girl thing. In B. Leadbeater & N. Way (Eds.), *Urban girls: Resisting stereotypes, creating identities* (pp 15–34). New York: New York University Press.

Rhodes, J., & Davis, A. (1996). Supportive ties between nonparent adults and urban adolescent girls. In B. Leadbeater & N. Way (Eds.), *Urban girls: Resisting stereotypes, creating identities* (pp. 213–225). New York: New York University Press.

Rigsby, L. (1994). The Americanization of resilience: Deconstructing research practice. In M. Wang & E. Gordon (Eds.), *Educational resilience in inner-city America: Challenges and prospects* (pp. 85–94). Hillsdale, NJ: Erlbaum.

Robinson, T., & Ward, J. V. (1991). "A belief in self far greater than anyone's disbelief": Cultivating resistance among African American female adolescents. In C. Gilligan, A.G. Rogers, & D. L. Tolman, (Eds.), *Women, girls, and psychotherapy: Reframing resistance* (pp. 87–103). Binghamton, NY: Harrington Park Press.

Staiger, A. (2005). Whiteness as giftedness: Racial formation at an urban high school. *Social Problems, 51,* 161–181.

Taylor, R. (1994). Risk and resilience: Contextual influences on the development of African American adolescents. In M. Wang & E. Gordon (Eds.), *Educational resilience in inner-city America: Challenges and prospects* (pp. 119–130). Hillsdale, NJ: Erlbaum.

U.S. Census Bureau. (2000). *Population, housing units, area, and density: 2000—New Mexico.* Retrieved February 2, 2006, from http://factfinder.census.gov/servlet/GCTTable?_bm=y&-geo_id=04000US35&-_box_head_nbr=GCT-PH1&-ds_name=DEC_2000_SF1_U&-format=ST-7

Valenzuela, A. (1999). Subtractive schooling: U.S.-Mexican youth and the politics of caring. Albany: State University of New York Press.

Wang, M., & Gordon, E. (Eds.). (1994). *Educational resilience in inner-city America: Challenges and prospects.* Hillsdale, NJ: Erlbaum.

Ward, J. (2002). School rules. In *The Jossey-Bass reader on gender in education* (pp. 510–542). San Francisco: Wiley.

Ybarra, R., & López, N. (2004). *Creating alternative discourses in the education of Latinos and Latinas: A reader.* New York: Peter Lang.

To Stay or to Leave?

How Do Mentoring Groups Support Healthy Dating Relationships in High-Risk Girls?

Elizabeth Banister and Bonnie J. Leadbeater

Safe spaces where girls can explore their own hopes, values, and choices with each other and with adult women are a core feature of contexts that build resistance and resilience for urban girls (Pastor, McCormick, & Fine, this volume). In this chapter, we focus in particular on the need for places to explore and understand heterosexual romantic relationships. How do girls learn about healthy relationships? How do young women learn how to both share and protect themselves in relationships with men?

The development of intimate relationships is a marker of the entrance to young adulthood in most societies. However, we live in a social world that both idealizes and vilifies romantic relationships and sexuality, overstating both their appeal and their dangers to women. At the same time, social norms privatize intimacy in individual relationships and create walls of silence around what it means to love and be loved. This privacy also hides unhealthy aspects of relationships that are characterized by interpersonal violence, sexually transmitted diseases, and disruptions.

This chapter will briefly review past research on the development of romantic relationships in adolescents, particularly demonstrating the central role of friendships and discussions with peers in girls' early efforts to establish healthy intimacy with members of the opposite sex. We will also describe a mentoring program that attempts to create safe spaces for high-risk girls and women to discuss sexual health, problematic relationships, and dating violence. Preliminary evidence of the program's success is given, and qualitative data recorded from mentoring group sessions are examined to illuminate the processes of decision making that are enhanced by dialogues among girls and between girls and women mentors. Early findings suggest that open dialogue allows girls to weigh the distinctions in their relationships between those that are loving and lasting and those built on the "lines" boys use to trap girls into staying in unhealthy relationships.

The Development of Romantic Relationships

Almost half a century ago, Erik Erikson (1968) suggested that the developmental task of late adolescence is to resolve the "psychosocial crisis" bound by the poles of intimacy versus isolation. Adolescents themselves have many strengths to help them balance their emerging emotional and physical needs for closeness and relief from loneliness with their equally pressing need to preserve newly forming identities and sometimes fragile self-esteem. These new relationships build on working models of attachment established in relationships with parents. Early relationships with parents set the stage for our ability to be close to others, but we continue to develop this capacity in relationships with peers and romantic partners. As Furman and his colleagues (Furman, Simon, Shaffer, & Bouchey, 2002) so aptly put it:

> Parent-child relationships may lay the foundation for the ability to be close to and intimate with others, but friendships are expected to contribute to the development of reciprocity and mutual intimacy that are central to romantic relationships. Characteristics of the affiliation system such as collaboration, co-construction, reciprocity, and symmetrical interchanges are central features of both friendships and romantic relationships. (p. 242)

Changes in the quality of peer relationships in adolescence can provide a foundation for the establishment of healthy romantic relationships. Compared with childhood friends, the quality of friendships in adolescence builds on enhancements in interpersonal understanding that reflect increased abilities to take others' perspectives and to show concern about their futures (Selman & Schultz, 1990). Moreover, mutual affirmation of self-worth, intimacy, and self-disclosure become important characteristics of close peer relationships in adolescents (Buhrmester, 1996). Peers appear to be important confidants and advisers as young people begin to engage in romantic relationships. Indeed, research has demonstrated that the development of romantic relationships is related to the quality of adolescents' friendships with their peers (Furman et al., 2002). However, exchanges with close friends of affection, self-disclosure, sophisticated conflict resolution strategies, and mutual affirmation can also contribute to problematic exchanges of jealousy, aggression, and sexual harassment (Leadbeater, Sangster, Foran, Hoglund, & Yeung, 2005). Withdrawn or aggressive youth may also lack the peer support needed for negotiating romantic relationships (Connolly & Goldberg, 1999).

Widening social networks in adolescence also normatively increases access to nonparent adults, including relatives, coaches, and advisers, who can provide mentorship and support to adolescents (Rhodes, 2002). The importance of relationships between adult women and girls for girls' healthy development has been emphasized by many researchers (Pastor et al., this volume); however, the participation of nonparent adults in the worlds of adolescents is typically through relationships defined by differences in power and control rather than by mutual concern and collaborative engagement. Yet participation with nonparent adults can facilitate youth development (Rhodes, Davis, Prescott, & Spencer, this volume). Mentors have been shown to promote positive development through role modeling and emotional support; facilitate improvements in adolescents' attitudes, self-perceptions, and behaviors (Walker & Freedman, 1996); and reduce risky sexual behavior among adolescent women (Taylor-Seehafer & Rew, 2000). In a meta-analysis of the effectiveness of mentoring programs, Dubois, Holloway, Valentine, and Cooper (2002) note that such programs offer the greatest potential for youth whose backgrounds include significant environmental risk and disadvantage (e.g., low family socioeconomic status).

But how does the combination of past and present experiences with parents, peers, and nonparent adults help girls and young women build healthy romantic relationships? There is no user manual and no instruction book for creating collaboration, mutual intimacy, and respectful reciprocity in romantic relationships. Girls learn much of what they need to know about romantic relationships as they happen, without much reflection or assistance from adults. This learn-as-you-go, peer-supported approach to healthy relationships does not work for everyone. Current rates of dating violence, unprotected sex, sexually transmitted diseases, and unwanted pregnancies all confirm that there can be sharp rocks on the path to building healthy romantic relationships. In their research that focused on gender-related violence in the lives of youth, Berman, Straatman, Hunt, Izumi, and MacQuarrie (2002) found that adolescent women were pessimistic about adults' willingness to confirm the young women's experiences of violence.

Research has also begun to show what supports are needed to respond to girls and women who seek help to leave abusive relationships. Next, we review the evidence for problems in romantic relationships. We also describe what is known about the help-seeking strategies of girls and women who leave violent relationships in order to frame the parameters of social response that could support their help seeking.

Evidence for Problems in Romantic Relationships in Adolescents

Domestic Violence

Intimate violence is a leading cause of injuries in both adult and adolescent women. Reported rates of dating violence in high school students range from 9% to 45% (Downey, Bonica, & Rincon, 1999), with significant numbers of students continuing such relationships despite the abuse. A U.S. national survey reveals that almost one in four (23%) women aged 18 to 24 were assaulted by a date, boyfriend, acquaintance, or stranger (U.S. Department of Justice, 1997). In our own population-based survey of dating experiences of 664 Canadian youth (Healthy Youth Survey, 2004) aged 12 to 18, 22% were currently dating ($n = 149$). The majority of those dating were girls (67%), and most were 15 or older (79%). Seventy percent of the relationships were of less than 6 months' duration. Few (1% to 3%) reported worrying about or experiencing physical victimization (threats, physical intimidation, pushing, and shoving). More of these young people were concerned about their romantic partners' reactions to them when angry: These included trying to make them jealous (8%), excluding them from activities with friends (9.5%), ignoring them (28%), or giving them the silent treatment (36%).

Abusive experiences associated with adolescent dating disrupt normal developmental processes such as the development of a stable self-concept and integrated body image (Ackard, Neumark-Sztainer, & Hannan, 2003) and may lead to impairments in behaviors, thoughts, and feelings (Grasley, Wolfe, & Wekerle, 1999). Problematic romantic relationships can have multiple negative effects, for example, on adolescents' self-esteem (Ackard et al., 2003) and emotional health (Compian, Gowen, & Hayward, 2004).

Despite this picture of women's victimization, there is also evidence that women can play a role in perpetrating and sustaining violence (and, by implication, could be empowered to regulate aggression). Interpersonal aggression in nonromantic relationships is more typical of males than females, but research shows that both women and men perpetrate and experience similar levels of violence in romantic relationships (Moffit, Caspi, Rutter, & Silva, 2001). Moffit et al. (2001) argue that gender differences have been overstated in the past due to reporting biases, failures in asking women about their experiences as perpetrators and men about their victimization, hypotheses that women's violence is motivated only by self-defense, and trivializations of the significance of women's violence due to their inferior strength.

Sexual Health Concerns

Adolescent women face a number of serious health issues related to sexuality and relationships. Unplanned pregnancy, HIV/AIDS, and sexually transmitted diseases are a major public health concern (Health Canada, 2002). The Centers for Disease Control and Prevention (CDC; 2004) identified risky sexual behavior as one of six health behaviors most associated with mortality, morbidity, and social problems among youth. For example, early sexual intercourse increases the risk of sexually transmitted infection and cervical cancer (Stone et al., 1995) and has been associated with depression and suicide (Hallfors et al., 2004).

In 2003, nearly 46.7% of high school students in the United States had engaged in sexual intercourse, and 37% who were sexually active had not used a condom at last sexual intercourse (CDC, 2004). Conflicting social pressures continue to affect adolescents' abilities to make decisions about contraceptive use and safe sex and contribute to risk-taking behaviors in heterosexual intimate relationships. For example, Hutchinson (1998) found that for 59% of young women, sexual risk history was not discussed with their partners prior to having sexual relations for the first time.

Despite considerable funding, few intervention programs have resulted in a substantial increase in postponing sexual initiation or curtailing pregnancy among adolescents. For example, programs that advocate saying no to having sex assume that young women have an assertive sexual identity and confidence in negotiating safe sex. Asking young women to talk about sex in advance and to produce condoms places them at risk for losing the relationship.

Leaving Abusive Relationships: What Helps?

Research and anecdotes about women in abusive relationships traditionally depict them as having learned helplessness or as passive and unable to cope; however, recent research with adult women demonstrates that the vast majority of women who experience domestic violence do leave these relationships (Cook, Woolard, & McCollum, 2004). Indeed, in one study in Charlotte, North Carolina, 98% of the 419 women involved had called the police and at least one other source for help, and most had sought help from a diverse set of formal and informal sources. Leaving was not a discrete event but rather occurred over time as resources accumulated and obstacles to leaving diminished.

There is almost no research on adolescents' efforts to end unhealthy relationships, the obstacles to their leaving, or the resources available to respond to their help seeking. In a 6-year study of 93 adolescent mothers, Leadbeater and Way (2001) report that 41% (38) had experienced abuse by a male partner (including physical or sexual abuse or excessive controlling of resources, friends, etc.). The majority (71%, $n = 27$) of these young women left these relationships. At the 6-year follow-up, compared with the small group who stayed in abusive relationships ($n = 11$), women who left were less likely to be on welfare, more likely to be living with their own mothers, more likely to be employed, and more likely to have graduated from high school. Those who left also reported fewer depressive symptoms and were less likely to have reported histories of childhood abuse, trauma, or severely limited personal and social resources. In the qualitative interviews, the women who left abusive relationships first described their feelings of increasing immobilization within the abusive relationship. They talked of losing self-control and of emptying themselves of thoughts and self-respect as they spiraled into these relationships. As one young woman says, "He just had me so I was dumb. I was stupid" (p. 125). For some, these women's own anger fueled the abuse as they fought back or even initiated attacks. The process of leaving was abrupt for some who broke off relationships after single episodes of physical or sexual assault and for those women who could move quickly to another residence, generally with relatives. For others, the process of leaving was long and difficult. It involved choosing among bad alternatives that included homelessness, loneliness, and fear of further assaults. Most women who left were economically self-supporting though welfare or work, and they felt efficacious in being able to support their children. Women who left also described the dynamics of their recovery as gaining self-control, learning to manage their anger, and not depending on anyone for help. Paradoxically, however, the process of replacing being controlled by a male partner with self-control made trusting new supports very difficult. One young woman describes a determination to be self-sufficient that is accompanied by a lack of trust in others when she talks about what it means to her to be a woman:

> Just like taking on your own responsibilities, and not letting everybody else control you. . . . I think that I've always felt that when you start taking care of yourself, that's when you're really a woman, . . . I mean financially and emotionally, everything. Just making sure that you have control of your life and not anybody else. (p. 131)

Resources available to the women who left included family support and financial self-sufficiency, but no women who left talked about accessing formal supports. Indeed, the total absence of references to formal resources to address the relationship problems is alarming. Although some of the women who remained in abusive relationships turned to emergency room services to deal with injuries or overwhelming anxiety, better resources to support adolescents are overdue. The following section describes a mentoring program that is theoretically based in our knowledge of the development of healthy relationships and that seeks to support girls who show risks for problematic relationships.

Adolescent Girls' Mentorship Program

Our community-based study used a respectful and participatory approach based on principles of feminist ways of knowing. Feminist approaches focus, in particular, on assessing power differentials and oppression (gendered or otherwise) and on the relational nature of the research process itself. Feminist values, characterized by respect for others' experience, values, and differences, were also central to this effort to illuminate women's dating health concerns and best practices for addressing them.

Forty participants were accessed through three public urban high schools, an urban youth health clinic, and a rural Aboriginal secondary school. Initially, participants were 14 to 16 years of age and either White (N = 30) or Aboriginal (N = 10). The majority were from families with low socioeconomic status and were at risk for dropping out of school. Participants from the four urban sites were recruited through school counselors, teachers, and a clinic nurse. An Aboriginal elder facilitated access to Aboriginal participants. The staff and adolescents at each site took seriously adolescent women's dating-related health concerns and were motivated to learn more about them.

The study was conducted in two phases: In phase 1, focus groups were conducted with five groups of girls (one at each site) to obtain ethnographic data on their dating health concerns. Findings from the focus groups provided the foundation for the development of the mentoring program used in phase 2. We designed the initial focus groups to create space where participants could be an audience for each other while at the same time co-constructing the meaning of their dating experiences. Prompts used in the focus groups to generate discussion included "Please describe your experience of your dating relationships" and "How might these experiences relate to your health?" Examples of issues identified by participants included substance abuse, having unprotected sex, and physical and emotional abuse by an intimate partner.

Results of the analyses of the focus group phase 1 data are reported in more detail elsewhere (Banister, Jakubec, & Stein, 2003); however, themes revealed the complex interaction of power dynamics and socialization processes in the girls' relationships with men. Girls frequently blamed themselves for their boyfriends' abuse and lack of commitment, and this, in turn, impeded their ability to speak in their own interests. Many of the adolescent women experienced the impossible choice between compromising themselves to maintain the relationship or compromising the relationship to maintain themselves.

During the second phase of the study, with the same girls who participated in the focus groups, we conducted a weekly mentoring program for 16 weeks, in 1.5-hour sessions. Each intervention group was made up of approximately eight girls, an adult woman mentor, and a research assistant. Building on data generated in phase 1 helped to ensure program relevance for the participants. Participants in three of the intervention groups interviewed potential mentors to determine their fit with participants' shared experiences. The four school sites incorporated the program into their regular school hours, facilitating a low attrition rate (only two girls dropped out because of scheduling conflicts).

We spent considerable time stressing the importance of maintaining confidentiality within the group, but we were aware that we did not have control over information participants may have disclosed outside of the group. We reviewed the issue of confidentiality and anonymity on an ongoing basis, and each group developed rules pertaining to both areas of concern (see Banister & Daly, in press). Following policies at three of the sites (the rural Aboriginal school, an urban high school, and the local youth clinic), a staff member was included as the mentor. This also created ethical concerns about confidentiality and dual roles when the mentoring role could be confused with the mentors' service roles (as nurses and teachers). However, we found that the benefits of having a staff member as mentor outweighed the potential risks. The mentors were respectful of the girls' need for privacy concerning all information shared in the group and also afforded the girls extra support outside of the group. As one mentor said, "[The girls] feel comfortable with me now outside the group . . . if there's something wrong [they] can call me."

Designing an Empowerment Curriculum

The mentoring curriculum included feminist strategies designed to facilitate egalitarian relationships in the groups, including circling, where each person takes a turn to speak while others in the group listen in situations involving decision making or conflict, and closing, where participants shared a critical reflection about the group's process at the end of a meeting. Aspects of Wolfe, Wekerle, and Scott's (1997) youth relationship project that use information, skill building, and social action to empower youth to end relationship violence were also included to increase learning about unhealthy power imbalances and visits to local community resources to gain information and report back to the group (e.g., family planning clinic, sexual assault center). We also adapted a pedagogical approach referred to as *multiliteracies* (New London Group, 1996) to enhance participants' learning (see Banister & Begoray, 2004). Activities such as free writing and tracing the body are used to invite participants to use a variety of sign systems (e.g., kinetics and visual design systems) for exploring multiple aspects of self and for expression. Tracing the body, for example, focused on exploring inner and outer selves on penciled outlines of each person's body traced on large sheets of paper. A mentor explains: "Yes, not everyone always sees their inside you know, they see the outer." Through the use of informal artwork and other creative activities, the adolescent women opened up and were more willing to examine their intimate relationship concerns.

What Works? An Examination of the Intervention Groups' Data

Following completion of the program, the research team conducted a 1-hour interview with each group and a half-hour, confidential interview with each participant, mentor, and site gatekeeper (principals, clinic nurse). Interviewees were asked to share their perception of the program and to offer suggestions for improving it. All responded positively about the program and provided helpful suggestions that will be incorporated into the manual for future mentoring groups. Our analyses of data gathered through recordings of the group discussions, process notes collected by research assistants who participated in the groups, and follow-up interviews with all participants suggest that the mentoring groups were effective in raising and changing participants' awareness of dating health concerns in particular by:

helping the girls express their concerns out loud in their own voice,
learning to identify problems in relationships, including health risks and partner abuse,
crossing boundaries previously formed by peer cliques and allegiances outside of the mentoring groups,
revealing others' (peers' and adults') views about relationships in acceptable ways that helped them see alternative perspectives and understandings about the functioning of healthy relationships, and
increasing adult participation in girls' lives by helping adult mentors to demonstrate positive role modeling and supportive relationships.

Illustrations of each of these strategies for change follow, with examples of the participants' own ways of expressing these changes.

Voicing Concerns Out Loud

Voicing concerns out loud included first gaining the trust to speak openly with the group. The mentoring environment facilitated the adolescent women's ability to use what Tolman (2002) calls their authentic voice. One mentor identified the importance of participants' voice directly in terms of leaving abusive relationships: "Just have a voice and say what you want to say and especially getting out of the bad relationships, you know, was helpful for the girls because they try to stay in it." Another mentor described how the group environment helped the girls gradually open up: "From the beginning some of the girls would not talk, not even say 'good morning,' but now they are so open and they are socializing more." Through mutual dialogue, a shared consciousness about dating violence was co-constructed which helped to reduce the girls' isolation: "You hear everybody else's problems . . . you don't feel so alone."

The mentoring groups established a safe environment for participants to discuss sexual health and intimate relationship concerns such as dating violence and also to critically reflect upon, analyze, and evaluate their own relationships: "Yeah, it helped [me by] listening to them talk about their serious relationships and I would learn a little bit more." The mentors' openness in sharing their own dating health experiences also served to build rapport and trust in the group, which helped the girls open up. A mentor explained: "Have the mentor go first and say something that you wouldn't know if [the girls] could say." A supportive, questioning, and meaning-making environment facilitated participants' critical reflection on problematic relationships. Some participants reported benefits from talking openly about topics that for many were considered taboo (such as dating violence). In other cases, the benefits came from sharing useful information. As one young woman said: "There would be a lot of stuff that young girls don't know yet about being overcontrolled or your boyfriend not wanting to do this or do that." Participants also reported an increased awareness of sexual health strategies. As one concluded: "Try to be on the safe side and carry a whole bunch of condoms around with you."

Identifying Risks

Virtually all participants were able to identify intimate partner abuse and learned "how to get out of an abusive relationship." As one participant reported on her growing independence within her relationships, "It was like, 'I can't live without a boyfriend.' So I was, like, when we would get in a big fight and he'd threaten to dump me or whatever and I'm like, 'Oh no I'll kill myself!' But now I'm like, 'whatever, fine. If you want to go . . . go! That's fine! I don't need you!'"

Crossing Boundaries

It has been well documented that adolescent culture is characterized by many subcultures, often organized in rigid, hierarchal, ascending levels of status (Brown, Way, & Duff, 1998). The mentoring program also contributed to boundary crossing among diverse adolescent subgroups (e.g., cool group, nerds). The advantages to youth of getting outside of the expectations (and limitations) of their social groups were highlighted in the movie *The Breakfast Club*. It is possible that mentoring groups, over the long term, allow for the establishment of relationships that can open possibilities for new expectations, empathy, tolerance for differences, and mutual caring that may not have previously existed. As one mentor observed:

> Here was this group of very different girls from very different groups in the school who were in a school where kids don't tend to stick around very long, and we had this group of nine girls, and they all stayed right through to the end, they all stayed in school, they became very committed to each other, committed to the group, despite whatever they thought about each other coming into the group. So in the end they could joke about it, and say, "You know, I used to think you were a bitch."

Gaining Perspectives

Peer sharing also facilitated shifts in perspectives and provided opportunities for the adolescent women to consider alternative ways of interacting and behaving. In the words of one of the adolescent girls: "I like hearing other people's point of view, so I think it kind of sometimes changes your point of view as well, which is good sometimes, or it just kind of makes you think of what you think."

Increasing Adult Participation

The presence of a caring adult was an important part of the program. Through the course of the research, many of the girls constructed an understanding of the features and functions of this alternative sort of relationship. One participant said:

> Like, adults don't want to listen to you about telling them about drugs; they don't want to listen if you tell them you have an STD or you're pregnant or something. A lot of kids are scared to say something, right? And I think that it's really good to incorporate all of that [into the program] because kids are looking for someone to talk to and adults are the wisest and if a kid is telling you something and an adult is listening and not judging, that can be the best thing for them.

Moreover, the mentors enjoyed offering positive role modeling and emotional support for the adolescents. As one mentor said: "I just liked sitting there, hearing the girls' problems and voices and some of them had experiences similar to what I'd had. So we could share our experiences." The mentors shared their own stories about relationships in order to positively influence the girls' relationship choices. As one mentor said: "Just to be able to tell my story because a lot of the things that they are doing is what I did and I regret. . . . how I wish I didn't do that back then and they are all the same, what they are all talking about, their actions and why they are doing it for the relationship."

Aboriginal Girls' Project: Addressing the Need for Cultural Sensitivity

Because of the reported benefit of the mentoring program by the 10 Aboriginal participants in the initial focus groups and program and because of the greater health risks related to relationships among Aboriginal women, we sought to create a second version of the curriculum that was sensitive to Aboriginal cultures (see Banister & Begoray, in press). A new group of adolescent Aboriginal women ($N = 9$, aged 15 to 17) was accessed from the same rural Aboriginal secondary school as before. The first group to use the Aboriginal curriculum showed differences in ways of using the program that aligned it and connected it more directly with Aboriginal cultural values and the wider community.

The roles of the mentors, in particular, underwent changes. Two female Aboriginal school staff members (a secretary aged 30 and a learning assistant aged 27) were chosen as mentors, and each covered for the other when necessary, for example, when one was unexpectedly required to attend 3 weeks of traditional ceremonies held at the local band's longhouse. The same elder who participated in the previous group as before attended as many group sessions as possible, saying, "I can encourage them. It's an opportunity for me to be able to speak to the girls, to share more. They're just young kids, and they need to keep hearing from the older people." She offered suggestions for group activities that were culturally appropriate; for example, participants created a wild woman necklace as a concrete symbol to remind them of their authentic voice and inner wisdom. The elder's mentor role in the Aboriginal community at large and her wise council also lent her esteem to the other group mentor: "I liked having Diane (the elder) being there and [telling us about] having your voice."

Given that relationships are central to being and becoming within Aboriginal contexts, the mentoring group also took on meaning beyond that of the group itself. The elder's presence helped to remind the mentors and girls of their interconnectedness to the larger community and prepared the participants for their mentoring responsibilities within their Aboriginal community:

> That's how it's going to benefit the whole community. It's by them saying, "I talked about this, I learned this and that in the mentoring program." And it's only going to help somebody else if they keep sharing it . . . we have to keep reminding them to share it. We'll fix it so they'll have those opportunities. That's how it's going to benefit us.

The mentoring program helped build community both within and outside of the group. According to the school principal:

> Having the group coming into the school on Friday mornings gave an opportunity for a small cavalry of young women as well as staff members to get together and in an informal circumstance. So I was very, very supportive of that process. To watch it through the four to five months gave me an opportunity to see growth and development of the girls individually and collectively. Friendships were made that weren't there before, old prejudices were broken and then, particularly among certain staff members that joined in, they too became not only mentors on Fridays but mentors throughout the week so there was a larger support network built through that. That was wonderful. I saw young women being more able to speak to me on an equal

basis and then I also saw them seeking out their mentors both just for the eye contact and for various issues.

During the final group meeting, participants were invited to create their own posters about their learning in the group. Many reported a greater awareness of dating violence and of the importance of having safe sex. Participants' comments recorded on the posters included the following: "Learned a lot of stuff about sex and birth control," "Don't stay with a guy that is really controlling," and "We're empowered to appreciate having safe sex."

According to the elder, the mentoring program's success was measured by the girls' increased awareness of healthy and unhealthy dating relationship dynamics: "They would figure out there's healthy relationships and bad relationships and that's the importance of doing this for me, it was bringing that awareness to the girls that there is such a thing. That's what it was all about." The elder also believed that the consequences would be wide-reaching:

> This didn't just happen because the girls were going to get into a group and talk every week and do arts and crafts. This happened because something was going on with the girls and we want the people to know what was going on with those girls. And we also want the young boys to know that the girls said this happened. We have girls that have gone through research projects and they've talked about their relationships with their boyfriend and so that the boyfriend knows that he can't do this anymore. He can't hang on to that relationship anymore because he's threatening her with a suicide.

Fostering Empowerment, Resilience, Social Action, and Strengths

What are the characteristics of safe spaces? Data from the mentoring groups revealed participants' need for forms of support that were unavailable within their existing peer and romantic relationships. Over time, the groups became increasingly characterized by trust, mutual respect, and reciprocal support. The growth of trusting, reciprocal relationships in groups of adolescent girls and committed women also offered alternative ways of being in relationships that could be seen as a model for other relationships. The group environment helped participants engage in reciprocity and authentic dialogue without being judged. A respectful and empathic listening environment, made safe by the presence of caring adults, helped the girls feel more at ease with opening up over time. As one participant said: "It's just as soon as someone opens up that's something you've really got to take into consideration because for a lot of people it's so hard to open up . . . just listen while you can."

As participants engaged in mutual and empathic dialogue, relationships within the group itself took on new meaning. As they openly shared their experiences, bonds of empathic understanding were generated, setting up new expectations for and new possibilities in supportive relationships with peers and nonparent adults. Once trust was established, the girls turned more to each other both within and outside the group context. As one mentor reported: "I saw them come together more as support for each other. They were turning to each other and talking about what was going on in their lives." Early on in the program, a participant acknowledged the support she received from a group member outside of the group: "I just wanted to say thank you to Jean [pseudonym] for, I guess the last time I was here when I was really upset. After class she came over and she said, "If you ever want to talk about anything, blah, blah." I thought that was really sweet because, like, I hardly even know her!"

The opportunity to experience reciprocity, caring, and mutual respect within and outside the group helped to motivate some participants to take positive action. A mentor observed: "That's what helped get the girls motivated—to share their own experiences or [listen to] someone else's." The mentors' empathy affirmed the girls' self-worth and helped them to open up. One mentor explained: "I see how their reactions are, when they talk to me I know what they are thinking or feeling, and I know it is similar to what I used to feel and think when I was their age." Participants witnessed respectful ways of being in relationships through the adults' example. A participant states that she was more inclined to listen to a nonparental adult: "Of course you listen more to somebody else on the outside than your own mother. You're just like, 'oh, whatever mum, go away!' But when you hear somebody else say it, then you're like, 'oh, maybe she's right.'"

The following excerpt of a dialogue, recorded 8 weeks into the program, illustrates how supportive responses to one participant's disclosure about her initially passive response to her boyfriend's abuse are informed by the other girls and the shifts in her thinking that occur as a result of their support:

Participant 1: Anyway, Mike [pseudonym] thought that I said that I'd slept over at [Dan's] house, or something like that. So he got all drunk, or he was pissed. And he was flipping out and I didn't know what he was going to do. He came into the kitchen and he threw his drink in my face.

Participant 3: Oh, God! Didn't you slap him in his face?

Participant 1: I never had to do nothing. Like, he just walked by me and threw his drink in my face and just walked out. I wasn't even paying any attention. I didn't even know he was mad at me.

Participant 5: You were so shocked!

Participant 1: Yeah. Because, like, I don't know, he went off into another room and was talking to [John] about it. When he got in a better state of mind, he was sitting, like, bawling his eyes out.

Participant 6: They always do that!

Participant 5: They always do that! I've been there where it's just like they've bawled their eyes out and the next day they're jerks again.

Participant 1: But, like, I don't know, it's just like our relationship is oddly like better now. But I'm still, there's that one part that keeps running through in my mind of what he did.

Participant 6: This guy, like if he keeps it up you should break up with him.

Participant 1: I'm just going to, like next time I'm just going to leave, and if he phones I'm just going to hang up. I'm just going to not talk to him any more.

(all speaking at once)

Participant 4: I can play it too buddy.

Participant 3: Exactly.

Participant 6: No, but that's how it always starts. Like, it always, like the first time there's any abuse. They go, "Oh, I'm so sorry," and then it might even be like a year or two later and it'll happen again. Especially, much more than the first time.

Participant 5: So how is it for you, dealing with that?

Participant 1: Well, it's just sitting there and it reruns in my head every night.

Real changes in our thinking and beliefs are hard-won, and they are unlikely to be found through rules, edicts, or catchy phrases that attempt to mold or restrict behaviors. Nevertheless, they do appear to occur through dialogue in the supportive environments of mentoring groups that are legitimized by adult participation and role modeling.

Summary

The mentoring program was designed to create a safe forum for girls to express their authentic voice and to engage fully in meaningful, mutual interactions with peers and nonparental adult mentors. The growth in voice and expansion of peer and adult connections made possible through the mentoring group may be particularly salient to girls' long-term development. Girls who lack supports because of alienation from school, families, work, and even peers, or who are isolated by abusive relationships, can benefit from the mentoring group experience.

Longitudinal data are needed to study the durability of changes that we observed. While also limited in its generalizability to the small samples we have worked with, this qualitative research points to the need for further work on the protective mechanisms engendered by mentoring groups.

It was also apparent that both the adolescent girls and the mentors benefited from the program. These effects for the mentors were particularly important within the Aboriginal context, since mentoring and building community are congruent with indigenous ways of knowing. A mentor expressed appreciation for her role in the study: "Well, I feel like I fulfilled something in me. The mentoring program was one of the most positive things for this year. Kind of snuck up on me, but I am glad that it did."

For some youth, safe spaces are part of their everyday home, sports, and school lives; for others, these need to be created through active adult participation and effort. Bringing adults into relationships with young people through structured mentoring groups is only one way of creating the respectful, trusting, empowering relationships that are at the foundation of safe spaces for girls. Uncovering and overcoming barriers to providing these kinds of services to young women is overdue. Educational materials on dating violence for Aboriginal and nonminority youth are available at www.youth.society.uvic.ca. We are continuing to work to create manuals for the girls' mentoring program and to disseminate and evaluate it so that it can be widely accessed and utilized by groups of girls and women with confidence in its efficacy.

NOTE

The adolescent girls' mentoring project was part of a 5-year Community Alliance for Health Research (CAHR) project focusing on preventing youth injury, funded by the Canadian Institutes of Health Research (CIHR).

REFERENCES

Ackard, D. M., Neumark-Sztainer, D., & Hannan, P. (2003). Dating violence among a nationally representative sample of adolescent girls and boys. *Journal of Gender Specific Medicine, 6*(3), 39–48.

Banister, E., & Begoray, D. (2004). Beyond talking groups: Strategies for improving adolescent health education. *Health Care for Women International, 25,* 481–488.

Banister, E. M., & Begoray, D. L. (in press). Adolescent girls' sexual health education in an Indigenous context. *Canadian Journal of Native Education.*

Banister, E., & Daly, K. (in press). Walking a fine line: Negotiating dual roles in a study with adolescent girls. In B. Leadbeater, E. Banister, C. Benoit, M. Jansson, A. Marshall, & T. Riecken (Eds.), *Research ethics in community-based and participatory action research with children, adolescents, and youth.* Toronto, Ontario, Canada: University of Toronto Press.

Banister, E., Jakubec, S., & Stein, J. (2003). "Like, what I suppose to do": Power, politics and public health concerns in adolescent women's dating relationships. *Canadian Journal of Nursing Research, 35*(2), 16–33.

Berman, H., Straatman, A., Hunt, K., Izumi, J., & MacQuarrie, B. (2002). Sexual harassment: The unacknowledged face of violence in the lives of girls. In H. Berman & Y. Jiwani (Eds.), *In the best interests of the girl child* (pp. 15–44). London, ON: Alliance of Five Research Centres on Violence, Status of Women Canada.

Brown, L. M., Way, N., & Duff, J. L. (1998). The others in my I: Adolescent girls' friendships and peer relations. In N. G. Johnson, M. C. Roberts, & J. Worell (Eds.), *Beyond appearance: A new look at adolescent girls* (pp. 205–225). Washington, DC: American Psychological Association.

Buhrmester, D. (1996). Need fulfillment, interpersonal competence, and the developmental context of early adolescent friendship. In W. Bukowski, A. Newcomb, & W. Hartup (Eds.), *The company they keep. Friendship in childhood and adolescence* (pp. 158–185). Cambridge: Cambridge University Press.

Centers for Disease Control. (2004). *Youth risk behavior surveillance—United States.* Retrieved June 25, 2005, from http://www.cdc.gov/mmwr/PDF/SS/SS5302.pdf

Compian, L., Gowen, L. K., & Hayward, C. (2004). Peripubertal girls' romantic and platonic involvement with boys: Association with body image and depression symptoms. *Journal of Research on Adolescence, 14,* 23–47.

Connolly, J., & Goldberg, A. (1999). Romantic relationships in adolescence: The role of friends and peers in their emergence and development. In W. Furman, B. B. Brown, & C. Feiring (Eds.), *The development of romantic relationships in adolescence* (pp. 266–290). Cambridge, England: Cambridge University Press.

Cook, S. H., Woolard, J. L., & McCollum, H. C. (2004). The strengths, competence and resilience of women facing domestic violence: How can research and policy support them? In K. Maton, C. Shellenbach, B. Leadbeater, & A. Solzar (Eds.), *Investing in children, youth, families and communities: Strengths-based research and policy* (pp. 97–115). Washington, DC: American Psychological Foundation.

Downey, G., Bonica, C., & Rincon, C. (1999). Rejection sensitivity and adolescent romantic relationships. In W. Furman, B. B. Brown, & C. Feiring (Eds.), *The development of romantic relationships in adolescence* (pp. 148–174). Cambridge, England: Cambridge University Press.

DuBois, D. L., Holloway, B. E., Valentine, J. C., & Cooper, H. (2002). Effectiveness of mentoring programs for youth: A meta-analytic review. *American Journal of Community Psychology, 30,* 157–197.

Erikson, E. (1968). *Identity: Youth and crisis.* London: Faber and Faber.

Furman, W., Simon, V. A., Shaffer, L., & Bouchey, H. A. (2002). Adolescents' working models and styles for relationships with parents, friends, and romantic partners. *Child Development, 73,* 241–255.

Grasley, C., Wolfe, D. A., & Wekerle, C. (1999). Empowering youth to end relationship violence. *Children's Services: Social Policy, Research, and Practice, 2,* 209–223.

Hallfors, D. D., Waller, M. W., Ford, C. A., Halpern, C. T., Brodish, P. H., & Iritani, B. (2004). Adolescent depression and suicide risk: Association with sex and drug behavior. *American Journal of Preventative Medicine, 27,* 224–231.

Health Canada. (2002). *Women and sexual and reproductive health.* Retrieved June 25, 2005, from Government of Canada, Health Canada Web site: http://www.hc-sc.gc.ca/english/women/facts_issues/facts_sexual.htm

Healthy Youth Survey. (2004). *Healthy Youth Survey: Project update.* Retrieved July 15, 2005, from University of Victoria, Centre for Youth and Society Web site: http://www.youth.society.uvic.ca/activities/research/cahr/survey.html.

Hutchinson, M. K. (1998). Something to talk about: Sexual risk communication between young women and their partners. *Journal of Gynecologic and Neonatal Nursing, 27,* 127–133.

Leadbeater, B. J., Sangster, N., Foran, K., Hoglund, W., & Yeung, R. (2005). *Changes in the developmental course and functions of aggression from childhood to adolescence: Implications for prevention programs.* Manuscript submitted for publication.

Leadbeater, B. J., & Way, N. (Eds.). (1996). *Urban girls: Resisting stereotypes, creating identities.* New York: New York University Press.

Leadbeater, B. J., & Way, N. (Eds.). (2001). *Growing up fast: Early adult transitions of inner-city adolescent mothers.* Mahwah, NJ: Erlbaum.

Moffitt, T. E., Caspi, A., Rutter, M., & Silva, P. A. (2001). *Sex differences in antisocial behavior: Conduct disorder, delinquency, and violence in the Dunedin Longitudinal Study.* Cambridge, England: Cambridge University Press.

New London Group. (1996). A pedagogy of multiliteracies: Designing social futures. *Harvard Educational Review, 66,* 60–92.

Rhodes, J. E. (2002). *Stand by me: The risks and rewards of mentoring today's youth.* Cambridge, MA: Harvard University Press.

Selman, R. L., & Schultz, L. H. (1990). *Making a friend in youth: Developmental theory and pair therapy.* Chicago: University of Chicago Press.

Stone, K. M., Zaidi, A., Rosero-Bixby, L., Oberle, M. W., Reynolds, G., Larsen, S., Nahmias, A. J., Lee, F. K., Schachter, J., & Guinan, M. E. (1995). Sexual behavior, sexually transmitted diseases, and risk of cervical cancer. *Epidemiology, 6,* 409–414.

Taylor-Seehafer, M., & Rew, L. (2000). Risky sexual behavior among adolescent women. *Journal of the Society of Pediatric Nurses, 5,* 15–25.

Tolman, D. L. (2002). *Dilemmas of desire: Teenage girls talk about sexuality.* Cambridge, MA: Harvard University Press.

U.S. Department of Justice. (1997). *National Crime Victimization Survey.* Washington, DC: Bureau of Justice Statistics, U.S. Department of Justice.

Walker, G., & Freedman, M. (1996). Social change one on one: The new mentoring movement. *American Prospect, 27,* 75–81.

Wolfe, D. A., Wekerle, C., & Scott, K. (1997). *Alternative to violence: Empowering youth to develop healthy relationships.* Thousand Oaks, CA: Sage.

Caring Connections
Mentoring Relationships in the Lives of Urban Girls

Jean E. Rhodes, Anita A. Davis,
Leslie R. Prescott, and Renée Spencer

Adolescents who have adjusted well in spite of profound and persistent stress often attribute their success to the influence of a natural mentor, such as a special aunt, neighbor, or teacher. Anecdotal reports of mentors' protective qualities are corroborated by a growing body of literature that has underscored the positive influence of nonparent adults in the lives of adolescents. Despite the promise of mentoring, as well as the recent rapid proliferation of volunteer programs across the United States, many questions remain concerning the nature and effects of mentor relationships. In this chapter we will discuss a developing model of the processes through which mentoring is likely to promote positive development for adolescents, and present findings from a series of studies examining the influence of natural and formal mentors. Implications of these findings for future research and preventative intervention are discussed.

Background

Although adolescents' relationships with their parents clearly play key roles in their development, nonparent adults can also be quite prominent in adolescents' lives. In a study of urban youth with diverse racial and ethnic backgrounds, 82% reported having a nonparent adult who they could count on and who was a significant influence on them (Beam, Chen, & Greenberger, 2002). In another study of urban youth, predominantly

African American, almost 54% indicated they had a natural mentor, and those with mentors reported engaging in fewer problem behaviors and having more positive attitudes toward school (Zimmerman, Bingenheimer, & Notaro, 2002).

Research on resilience has called attention to the strong positive force that nonparent adults can be in youths' lives. Nonparent adults and other extrafamilial sources of support have been consistently identified as contributing to resilience among youth faced with a wide array of challenges, from divorce to maltreatment (Cowen & Work, 1988; Garmezy & Neuchterlein, 1972; Luthar & Ziglar, 1991; Masten & Coatsworth, 1998). Werner and Smith (1982), for example, conducted a longitudinal investigation of children who were exposed to poverty, biological risks, and family instability. Those who developed into competent and autonomous young adults showed an ability to locate an adult in addition to their parents for support.

Unfortunately, many of today's youth cannot easily find supportive nonparent adults in their communities. Shifting family and marital problems, overcrowded schools, and less cohesive communities have dramatically reduced the availability of caring adults (Furstenberg, 1994; Putnam, 2000). The problem is particularly acute in urban centers where many of the middle-class adults who once served as respected authority figures have moved to suburbs, leaving far fewer adults in these communities who are able to pass along vital information and resources to youth who are struggling educationally or economically (Anderson, 1999).

A growing body of literature points to relationships with adults, particularly adult women, as being especially important to the healthy psychological development of adolescent girls (Brown & Gilligan, 1992; Debold, Brown, Weseen, & Brookins 1999; Sullivan, 1996; Taylor, Gilligan, & Sullivan, 1995). Gilligan (1990) contends that "relationships between girls and adult women may be particularly critical during the transition into adolescence" because girls at this juncture are eager to "seek out and listen attentively to advice from women" (p. 6). Nonparent adults may play a critical role in mediating adolescent girls' dual needs for both independence and guidance. With adults other than their parents, adolescents can gain some autonomy while simultaneously obtaining needed emotional support and advice (Allen, Aber, & Leadbeater, 1990). Chodorow (1992) also notes the influential role of nonparent adults in the lives of adolescent girls. From childhood, girls are more likely than boys to participate in an intergenerational world of women, including their mothers, grandmothers, aunts, and other female kin. Older women "become mediators between mother and daughter, by providing a daughter with alternative models for personal identification and objects of attachment" (p. 6).

Intergenerational relationships have long been recognized as an important resource in many urban African American communities (Martin & Martin, 1978; Wilson, 1997). Collins (1987), for example, has described the protective influence of African American women, referring to them as "othermothers." These women provide guidance to younger members of the community, often acting as surrogate parents. Women-centered networks typically extend beyond the boundaries of biologically related extended families to include "community othermothers" and "fictive" kin (i.e., non-kin who have been absorbed into an existing family structure; Collins, 1987; Stack, 1974).

Many Latino families are embedded similarly in extended kinship systems that include not only blood relatives but also other important adults (de Anda, 1984; Escobar & Randolph, 1982; Ramirez, 1989). For example, godparents often function as substitute parents (*padrinos/madrinas*) for children and adolescents or as "co-parents" (*compadres/commadres*) to young mothers (Mindel, 1980; Sena-Rivera, 1979; Becerra & de Anda, 1984). These relationships are often formalized through the ritual of infant baptism, which obligates godparents to provide the children and their families with economic assistance, encouragement, and guidance (Garcia-Preto, 1982). "Child-keeping," or the informal fostering of children, is also common in both African American and Latino families (Dore & Dumois, 1990).

Despite their prominence, little is known about the role that intergenerational ties play in the lives of urban adolescent girls. Research on girls' development suggests that such relationships hold the potential to contribute to girls' developing sense of self by meeting their high needs for connection and relationship (Brown & Gilligan, 1992). Mentors, who are well positioned to offer guidance and growth-promoting challenges as girls strive to develop their full potential, may be particularly important.

How Mentoring Works

Close connections with nonparent adults, including either adults in their families and communities or volunteer mentors in a formal mentoring program, are likely to promote overall positive development in girls in several ways. Although little empirical study of the mentoring process has yet been undertaken, Rhodes (2002) proposes that mentoring affects youth through three interrelated processes: (a) by enhancing youth's social relationships and emotional well-being, (b) by improving their cognitive skills through instruction and meaningful conversation, and (c) by promoting positive identity development by serving as role models and advocates. These processes are described in the following and illustrated by a brief case that is drawn from a qualitative interview study of urban youth and their adult mentors.

Social-Emotional Development

A frequent observation among mentors and parents is that close connections with mentors can foster improvements in adolescents' sense of self and in their ability to connect with others. When adolescents sense that their mentors hold them in positive regard, they may internalize this positive appraisal, perhaps contributing to their own feelings of self-worth. Through consistently warm and accepting interactions with their mentors, youth may begin to recognize the potential that exists in close relationships and open themselves to the people around them, particularly their parents. In some cases, mentors can serve as alternative or secondary attachment figures, helping girls to realign their conceptions of themselves in relation to other people. In other cases, mentors may act as a sounding board, providing a model for effective communication and helping adolescents to better understand, more clearly express, and more effectively control both their positive and their negative emotions (Pianta, 1999).

In a national longitudinal evaluation of the Big Brothers Big Sisters program, which included 1,138 boys and girls aged 10 to 16 years, Rhodes, Grossman, and Resch (2000) tested some of these social and emotional processes. Mentoring relationships led to improvements in adolescents' perceptions of their relationships with their parents (i.e., higher levels of intimacy, communication, and trust). These improvements, in turn, led to positive changes in adolescents' sense of self-worth, scholastic competence, and scholastic achievement.

Cognitive Development

Adolescence is a time of significant cognitive growth, during which youth become more self-reflective and self-aware. A trusting relationship with a mentor can thus provide a framework in which girls acquire and refine new thinking skills. Vygotsky (1978) described a "zone of proximal development" in which learning takes place: the range between what a youth can attain when problem solving independently and what he or she can accomplish while working under adult guidance or with more capable peers. To the extent that interactions with a mentor occur within this zone of challenging but attainable pursuits, the mental capacities of girls may increase and improve. Opportunities for authentic conversation are particularly important for girls, who often hide their true feelings from their parents, teachers, and others in their efforts to gain some autonomy (Darling, Hamilton, & Hames, 2003).

Identity Development

Profound changes in girls' behaviors and expectations for the future also occur in adolescence. Adults who exemplify desired knowledge, skills, and behavior often facilitate these changes. Indeed, many lower-income girls in particular have limited personal contact with positive role models outside the immediate family and believe that their opportunities for success are restricted. Mentors can serve as concrete models of success, demonstrating qualities that girls might wish to emulate and providing guidance and information about the necessary steps to achieve various goals. Through mentors' support, feedback, and encouragement, this modeling process is thought to be reinforced (Kemper, 1968).

Case Example

These interrelated processes are exemplified in the relationship between 12-year-old Leigh, a White working-class girl, and her Big Sister, Julie, who is White and middle-class, who were matched for more than 5 years. Leigh's long-term relationship with Julie became important to her in new ways when Leigh's mother remarried. Leigh felt that her mother "just didn't have time" for her anymore because so much of her attention was now directed at the newest family members (her mother's husband's children). Leigh felt she could talk to Julie about anything, even "feeling pushed away" by her mother. Julie also felt that it had been vital during this time that Leigh had someone "outside the family . . . to talk to that doesn't judge a lot." Leigh saw a link between being able to "spill everything out" with Julie and her overall sense of competence. Without Julie to talk to, Leigh thought she would not have had as much self-confidence. Their mentoring relationship also helped to preserve closeness between Leigh and her mother, as Leigh began to reinterpret her mother's actions through a less hurtful, rejecting lens. Julie helped Leigh to understand her mother's perspective and conflicting roles. Julie also got married since first being matched with Leigh and demonstrated concretely how the addition of a new person to her family life did not inevitably diminish her preexisting relationships.

Another important dimension of their relationship was Julie's discussion with Leigh of the girl's future. None of Leigh's family members had attended college. Julie, however, could speak to the benefits of a college education and took Leigh to alumni events at her alma mater that, in Julie's words, "put it into her head that college is even an option." Although Leigh was not sure whether she wanted to attend college ("it might benefit me, it might not"), she did consider it as a possible choice.

Informal Mentors

In a series of studies, we have examined how informal or natural mentors affect the lives of African American adolescent mothers. Over the course of 5 years, young mothers who were residing in low-income Chicago neighborhoods throughout the 1990s were asked, "Other than your parents or whoever raised you, is there an older person in your life (a mentor or positive role model) who you go to for support and guidance?" Four characteristics of the relationship were then listed as criteria for persons to be nominated as mentors. These included: (a) You can count on this person to be there for you, (b) he or she believes in you and cares deeply about you, (c) he or she inspires you to do your best, and (d) knowing him or her has really influenced what you do and the choices that you make. Participants who nominated natural mentors were then asked how long and in what capacity they had known them, what the qualities and importance of the relationships had been, and what had been their frequency of interaction.

Several additional measures were employed, including the depression subscale of a self-report symptom inventory (the SCL-90-R; Derogatis, 1983), a checklist of major stressors occurring in the past year (Life Events

Survey; Sarason, Johnson, & Siegel, 1979), economic strain (Pearlin, Menaghan, Lieberman, & Mullan, 1981), as well as questions about participants' aspirations, expectations, and barriers to education. In addition, participants were asked to nominate individuals from whom various types of support (i.e., tangible, emotional, social, cognitive, instrumental, or child care) were elicited in the past month, to rate their satisfaction with this support, and to cite any problems that they experienced in their relationships (i.e., conflict, disappointment, criticism, or intrusiveness). The amount of support was calculated as the total number of persons who were nominated as providing support. (Further details about the measures and procedures are reported in Rhodes, Ebert, & Fischer, 1992; and Rhodes, Contreras, & Mangelsdorf, 1994.)

Forty-five percent of the participants in this study nominated natural mentors, ranging from their boyfriends' female relatives to their grandmothers, aunts and uncles, older friends, sisters, teachers, church staff, counselors, and neighbors. Most (85%) of the mentors were women, more than half (53%) lived in the same neighborhood as the adolescent, and 95% were seen at least once per week. Adolescents with and without mentors were exposed to comparable levels of life stress and economic strain, and when mentor support was removed from the analyses, there were no group differences in the amount of social support that was available to the participants. Nonetheless, adolescents with mentors were less depressed than adolescents without mentors.

Similar findings emerged in a study of mentoring relationships among adolescent Latina (predominantly Puerto Rican and Mexican) mothers (Rhodes et al., 1994). Thirty-five percent of the participants in the study nominated natural mentors, most of whom (89%) were women. Nearly all the participants (94.7%) interacted with their mentors at least once per week, roughly half (46.4%) had known their mentors for at least 16 years, and most (82.4%) expected to maintain the relationships for the rest of their lives. Although mothers with and without mentors reported similar levels of stress exposure and overall support, those with mentors reported lower levels of depression and anxiety and greater satisfaction with support resources. For the group with mentors, none of the predictor variables (i.e., amount of support, satisfaction with support, problems in relationships) were related to anxiety or depression. For the group without mentors, however, relationship problems significantly predicted anxiety and depression. This suggests that mentor support serves to buffer young mothers from the negative effects of relationship problems. This pattern is consistent with Collins's (1987) observations concerning othermothers, who "often play a central role in defusing the emotional intensity between bloodmothers and their daughters" (p. 8). Thus, mentors may enhance the young women's capacity to elicit and appreciate the positive aspects of their social support networks and more effectively cope with relationship problems.

We have examined the extent to which mentors are associated with educational and vocational outcomes. As noted earlier, many of the urban girls experience a widening gap between their career aspirations and their actual expectations, and mentors can help to alter beliefs about available opportunities (Bowman, 1991; Leadbeater & Way, 2001). We have found that African American adolescents who identified natural mentors were more likely to be engaged in activities related to their career goals (Klaw & Rhodes, 1995). Moreover, mentor support was associated with the girls' belief in education as a link to opportunities with their heightened optimism about the future (Klaw & Rhodes, 1995), and with a greater likelihood of graduating from high school (Klaw, Rhodes, & Fitzgerald, 2003). This suggests the presence of a more positive future orientation in the identities of mentored youth. Along these lines, Hellenga, Rhodes, and Aber (2002) used discriminate function analysis to distinguish between urban girls whose vocational aspirations and expectations for the future were discrepant and those that were consistent. In other words, girls with mentors expected that they would achieve their goals.

Formal Mentors

Although these findings are promising for those adolescents with natural mentors, many adolescents do not identify natural mentors. To address the needs of these young women, efforts have been made to pair them with volunteer mentors, and hundreds of mentoring programs, modeled after the Big Brother Big Sister prototype, have emerged in recent years. Many of these programs have been designed to meet the needs of pregnant and parenting adolescents. Although such programs tend to engender considerable enthusiasm, we know too little about their effectiveness (Freedman, 1993). It is also unclear whether assigned mentoring relationships can be as protective as natural mentor relationships. Whereas natural mentor relationships typically emerge from within the youth's social support system, assigned mentor relationships tend to be grafted onto the extant network. These and other differences may influence the nature and course of the relationship.

A meta-analysis of mentoring program evaluations (DuBois, Holloway, Valentine, & Cooper, 2002) concluded that formal mentoring programs have the potential to offer youth some of the same benefits that have been found to be associated with natural mentoring relationships. Such benefits include improvements in self-concept and interpersonal relationships, decreases in substance use, and improved school attendance (DuBois, Neville, Parra, & Pugh-Lilly, 2002; Rhodes, 2002). Simply being matched with a mentor, however, does not lead to positive results. Growing evidence suggests that a close and enduring connection must form in order for youth to benefit from a mentoring relationship. Relationships that are less close tend to have little effect, and those of short duration can actually make matters worse for some youth. For example, Grossman and Rhodes (2002) found that the associations of mentor relationships with outcomes varied as a function of their duration. Relative to controls, youth whose relationships terminated within a year appeared to derive the fewest benefits. Those in short matches (i.e., terminating within the first 3 to 6 months) actually suffered declines in reported levels of feelings of self-worth and perceived scholastic competence. For boys and girls who were in matches that lasted more than a year, however, positive effects were evident on levels of self-worth, perceived social acceptance, scholastic competence, parental relationship quality, school value, and levels of both drug and alcohol use. These findings are consistent with other studies (DuBois, Neville, et al., 2002; Lee & Cramond, 1999). Unfortunately, estimates show that as many as half of all assigned mentoring relationships terminate within the first few months (Rhodes, 2002).

Many questions remain about natural mentoring relationships. It is unclear, for example, how natural mentoring relationships are initiated and maintained. That is, are mentors "choosing" mentees and taking more responsibility for maintaining the relationship? Or do mentors and mentees share equal responsibility in establishing and maintaining the relationship? It is possible, for example, that there is an ebb and flow in these relationships and that for longevity to occur each member of the dyad takes more responsibility for its continuation at some point in time. It is also interesting to consider the possibility that although the adolescent starts out in a less "powerful" position in the dyad, this relationship might undergo a transformation over the long term in which it becomes more egalitarian. It may be that this type of transformation actually helps to account for long-term relationships because it offers the adolescent an opportunity to mature and contribute to a more balanced relationship. An understanding of if and how such transformations occur could be extremely useful to novice mentors who are feeling their way through this process.

Conclusions

Enthusiasm for mentoring adolescent girls must be tempered with realism about the potential limitations of mentoring relationships. Despite some clear successes, our data also suggest that volunteer relationships may not be as influential or enduring as those that form naturally. For example, a sizable proportion of volunteer relationships terminate after only a few months. High termination rates are common in mentoring programs and appear to be partially influenced by the expectations and characteristics of the volunteers. Whereas some mentors allow their partners to take an active role in determining the direction and activities of the relationship, others enter the project with more rigid prescriptive agendas (Styles & Morrow, 1995).

Similarly, some young women complain that their mentors seem out of touch with their experiences and problems. This problem sometimes stems from the social distance that exists between middle-class volunteers and urban adolescent girls. Flaxman, Ascher, and Harrington (1988) have noted that in settings where middle-class adults are attempting to work with urban adolescents, the mentors' world can easily seem "irrelevant or even nonsensical" to the youngsters, "and their goals for mentees naïve" (p. 3). Adults who live or work in urban communities, and who are familiar with the circumstances confronting youth, are likely to be better able to give advice that is consistent with the cultural norms, options, and constraints of a given setting.

In addition to issues concerning socioeconomic status, programs tend to gloss over the particular needs related to gender. Single-sex programs (e.g., Big Sisters of Greater Boston) are finding themselves under increased pressure to become coeducational, despite evidence that they may be more advantageous to adolescent girls. The mentoring movement has grown so rapidly that research has lagged behind, particularly in the area of gender differences. Yet gender may play a critical role in mentoring—particularly since girls and boys may form and view relationships very differently

(Bogat & Liang, 2005). Girls and boys may thrive with different types of mentoring and form different sorts of relationships with their mentors. For example, instrumental mentoring, with its more problem-focused, goal-oriented approach, may appeal more to boys, whereas psychosocial mentoring, which relies primarily on the interpersonal relationship between the mentor and mentee, may be a better match for girls (Bogat & Liang, 2005; Rhodes, 2002). Such differences may not be directly addressed in the pre-match training that goes on at coeducational programs, diminishing the likelihood that mentors are adequately prepared to build strong relationships with their little sisters.

More generally, gender-specific programs may be particularly useful for girls, who tend to get lost in the shuffle if their needs are not a specific focus of attention. Much coeducational youth programming is provided by agencies that formerly catered solely to boys, which may continue to place boys' needs and interests first, even after going coeducational (Mead, 2001; Deutsch & Hirsch, 2004). In a 4-year study of youth programming, Mead (2001) concluded that many programs did not serve girls as effectively as boys: "The result was a mismatch between the program's design and the girls' interests and concerns—a mismatch that caused girls to be marginalized, their needs to be unmet, and their potential to be unrealized" (p. 23). Although less of a concern in the more individual-oriented mentoring programs, biases remain.

Beyond these considerations, a more effective intervention approach may ultimately lie in teaching adolescents techniques for recruiting support from helpful adults within their own social networks. This may be particularly important for those girls who have experienced difficulties in their early relationships and are less likely to trust the overtures of caring adults. Caring older women are already embedded in extended families, schools, churches, and neighborhoods, but many girls appear hesitant to approach them. With training and encouragement, adolescents might be taught techniques for identifying, meeting, and establishing relationships with existing sources of support (Balcazar & Fawcett, 1992). Adolescents can then use their acquired skills to find different adults to assist them in dealing with various concerns in different contexts over time.

It is also important to consider that, despite its promise, mentoring cannot redress the many challenges facing urban girls today. Until the basic resources in urban communities are improved—the schools, neighborhoods, health and child care settings, employment opportunities, and so forth—the influence of adult supports or any other supplementary resources on the life trajectories of most youths will remain limited. On the other hand, we should not minimize mentors' potentially positive influences. Indeed, our findings and observations provide us with considerable hope about the capacity of mentors to transform some young women's lives. These observations challenge us to further understand the complexities of nonparent adult relationships and the conditions under which they have protective effects.

References

Allen, J. P., Aber, L., & Leadbeater, B. L. (1990). Adolescent problem behaviors: The influence of attachment and autonomy. *Psychiatric Clinics of North America, 13,* 455–467.

Anderson, E. (1999). *Code of the street: Decency, violence, and the moral life of the inner city.* New York: Norton.

Balcazar, F. E., & Fawcett, S. B. (1992). *Recruiting mentors and potential helpers.* Lawrence: University Press of Kansas.

Beam, M. R., Chen, C., & Greenberger, E. (2002). The nature of adolescents' relationships with their "very important" nonparental adults. *Journal of Community Psychology, 30,* 305–325.

Becerra, R., & de Anda, D. (1984). Pregnancy and motherhood among Mexican adolescents. *Health and Social Work, 9,* 106–123.

Bogat, G. A., & Liang, B. (2005). Gender in mentoring relationships. In D. L. DuBois & M. J. Karcher (Eds.), *Handbook of youth mentoring* (pp. 205–218). Thousand Oaks, CA: Sage.

Bowman, P. J. (1991). Joblessness. In J. S. Jackson (Ed.), *Life in Black America* (pp. 156–178). Newbury Park, CA: Sage.

Brown, L. M., & Gilligan, C. (1992). *Meeting at the crossroads: Women's psychology and girls' development.* Cambridge, MA: Harvard University Press.

Chodorow, N. (1992). *Feminism and psychoanalysis.* San Francisco: Jossey-Bass.

Collins, P. H. (1987). The meaning of motherhood in Black culture and Black mother/daughter relationships. *Sage, 4,* 3–10.

Cowen, E. L., & Work, W. (1988). Resilient children, psychosocial wellness, and primary prevention. *American Journal of Community Psychology, 16,* 591–607.

Darling, N., Hamilton, S. F., & Hames, K. (2003). Relationships outside the family: Unrelated adults. In G. R. Adams & M. D. Beronzsky (Eds.), *Blackwell handbook of adolescence* (pp. 349–360). Oxford, England: Blackwell Publishing.

de Anda, D. (1984). Informal support networks of Hispanic mothers: A comparison across age groups. *Journal of Social Service Research, 7,* 89–105.

Debold, E., Brown, L. M., Weseen, S., & Brookins, G. K. (1999). Cultivating hardiness zones for adolescent girls: A new conceptualization or resilience in relationship with caring adults. In N. G. Johnson, M. C. Roberts, & J. Worell (Eds.), *Beyond Appearance: A new look at adolescent girls* (pp. 181–204). Washington, DC: American Psychological Association.

Derogatis, L. R. (1983). *SCL-90-R: Administration, scoring, and procedures manual—for the R version.* Baltimore: Author.

Deutsch, N. L., & Hirsch, B. J. (2004). A place to call home: Youth organizations in the lives of inner city adolescents. In T. M. Brinthaupt & R. P. Lipka (Eds.), *Understanding early adolescent self and identity: Applications and interventions* (pp. 293–320). Albany: State University of New York Press.

Dore, M. M., & Dumois, A. O. (1990). Cultural differences in the meaning of adolescent pregnancy. *Journal of Contemporary Human Services, 2,* 93–102.

DuBois, D. L., Holloway, B. E., Valentine, J. C., & Cooper, H. (2002). Effectiveness of mentoring programs for youth: A meta-analytic review. *American Journal of Community Psychology, 30,* 157–197.

DuBois, D. L., Neville, H. A., Parra, G. R., and Pugh-Lilly, A. O. (2002). Testing a new model of mentoring. In J. E. Rhodes (Ed.), *A critical view of youth mentoring* (Vol. 93, pp. 21–58). San Francisco: Jossey-Bass.

Escobar, J. I., & Randolph, E. T. (1982). The Hispanic and social networks. In R. M. Becerra, M. Karno, & J. I. Escobar (Eds.), *Mental health and Hispanic Americans: Clinical perspectives* (pp. 89–105). New York: Grune and Stratton.

Flaxman, E., Ascher, C., & Harrington, C. (1988). *Youth mentoring programs and practices.* New York: Institute for Urban and Minority Education, Teachers College, Columbia University.

Freedman, M. (1993). *The kindness of strangers: Adult mentors, urban youth, and the new volunteerism.* San Francisco: Jossey-Bass

Furstenberg, F. F. (1994). How families manage risk and opportunity in dangerous neighborhoods. In W. J. Wilson (Ed.), *Sociology and the public agenda.* Newbury Park, CA: Sage.

Garcia-Preto, N. (1982). Puerto Rican families. In M. McGoldrick, J. K. Pearce, & J. Giordano (Eds.), *Ethnicity and family therapy.* New York: Guilford.

Garmezy, N., & Neuchterlein, N. (1972). Invulnerable children: The fact and fiction of competence and disadvantage. *American Journal of Orthopsychiatry, 42,* 328–329.

Gilligan, C. (1990). *Girls at 11: An interview with Carol Gilligan* (pp. 5–7). Cambridge, MA: Harvard Graduate School of Education, in association with Harvard University Press.

Grossman, J. B., & Rhodes, J. E. (2002). The test of time: Predictors and effects of duration in youth mentoring relationships. *American Journal of Community Psychology, 30,* 199–219.

Hellenga, K., Rhodes, J. E., & Aber, M. S. (2002). African American adolescent mothers' vocational aspiration-expectation gap: Individual, social, and environmental influences. *Psychology of Women Quarterly, 26,* 200–212.

Kemper, T. (1968). Reference groups, socialization, and achievement. *American Sociological Review, 33,* 31–45.

Klaw, E., & Rhodes, J. E. (1995). Mentor relationships and the career development of pregnant and parenting African-American teenagers. *Psychology of Women Quarterly, 19,* 551–562.

Klaw, E. L., Rhodes, J. E., & Fitzgerald, L. F. (2003). Natural mentors in the lives of African-American adolescent mentors: Tracking relationships over time. *Journal of Youth and Adolescence, 32,* 223–232.

Leadbeater, B. J. R., & Way, N. (2001). *Growing up fast: Transitions to early adulthood of inner-city adolescent mothers.* Mahwah, NJ: Erlbaum.

Lee, J., & Cramond, B. (1999). The positive effects of mentoring economically disadvantaged students. *Professional School Counseling, 23,* 172–178.

Luthar, S. S., & Ziglar, E. (1991). Vulnerability and competence: A review of research on resilience in childhood. *American Journal of Orthopsychiatry, 61,* 6–22.

Martin, E. P., & Martin, J. M. (1978). *The Black extended family.* Chicago: University of Chicago Press.

Masten, A. S., & Coatsworth, J. D. (1998). The development of competence in favorable and unfavorable environments: Lessons from research on successful children. *American Psychologist, 53,* 205–220.

Mead, M. (2001). *Gender matters: Funding effective programs for women and girls.* Medford, MA: Lincoln Filene Center, Tufts University.

Mindel, C. H. (1980). Extended familism among urban Mexican Americans, Anglos, and Blacks. *Hispanic Journal of Behavioral Sciences, 2,* 21–34.

Pearlin, L., Menaghan, E. G., Lieberman, M. A., & Mullan, T. J. (1981). The stress process. *Journal of Health and Social Behaviors, 22,* 337–356.

Pianta, R. C. (1999). *Enhancing relationships between children and teachers.* Washington, DC: American Psychological Association.

Putnam, R. D. (2000). *Bowling alone: The collapse and revival of American community.* New York: Simon and Schuster.

Ramirez, O. (1989). Mexican American children and adolescents. In J. T. Gibbs & L. N. Huang (Eds.), *Children of color: Psychological interventions with minority youth* (pp. 224–250). San Francisco: Jossey-Bass.

Rhodes, J. E. (2002). *Stand by me: The risks and rewards of mentoring today's youth.* Cambridge, MA: Harvard University Press.

Rhodes, J. E., Contreras, J. M., & Mangelsdorf, S. C. (1994). Natural mentor relationships among Latina adolescent mothers: Psychological adjustment, moderating processes, and the role of early parental acceptance. *American Journal of Community Psychology, 22,* 211–228.

Rhodes, J. E., Ebert, L., & Fischer, K. (1992). Natural mentors: An overlooked resource in the social networks of adolescent mothers. *American Journal of Community Psychology, 20,* 445–461.

Rhodes, J. E., Grossman, J. B., & Resch, N. R. (2000). Agents of change: Pathways through which mentoring relationships influence adolescents' academic adjustment. *Child Development, 71,* 1662–1671.

Sarason, I. G., Johnson, J. H., & Siegel, J. M. (1979). Assessing the impact of life changes: Development of the life experiences survey. In I. G. Sarason & C. D. Spielberger (Eds.), *Stress and anxiety* (Vol. 46, pp. 932–946). New York: Wiley.

Sena-Rivera, J. (1979). Extended kinship in the United States: Computing models and the case of the la familia Chicana. *Journal of Marriage and the Family, 41,* 121–129.

Stack, C. B. (1974). *All our kin.* New York: Harper and Row.

Styles, M. B., & Morrow, K. B. (1995). *Understanding how youth and elders form relationships: A study of four Linking Lifetimes Programs.* Philadelphia: Public/Private Ventures.

Sullivan, A. (1996). From mentor to muse: Recasting the role of women in relationship with urban adolescent girls. In B. Leadbeater & N. Way (Eds.), *Urban girls: Resisting stereotypes, creating identities.* New York: New York University Press.

Taylor, J. M., Gilligan, C., & Sullivan, A. M. (1995). *Between voice and silence: Women and girls, race and relationship.* Cambridge, MA: Harvard University Press.

Vygotsky, L. S. (1978). *Mind in society.* Cambridge, MA: Harvard University Press.

Werner, E. E., & Smith, S. (1982). *Vulnerable but invincible: A study of resilient children.* New York: McGraw-Hill.

Wilson, W. (1997). *When work disappears: The world of the new urban poor.* New York: Vintage.

Zimmerman, M. A., Bingenheimer, J. B., & Notaro, P. C. (2002). Natural mentors and adolescent resiliency: A study with urban youth. *American Journal of Community Psychology, 30,* 221–243.

Latina Girls
"We're Like Sisters—Most Times!"

Jill McLean Taylor, Carmen N. Veloria, and Martina C. Verba

Familiar and dominant narratives about Latina girls in urban settings include reports of early sexual activity and pregnancy, low academic expectations, and poor performance in high school followed by failure to graduate. Over the last 10 years, there have also been more reports of urban girls involved in conflict with other girls, giving rise to stereotypes about lack of trust, betrayal, and competition in relationships with boys and with one another. Counternarratives are produced by the girls in the study described in this chapter as they negotiate cultural conventions about their own sexuality, success in school, and strong, lasting friendships, ones in which they are forthright and outspoken as well as supportive and protective: "like sisters."

In *Urban Girls: Resisting Stereotypes, Creating Identities,* the chapter "Cultural Stories: Latina and Portuguese Daughters and Mothers" (Taylor, 1996) ended with a query about the possibility of "providing a safe space for girls so they would be able to experience a range of emotions—often contradictory and confusing—that include anger, sadness, joy, pleasure, and love, a place where someone from the girls' own cultural background verified girls' perceptions of reality" (p. 129). Mothers, according to their daughters, often did not understand their dilemmas at school and with friends, particularly around sexuality. And friends, often a source of comfort and support, also caused girls to feel hurt and betrayed.

In the years since the Understanding Adolescence Study on which the earlier chapter was based (Taylor, Gilligan, & Sullivan, 1995), numerous researchers from different disciplines have studied girls from diverse back-grounds. Films, television series, books, guides for parents and educators, and out-of-school programs have been based on findings from these girl-hood studies (Harris, 2004a). Girl power is a force to be reckoned with. The "at-risk" girl has become the "can-do" girl (Harris, 2004b), and the benefits of a safe space for girls to speak about what was previously taboo have become widely accepted (Weis & Fine, 2000; Tolman, 2002; Harris, 2005). Girls as consumers are sought after, and more than 50% of the undergraduate college population nationwide is composed of young women, although race, ethnicity, and social class differences continue to exist (www.nces.ed.gov/pubs).

Social class, gender, race, ethnicity, religion, and other factors intersect with the dominant culture's expectations of urban youth, including expec-tations of gender-specific roles and behavior. Educator Pedro Noguera posits that due to the demographic and economic transformations that have occurred in cities throughout the United States during the past 50 years, there has been a significant shift in the way society thinks about the term *urban*. It has become associated with people who are poor and non-White. It is less likely to be used as a geographic concept that delineates a physical location than as a social or cultural construct used to describe certain people (Noguera, 2003, p. 19).

The underachievement of students from diverse cultural and linguistic backgrounds (compared with their mainstream peers) continues to be a pervasive problem in urban education. Many urban students come from low-income families, are African American or Latino American, and speak a primary language other than standard American English (Campbell, Hombo, & Mazzeo, 2000). Urban schools are also increasingly home to students whose lives and experiences are vastly different from those of their teachers, who are overwhelmingly White, middle-class, and mono-lingual English speakers (Futrell, 1999).

Gearing Up

In Boston, girls are graduating from public high schools at a higher rate than boys (Khatiwada & Sum, 2002). Girls hold more leadership positions and make up a larger percentage of the top 20% of the class (Tench, 2005). At the same time, a Citizens for Juvenile Justice report (2005) notes that the overall arrest rate for girls in Massachusetts nearly tripled from 1991 to

2001, and the number of female delinquents more than doubled from 1996 to 2003 (Girls' Coalition of Greater Boston, 2005). This is echoed by news reports of "mean girls," "girl fighting" (Brown, 2003), and the sharp increase nationally in the numbers of girls involved in the juvenile criminal justice system (Chesney-Lind & Shelden, 2003). Educators, psychologists, and parents are concerned about girls' increasingly competitive and aggressive behavior, and girl's friendships are both idealized in our culture and understood as potentially harmful and divisive (Brown, 2003).

This study took place in the context of the federally funded program called Gaining Early Awareness and Readiness for Undergraduate Programs (GEAR UP), designed to reduce the differences in achievement between suburban and urban students and between White students and Black and Latino students. This program emerged from the Higher Education Amendments of 1998 (Public Law 105–244), signed by President Clinton on October 7, 1998, with the goal of increasing the number of low-income students who participate in postsecondary education. GEAR UP, which is based on partnerships between universities and colleges and urban school systems, is aimed at enabling low-income communities and states to strengthen their schools and provide opportunities for low-income students to attend postsecondary institutions (www.ed.gov).

Locally, GEAR UP consists of a partnership among two small private universities and a middle and high school. The model is derived from relational psychology (Gilligan, 1982; Noddings, 1992) and from the school development model of James Comer (1980, 2004). It is holistic in the sense that it includes direct academic services (in-school/after-school tutoring, college campus Saturday academic program, school vacation and summer programs), mentoring, college advising, professional development for school staff, parent outreach services, community involvement initiatives, and various enrichment programs. The students who participate in the program also gain "cultural capital," Pierre Bourdieu's "notion of a socially inherited cultural competence that facilitates achievement in school" (Perry, Steele, & Hilliard, 2003, p. 70), because they have spent a considerable amount of time on the university campuses and worked in department offices during the summer. The continuity of key personnel has enabled students and adults to develop strong relationships. Participants identify themselves as GEAR UP students.

This study, which came to be called El Coro by the girls, was in the context of the Boston GEAR UP program and the many activities and long-term relationships involved. El Coro, or El Corito, the name used by the

Dominican girls, means "choir" or "chorus" and refers to being part of a specific conversation. In their sophomore year, six Latina girls sought out the GEAR UP coordinator, Carmen Veloria, to ask if they could meet and talk, in effect asking for "a safe space" in which to they could "speak their minds" (Denner & Dunbar, 2004). This chapter presents themes that emerged from these safe spaces with girls over a period of 13 months.

Participants

The six Latina girls who participated in the study had been in the GEAR UP program since seventh grade. Five of the girls are of Dominican descent, and one is from Central America. All are 16 or 17 years old, and they consider themselves friends.[1] Two of the girls are cousins. All live in the same low-income community; five girls are living in female-headed households, although two mothers have live-in boyfriends. All actively demonstrate a desire to persist with their education by actively researching colleges, keeping track of their academic requirements, communicating their desire to attend college, and continuing to be part of the GEAR UP program. At first, the open-ended questions were used to explore their academic experiences and to learn what they were thinking about school and their aspirations for the future. However, after the first group session, when the girls took the discussion in the direction of race, gender, and their experiences in relationships, we followed the girls' lead, talking about relationships with mothers, friends, and boys, including their brothers, and about sexuality.

Method

The ethnographic, action-based El Coro study was originally designed to have four focus group meetings in May and June 2004 when the girls were at the end of 10th grade, but in December 2004 the girls asked to begin meeting again. Six meetings followed until May 2005, when two final meetings for the year took place.

The authors facilitated the discussions. Jill McLean Taylor is a Pakeha New Zealander researcher and teacher and has been her institution's coordinator of the GEAR UP grant since 1999.[2] Carmen Veloria is a Latina doctoral candidate and the on-site project director of GEAR UP; she has been with the program since 2000. She shares a similar background in terms of race, ethnicity, language, and socioeconomic upbringing as the girls. Martina Verba is a Jewish Caucasian master's-level social worker who worked as a counselor with other GEAR UP students. Permission slips to participate were signed by both students and their mothers. The girls chose their own pseudonyms, which we use here.

The groups were conducted in an open ended, semistructured manner in which the participants both raised and focused on topics they felt were important, and explored topics introduced by group facilitators. The group met in a GEAR UP office or in a small dining room at the university. Most of the meetings included food. Each discussion session lasted 1.5 to 2 hours. Carmen Veloria participated in all 12 meetings; Martina Verba also participated in the first 4 meetings, and Jill Taylor in the final 2. Six sessions (the first four and the final two) were audiotaped and transcribed; six others were recorded in field notes taken by a program intern. The girls often pursued questions that were generated from previous discussions in follow-up meetings.

The authors reviewed the tapes, transcripts, and field notes to identify and analyze themes that recurred throughout the sessions. We adapted the interpretive method of the Listening Guide developed by Lyn Brown, Carol Gilligan, and others of the Harvard Project on Women's Psychology and Girls' Development (see Brown, Debold, Tappan, & Gilligan, 1991; Taylor et al., 1995; Tolman, 2002). The method involves at least four readings of the interviews: the first for the overall story told by the participant and the role of the researchers; the second for individual voices or how the participants speak about themselves; the third and fourth for the contrapuntal voices, in this particular case, for psychological health and resilience, as well as psychological distress (see Gilligan, Spencer, Weinberg, & Bertsch, 2003, for a more thorough description of this method). The predominant themes focused on sexuality, relationships with the girls' mothers, negotiating school, and negotiating cultural expectations.

Findings

In group discussions, we heard collective gender and ethnic identity emerge (Weiler, 2001) as the girls spoke about their experiences at school, at home, and with mothers and boyfriends. They made frequent references to the meanings attached to having a "Latina mother" or, more specifically, a "Dominican mother," and to their expectations for daughters. We also heard the girls' critiques of school and their strategies for negotiating school requirements and barriers. To borrow Nancy López and Chalane Lechuga's term (this volume), we heard "hopeful girls" who were determined to succeed despite the many challenges they face, both inside and outside school.

"For Latinas, the Big Stereotype Is That You'll Become Pregnant"

As in the earlier Understanding Adolescence Study, the girls in this study described their relationships with their mothers and brothers against a backdrop of protectiveness and restricted freedom, along with concerns about reputation and fear of pregnancy. As Clara says, "My mother's always in the window." This metaphor describes the perceived constant surveillance both at home and in the neighborhood. Wanda, who lives with her grandmother, tells a story of how her grandmother knows everyone in the community, saying, "I can't do anything!" Rebeca described how her mother defended her honor when a boy at church started spreading rumors about her and how this made her feel relieved and supported.

On the other hand, the girls describe frustration at not being able to "make their own mistakes . . . to learn from them" and at not being able to talk to their mothers honestly and openly. Studies of communication about sex between Latina adolescent girls and their mothers also indicate that adolescent girls are reluctant to disclose information about dating and sexuality to their mothers (O'Sullivan, Meyer-Bahlburg, & Watkins, 2001; Tolman, 2002; Denner & Dunbar, 2004). Even though their mothers recommend that they talk to them if and when they become sexually active, none of the girls in this study have. In May 2004, some girls expressed the fear of their mothers finding out they were sexually active. In most cases their mothers had told them that they would be able to tell if and when they became sexually active. Both Wanda and Maria talked about their mothers telling them that they "would walk differently, and that their legs would be further apart." In May 2005, Jessie shared that her mother somehow knew; she said her mom had said she "got thicker." This revelation was met with laughter and awe, as if the girls understood both the absurdity and the value of such warnings.

In May 2004, the girls perceived power in expressing their sexual feelings as long as they were still in control. Although they were quick to clarify that they were not "easy," they liked the idea of "not being tied to any-one" and not having "to go all the way." The girls talked about "saving face" when a boy did something that was inappropriate. Even when they felt enjoyment, they also felt obligated to ask the boy to stop, and in some cases slap his face. According to their understanding of Latina femininity, this is what one must do. By May 2005, the girls who were sexually active sounded as though they had integrated this into their lives and were using birth control and taking care of themselves. Their mothers seemed to be having more difficulty as their daughters matured, particularly the moth-ers with boyfriends. These women were most apprehensive about their daughter's sexuality, getting angry with them for wearing tank tops or shorts when their own boyfriends were around. The girls clearly have to manage the men's sexuality. Carmen asks if the girls are worried about the men in the house, and discussion follows about mothers and why they might make the choices they have.

Maria talked about a "culture clash"—"living in two worlds." None of the mothers had been formally educated in the United States. Their Eng-lish skills were also limited. As a result, the girls found themselves navigat-ing between two cultures. In one, their world revolves around Dominican dialect, customs, views, and values that include submissiveness toward husbands or partners. The other centered on middle-class American val-ues needed to learn to navigate for upward mobility in the context of this society. Most of them felt that despite their mothers' push for them to continue with their education, it would not surprise their mothers one bit if one of them was to become pregnant. The girls viewed the fact that they had not become pregnant as an accomplishment and a motivator to "prove them wrong."

"This School, Miss . . ."

In the context of No Child Left Behind, MCAS, PSATs, and SATs, stan-dardized tests have taken over the curriculum. In Boston, administrators, teachers, and students are anxious about test scores for reasons that have to do with evaluation of the school as a whole, as well as individual evalu-ations of school administrators and teachers. As GEAR UP staff, we were also concerned about the impact of testing and the pressure that many of the students experienced, as well as the lack of resources at the high school. Despite our disagreement with the emphasis on tests and results, we are constrained by what is necessary for students to do to attend post-secondary institutions. When the girls talked about school and college, some in the group were aware that their academic records over the past 3 years were uneven, but they were also aware of the part the school played in their lack of success.

Clara is both indignant at and resigned to practices that are common in her school. In May 2004, recalling an experience with a teacher who taught a required course, Clara commented:

> Remember Mr. G's class? He did not know what to do . . . we were teaching him what to do! I went there like twice, and the rest of the time I was in Mr. X, Mr. A, and Mrs. B's [administrator's] offices complaining—saying that we need to get changed! I complained all of ten thousand times. How are we going to pass MCAS if we are teaching the teacher what we are supposed to do?

Others in the group talked about advocating for themselves, needing interventions by GEAR UP staff, or having their mothers come to the school to argue for class reassignment when they encountered teachers who did not teach.

The strong connection between poverty and school inequality is apparent. The girls are exposed to situations and are involved in conversations that highlight the gaps in the expectations between their school and colleges. During college tours, for example, as admission representatives talk about the importance of a rigorous curriculum in high school and challenging classes, the girls are critical of their own educational shortcomings and their lack of access to certain classes. Their school offers only one foreign language option—Spanish. At the same time, however, they are learning to voice those critiques to invoke change and are strategically planning for their futures. For example, the girls discuss their plans to load up on Advanced Placement (AP) courses during their senior year because they believe that AP courses at their school are "like regular courses elsewhere."

The girls frequently introduce the idea of time wasted, "where teachers go over the same thing over and over" during the course of the year. It is sometimes used as an excuse for skipping classes. In May 2005, Jessie complained about her English class, "All we get are worksheets." She explained, "I need to work on my writing . . . especially with the new SAT." Her self-assessment is correct: She has yet to pass the English Language Arts section of the MCAS.

Yolanda, Rebeca, and Maria joined the heated discussion about how they are all doing poorly in English classes this year, and Maria introduced a more specific criticism: "Black, black, black history, that's all we hear about. . . . I'm like, [to the teacher] look around you, look who's sitting in front of you. . . . and it's not a history class, it's an English class!" Maria, who is taking an AP class as a junior, describes an ongoing discussion about diversity in the curriculum that presents only information about African American authors, history, and achievements. She cites other examples of teachers speaking as though there is no difference between Latinos, Puerto Ricans, and Dominicans. Clara mentions one teacher specifically using the term *Banilejos* when referring to them. "All ya'll Banilejos need to get to class," implying that they all come from the province of Bani and that they are all "loud and from el campo." Within the group, the girls acknowledge that Carmen is a "light-skinned" Puerto Rican and in lighthearted conversations occasionally poke fun at her. For Dominicans in the community and at the school, the politics of skin color and difference in darkness is a sensitive issue relating to heritage. Clara says, "In our school they think that if you are light skinned you are Puerto Rican and if you are dark skinned you are Dominican. . . . That's stupid because I am light skinned but I am Dominican." Similarly, Maria becomes angry when people assume that she is an African American because "it's a pride thing"; she does not want to be judged or to have others make assumptions about her. She says: "Miss, it's as if people assumed you are White and Puerto Rican." Issues of identity, stereotyping, and skin color are evident throughout the girls' discussion of their school experiences.

"My Mother's Been Through a Lot, a Lot"

Even though all the girls talked about not being able to "have a serious conversation with their mothers," most of them acknowledge insight into what their mothers have had to go through and the strength that they have. For most, their mothers' experiences serve as reminders of what is possible even with barriers and setbacks; for others, these experiences serve as a motivator to move away from a life they want to escape.

Although the girls readily acknowledge their mothers' hardships, they are also critical of some of their actions—particularly as they pertain to mixed messages of "you better do good in school," while requiring the girls to clean the house and help out with younger siblings. Jessie talks about child care responsibilities that are clearly interfering with her education. Her mother works from early in the morning until late evening, so Jessie is responsible for taking care of her younger brother and sister. She missed school to take her brother to school when he was not allowed on the bus. She says: "My brother's principal said she needs to see my mother in school, not me, and that I should be in school." Jessie acknowledges this is "a huge problem" and insists she will tell her mom "it has to stop." But Jessie knows that her mother works two jobs, frequently has car trouble, and cannot get to the school early in the day. Her mother may also not feel welcome at her daughter's school.

The dual messages Latina mothers give their daughters—to be a *mujer de hogar* (woman of the home) and to *valerse por si misma* (to be self-reliant)—are discussed by researchers Villenas and Moreno (2001). They assert that the women in their study affirm their cultural values by taking pride in their homes and maintaining a sense of honor. The mothers talk about being *buenas hijas* (good daughters) and *buenas esposas* (good wives) and transmit these cultural messages to their daughters. At the same time, mothers teach their daughters through *consejos* (advice), *cuentos* (stories), and *experiencia* (experience) that the girls must learn self-reliance, that they need to learn to survive without a man because the man might leave, that they must focus on their educations and dream of opportunities beyond what their mothers have had. The mothers teach the daughters both to survive in the system and to survive the system.

The mothers are also criticized for their own action concerning boyfriends. Maria and Jessie are critical of how their mothers give traditional and preferential treatment to the men. Special food is prepared and served, and "insane cleaning" takes place. Latina daughters who witness the devaluation of their mothers' knowledge and roles in a culture that glorifies traditionally masculine achievement simultaneously recognize the sacrifices that their mothers make to meet the demands of family life (Andrade & Gonzalez, 1999).

Yolanda, however, describes her nontraditional mother's resistance if her father does not want the food that has been prepared for the family. "Please yourself," she says. "Go and get something else." Asked where that attitude comes from, Yolanda shrugs and says, "My mother doesn't take that from anyone." Yolanda's mother is renowned for her strictness and for taking a stand with teachers and administrators, and Yolanda and the others admire her strength and independence. Maria's mother emphasizes the values of honor and being a *buena hija,* and the importance of emotional strength. Maria describes watching multiple conflicts between her mother and stepfather, as well as her mother and brothers. Maria reports that at times her stepfather leaves, but her mother never cries, demonstrating for Maria her emotional strength in the face of conflict with her husband and sons.

"You Know What It's Like, Miss"

How do stories function in culture? Because we produce and communicate stories within a social context, the stories we tell are those that are "culturally available for our telling" (Ewick & Silbey, 1995). "You know you were raised like that, too, miss," exclaimed Maria during an animated discussion of "what happens at home" and being reared in a Latina household. "Latinas are raised like that. . . . like if you are being screamed at you just go like this (looked down) and listen to it," Maria continued.

In the retelling of stories about growing up in a Latina household, the girls often looked to Carmen for affirmation. These occasions were often met with laughter, awkwardness, and shouts of validation from the other girls. However, they also provided opportunities to explore the deeper meaning of "that's just the way it is" and the motivation to transcend oppressive experiences. During a discussion about being yelled at and sometimes hit at home, Carmen says she was not allowed to answer back, but rather had to "show respect." She asks, "How do you then break away from the mold of how you are raised at home? How does one learn to advocate for oneself when at home one learns to stay quiet, look down, and show respect?" She went on to share a story: While attending a new elementary school in the United States, she was placed in a bilingual class with a teacher who shared her ethnicity. This teacher gave her a nickname—sort of like a "chatterbox"—except that the term in Spanish had a negative connotation. Carmen did not like it, and neither did her mother. Despite having limited English skills, her mother went to school and asked the teacher to stop calling her daughter that name; she also told Carmen never to allow anyone to call her names. The teacher stopped. Carmen reflected on how seeing her mother's action that day empowered her to advocate for herself—even if that rule did not necessarily apply at home. Most of the girls responded that they, too, are able to challenge the status quo outside of the home. Their mothers regularly communicate to them that they should "put up with nothing." Yet the implicit understanding that this rule does not necessarily apply at home frustrates the girls, and they understand the negative effects of such a contradiction. When discussing the fact that they are yelled at and sometimes hit by their mothers, Mari said: "But I think that hurts us, because whatever we have to say we are keeping it to ourselves and if that happens continuously, right, that's more things to keep inside, and that affects your school, that affects how you think, that affects who you are, and how you are going to act."

Summary

Here, stories allow girls "to name and reclaim, over and over, the connections we are taught to ignore and the dynamics we are told do not exist" (Morales, 1988, p. 5). During discussions, the girls shared their stories of not being allowed to go out before cleaning the house, of their inability to spend time on their studies while watching over younger siblings, and their perception that "my mom just does not understand" about school and work. They also told stories of their mothers' resistance, strength, and courage in school and home contexts. These two types of stories ran throughout their discussions of their lives and formed a critical part of who they were and who they wanted (or did not want) to be.

Discussion

In the context of talk of "mean," "backstabbing," "untrustworthy" girls in a school where there are many rumors and fights, the girl's willingness to trust one another as they talk about their sexual experiences, relationships with families and boyfriends, and concerns about school and the future strengthens their mutual resolve to "be successful." They express different opinions, make judgments, and have arguments. The facts that they have known each other since sixth grade and have very similar backgrounds are considered important components of their friendships. In GEAR UP they have shared rooms on three-day trips and have been on college tours, adding to the idea that they know each other very well. In typical adolescent language, "They are there for one another," around crises with boyfriends, fights with mothers, and disappointments and successes at school.

The topics that are discussed by the group are familiar—sexuality, relationships with mothers, schooling. What is different, however, from previous work is the critique and "double vision" the girls now use to discuss these topics. They do not, for example, seem confused about decisions they have made regarding their own sexuality and sexual behavior. They are very aware of the level of anxiety around sexuality, and their mother's live-in boyfriends. They recognize the contradictions between their mothers' submissiveness and strength, and they place this in a cultural context of roles for Dominican women and men. In a less well-articulated theme, girls look at how their own relationships with boyfriends have at times mirrored those of their mothers: they, too, have been treated harshly and "put up with it," even though they have asked their mothers why they would live with this. Here the benefits of a group were clear, as girls spoke directly to one another and tried to understand and dissuade their friends from continuing in relationships that were unhealthy.

The difficulties of a large urban high school are highlighted. Issues of decisions regarding scheduling, overburdened teachers, and limited access to rigorous courses all come up on a regular basis. As adults in the group, we reminded students of the context in which they were complaining about teachers, so that their critique became grounded in issues of limited resources and equity rather than personal accusations. As in previous studies, adolescents' ability to name what is indeed unfair is clear—why does their school not have science labs or another modern language offering? Their ability to see what was necessary to succeed enables them to live with the contradictions, to advocate for themselves, to find others to do so, and to demand to be taken seriously as students.

The girls' belief that they are heard and understood allows them to speak about experiences that they might otherwise keep to themselves. The expression "You know, Miss" (sometimes with an exclamation point) was used frequently in discussions ranging from mothers, to teachers, to the future. Because conversations occurred within the context of GEAR UP, our roles as researchers and staff associated with the program were intertwined, and we were situated to "provide . . . moments of contestation, challenge, and social change" (Lareau & Horvat, 1999, p. 38). Facilitator Carmen Veloria played a crucial role as an adult in the group and with the Latina girls in GEAR UP generally. Carmen's epistemological premise is grounded on her own experiences as a self-identified Latina who came of age in the United States under socioeconomic conditions similar to those of the girls in the group. She is a native of Puerto Rico, whose status as a commonwealth of the United States had different political implications, and considers herself a woman of color due to the racially mixed ancestry of the island. In the racialized U.S. context, Puerto Ricans grapple with the perils of racism (Flores, 2002; Nieto, 2000). Due to similarities in terms of race, ethnicity, language, socioeconomic background, and experiences of growing up in the United States as Latinas attending an urban school, Carmen's gendered, race-based epistemology and methodology helped her to analyze and theorize about the data (audiocassettes, written artifacts, field notes, etc.). According to López (2003), "The race, gender, and class locations of the researcher and participants always shape the framing of an issue, the questions asked, and the dynamics of the interview, regardless of whether one utilizes qualitative or quantitative data or a combination thereof" (p. 11). In Clara's words, "Not everyone understands." Maria continued by saying, "If it would have been—no offense—a white person—no offense—I think we would not have been able to connect like that—like we did with you," as she looked at Carmen. Clara elaborated on this point:

> To encourage you, you need someone who is going to understand you because if it is someone who is just trying to encourage you, but they don't understand what you are going through, they don't understand where you've been—if they have not been through it—something like that—then you're like you don't understand where I'm coming from.

The group also allowed the girls to develop a realistic critique of the educational system and at the same time to learn ways to negotiate it and do what they have to do. The emerging "collective gender and ethnic identity" acts as a buttress against low expectations. The "safe space" of the group became a place where the girls were able to articulate the trajectory of their academic lives by interacting with trusted adult women, who shared their own stories (lived experiences), knowledge, and expertise about adolescent development and college access.

Ward and Benjamin (2004) call on adult women to commit themselves to providing a new generation of adolescent safe harbors from the painful losses weathered by their mothers, mentors, and teachers. In this action-based, ethnographic research, women were able to connect with the girls across cultural differences with a common purpose, that of supporting and encouraging girls' hopes and plans for a future, validating their critique of the educational system, and intervening where necessary.

The girls use the "safe space" to question, explore, and critique but also to bring about changes in their lives. By the last session in May 2005, all but one of the girls had indicated that their mothers no longer slapped or hit them. Maria indicated that she had stopped her mom from slapping her, and that since that day, there had been no incidence of hitting or slapping. Several of the girls indicated that they are more outspoken at home, and have started to demand time to study. Jessie articulated her plans to do the same. Others have become more proactive in terms of self-advocacy and have already arranged for additional help with the college application process. They are also urging the others in the group to do the same. We believe it is this shared safe space, where someone from the girls' own cultural background could verify the girls' perceptions of reality, where girls could see adult women collaborating to find solutions, and where they could experience a range of emotions—often contradictory and confusing—that included anger, sadness, joy, pleasure, and love, that created an environment that encouraged self-advocacy at home and school and allowed the girls to identify and voice their needs and wishes. Girls can develop a critical consciousness when they are recognized and supported by adult women who can intervene in school where necessary, strongly suggest change at home, and provide academic support. GEAR UP helps the girls maintain hope and excitement for their futures.

Discussion Questions

1. How can schools or community organizations build into their programming discussion groups that are led by adult women and that support a constructive critique of schools; allow for conversations about race, ethnicity, sexuality, and social class; and intervene when necessary?
2. Why do group discussions help these Latina girls?

NOTES

1. As per the group's definition of "friends"—"Nos tenemos confianza" (we trust each other), we are "cool" with each other in and outside of school, we have "each other's back."

2. Pakeha is the Maori word for Whites. White New Zealanders had traditionally referred to themselves as New Zealanders, but as Maori women and men pointed out, they too are New Zealanders, and were so long before European settlers arrived. The Maoris ask that white New Zealanders refer to themselves as Pakehas.

References

Andrade, R., & Gonzalez, H. (1999). The formation of a code of ethics for Latina/Chicana scholars: The experience of melding personal lessons into professional ethics. *Frontiers: A Journal of Women's Studies, 20,* 151–160.

Bell, L. A. (2003). Telling tales: What stories can teach us about racism. *Race, Ethnicity and Education, 6*(1), 3–28.

Brown, L. M. (2003). *Girlfighting.* New York: New York University Press.

Brown, L. M., Debold, E., Tappan, M., & Gilligan, C. (1991). Reading narratives of conflict for self and moral voice. In W. Kurtines & J. Gewirtz (Eds.), *Handbook of moral behavior and development* (pp. 25–61). Hillsdale, NJ: Erlbaum.

Campbell, J. R., Hombo, C. M., & Mazzeo, J. (2000). *NAEP 1999 trends in academic progress: Three decades of student performance (NCES 2000–469).* Washington, DC: U.S. Department of Education, National Center for Education Statistics.

Chesney-Lind, M., & Shelden, R. G. (2003). *Girls, delinquency, and juvenile justice* (3rd ed.). Boston: Wadsworth.

Citizens for Juvenile Justice. (2005). *Massachusetts girls fact sheet.* Boston: Citizens for Juvenile Justice. Retrieved May 2006, from http://www.cfjj.org/Pdf/MASSACHUSETTS%20GIRLS%20FACT%20SHEET.pdf

Comer, J. P. (1980). *School power: Implications of an intervention.* New Haven, CT: Yale University Press.

Comer, J. P. (2004). *Leave no child behind: Preparing today's youth for tomorrow's world.* New Haven, CT: Yale University Press.

Denner, J., & Dunbar, N. (2004). Negotiating femininity: Power and strategies of Mexican American girls. *Sex Roles, 50,* 301–314.

Ewick, P., & Silbey, S. S. (1995). Subversive stories and hegemonic tales: Toward a sociology of narrative. *Law and Society Review, 29,* 197–226.

Flores, J. (2002). Islands and enclaves: Caribbean Latinos in historical perspective. In M. Suarez-Orozco & M. Paez (Eds.), *Latinos: Remaking America* (pp. 59–74). Berkeley: University of California Press.

Futrell, M. H. (1999). The challenge of the 21st century: Developing a highly qualified cadre of teachers to teach our nation's diverse student population. *Journal of Negro Education, 68,* 318–334.

Gilligan, C. (1982). *In a different voice.* Cambridge, MA: Harvard University Press.

Gilligan, C., Spencer, R., Weinberg, M. K., & Bertsch, T. (2003). On the listening guide: A voice-centered relational method. In P. M. Camic, J. E. Rhodes, & L. Yardley (Eds.), *Qualitative research in psychology: Expanding perspectives in methodology and design* (pp. 157–172). Washington, DC: American Psychological Association.

Girls' Coalition of Greater Boston. (2005, December). *Where are the girls? The state of girls' programming in Greater Boston.* Retrieved May 2006, from http://www.girlscoalition.org/uploads/pdf/COPY%20FOR%20PRINTING--Where%20Are%20the%20Girls%20report%2012.29.05%20FINAL.pdf

Harris, A. (Ed.). (2004a). *All about the girl: Culture, power, and identity.* New York: Routledge.

Harris, A. (2004b). *Future girl: Young women in the twenty-first century.* New York: Routledge.

Harris, A. (2005). Discourses of desire as governmentality: Young women, sexuality and the significance of safe spaces. *Feminism and Psychology 15,* 39–43.

Khatiwada, I., & Sum, A. (2002). *Gender differences in high school graduation rates and college enrollment rates of graduation from Boston public high school in recent years: Findings of the follow-up surveys for the classes of 1999, 2000, and 2001 and agenda for future research.* Paper prepared for the Boston Private Industry Council and Boston Public Schools. Boston, MA.

Lareau, A., & Horvat, E. M. (1999). Moments of social inclusion and exclusion: Race, class, and cultural capital in family-school relationships. *Sociology of Education, 72,* 37–53.

López, N. (2003). *Hopeful girls, troubled boys: Race and gender disparity in urban education.* New York: Routledge.

Morales, A. L. (1988) *Medicine stories: History, culture and the politics of integrity.* Cambridge, MA: South End Press.

Nieto, S. (2000). Puerto Rican students in U.S. schools: A brief history. In S. Nieto (Ed.), *Puerto Rican students in U.S. schools* (pp. 5–38). Mahwah, NJ: Erlbaum.

Noddings, N. (1992). *The challenge to care in schools: An alternative approach to education.* New York: Teachers College Press.

Noguera, P. (2003). *City schools and the American dream: Reclaiming the promise of public education.* New York: Teachers College Press.

O'Sullivan, L., Meyer Bahlburg, H. F. L., & Watkins, B. X. (2001). Mother-daughter communication about sex among urban African American and Latino families. *Journal of Adolescent Research, 16,* 269–292.

Perry, T., Steele, C., & Hilliard, A. (2003). *Young, gifted, and Black.* Boston: Beacon Press.

Taylor, J. M. (1996). Cultural stories: Latina and Portuguese daughters and mothers. In B. Leadbeater & N. Way (Eds.), *Urban girls: Resisting stereotypes, creating identities* (pp. 117–131). New York: New York University Press.

Taylor, J. M., Gilligan, C., & Sullivan, A. M. (1995). *Between voice and silence: Women and girls, race and relationship.* Cambridge, MA: Harvard University Press.

Tench, M. (2005, June 5). Faces of excellence. *Boston Globe,* City and Region, pp. B1, 3.

Tolman, D. L. (2002). *Dilemmas of desire: Teenage girls talk about sexuality.* Cambridge, MA: Harvard University Press.

Villenas, S., & Moreno, M. (2001). "To *valerse si misma* between race, capitalism, and patriarchy: Latina mother-daughter pedagogies in North Carolina." *Qualitative Studies in Education, 14,* 671–687.

Ward, J., & Benjamin, B. C. (2004). Women, girls, and the unfinished work of connection: A critical review of American girl's studies. In A. Harris (Ed.), *All about the girl* (pp. 15–28). New York: Routledge.

Weiler, J. (2001). Alternative visions: (Re)fashioning female gender identities within an urban classroom. *Race, Gender, and Class, 8,* 162–183.

Weis, L., & Fine, M. (Eds.). (2000). *Construction sites: Excavating race, class, and gender among urban youth.* New York: Teachers College Press.

Part III

Culture, Parents, and Protection

Changes in African American Mother-Daughter Relationships During Adolescence

Conflict, Autonomy, and Warmth

Catherine L. Costigan, Ana Mari Cauce, and Kenyatta Etchison

> They were uppity Black women, our mothers and grand-mothers, women who tossed their head and crossed their legs, read Fanon and dealt with dream cards, wore felt head huggers and high-top shoes. Bold, audacious women of indomitable spirit who believed that all things are possible, they taught their daughters respect for the possibilities in themselves and in others.
>
> DeCosta-Willis (1991, p. 36)

During adolescence, children strive to move from a position of dependence to one of autonomy and individuation (Smetana, 1995). They are expected to seek greater independence from their parents, and parents are expected to gradually relinquish control. To accomplish this, parent-child relationships need to be realigned so that unilateral parental authority shifts toward more mutuality in decision making (Youniss & Smollar, 1985). Parents do not abdicate control altogether or withdraw entirely; rather, this process of realignment is gradual, slowly resulting in more shared control over time.

There is also considerable stability in parent-child relationships, particularly in terms of affective relationships. The individuated adolescent does not reject the parent but instead sees the parent more realistically (Smollar

& Youniss, 1989). For most adolescents, transformations in parent-child dynamics take place in the context of continued warmth and feelings of relatedness. Although adolescents seek greater freedom, they remain responsive to their parents' guidance and advice (Steinberg, 1990). Thus, the adolescents' task of individuation and autonomy seeking leaves room for the continuity of warmth and closeness between parents and adolescents (Allen, Hauser, Eickholt, Bell, & O'Connor, 1994; Cooper, Grotevant, & Condon, 1983). The task of the parent of an adolescent, however, remains undeniably difficult, requiring them to support the child at the same time that the child is pulling away.

The current study explores these relationship changes with a focus on mothers and daughters. Mothers are the parent most responsible for establishing and maintaining connectedness and warmth through caregiving and are also typically the caretakers who provide children with the most control and supervision (DiClemente et al., 2001). In addition, compared with other parent-child dyads in the family, mother-daughter relationships are typically the most emotionally charged (Steinberg, 1990) and involve the highest levels of conflict (Montemayor, 1986; Smetana, 1989).

This chapter builds on our previous work in which we evaluated how conflict, autonomy, and warmth are manifested in African American mother-daughter relationships when the girls were in early adolescence (Cauce et al., 1996). Here, we examine how these relationships change over time in the same sample of mothers and daughters.

African American Mothers and Daughters: A Unique Relationship

The distinctiveness of African American mother-daughter relationships is a subject that has captivated both novelists and poets (see Bell-Scott et al., 1991, for one example). Appreciating the unique sociocultural niche of African American mothers and daughters is essential to understanding their relationship (Cauce et al., 1996). Within African American families, daughters describe mother-daughter relationships as the closest and most supportive in early adolescence compared with relationships with fathers or peers (Cauce et al., 1996). African American mothers also appear to be especially focused on making sure that their daughters are prepared to be self-supporting and independent, communicating that attitude to them through their words and actions. As one of the mothers in our study put it, "You just can't count on no man taking care of you. You need to be ready to do for yourself." Similarly, in an especially rich and nuanced qualitative study of urban teenagers, Way (1998) quotes Chantal, an African American adolescent describing her mother and herself: "She's independent. . . . It's like she doesn't depend on anybody to take care of her. It's like she's on her own. . . . Everybody tells me I act just like my mother . . . very independent. . . Don't wait for everybody to do for you 'cause you'll have nothing" (p. 37).

This independence training by African American mothers is likely a key protective factor that fosters resilience in young African American females in the face of multiple risks. That is, while wanting to help their daughters become strong and independent, African American mothers are also very aware of the dangers facing their daughters, especially when they are growing up in dangerous and/or impoverished neighborhoods. Compared with their White counterparts, African Americans are more likely to grow up in a neighborhood characterized by concentrated poverty (25% vs. 3%; Jargowsky, 1997) and also are more likely to live in poverty for an extended period of time (29% of African American youth live in poverty for periods of 10 years or longer, compared with 1% of White youth; Lewit, 1993). The neighborhoods African Americans live in are also characterized by more violence and crime (Duncan, Brooks-Gunn, & Klebanov, 1994; Pinder-hughes, Nix, Foster, Jones, & CPPRG, 2001).

The risks that African American teenage girls face are not only there for those growing up in poverty. Even in middle-class situations, African American teens may be viewed through the lenses of prejudice and discrimination, making it more difficult for them to navigate the rocky waters of adolescence. Stereotypes about African American urban teens as drug addicted and violent abound. African American girls also suffer from sexist stereotypes about early pregnancy and loose sexual mores (Leadbeater & Way, 1996; Way, 1998). Thus, African American mothers face unique challenges in raising their adolescent daughters to feel good about who they are in the face of these negative messages and barriers (Turnage, 2004).

Can African American mothers protect their children in this context while not interfering with their move toward autonomy (Thornton, Chatters, Taylor, & Allen, 1990; Thornton, 1997; Turnage, 2004)? The answer is, of course, yes. African American mothers routinely raise healthy, happy, smart, courageous, independent, and accomplished daughters. Given this fact, the more interesting question relates to how African American mothers promote resilience in their daughters in a societal context that presents so many challenges. In her ethnographic study of urban African American youth, Jarrett (1997, 1999) provides powerful examples of how mothers work to protect their children from the dangers that surround them. One key strategy involves very close monitoring of their activities, and at times even confining their child. We saw this strategy in the current sample. For example, one of the mothers described how, while she hated doing it, she required her daughter to stay in their apartment until the mother came home from work.

In order to better understand how African American mothers realign their relationships with their adolescent daughters to help them manage the obstacles that they may encounter in their path toward adulthood, we explore in detail how these relationships change during adolescence, focusing on three areas: conflict, autonomy, and warmth.

The Role of Conflict in Adolescent Individuation and Adjustment

Although parent-child conflict is popularly considered a hallmark of adolescent development, the extent of conflict varies considerably across families (Collins, 1990; Steinberg, 1990). Research consistently suggests that most parent-adolescent conflict involves everyday issues such as chores around the house or completing homework (Montemayor, 1983; Smetana, 1989). There is less consensus, however, regarding the developmental course of parent-adolescent conflict. For instance, some research has found that parent-adolescent conflict peaks in early adolescence, around the time of puberty, and declines thereafter (e.g., Collins, 1990; Galambos & Almeida, 1992; Holmbeck & Hill, 1991; Maggs & Galambos, 1993; Laursen, Coy, & Collins, 1998; Paikoff & Brooks-Gunn, 1991; Rutter & Conger, 1995; Smetana & Asquith, 1994; Smetana & Gaines, 1999; Steinberg, 1988). Other researchers, however, have found weak or inconsistent links between puberty and conflict (e.g., Anderson, Hetherington, & Clingempeel, 1989; Laursen & Collins, 1994), and still others report consistently high levels of conflict across adolescence (Furman & Buhrmester, 1992; Smetana, 1988).

One potential reason for these discrepant findings is that previous research has employed different definitions of conflict. For instance, conflict has been defined by its frequency (e.g., Rutter & Conger, 1995), its intensity (e.g., Papini, Clark, Barnett, & Savage, 1989), or a combination of the two (Galambos & Almeida, 1992). It is possible that these different aspects of conflict may show different trajectories of change and stability across adolescence. Furthermore, some researchers have defined conflict in terms of the overall amount of disagreement across a broad range of topics (e.g., Rutter & Conger, 1995), whereas others have examined conflict across specific content areas (e.g., Papini et al., 1989; Smetana, 1988, 1989; Smetana, Daddis, & Chaung, 2003). Different areas of conflict show different patterns of change. For instance, conflicts about chores, appearance, and politeness decrease from sixth to eighth grade; conflicts around substance use and finances show no change (Galambos & Almeida, 1992); and conflicts about homework and achievement increase from middle to late adolescence (Smetana et al., 2003).

A second area of debate within this literature concerns the role of conflict in either promoting or hindering positive developmental outcomes. Two primary hypotheses have been proposed. The first is that parent-adolescent conflict is problematic because it is associated with poorer adjustment for adolescents. Higher levels of conflict have been related to a variety of adjustment problems, including low self-esteem and higher levels of aggression and delinquency. Conflict may hinder adolescent development by decreasing feelings of warmth in the family (Steinberg, 1990). Lower levels of warmth within the family may also establish an environment in which conflicts are not resolved effectively, thereby increasing the probability of further conflict and maladaptive adolescent outcomes (Rutter & Conger, 1995).

An alternative theory regarding the role of conflict in adolescent development argues that parent-adolescent conflict serves an adaptive function by facilitating adolescent autonomy (Montemayor, 1983; Smetana, 1989). Conflicts, either directly or more subtly, involve the negotiation of freedom and independence for adolescents (Smetana & Asquith, 1994). Through conflict, adolescents communicate their increasing desire for autonomy and increasing ability to handle new responsibilities, resulting in greater awareness of differences in perspectives and requiring parents to reevaluate the extent of their authority (Papini & Sebby, 1988). When disagreements take place in the context of supportive relationships, they lead to new areas of control for adolescents, new limits on parental authority, and new patterns of relating between parents and adolescents. Thus, the end result of conflict is increased control and freedom for the adolescent and increased mutuality in parent-adolescent relationships.

A limitation of existing research on parent-adolescent conflict is its almost exclusive focus on European American, middle-class to upper-middle-class families, and/or two-parent families. Little is known about the generalizability of findings to economically disadvantaged families of color, where the challenges to parenting may be greatest. Moreover, with few exceptions (e.g., Smetana et al., 2003; Smetana, Campione-Barr, & Daddis, 2004), this research has relied on cross-sectional data to draw developmental conclusions. In the current study, we explore the longitudinal relations among conflict, autonomy, and warmth in adolescence with a sample of African American mothers and daughters from predominantly lower-income working-class backgrounds and various family structures. We examine several definitions of conflict, including the number of topics of conflict, as well as their intensity and frequency. In addition, we examine change in conflict and autonomy within specific content domains. Finally, we assess the function of mother-daughter conflict in these families. We hypothesize that parent-adolescent conflict is a mechanism by which adolescents negotiate new roles and relationships with parents, resulting in increased independence, despite the context of adversity created by discrimination and economic disadvantage.

Study Methods Used in Examining Changes in Conflict, Autonomy, and Warmth

The Sample

The sample consists of 39 mother-daughter pairs who were seen twice as part of a larger study of parent-child relationships during adolescence (Cauce et al., 1996). The Time 1 assessment occurred when the girls were in seventh or eighth grades and were on average 13.50 years old ($SD = .80$). The Time 2 assessment was conducted approximately 2 years later when the girls were in 9th, 10th, or 11th grades and were on average 15.75 years old ($SD = .87$).

The sample represents an array of educational and economic backgrounds. Twenty-five percent of the families earned less than $15,000 a year; 25% earned more than $35,000. The average family income was $23,000 ($SD = $12,000$), indicating a lower-income working-class household. A small number (13.2%) of the mothers did not complete high school, 23.7% had a high school degree, 52.6% completed some college or

TABLE 8.1
*Items from the Issues Checklist Categorized Within Each Domain
of Parent-Adolescent Conflict*

PERSONAL DOMAIN
1. Watching TV
2. Which clothes to wear
3. How neat clothes look
4. Picking books or movies
5. Buying records, toys, games, and things
6. Selecting new clothes
7. Cleaning bedroom
8. Putting away clothes
9. Cleanliness (e.g., washing, showers)

PRUDENTIAL DOMAIN
1. Drugs
2. Alcohol
3. Sex
4. Smoking

MONITORING DOMAIN
1. Going places without parents
2. Going on dates
3. Coming home on time
4. How to spend free time
5. Earning money away from home
6. Who friends should be
7. Telephone calls
8. How money is spent
9. Lying

SCHOOL DOMAIN
1. Homework
2. Getting to school on time
3. Getting low grades in school
4. Getting in trouble at school

vocational training, 5.3% held university degrees, and 5.3% held graduate degrees. At Time 1, approximately half (48%) of the mothers were married or living with a partner, and half (52%) were single parents. The majority of the mothers (85%) worked outside of the home.

Assessment Instruments

PARENT-ADOLESCENT CONFLICT

Mothers and daughters completed a modified version of the Issues Checklist (Robin & Foster, 1989) at both assessments. This instrument includes 44 topics that are potential areas of conflict between parents and adolescents. Three ratings are made for each topic. First, respondents indicate whether or not the topic has been a source of disagreement in the past 4 weeks (*yes* or *no*). Next, if the topic has been discussed, the respondent indicates how many times in the past 4 weeks the topic was discussed (frequency) and how intense the discussion was, from 1 (*calm*) to 5 (*very angry*). *Number of topics* is measured by summing the number of topics that were a source of disagreement in the past month. *Frequency* is measured by summing the frequency ratings and dividing by the number of topics that were discussed. *Intensity* is measured by averaging the intensity ratings given for the topics that were discussed. Drawing on the work of Smetana (1988, 1989), we also categorize conflicts into specific domains. The *personal domain* consists of conflict topics that have consequences

TABLE 8.2
Items from the Decision-Making Questionnaire Categorized Within Each Domain

PERSONAL
1. What hairstyle or haircut teen gets
2. What clothes teen buys
3. How much TV teen watches
4. Which TV shows, videos, or movies teen watches
5. What sorts of clothes teen wears to school
6. How much time teen spends with friends
7. What activities teen can take part in

MONITORING
1. What time teen has to be home at night on weekends
2. When teen can begin dating
3. Whether teen has to be home for dinner
4. Which friends teen spends time with
5. Whether teen tells parents where she is when she goes out
6. Whether teen can have friends over when parents aren't home
7. How late teen can stay out on weeknights
8. Whether teen stays overnight outside the home

SCHOOL
1. Whether teen is too sick to attend school
2. How much time teen spends on homework
3. When teen has to do homework
4. What time teen has to go to sleep on school nights

only for the adolescent and which adolescents perceive as matters of their own personal discretion (e.g., choice of hairstyle). Topics in the *prudential domain,* in contrast, have potentially serious consequences and moral implications (e.g., alcohol use). Topics in the *school domain* pertain to the adolescent's academic experience (e.g., getting poor grades). The *monitoring domain* consists of topics related to the parent's authority to supervise and monitor the child's activities and friendships. The specific topics included in each domain are shown in Table 8.1.

AUTONOMY

Daughters reported on the degree of autonomy allowed by parents with the Decision Making Questionnaire (Steinberg, 1987), a measure that consists of 28 areas of decision making (e.g., curfew on weekends). Respondents indicate whether each issue is typically decided by parents alone, by parents and the adolescent jointly, or by the adolescent alone. Higher levels of adolescent decision making and lower levels of parental decision making indicate more adolescent autonomy.[1] We also categorize decision-making items into three of the four domains used to categorize parent-adolescent conflict: *personal, school,* and *monitoring* domains. The items constituting these domains are shown in Table 8.2.

WARMTH

The affective quality of the mother-daughter relationship is assessed with the Inventory of Parent and Peer Attachment (Armsden & Greenberg, 1987), a scale that measures daughters' feelings of closeness to their mothers, fathers, and peers. Only the scale regarding feelings of attachment toward mothers is used here. This scale consists of 25 items and assesses the extent to which the adolescent feels she has a close and trusting relationship with her mother.

ADOLESCENT ADJUSTMENT

Two scales are used to index adolescent adjustment. First, adolescent self-esteem is assessed with the 5-item Behavioral Self-Esteem subscale of the Perceived Social Competence Scale (Harter, 1982). Each item consists of two conflicting statements (e.g., "Some teenagers are usually pleased with the way they act" vs. "Other teenagers are often ashamed of the way they act"). Respondents choose which statement best describes the way they feel about themselves and then indicates how much they agree with the statement (*really true for me* vs. *sort of true for me*). Scores for each item can range from 1 to 4, with higher scores indicating higher behavioral self-esteem. Second, feelings of depression are assessed with the 18-item Children's Depression Inventory (Kovacs, 1983). Each item consists of three statements, and respondents choose the statement that most closely matches their experience in the past 2 weeks (e.g., "I feel like crying every day" vs. "I feel like crying many days" vs. "I feel like crying once in awhile"). Higher scores indicate more depressive feelings.

What Did We Find?

Changes in Conflict

The first set of analyses assesses change in mother-daughter conflict from early adolescence to middle adolescence. For all analyses, the significance level was set at $p < .01$ unless otherwise indicated. First, the overall number of topics, conflict frequency, and conflict intensity were submitted to a series of time period (Time 1, Time 2) by reporter (mother, daughter) repeated measures ANOVAs. For the number of topics, there was a significant main effect for time, $F(1,36) = 24.41$, and no difference between the

TABLE 8.3
Changes in Conflict, Autonomy, and Warmth: Means and Standard Deviations

Variable	Time 1		Time 2		Range	Effect
	Mothers	Teens	Mothers	Teens		
Conflict						
Number of topics	20.51	19.22	15.78	15.19	0–44	Time 1 > Time 2
	(8.00)	(7.95)	(7.40)	(5.77)		
Frequency	6.54	8.80	4.49	7.92	Past month	Daughters > mothers
	(5.47)	(9.46)	(3.78)	(7.44)		
Intensity	2.04	2.15	2.08	2.37	1–5	Daughters > mothers
	(.50)	(.69)	(.78)	(.73)		
Decision-Making Autonomy						
Teen decides		34.64		50.11	0–100	Time 2 > Time 1
		(16.18)		(18.82)		
Parent decides		30.04		21.36	0–100	Time 1 > Time 2
		(16.18)		(16.82)		
Mother Warmth						
Warmth		3.89 (.73)		3.69 (.82)	1–5	None

reports of mothers and daughters. Both mothers and daughters report more topics of conflict at Time 1 than Time 2 (see Figure 8.1). As shown in Table 8.3, mothers and daughters report disagreeing on an average of 20 issues a month at Time 1 and an average of 15 issues a month at Time 2.

The frequency and intensity of conflict did not change significantly over time. However, there was a significant difference between the reports of mothers and daughters, with daughters reporting more frequent conflict, $F(1,36) = 7.79$, and more intense conflict, $F(1,36) = 6.26$, than mothers. As shown in Table 8.3, the daughters report disagreeing approximately eight times a month, whereas the mothers report disagreeing approximately five times a month. Although daughters report significantly more intense conflicts than mothers, the average intensity ratings for mothers and daughters fall toward the "calm" end of the spectrum.

We next examined changes in conflict in specific domains with a series of time (Time 1, Time 2) by reporter (mother, daughter) repeated measures ANOVAs. These analyses show that the overall decline in the number of topics is accounted for by decreases in the personal domain, $F(1,32) = 16.51$, and the school domain, $F(1,34) = 4.07$, $p < .05$. In contrast, there are no significant changes over time in the number of conflicts in the prudential or monitoring domains. Figure 8.1 displays the percentage of topics in each domain endorsed as conflicts at Time 1 and Time 2. In the figure, the reports of mothers and daughters are averaged because they do not differ

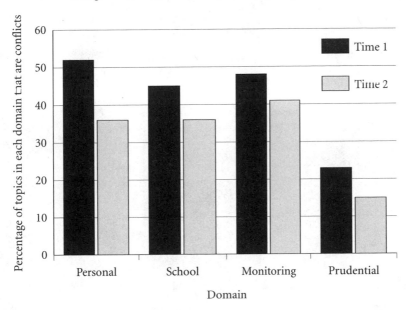

FIGURE 8.1.
Change in the Number of Conflictual Topics by Domain

in any domain. A domain (personal, school, monitoring, prudential) by reporter (mother, daughter) repeated measures ANOVA at each time period reveals that a significantly higher percentage of topics in the personal, school, and monitoring domains are conflicts compared to the prudential domain at Time 1, $F(3,29) = 23.59$ and at Time 2, $F(3,30) = 11.88$.

Change in Decision-Making Autonomy

We evaluated changes in adolescents' reports of decision-making autonomy with a series of paired t-tests. These analyses show a significant increase in the percentage of issues the daughters decide on their own, $t(35) = -4.71$, and a significant decrease in the percentage of issues where parents have exclusive authority to decide, $t(35) = 2.55$. As shown in Table 8.3, the daughters decided approximately 35% of the issues at Time 1 and 50% of the issues at Time 2. The number of issues over which parents retain decision-making authority dropped from 30% at Time 1 to approximately 21% at Time 2.

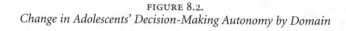

FIGURE 8.2.
Change in Adolescents' Decision-Making Autonomy by Domain

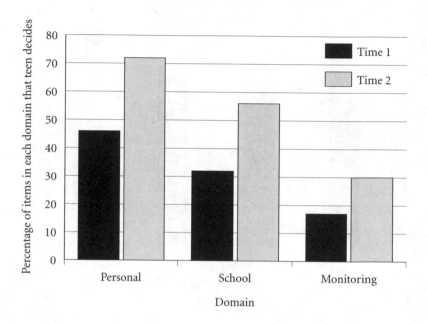

As shown in Figure 8.2, the percentage of issues that teens decide alone increased significantly in all three domains: personal, $t(38)$ =−4.86, school, $t(38)$ =−4.17, and monitoring, $t(38)$ =−2.91. However, a time (Time 1, Time 2) by domain (personal, school, monitoring) repeated measures ANOVA indicated that these increases were not equally distributed across domains, $F(2,56)$ = 40.17. Adolescents report the highest amounts of decision-making autonomy for items in the personal domain, intermediate amounts in the school domain, and the lowest levels of decision-making autonomy in the monitoring domain. All differences are statistically significant.

Change in Warmth

There were no significant differences in adolescents' feelings of warmth toward their mothers between Time 1 and Time 2, $t(37)$ = 1.79. The adolescents' feelings of warmth and closeness toward their mothers were generally high, with means greater than 3.6 on a 5-point scale (see Table 8.3).

TABLE 8.4
Correlations Among Study Variables at Time 1 and Time 2

	1	2	3	4	5	6	7	8
1. Number of Topics	—	.37*	.34*	-.35*	.35*	-.05	-.14	.24
2. Conflict Intensity	.02	—	.38*	-.26	.18	-.35*	-.34*	.48***
3. Conflict Frequency	.01	.11	—	-.07	.14	.01	-.07	.11
4. Teen Decides	-.31a	-.11	-.13	—	-.71***	.45**	.08	-.39*
5. Parent Decides	.26	.35	.07	-.59***	—	-.31a	.11	.31a
6. Warmth	-.21	-.31***	.05	.01	.31a	—	.24	-.47***
7. Self-esteem	-.30a	-.52***	-.45**	.10	-.12	.34*	—	-.58***
8. Depression	.15	.48***	-.03	.12	.07	-.56***	-.55***	—

Note: Time 1 is above the diagonal; Time 2 is below the diagonal
[a]$p < .10$. *$p < .05$. **$p < .01$. ***$p < .001$.

Relations Among Conflict, Decision-Making Autonomy, Warmth, and Adolescent Adjustment

The bivariate correlations among conflict, decision-making autonomy, warmth, and adolescent adjustment at Time 1 and Time 2 are presented in Table 8.4.

CONFLICT IS MALADAPTIVE

To evaluate the hypothesis that conflict erodes feelings of warmth between mothers and daughters, cross-lagged panel designs were used to assess the reciprocal relations between conflict and *warmth*. These analyses allow us to control for the stability of each construct over time while examining reciprocal influences. The general fit of each model is evaluated using the chi-square test of fit and the recommended cutoff of .90 for the Normed Fit Index (NFI; Bentler & Bonett, 1980). Also, the significance of individual path coefficients is assessed with the T-statistic, which evaluates the size of the coefficient in relation to its standard error. Reciprocal relations between the *number of conflictual topics* (the number of topics with intensity ratings above 2) and warmth are evaluated first. The chi-square test of general fit was not significant, $\chi^2(1) = 2.77$, *ns*, indicating a good fit of the model to the data, as did the NFI = .90. Of particular interest in these analyses are the cross-lagged relations. As shown in Figure 8.3, higher levels of warmth at Time 1 are significantly associated with a fewer conflictual topics at Time 2 ($B = -.32$). On the other hand, contrary to the hypothesis, the number of conflictual topics at Time 1 is not significantly associated with decreases in warmth over time ($B = -.21$). The results with average conflict *intensity* and warmth, shown in Figure 8.4, paint a different picture. Both the chi-square

FIGURE 8.3

Reciprocal Relations Between Number of Topics of Conflict and Warmth

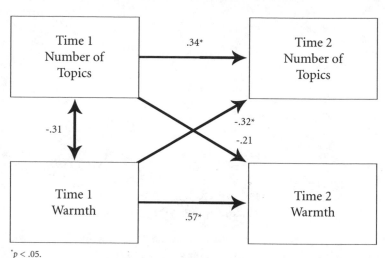

$^*p < .05.$

test, $\chi^2(1) = 1.75$, *ns,* and the NFI = .96 indicate a good fit. Consistent with the hypothesis that conflict erodes feelings of warmth, the cross-lagged path coefficients show that higher-intensity conflict at Time 1 is significantly associated with decreases in warmth over time ($B = -.26$). There are no significant cross-lagged relationships between the *frequency* of conflict and warmth.

Regression analyses were used to evaluate the relations between conflict and adolescent adjustment (Table 8.5). The adolescent outcome variable at Time 1 (self-esteem or depression) was entered in the first step, and conflict and warmth variables were entered in the second step. Thus, the second step assesses whether conflict and warmth predict changes in adolescent adjustment over time. Consistent with the maladaptive effects hypothesis, more intense and more frequent conflict is significantly associated with decreases in self-esteem over time. In addition, more intense conflict and less warmth are significantly associated with increases in feelings of depression over time. However, the number of topics of conflict is unrelated to changes in adolescent adjustment.

CONFLICT IS ADAPTIVE

To evaluate the hypothesis that parent-adolescent conflict promotes autonomy, and therefore may serve an adaptive function, two relations are

FIGURE 8.4
Reciprocal Relations Between Intensity of Conflict and Warmth

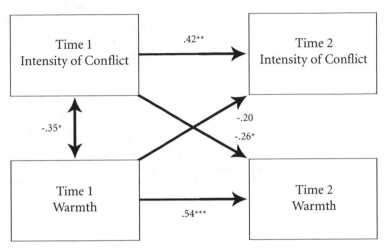

$^*p < .05.$ $^{**}p < .01.$ $^{***}p < .001.$

FIGURE 8.5
*Reciprocal Relations Between Number of Topics of
Conflict and Decision-Making Autonomy*

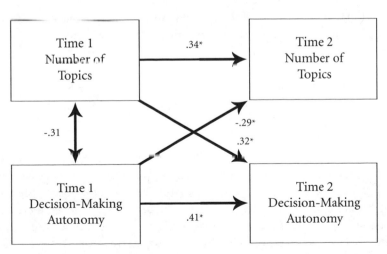

$^*p < .05.$

TABLE 8.5

Predicting change in Adolescent Adjustment from Time 1 Conflict, Warmth, and Decision-Making Autonomy

	Time 2 Self-Esteem			Time 2 Depression		
	R^2	ΔR^2	Beta[b]	R^2	ΔR^2	Beta[b]
Step 1	.14			.31		
Time 1 Adjustment			.38*			.56***
Step 2	.48	.34*		.44	.13	
Time 1 Number of topics			-.13			.11
Time 1 Conflict intensity			-.46*			.31*
Time 1 Conflict frequency			-.54**			.09
Time 1 Warmth			.01			-.30[a]
Step 3	.59	.11[a]		.47	.03	
Time 1 Teen decides			.38*			-.09
Time 1 Parent decides			-.34*			.18

[a] $p < .06$, * $p < .05$, ** $p < .01$, *** $p < .001$; [b] Beta weights at the time of entry after accounting for variables in previous steps

examined: (a) the relation between conflict and decision-making autonomy over time and (b) the relation between decision-making autonomy and changes in adolescent adjustment.

First, we evaluate the hypotheses that conflict at Time 1 is associated with greater decision-making autonomy over time and that greater decision-making autonomy at Time 1 is associated with less conflict over time. The cross-lagged panel design evaluating the relations between the *number of conflictual topics* and adolescents' *decision-making autonomy* demonstrated good fit, $\chi^2(1) = .15$, *ns*, NFI = .99. As shown in Figure 8.5, and consistent with the adaptive effects hypothesis, disagreeing on a greater number of topics at Time 1 is significantly associated with increasing levels of adolescent autonomy over time ($B = .32$). Also, higher decision-making autonomy at Time 1 is significantly associated with decreases in the number of topics of conflict over time ($B = -.29$). There were no reciprocal relationships between decision-making autonomy and the intensity or frequency of conflict.

These findings support the idea that disagreements may help adolescents negotiate greater autonomy. But is autonomy, bought by disagreements, adaptive? It is possible that mothers give in or give up as a result of adolescents wearing them down, and that they grant adolescents freedoms that they are not prepared to handle. In order to consider increasing autonomy *adaptive*, it should be associated with better adolescent adjustment. We used regression analyses to assess the relations between decision-making autonomy at Time 1 and changes in adolescents' adjustment over time. Results are presented in the final three rows of Table 8.5. After accounting for the effects of conflict and warmth on changes in adolescents' adjustment, greater adolescent decision-making autonomy at Time 1 is significantly associated with increases in self-esteem over time. There were no significant relations between adolescent autonomy and changes in feelings of depression.

Changes in the Mother-Daughter Relationship: What Do They Mean?

Black women's feminist and literary traditions have described with a great deal of poignancy the ways in which African American mothers prepare their daughters to take their place in adult society and how this affects their relationships with each other (see Hinton-Johnson, 2004, for an especially compelling recent overview). The current study empirically examined how changes in mother-daughter relationships may affect adolescent girls.

Mothers and daughters reported a similar number of topics of conflict, but daughters reported greater conflict intensity and frequency. The overall rate of conflict in this sample was fairly similar to means reported in other samples (Maggs & Galambos, 1993; Steinberg, 1990). Contrary to our findings, one longitudinal study of middle-class African American boys and girls found that mothers reported more conflictual topics than did their adolescents (Smetana et al., 2003). However, consistent with our findings, this same study found that the adolescents reported more conflict intensity than the mothers.

We found that different aspects of conflict change at different rates across adolescence. Although the overall number of topics of conflict decreases steadily from early to middle adolescence, the frequency and intensity of conflicts that do occur remain stable. Previous studies that have shown that conflict peaks in early adolescence are supported to the extent that early adolescence appears to be the time when the greatest number of topics is discussed. However, our results also indicate that some areas of conflict persist into middle adolescence, and that these issues are debated as frequently and intensely as before.

Examining areas of conflict according to their domain also reveals important insights into the pattern of change in conflict. Specifically, conflict involving issues of personal choice and academic performance decreases, whereas conflict involving parental monitoring of the adolescent's activities remains high. The only other longitudinal study with African American adolescents also found that conflict in the personal domain decreased over time; however, contrary to our findings, conflict about school and homework increased from early to middle adolescence (Smetana et al., 2003). That study examined a more middle-class African American sample of mothers and included both boys and girls. Thus, it is possible that academic aspirations are higher in those more uniformly middle-class homes, so that issues around school achievement are more charged.

Importantly, conflict and autonomy appear to change in concert, as the domain with the greatest decline in conflict shows the greatest increase in decision-making autonomy (the personal domain), and the domain with the least change in conflict shows the smallest gain in decision-making autonomy (the monitoring domain). This correspondence supports the notion that parent-adolescent conflict is a means by which adolescents express their growing desire for more independence. Consistently, a recent qualitative study of social cognitions associated with development among urban, low-income African American and Latina girls and mothers showed that more distant and strained relationships with their mothers are the price that postpubertal girls pay for their increasing independence (O'Sullivan, Meyer-Bahlburg, & Watkins, 2000). Although it may not be exactly comforting to those in the midst of it, both mothers and adolescents may find it well worth knowing that negotiating conflicts has a role in the natural and normal process of the adolescent transition.

Our findings speak to the challenge that African American mothers face in balancing the demands of protecting children while also fostering a sense of competence. For example, mothers retained a higher amount of decision-making autonomy around important monitoring issues, despite persistent levels of conflict in this domain. This suggests that the mothers are strategically granting greater freedom, rather than giving in and granting autonomy simply in order to decrease conflict. In light of the socio-ecological niche that these families inhabit (see Cauce et al., 1996, for a fuller description), the mothers' focus on monitoring seems especially wise for promoting resilient outcomes for their daughters.

Perhaps these mothers can best be described as practicing "no-nonsense parenting," a term coined by Brody and colleagues (Brody, Flor, & Gibson, 1999) to describe the more highly restrictive, but still appropriate and involved, parenting of African American families in risky environments. Mothers may be letting go, but they are retaining a close watch on safety areas, ready to intervene should problems become evident. As one mother in our study said to her daughter, "Of course I trust you, and of course you need to make your own mistakes, that's how you learn. I just need to make sure the mistakes aren't big ones." The need to keep their children free of "big" mistakes may be especially important for African Americans, in light of the evidence from the criminal justice system that the price they pay for errors is high (Alexander & Gyamerah, 1997; Sampson & Lauritsen, 1997). Striking a balance between retaining parental control and granting autonomy, although difficult to achieve, may be a key protective factor in raising strong and competent daughters in the context of risks related to lower socioeconomic resources, discrimination, and negative stereotypes.

There was evidence that mother-daughter conflict may be both adaptive and maladaptive. Conflict may be a risk for poorer adjustment when it is frequent and intense. Our findings suggest that greater conflict *intensity* erodes feelings of warmth and leads to lower self-esteem and higher levels of depression over time. Greater conflict *frequency* at Time 1 is also associated with lowered self-esteem over time. In contrast, the *number of topics* of conflict in early adolescence is not related to warmth at Time 2 or adjustment over time. This suggests that the occurrence of disagreement, in and of itself, is not a sign of problems. In fact, a higher number of topics of conflict appears to facilitate the development of adolescent autonomy, and consistent with the work of others (Smetana et al., 2004), greater adolescent autonomy is associated with stronger feelings of self-esteem. Thus, the ability to acknowledge multiple areas of disagreement may be an important strength that fosters positive adaptation.

The key to whether conflict is adaptive may be related to whether families are able to effectively resolve conflict. Effective management of conflict involves addressing areas of conflict rather than avoiding them, and doing so in a way that prevents an escalation into arguments that are frequent and intense. Achieving this difficult balance is likely aided by strong feelings of warmth in the mother-daughter relationship. In general, a high level of warmth in African American mother-daughter relationships is a critical strength that allows mothers to serve as a "refueling station" (Turnage, 2004, p. 159) for their daughters as they make their way through a society that is often less than friendly and supportive. With respect to conflict specifically, perceived parental warmth in early adolescence may facilitate the healthy negotiation of conflict. For example, in this study, higher feelings of warmth at Time 1 were associated with fewer topics of conflict at Time 2. Thus, consistent with Rutter and Conger (1995), it may be that warm family relationships initiate a positive cycle among disagreements, resolution, autonomy, and adaptation. Developing warm parent-child relationships well before adolescence may enable families to avoid the damaging aspects of conflict escalation, while benefiting from the growth in adolescent autonomy and self-esteem that result from successful conflict negotiation.

Our small sample size does not allow us to test more complex, integrated models. Also, longer-term effects cannot be studied because we have only two assessment points, both within adolescence. Despite these limitations, the results of this study highlight aspects of mother-daughter relationship in African American families that promote resilience and competence in young females despite the considerable risks they face in contemporary society. The ability to discuss disagreements without escalating to frequent and intense conflict, the ability to judiciously grant adolescents greater autonomy while maintaining parental control over the teens' activities, and the ability to maintain strong feelings of warmth in the mother-daughter relationship all contribute to positive developmental outcomes for urban African American adolescent females. Granting autonomy is often a difficult issue for African American mothers because the costs of losing control of their daughters may be especially high. In the face of an unforgiving world, it is hard to be a flexible parent. But it is clear that these mothers are being flexible, at least in those areas where they believe they can.

Discussion Questions

1. The authors state that African American mothers face some unique challenges in raising their daughters. What are these challenges, and why are they unique, or at least more common, for African American than for White mothers?
2. Much of the research on parent-child conflict looks only at the frequency and intensity of conflict. In this study, the authors looked at conflict in different domains—personal, prudential, school, and monitoring domains. Define the types of conflicts that we would find in each domain. Discuss whether or not you think there is anything to be gained by looking at conflict in this detailed manner.

3. Based on the findings in this study, how would you describe the relations between parent-child conflict and adolescent autonomy? Is conflict greatest in those areas where autonomy is increasing or decreasing? Why do you think this might be the case? Do these findings fit with your memories about your adolescent years and your relationships with your parents during that time?

4. Do you think the relationships, and the changes in the relationships, described in this chapter would have been different if the authors had examined a sample of fathers and daughters? Fathers and sons? White mothers and daughters? Which findings do you think would have been similar, and which would have been different? Why?

5. Based on the findings in this chapter, what aspects of the parent-child relationship would you describe as "protective"? What aspects would you describe as "risk" factors? Is there any evidence in this chapter that these factors interact, such that protective factors decrease the impact of risk factors? If yes, describe that evidence. If not, how might you design a study that would test a risk-protective factor model of parenting an adolescent?

NOTE

1. Previous research has interpreted this measure from the perspective of the parent as an indication of parental control and parenting style (e.g., Lamborn, Dornbusch, & Steinberg, 1996; Radziszewska, Richardson, Dent, & Flay, 1996). That is, a high amount of unilateral parental decision making is equated with authoritarian parenting, whereas a high amount of unilateral adolescent decision making is equated with permissive parenting. However, we expect the parent's level of involvement in decision making to be more responsive to developmental changes in the adolescent than would be implied by a relatively static definition of parenting style, such that some shifts from unilateral parental authority toward unilateral adolescent authority should be developmentally appropriate. Therefore, we interpret this measure from the adolescent's perspective as an indication of the level of autonomy that she is granted.

REFERENCES

Allen, J. P., Hauser, S. T., Eickholt, C., Bell, K. L., & O'Connor, T. G. (1994). Autonomy and relatedness in family interactions as predictors of expressions of negative adolescent affect. *Journal of Research on Adolescence, 4,* 535–552.

Alexander, R. J., & Gyamerah, J. (1997). Differential punishing of African Americans and Whites who possess drugs: A just policy or a continuation of the past? *Journal of Black Studies, 28,* 97–111

Anderson, E. R., Hetherington, E. M., & Clingempeel, W. G. (1989). Transformations in family relations at puberty: Effects of family context. *Journal of Early Adolescence, 9,* 310–334.

Armsden, G. C., & Greenberg, M. T. (1987). The Inventory of Parent and Peer Attachment: Individual differences and their relationship to psychological well-being in adolescence. *Journal of Youth and Adolescence, 16,* 427–453.

Bell-Scott, P., Guy-Sheftall, B., Jones Royster, J., Sims-Wood, J., DeCosta-Willis, M. & Fultz, L. P. (1991). *Double stitch: Black women write about mothers and daughters.* Boston: Beacon Press.

Bentler, P. M., & Bonett, D. G. (1980). Significance tests and goodness of fit in the analysis of covariance structures. *Psychological Bulletin, 88,* 588–606.

Brody, G. H., Flor, D. L., & Gibson, N. M. (1999). Linking maternal efficacy beliefs, developmental goals, parenting practices, and child competence in rural single parent African American families. *Child Development, 69,* 803–816.

Cauce, A. M., Hiraga, Y., Graves, D., Gonzales, N., Ryan-Finn, K., & Grove, K. (1996). African American mothers and their adolescent daughters: Closeness, conflict, and control. In B. J. Leadbeater & N. Way (Eds.), *Urban adolescent girls: Resisting stereotypes, creating identities* (pp. 100–116). New York: New York University Press.

Collins, W. A. (1990). Parent-child relationships in the transition to adolescence: Continuity and change in interaction, affect, and cognition. In R. Montemayor, G. R. Adams, & T. P. Gullotta (Eds.), *From childhood to adolescence: A transitional period?* (Vol. 2, pp. 85–106). Newbury Park, CA: Sage.

Cooper, C. R., Grotevant, H. D., & Condon, S. M. (1983). Individuality and connectedness in the family as a context for adolescent identity formation and role-taking skill. *New Directions for Child Development, 22,* 43–59.

DeCosta-Willis, M. (1991). The meaning of motherhood in Black culture and Black mother-daughter relationships. In P. Bell-Scott, B. Guy-Sheftall, J. Jones Royster, J. Sims-Wood, M. DeCosta-Willis, & L. P. Fultz (Eds.), *Double stitch: Black women write about mothers and daughters* (pp. 36–49). Boston: Beacon Press.

DiClemente, R. J., Wingood, G. M., Crosby, R., Sionean, S., Cobb, B. K., Harrington, K., et al. (2001). Parental monitoring: Association with adolescents, risk behaviors. *Pediatrics, 107,* 1361–1368.

Duncan, G. J., Brooks-Gunn, J., & Klebanov, P. K. (1994). Economic deprivation and early childhood development. *Child Development, 65,* 296–318.

Furman, W., & Buhrmester, D. (1992). Age and sex differences in perceptions of networks of personal relationships. *Child Development, 63,* 103–115.

Galambos, N. L., & Almeida, D. M. (1992). Does parent-adolescent conflict increase in early adolescence? *Journal of Marriage and the Family, 54,* 737–747.

Harter, S. (1982). The Perceived Competence Scale for Children. *Child Development, 53,* 87–97.

Hinton-Johnson, K. V. (2004). African American mothers and daughters: Socialization, distance, and conflict. *ALAN Review, 31,* 51–63.

Holmbeck, G. N., & Hill, J. P. (1991). Conflictive engagement, positive affect, and menarche in families with seventh-grade girls. *Child Development, 62,* 1030–1048.

Jargowsky, P. (1997). *Poverty and place.* New York: Russell Sage Foundation.

Jarrett, R. L. (1997). African American family and parenting strategies in impoverished neighborhoods. *Qualitative Sociology, 20,* 275–288.

Jarrett, R. L. (1999). Successful parenting in high-risk neighborhoods. *The Future of Children: When School Is Out, 9,* 45–50.

Kovacs, M. (1983). *The Children's Depression Inventory: A self-rated depression scale for school-aged youngsters.* Unpublished manuscript, University of Pittsburgh.

Lamborn, S. D., Dornbusch, S. M., & Steinberg, L. (1996). Ethnicity and community context as moderators of the relations between family decision making and adolescent adjustment. Child Development, 67, 283–301.

Laursen, B., & Collins, W. A. (1994). Interpersonal conflict during adolescence. *Psychological Bulletin, 115,* 197–209.

Laursen, B., Coy, K., & Collins, W. A. (1998). Reconsidering changes in parent-child conflict across adolescence: A meta-analysis. *Child Development, 69,* 817–832.

Leadbeater, B., & Way, N. (1996) *Urban girls: Resisting stereotypes, creating identities.* New York: New York University Press.

Lewit, E. M. (1993). Children in poverty. *The Future of Children: When School Is Out, 3,* 176–182.

Maggs, J. L., & Galambos, N. L. (1993). Alternative structural models for understanding adolescent problem behavior in two-earner families. *Journal of Early Adolescence, 13,* 79–101.

Montemayor, R. (1983). Parents and adolescents in conflict: All families some of the time and some families most of the time. *Journal of Early Adolescence, 3,* 83–103.

Montemayor, R. (1986). Family variation in parent-adolescent storm and stress. *Journal of Adolescent Research, 1,* 15–31.

O'Sullivan, L. F., Meyer-Bahlburg, H. F., & Watkins, B. X. (2000). Social cognitions associated with pubertal development in a sample of urban, low-income, African-American and Latina girls and mothers. *Journal of Adolescent Health, 27,* 227–235.

Paikoff, R. L., & Brooks-Gunn, J. (1991). Do parent-child relationships change during puberty? *Psychological Bulletin, 110,* 47–66.

Papini, D. R., Clark, S., Barnett, J. K., & Savage, C. L. (1989). Grade, pubertal status, and gender-related variations in conflictual issues among adolescents. *Adolescence, 24,* 977–987.

Papini, D. R., & Sebby, R. A. (1988). Variations in conflictual family issues by adolescent pubertal status, gender, and family member. *Journal of Early Adolescence, 8,* 1–15.

Pinderhughes, E. E., Nix, R. L., Foster, E. M., Jones, D., & Conduct Problems Prevention Research Group. (2001). Parenting in context: Impact of neighborhood poverty, residential stability, public services, social networks, and danger on parental behavior. *Journal of Marriage and the Family, 63,* 941–953.

Radziszewska, B., Richardson, J. L., Dent, C. W., & Flay, B. R. (1996). Parenting style and adolescent depressive symptoms, smoking, and academic achievement: Ethnic, gender, and SES differences. Journal of Behavioral Medicine, 19, 289–305.

Robin, A. L., & Foster, S. L. (1989). *Negotiating parent-adolescent conflict: A behavioral-family systems approach.* New York: Guilford.

Rutter, M. A., & Conger, R. D. (1995). Antecedents of parent-adolescent disagreements. *Journal of Marriage and the Family, 57,* 435–448.

Sampson, R. J., & Lauritsen, J. L. (1997). Racial and ethnic disparities in crime and criminal justice in the United States. In M. Tonry (Ed.), *Ethnicity, Crime, and Immigration:* Comparative and Cross-National Perspectives (pp. 311–374). Chicago: University of Chicago Press.

Smetana, J. G. (1988). Adolescents' and parents' conceptions of parental authority. *Child Development, 59,* 321–335.

Smetana, J. G. (1989). Adolescents' and parents' reasoning about actual family conflict. *Child Development, 60,* 1052–1067.

Smetana, J. G. (1995). Parenting styles and conceptions of parental authority during adolescence. *Child Development, 66,* 299–316.

Smetana, J. G., & Asquith, P. (1994). Adolescents' and parents' conceptions of parental authority and personal autonomy. *Child Development, 65,* 1147–1162.

Smetana, J. G., Campione-Barr, N., & Daddis, C. (2004). Longitudinal development of family decision making: Defining healthy behavioral autonomy for middle-class African American adolescents. *Child Development, 75,* 1418–1434.

Smetana, J. G., Daddis, C., & Chaung, S. S. (2003). "Clean your room!" A longitudinal investigation of adolescent-parent conflict and conflict-resolution in middle-class African American families. *Journal of Adolescent Research, 18,* 631–650.

Smetana, J. G., & Gaines, C. (1999). Adolescent-parent conflict in married and divorced families. *Developmental Psychology, 27,* 1000–1010.

Smollar, J., & Youniss, J. (1989). Transformations in adolescents' perceptions of parents. *International Journal of Behavioral Development, 12,* 71–84.

Steinberg, L. (1987). Single parents, stepparents, and the susceptibility of adolescents to antisocial peer pressure. *Child Development, 58,* 269–275.

Steinberg, L. (1988). Reciprocal relation between parent-child distance and pubertal maturation. *Developmental Psychology, 24,* 122–128.

Steinberg, L. (1990). Autonomy, conflict, and harmony in the family relationship. In S. S. Feldman & G. R. Elliott (Eds.), *At the threshold: The developing adolescent* (pp. 255–569). Cambridge, MA: Harvard University Press.

Thornton, M. C. (1997). Strategies of racial socialization among Black parents: Mainstream minority and cultural messages. In R. J. Taylor, J. S. Jackson, & L. M Chatters (Eds.), *Family life in Black America* (pp. 201–215). Thousand Oaks, CA: Sage.

Thornton, M. C., Chatters, L. M., Taylor, R. J., & Allen, W. R. (1990). Sociodemographic and environmental correlates of racial socialization by Black parents. *Child Development, 61*, 401–409.

Turnage, B. F. (2004). African American mother-daughter relationships mediating daughters' self-esteem. *Child and Adolescent Social Work Journal, 21*, 155–173.

Way, N. (1998). *Everyday courage: The lives and stories of urban teenagers.* New York: New York University Press.

Youniss, J., & Smollar, J. (1985). *Adolescent relations with mother, fathers, and friends.* Chicago: University of Chicago Press.

The "Good" News and the "Bad" News

The "Americanization" of Hmong Girls

Stacey J. Lee

Hmong boys are privileged. At least in my family they are. First of all, compared to girls, they are more encouraged to do stuff; join sports, be involved in school, go away for college and they also have more rights and say in the family. The girls are supposed to be subservient and obedient, while the guys have the chance to go out with their friends and do whatever they want. I understand the fact that this cultural stigma has probably been in effect for centuries. It's just that now, here in the US, girls and guys alike are given more opportunities than the Hmong culture and its traditions cannot deal with. This isn't fair to anybody—it's not fair to the girls, to the guys, nor to the Hmong people itself because now THEY have to deal with this issue. It's really unfair because the boys get to do basically whatever they want. The girls, on the other hand, have to stay at home, cook, clean, and watch all of her 50 little brothers and sisters. Being a Hmong girl isn't that easy. I think that American girls have it so much easier.

Hmong Homepage Teen Feedback, retrieved May 26, 2001, from www.hmongnet.org/teenfeedback/index.html

As in other immigrant and refugee communities, the landscape of gender is being transformed within Hmong families in communities across the United States. Like the speaker in the epigraph, Hmong American adolescent girls are exploring new gendered opportunities in the United States and challenging what they believe to be the gender inequality in the Hmong culture. They are taking the lead in revising gender norms and roles within their families and their communities.

Many researchers of gender and the Asian American immigrant experience suggest that life in the United States offers Asian American women greater freedom and independence (Donnelly, 1994; Gibson, 1988; Lee, 1997; Smith-Hefner, 1999; Zhou & Bankston, 1998). The assumption is that American gender norms are more modern and progressive than Asian gender norms. Like these scholars, Hmong adolescent girls believe that Asian women in the United States have greater individual opportunities than in their native countries. They perceive American culture as offering personal freedom and unequaled educational opportunities for girls and women, and they assume that American girls and women enjoy gender equality. Not insignificantly, they believe that the adoption of mainstream American gender norms will lead to progressive changes within the Hmong American community.

In this chapter, I examine the ways Hmong American adolescent girls are negotiating new gender norms and roles in the United States, a process the girls refer to as *Americanization*. I pay particular attention to ways the girls' perceptions of gendered opportunities in the United States shape their aspirations and their creation of new gender norms. I consider whether life in the United States and the process of Americanization have indeed led to progressive change and greater empowerment for Hmong girls and women. My focus is on three areas where Hmong American girls and women are altering gender roles and patterns: (a) educational aspirations; (b) marriage, sexuality, and family relationships; and (c) ideals about beauty.

Methods

Data for this chapter were collected as part of a larger ethnographic study on the way race, class, and gender inform the process of "becoming American" for Hmong high school students (Lee, 2001a, 2001b, 2005). Ethnographic fieldwork was conducted at a public school I call University Heights High School (UHS) between January 1999 and June 2000. Located in a midsize city in Wisconsin, UHS enjoys an excellent academic reputation in the city and throughout the state. During the 1999–2000 academic year, UHS enrolled 2023 students, 29% of whom were classified as students of color and 14% of whom were identified as low income (receiving free or reduced-cost lunch).

Because the school district includes students from all Asian ethnic groups in one category, it was difficult to determine the exact number of Hmong students at UHS. According to estimates made by the various school staff, however, there were 54 Hmong students enrolled at UHS during the 1998–1999 school year and approximately 65 Hmong students enrolled during the 1999–2000 academic year. All the Hmong American students at UHS were the children of immigrants or refugees, and nearly 80% were second-generation. The remaining Hmong American students arrived in the United States during their elementary or middle school years and were members of the 1.5-generation. Although Hmong was the first language in the homes of all students, all spoke English at school. Most were from low-income families and received free or reduced-cost lunch.

The ethnographic fieldwork with Hmong American students at UHS included participant observation during lunch periods and study halls; interviews with Hmong American students and school staff; classroom observations; and analysis of site documents. On average, I spent two to three days per week at UHS. In addition to this fieldwork, I conducted observations at school district–sponsored meetings for Southeast Asian parents and observations of local Hmong community events. My identity, particularly assumptions about my identity, affected the way my informants responded to me. In my first encounters with Hmong American students, I was asked questions about my ethnicity, age, marital status, occupation, and place of birth. As a Chinese American woman, I share race and gender in common with the Hmong American girls, which helped in the negotiation of trusting relationships. Several girls, for example, asked me about gender roles for Chinese girls and women, specifically about my family's ideas regarding gender roles. They interpreted the fact that my family fully supported my pursuit of higher education as evidence that my family and I embraced "Americanized" gender constructs.

In addition to the data from ethnographic fieldwork, this chapter also draws data from Hmong Internet sites and from works of fiction by Hmong American women. I became interested in examining Internet sites when I learned how much time Hmong American youth at UHS spent surfing the Web and interacting with other youth in Hmong chat rooms. The quotation that opens this chapter, for example, was taken from a Web page for Hmong teens organized by a Hmong adolescent girl. The purpose of the site was to provide Hmong teens a forum to discuss concerns related to being Hmong teenagers in the United States. This comment was given in response to the question "What privileges do Hmong boys have that Hmong girls don't? Is it fair? What can be done to change this?" (www.hmongnet.org/teenfeedback/index.html). The use of these supplementary sources of data helps to situate the voices of Hmong American girls at UHS within the larger cultural context.

The Hmong in the United States

The first Hmong came to the United States as refugees from Laos in the late 1970s. During the Vietnam War, the Hmong served as U.S. allies in the "secret war" against communism in Laos. According to the 2000 U.S. census, 186,310 people identify as Hmong living in the United States, with the largest populations in California, Minnesota, and Wisconsin.

The Hmong culture is most often characterized as traditional, rural, preliterate, and patriarchal (Donnelly, 1994; Fass, 1991). Early studies of Hmong refugees focused on the differences between Hmong culture and mainstream American culture, particularly with regard to gender norms (Donnelly, 1994; Goldstein, 1985; Walker-Moffat, 1995). While Hmong gender norms were characterized as premodern and traditional, mainstream American gender norms were implicitly seen as modern and progressive. According to these early studies (Donnelly, 1994; Faderman & Xiong, 1998), Hmong society in Laos needed rigid gender roles for men and women where men were the undisputed leaders in the families. The patrilineal and patriarchal clan system shaped gender relations between husbands and wives and between parents and children, and Hmong girls were encouraged to marry during early adolescence.

In the last two decades Hmong women and men have been creating and revising gender roles in response to social, economic, and political conditions in the United States. Hmong men continue to be viewed as family and community leaders, but some Hmong women are also emerging as leaders in their communities. As noted earlier, researchers have characterized the changes in gender roles and norms in the Hmong community as leading to greater equality and empowerment for Hmong women (Donnelly, 1994).

Changing Gender Norms

Hmong American girls at UHS were uniformly interested in greater gender equality for Hmong girls, and they assumed that adopting more Americanized gender norms would lead to greater economic and personal independence. The centrality of gender issues, particularly issues regarding gender equality, for Hmong American girls and young women beyond UHS is supported by a review of Hmong Internet sites and by works of Hmong American fiction. In the first anthology of Hmong American writers, for example, 10 out of 22 contributors wrote pieces that address gender inequality in the Hmong community (Moua, 2002). Similarly, much of what the youth discussed on the Hmong Teen Feedback page revolved around issues of gender inequality in their families and in the larger Hmong American community (www.hmongnet.org/teenfeedback/index.html).

Education

Perhaps the biggest change in the Hmong community regarding gender concerns the education of girls and women. Early research on Hmong refugee students in the United States discovered that Hmong girls experienced serious problems in school, including significant dropout rates from middle and high school (Cohn, 1986; Goldstein, 1985). Researchers concluded that the emphasis on early marriage and motherhood within the Hmong community led to these high dropout rates among girls (Donnelly, 1994; Goldstein, 1985). Ethnographic research on Hmong women in the 1980s revealed that "educated girls quickly fell into disfavor as wives, since traditional parents wanted obedient daughters-in-law and urged their sons to choose compliant girls, often fitting their own preferences" (Donnelly, 1994, p. 139).

More recent research suggests that the Hmong community now believes that education is important for both girls and boys (Koltyk, 1998; Lee, 1997). One of the strongest indicators of the Hmong American community's investment in education is the growing number of Hmong men and women pursuing higher education. In 2001 there were approximately 6,500 Hmong students enrolled in undergraduate institutions across the country (Pobzeb, 2001). Women who interrupted their studies to marry as teenagers are also returning to school in order to get better jobs (Fass, 1991; Lee, 1997).

According to Hmong American girls at UHS, their parents encourage sons and daughters to study hard and graduate from high school (Lee, 2005). The importance of education for girls and young women can be seen in the Hmong community's new definition of "good girls." One of the bilingual resource specialists at UHS noted that most Hmong adults now define a "good girl" as someone who speaks Hmong, respects her elders, stays away from boys, and graduates from high school. This definition of a "good Hmong girl" is significantly different from the definition from the 1980s, when "good Hmong girls" often dropped out of high school to marry and have children. In many respects, the Miss Hmong contests held in Hmong American communities across the country reflect the new dominant Hmong view concerning the new ideal femininity. Hmong community leaders are generally the judges in these contests, and winners of the contests are described as Hmong role models. One student at UHS who competed in the Wisconsin Miss Hmong contest noted that the ideal Miss Hmong is beautiful, knows the Hmong culture, and works hard in school. Indeed, most of the recent Miss Hmong winners are college students, and most express a strong interest in the Hmong culture. For example, in an open letter to the Hmong American community, Miss Hmong International 2004–2005, a young woman from Stockton, California, expressed her interest in promoting higher education among Hmong people (http://www.laofamilyofstockton.org/Miss_hmong_internatio.htm).

Economic forces in the United States have had a particularly profound impact on attitudes regarding the education of Hmong girls and women. Adults in the Hmong community recognize that economic necessity will require most Hmong women to work outside the home. Hmong parents believe that education is central to helping their daughters secure high-paying jobs. Hmong girls at UHS consistently reported that their parents told them that education was the key to escaping poverty. One second-generation girl, for example, remarked, "My parents tell me go to school and become a doctor so I will make lots of money." Another second generation girl reported that her parents told her that if she did not stay in school she would end up poor.

Like their parents, Hmong girls at UHS view education as a route to social mobility. They assume that they will have to work outside the home, and that education will help them secure better jobs. Higher-achieving Hmong girls, in particular, noted that they aspire to go to college in order to secure professional jobs upon graduation. Still other girls believed that education would give them more power within their families. One girl, for example, remarked that she planned to "go to college and get a good job so that I don't have to depend on a man." A few girls mentioned that some Hmong boys are ambivalent about marrying educated Hmong women. The girls told stories they had heard from cousins and friends about Hmong women who could not find husbands because they were too educated. Despite the possibility that higher education might make them unpopular with Hmong men, most girls at UHS still believed that it was important to pursue their educations.

At UHS, Hmong girls outperform Hmong boys academically in both generations (Lee, 2005). For example, 1.5-generation and second-generation Hmong American girls were more likely to be on the honor roll than their male counterparts. Among the 1.5-generation students, both girls and boys held positive attitudes toward school, but girls were more likely to participate in compensatory educational programs for college-bound students and were more likely to have close relationships with their teachers. Among second-generation students, girls were generally more engaged in school than were boys. Whereas second-generation girls could be found doing their homework at lunch, I never observed a second-generation boy studying during the lunch period.

Beyond the walls of UHS, there is growing evidence that Hmong American women are surpassing Hmong American men in higher education. Informal conversations with administrators at midwestern colleges and universities suggest that Hmong women are among the majority of Hmong students to persist in school. Many in the national Hmong community believe Hmong women are more successful in pursuing higher education than Hmong men (Vang, 2004). Interestingly, this gender gap has been identified in other immigrant groups (López, 2003; Zhou & Bankston, 1998). Some researchers have suggested that traditional gender norms for girls may inadvertently support education by keeping girls from participating in delinquent behavior (Zhou & Bankston, 1998).

My research suggests that the growing achievement gap between Hmong American girls and boys is related to their perceptions of gendered opportunities in the United States. As noted earlier, Hmong American girls and women view the United States as being the land of gender equality. At UHS, girls uniformly believe that there are greater educational opportunities for girls and women in the United States than in Laos (Lee, 2005). In fact, they see education as one of the best things about life in the

United States. One girl, for example, asserted that "schools are great in America because everyone can go." In short, the girls have a positive dual frame of reference with regard to gender opportunities that motivates them to do well in school. In contrast to the girls, many Hmong American boys at UHS appeared to see themselves as being disadvantaged by life in the United States. In particular, boys were aware that they failed to live up to hegemonic notions of masculinity (Lee, 2004).

At UHS, teachers strongly supported the girls' desires to attain a quality education (Lee, 2005). Many members of the UHS faculty and staff expressed concern about the patriarchal nature of Hmong culture. These educators saw Hmong females as victims in need of saving. In comparing the position of boys and girls within Hmong families, one teacher asserted: "I think the girls have to grow up faster in terms of taking on home responsibilities. I think the work-load is inequitable outside of school. And then this whole issue of you know, who gets to decide when you marry, who you marry" (Lee, 2005, p. 93).

White female teachers, in particular, expressed sympathy for the position of girls in Hmong families and an interest in helping them take advantage of educational opportunities in the United States. They were particularly concerned about 1.5-generation girls because they assumed that newcomer girls were more vulnerable to traditional gender norms. Thus, they often went out of their way to provide 1.5-generation girls with extra academic assistance in the form of tutoring, and information about postsecondary options. On occasion, the teachers would share their own stories of overcoming gender inequality in an effort to demonstrate that it is possible to overcome adversity. Not insignificantly, Hmong American boys at UHS were rarely the recipients of extra academic assistance or encouragement. In fact, teachers at UHS either ignored the Hmong American boys or stereotyped them as gangsters (Lee, 2004). Thus, the girls' experiences with teachers appeared to confirm their optimism about education, and the boys' experiences appeared to contribute to their sense of marginalization in the United States.

Marriage, Sexuality, and Family Life

Marriage, sexuality, and family life are perhaps the most contested issues within Hmong American communities. Early research on Hmong refugee communities found that Hmong elders believed that sustaining a distinct

Hmong culture depended on adhering to traditional beliefs about gender roles, especially that women are subordinate to male authority, and that girls should marry and begin having children during early adolescence (Donnelly, 1994; Goldstein, 1985). The practices of early marriage and early childbearing have led to conflict between the Hmong community and the dominant society and to conflict within Hmong American families (Lee, 2001).

Despite the ongoing controversy surrounding these matters, there is significant evidence that attitudes regarding marriage have changed in recent years. In interviews with Hmong girls at UHS, I learned that parents held varied opinions regarding when girls should marry (Lee, 2001). A growing number of parents appear to be encouraging their daughters to postpone marriage until they graduate from high school. At UHS, teachers who work most closely with Hmong students reported that in the last 10 years fewer girls had dropped out of school to get married.

The changing ideas regarding marriage appear to be related to parents' perceptions of economic and social conditions in the United States (Lee, 1997). Economic realities, for example, have led Hmong adults to question the economic viability of young people getting married and having children prior to graduating from high school.

The dominant society's condemnation of marriage involving minors has also had an impact on attitudes regarding marriage in the Hmong American community. Stories of Hmong parents being prosecuted for forcing their minor children to marry are well known in Hmong American communities. Hmong American students at UHS also reported hearing about Hmong parents who "got in trouble" when their daughters married as minors. In a recent Wisconsin case, for example, a Hmong mother has been charged with a felony for allowing her 14-year-old daughter to engage in sexual relations with an adult male. According to the daughter, she is married to the man "in the Hmong tradition," and they live as husband and wife. (http://www.wisinfo.com/sheboyganpress/print/print_22782782.shtml). In response to cases like this, some in the Hmong American community have encouraged postponing marriage as a form of accommodation to dominant social norms and laws. There is also some evidence that early marriage has gone underground. I discovered, for example, that a few Hmong American girls at UHS were "married in the Hmong tradition" but hid their marriages from those outside of the Hmong community.

Like Hmong adults, Hmong American girls hold varied attitudes regarding when girls should marry. A recent issue of *Hmoob Teen,* one of the largest publications for Hmong teenagers, was devoted to the subject of Hmong marriage, reflecting the centrality of the marriage debate in their lives (http://www.hmong.org/displaycontentmenu.asp?ID=27). At UHS, the majority of girls reported that they wanted to wait to marry until after high school, and some even reported that they planned to postpone marriage until they completed college. Girls who were the best students and aspired to higher education were the ones most likely to express an interest in postponing marriage. Girls framed the postponement of marriage until after college as an Americanized choice.

A small minority of girls at UHS embraced early marriage. Interestingly, girls who were estranged from their families often viewed early marriage as a way to escape parental authority. In some cases, the girls married their boyfriends against their parents' wishes. Ironically, these girls appeared to be using a culturally accepted way to challenge parental restrictions regarding relationships with boys. In other words, they refused to stay away from boys, so they used early marriage as a way to get around their parents' rules. Similarly, in her study of Hmong American college students, Ngo (2002) discovered that some Hmong women "engage in or understand early marriage as an expression of defiance to parents' control and restrictions on social life" (170).

While girls have diverse opinions regarding the appropriate age for marriage, they are well aware that most teachers and non-Hmong students are critical of early marriage. Several girls complained that non-Hmong people mock Hmong people for getting married at young ages and for having large families. Even girls who are critical of early marriage are deeply offended when the dominant society judges the Hmong culture. Girls who were married hid their marital status from non-Hmong students and from adult authorities at the school. Even unmarried girls who criticized early marriage helped their married peers keep their secret.

The debate within the Hmong American families regarding marriage is also connected in complex ways to beliefs about girls' sexuality and relationships with boys. Although Hmong adults hold diverse attitudes regarding when girls should marry, they are consistent in their attitudes about controlling female sexuality. Male and female students asserted that Hmong parents believed that "good" Hmong girls must stay away from boys. Hmong parents perceive American society as particularly threatening to female sexuality and fear that their daughters will adopt its "loose" sexual mores. Although the importance of sexual purity among girls is a traditional value, research suggests premarital sex was not uncommon in Laos (Donnelly, 1994; Vang, 1982). The disparity between acceptance of premarital sex in native Laos and the strict adherence to standards of sexual "purity" in the United States suggests that life in the United States may have greater restrictions for girls and women. Similarly, in her research on Khmer refugees, Smith-Hefner (1999) found that "as a result of social pressures to preserve female virtue, Khmer girls in the United States may actually be marrying at younger ages" (181).

In efforts to protect their daughters' reputations, Hmong parents impose rigid restrictions on girls' dating and their after-school activities. Girls reported that their parents were generally suspicious of any after-school activities and often prohibited them from participating in extracurricular activities. When not in school, girls are expected to stay at home, whereas boys are allowed to go out to socialize with their peers. Hmong girls are generally forbidden to spend time alone with boys. One Hmong girl at UHS explained her mother's rules about dating like this: "My sister would have to go [on the date] or sometimes my mom, we would all have to go together."

Girls who break their parents' rules regarding contact with boys run the risk of being forced into early marriage. During one conversation with Hmong girls and boys, several students joked, "If you don't want to get married don't fool around." Girls commonly complained that whereas boys who "fool around" might be welcome back into the family, a girl who spends time alone with a boy must marry in order to save her reputation and the reputation of her family. Here, the threat of early marriage becomes a strategy to prevent girls from assimilating into American cultural norms regarding sexuality.

Another area of gender conflict within Hmong families involves girls' desire for greater equality regarding household chores. Girls at UHS regularly complained that they are expected to help with all household chores while their brothers are allowed to have fun. One UHS girl expressed her frustration with her parents' rules about household chores like this: "But then my brothers, they don't do anything, which gets me really upset. Every time, every time my mom tells us to like do the laundry I am always fighting. 'No—I am not doing their [brothers'] laundry, they are old enough to do their laundry'" (Lee 2005, 106). The girls asserted that girls and boys should have to do equal amounts of work around the house, and they stated that when they had children of their own they would have their sons and daughters share the domestic chores.

The girls' belief in the possibility of gender equality in the domestic realm was influenced by their perception that girls and boys in mainstream American families shared household chores. This assumption about gender equality in mainstream American families was influenced by the media (Lee & Vaught, 2003). One girl, for example, reported that she had learned from TV that "girls and guys in American families help with the dishes and other jobs around the house." Although the girls' perceptions of mainstream American families may not be entirely accurate, their perceptions of American gender norms are empowering them to dream of greater gender equality for their future children. Unfortunately, their perceptions of mainstream American families also led to greater discontent with their own families. Girls who question or challenge parents' expectations regarding household responsibilities run the risk of being characterized as "bad girls." One recent study of parent-child relationships in Hmong families, for example, found that mothers and daughters often have conflicts over household chores (Xiong, Eliason, Detzner, & Cleveland, 2005).

Ideals of Beauty

The desire to adopt more Americanized gender norms has also influenced Hmong girls' ideas about beauty. Many second-generation Hmong American girls, in particular, have internalized dominant messages regarding beauty. These young women attempt to alter their bodies to fit mainstream American ideals regarding attractiveness. Some Hmong girls, for example, bleach their hair and wear colored contact lenses in what appear to be efforts to look less Asian (Lee & Vaught, 2003; Vang, 2002). Although I met only one Hmong girl at UHS who wore colored contact lenses, many girls reported that this practice was becoming increasingly popular within the community.

Some Hmong girls are also beginning to aspire to achieve the superthin body types promoted by mainstream beauty standards. At UHS, for example, a group of self-described Americanized Hmong girls discussed their desire to diet down to size zero clothes. In her study of Hmong adolescent girls, Yang (2001) discovered that girls felt pressured by their parents to be thin in order to be viewed as good marriage material. It should be noted that the valuing of thinness reflects a significant shift in beauty standards away from standards in Laos, where full-figured women were prized because of the associations between fecundity and roundness (Lynch, 1999). Although I was not aware of any Hmong girls at UHS who had eating disorders, anecdotal evidence suggests that may be a growing issue within Hmong American communities.

Conclusions

My research on Hmong American girls supports the growing body of research on the fluid and complex nature of gender within immigrant communities (Gibson, 1988; Hall, 2002; López, 2003; Sarroub, 2005; Smith-Hefner, 1999; Zhou & Bankston, 1998). As in other immigrant communities, the transformation of gender norms is not simply a straightforward linear process. Hmong girls and women have successfully struggled for greater gender equality within their communities, but they have also faced some resistance to change.

In the realm of education, Hmong girls and women have made significant gains in gender equality. Like other Asian immigrant communities, the Hmong American community believes that girls and women need to be educated in order to achieve economic security (Bankston, 1995; Louie, 2004). Similarly, Louie (2004) found that among Chinese immigrant parents "there was a material incentive for parents to encourage their daughters to pursue higher education, both in the payoff for the daughters and in the minimal investment on the part of parents, since higher education was more available to begin with" (p. 69). Through education, Hmong girls and women have gained access to increased economic independence and power within the Hmong American community. Many Hmong American organizations now have female representation. Hmong National Development, a national nonprofit that does educational and political advocacy work for the Hmong community, has had women involved since it was established in 1993 (http://www.hndlink.org).

As is the case in other immigrant communities, gender arrangements within families are being transformed and maintained (López, 2003; Louie, 2004). With regard to marriage, it appears that the Hmong American community is increasingly encouraging girls to complete high school before marriage. In terms of domestic responsibilities, however, it appears that girls and women continue to carry the burden. Thus, Hmong American girls who aspire to higher education must juggle both schoolwork and housework. As in other immigrant communities where family honor depends on female sexual purity, adults in the Hmong community have responded to the perceived dangers of American norms regarding sexuality by further restricting girls' activities (Sarroub, 2005; Smith-Hefner, 1999).

While much of the gender transformation has led to greater empowerment and gender equality for Hmong girls and women, not all change is progressive. The internalization of dominant beauty standards is one aspect of Americanization that leads to greater oppression of girls and women. Studies suggest that Asian American girls and women are increasingly vulnerable to dominant White beauty standards (Hall, 1995; Kaw, 1998).

By observing Hmong American adolescent girls' interpretations of and responses to American gender ideologies, my research offers an opportunity to critically examine mainstream American gender constructs from the perspective of immigrant girls and young women. My research suggests that the "Americanization" of gender norms and roles for Hmong American girls and women has led to complicated outcomes, ones that both empower and limit the lives of Hmong females.

REFERENCES

Bankston, C. (1995). Gender Roles and Scholastic Performance Among Adolescent Vietnamese Women: The Paradox of Ethnic Patriarchy. *Sociological Focus, 28,* 161–176.

Cohn, M. (1986). Hmong Youth and Hmong Culture in America. In G. Hendricks, B. Downing, & A. Deinard (Eds.), *The Hmong in Transition* (pp. 197–201). Staten Island, NY: Center for Migration Studies.

Donnelly, N. (1994). *Changing Lives of Refugee Hmong Women.* Seattle: University of Washington Press.

Faderman, L., & Xiong, G. (1998). *I Begin My Life All Over: The Hmong and the American Immigrant Experience.* Boston: Beacon Press.

Fass, S. (1991). *The Hmong in Wisconsin: On the Road to Self-Sufficiency.* Milwaukee: Wisconsin Policy Research Institute.

Gibson, M. (1988). *Accommodation Without Assimilation: Sikh Immigrants in an American High School.* Ithaca, NY: Cornell University Press.

Goldstein, B. (1985). *Schooling for Cultural Transitions: Hmong Girls and Boys in American High Schools.* Unpublished doctoral dissertation, University of Wisconsin–Madison.

Hall, C. (1995). Asian Eyes: Image and Eating Disorders of Asian and Asian American Women. *Eating Disorders: The Journal of Treatment and Prevention, 3,* 8–18.

Hall, K. (2002). *Lives in Translation: Sikh Youth as British Citizens.* Philadelphia: University of Pennsylvania Press.

Hmong National Development, Inc. http://www.hndlink.org.

Hmoob Teen. http://www.hmong.org/index.asp.

Kaw, Eugenia. (1998). Medicalization of Racial Features: Asian-American Women and Cosmetic Surgery. In R. Weitz (Ed.), *The Politics of Women's Bodies: Sexuality, Appearance, and Behavior* (pp. 167–183). New York: Oxford University Press.

Koltyk, J. (1998). *New Pioneers in the Heartland: Hmong Life in Wisconsin.* Boston: Allyn and Bacon.

Lee, S. J. (1997). The Road to College: Hmong American Women's Pursuit of Higher Education. *Harvard Educational Review, 67,* 803–827.

Lee, S. J. (2001a). More Than "Model Minorities" or "Delinquents": A Look at Hmong American High School Students. *Harvard Educational Review, 71,* 505–528.

Lee, S. J. (2001b). Transforming and Exploring the Landscape of Gender and Sexuality: Hmong American Teenaged Girls. *Race, Gender and Class, 8,* 35–46.

Lee, S. J. (2004). Hmong American Masculinities: Creating New Identities in the United States. In N. Way & J. Chu (Eds.), *Adolescent Boys: Exploring Diverse Cultures of Boyhood.* New York: NYU Press.

Lee, S. J., & Vaught, S. (2003). "You Can Never Be Too Rich or Too Thin": Popular and Consumer Culture and the Americanization of Asian American Girls and Young Women. *Journal of Negro Education, 72,* 457–466.

Lee, S. J. (2005). *Up Against Whiteness: Race, School and Immigrant Youth.* New York: Teachers College Press.

López, N. (2003). *Hopeful Girls, Troubled Boys: Race and Gender Disparity in Urban Education.* New York: Routledge.

Louie, V. (2004). *Compelled to Excel: Immigration, Education, and Opportunity among Chinese Americans.* Stanford, CA: Stanford University Press.

Lynch, A. (1999). *Dress, Gender and Cultural Change: Asian American and African American Rites of Passage.* New York: Berg.

Mother Charged for Daughter's Sex. (2005, September 28). *Sheboygan Press.* http://www.wisinfo.com/sheboyanpress/pring/print 22782782.shtml

Moua, M. A.(2002). (Ed). *Bamboo Among the Oaks: Contemporary Writing by Hmong Americans.* Minnesota: Minnesota Historical Society Press.

Ngo, B. (2002). Contesting "Culture": The Perspectives of Hmong American Female Students on Early Marriage. *Anthropology and Education Quarterly, 33,* 163–188.

Pobzeb, V. (2001). *2001 Hmong Population and Education in the United States and the World.* Eau Claire, WI: Lao Human Rights Council.

Sarroub, L. (2005). *All American Yemeni Girls: Being Muslim in a Public School.* Philadelphia: University of Pennsylvania Press.

Smith-Hefner, N. J. (1999). *Kmer American: Identity and Moral Education in a Diasporic Community.* Berkeley: University of California Press.

Vang, H. (2004). Hmong American Women's Educational Attainment: Implications for Hmong American Women and Men In Hmong National Development Inc. and Hmong Cultural and Resource Center (Eds.), *Hmong 2000 Census Publication: Data and Analysis* (pp. 23–25). Washington, DC: Hmong National Development.

Vang, K. (1982). Hmong Marriage Customs: A Current Assessment. In B. Downing & D. Olney (Eds.), *The Hmong in the West: Observations and Reports.* Papers of the 1981 Hmong Research Conference at the University of Minnesota. Southeast Asian Refugee Studies Project & Center for Urban and Regional Affairs. Minneapolis: University of Minnesota.

Vang, K. (2002). Twinkies. In M. Moua (Ed.), *Bamboo Among the Oaks: Contemporary Writing by Hmong Americans.* St. Paul: Minnesota Historical Society Press.

Walker-Moffat, W. (1995). *The Other Side of the Asian American Success Story.* San Francisco: Jossey Bass.

Xiong, A., Eliason, P., Detzner, D., & Cleveland, M. (2005). Southeast Asian Immigrants' Perceptions of Good Adolescents and Good Parents. *Journal of Psychology, 139,* 159–175.

Yang, N. (2001). *The Bicultural Competency of Hmong Adolescent Girls: Negotiating Gender Messages in the Home Context.* Master's thesis, University of Wisconsin–Madison.

Zhou, M., & Bankston, C. (1998). *Growing Up American: The Adaptation of Vietnamese Adolescents in the United States.* New York: Russell Sage Foundation.

Part IV

Resistance
Personal and Political

"Don't Die With Your Work Balled Up in Your Fists"

Contesting Social Injustice Through Participatory Research

María Elena Torre, Michelle Fine, Natasha Alexander, and Emily Genao

We open this chapter with the performers of the theater piece *Echoes of Brown: Youth Documenting and Performing the Legacy of* Brown v. Board of Education. Picture five strong young women taking center stage, speaking back to social injustice. In the following we have spliced together the individual poetry of Ariane Ashley Gilgeous, Iralma Osorio Sorondo, Annique Roberts, Emily Genao, and Tahani Salah to call forth in your imagination their performance of a chorus—a collective social conscious.

I think I missed something—
"The Policy of Separating . . ."
There was a policy?
A strategy to segregate?
Yeah, there was and now it has moved from policy to normalcy.
Subway tourist maps don't go further than 125th Street = I'M NOT HERE.
No you shut up!
You—the miseducator and misinformer
You—the history rewriter that tries to contain my generation to one-sided tongues
You shut up because I've shut up so long
my down is wide open
gaping for voices hungry for words unspoken

Whose genetics exactly are inferior?
Whose genetics exactly are missing a few crossbars on the double helix?
Whose genetics are you examining though your microscope?
Now it is time for OUR *revolution!*

Young women are a global spectacle. Scholars, activists, policy makers, and feminists—those on the Left and those on the Right—pin our anxieties on their sexualities, our stereotypes on their souls, and our hopes on their futures (Cahill, 2004). With the broad sweep of global capital and militarized, racialized patriarchy, young women are being represented and simultaneously groomed as consumers, soldiers, HIV carriers, potential victims, virgins, whores, sweatshop workers, drug lord mules, sex workers, mothers, students—transmitting culture, capital, values, virtue, and disease. They are, allegedly, the reason the United States invaded Afghanistan, the shock of Abu-Ghraib, the ones who must bear their de-scarved heads in France, and those who must seek permission to get abortions. Feminist, queer, and critical race theorists have eloquently argued the ways in which young women's bodies and minds have come to represent a field of contested, global struggles (Carney, 2001; Harris, 2004; Lesko, 2001; Walkerdine, Lucey, & Melody, 2001). Rearticulated, at once, as victims and perpetrators, consumers and commodity, survivors and seductresses, they occupy a focal point for global gaze and surveillance.

Concerned with the commodification/consumerization of young women, in this chapter we enter a space in which young women, like those quoted earlier, speak back to the surround sound of global injustice and begin to articulate their demands for justice. These young women are tired of the mass-produced patriotic platitudes about democracy and freedom, as their bodies are tossed on the heap of the socially disposable. Challenging hegemonic representations of nation, democracy, and justice, these young women ask for recognition, redistribution, responsibility, and revolution, as evidenced by Iralma Osorio Sorondo, a youth performer who wrote to her hyperassimilating Latino teacher, draped in a *bandera Americana,* "Take that red, white and blue off and LOOK AT ME."

This chapter integrates fragments of spoken word pieces by young women crafted in a collective of young urban and suburban women, and some men, gathered by the Social Justice and the Arts Institute to pool their critical, situated knowledge about unjust distributions of resources, opportunities, and respect. Together, those in the institute created *Echoes,* a youth-based theater piece of research and resistance in which history, social inquiry, dance, and spoken word were performed by youth and elders for the anniversary of the *Brown v. Board of Education* decision. *Echoes* became what Fraser (1990) would call a "counter public space," where we assembled our distinct and collective "experiences" and social analyses, organized around our differences, and launched a common pro ject of producing research and performance on the persistence of social injustice in the lives of America's youth.

Refusing the fantasy that we live in a nation of justice as well as the alternative argument that we are equally affected by unjust social arrangements, we embraced instead a nuanced understanding of the differential consequences of structural injustice. Positioning ourselves, nevertheless, as collectively responsible to contest and to act against what Antonio Gramsci described as the "passive revolution" whereby "the interests of the dominant class are articulated with the needs, desires, and interests of subordinated groups," we set out to study patterns of naturalized, cumulative educational injustice and to disrupt taken-for-granted patterns of inequity, long justified and made to seem inevitable (Mouffe, 1979, p. 192).

From the larger *Echoes* collective, four of us—Natasha and Emily, María and Michelle—decided to write together for *Urban Girls.*[1] We write across, through, and, at times, from within our differences: two youth performers, two social psychologists, all researchers committed to social change. This chapter was produced with the same commitments that steadied our counter public space: commitments to a justice of redistribution and recognition (Fraser, 1990), an interrogation of difference and collectivity (Torre, 2005), and a developmental aim of moving from a "safe space" for critical work (Evans & Boyte, 1992; Pastor, McCormick, & Fine, 1996) toward a series of public and performative demands for action. As you read, you will note that we move between "we" and a rotating "I"—a reflection of our critical praxis of interrogating power and difference in our work—as we analyze interview and written data from the young women who participated in *Echoes,* as well as each of our experiences of the work. The "I" sections are named and italicized so our individual thoughts can be distinguished from our otherwise collective writing.

While the *Echoes* group as a whole included two young men, we focus here exclusively on the writings, performance, and experiences of the young women who made up the other eleven members of the collective. In a volume dedicated to the lives of urban girls, it is fair to ask how we understand young women's work when it is produced in a collective with young men. Our response is that this is precisely what we find interesting. The collective project of *Echoes* was organized around better understanding historic and present-day struggles for educational justice and civil rights. Our initial focus was on the persistence of segregation in allegedly desegregated schools. Yet the young women in the group consistently raised feminist critiques of science, the body, gendered violence, self-reflexivity, the politics of representation, and social responsibility.

That we write about the work of the young women from within this explicitly integrated group is a practical reflection of both the theory and the method of the *Echoes* project: first, our belief in the simultaneous need for segregated spaces while we work to sustain integrated ones, and, second, our belief in the potential of participatory democracy, a project that brings together all of us, in and *for* our differences. Our differences inspire us to produce, create, argue, and dream, informing our civic contribution to a resuscitated public sphere. Too often, in the case of young women, the paths to citizenship are paved with consumerism and exploitation (Harris, 2004). What we found exciting about the young women of *Echoes* is their passion to contest these trends and their deepening expectation and insistence—as researchers, writers, and performers—that their ideas, opinions, and actions be not only recognized within the public dialogue but incorporated and even built upon. In this chapter we take up the feminist and critical race consciousness of these young urban women and agitate for counter public spaces in which young women can grow, develop, and stretch their critical consciousness toward participatory research and action.

We refer readers interested in the theory, design, and practice of our participatory research project to some of our writings on method (Fine et al., 2005; Torre & Fine, 2003; Torre, 2005). For those interested in the full text of youth and elder spoken word, we invite you to browse our book and watch the DVD of *Echoes* (Fine et al., 2004). We urge those eager to hear the nature of young women's social critique, the power and strength of individually and collectively contesting social injustice, as well as the electricity of bringing together very differently situated young women and men to interrogate the shared effects of oppression and our collective responsibilities to act to read on.

Building Spaces for Counterwork

In creating the *Echoes* space, we worked from our understandings about power, privilege, oppression, participatory action research, and responsibility. Fed by the writings of Linda Thuwai Smith (1999), Nancy Fraser (1990), Amatrya Sen (2004), bell hooks (1984), and others, we sought to create a context in which high school and college students would come together, importing distinct situated knowledges, within very differently marked bodies, carrying heavy and light biographies of privilege, oppression, and racial injustice in schools. We took seriously the writings of Nancy Fraser (1990), trying to build a counter public space that "contested the exclusionary norms of the bourgeois public, elaborating alternative styles of political behavior and alternative norms of public speech" (p. 75). In this space we hoped that common concerns of contemporary youth could be elaborated alongside the vibrant, idiosyncratic stories of a few or even one, which, we would learn, represented so many others not in the room. We began, too, with an awareness that before we even entered the room, power dynamics were in play, which needed to be gracefully deconstructed if we were going to collaborate with trust across zip codes, ethnic backgrounds, communities, and generations.

Natasha: To be really honest with you I remember that after the first day at *Echoes*, my mother warned me about what to expect. She said "Natasha, I want you to just be aware that sometimes when White folks are working with you, they're caught up in a White man's burden kind of thing. They're wrapped in guilt and just want to do good for Black and Latino students, like make things right in school. Sometimes you might run across this." So I kind of had this in mind when we started. But then it changed. I saw that people here weren't really like that.

María: How did you know?

Natasha: It's hard to say. The kinds of conversations we had. The way you talked about high and low power groups, and how we weren't just talking about race. And then when we were talking about some groups wanting schools for just one kind of people, how Michelle said that although she really believes in integration, some of us in the room might feel strongly about the need for separate spaces. And that she'd be willing to work for low power groups to have spaces of their own—like a school for African American students, or all girls—but that she wouldn't do it for a high power group. That they wouldn't really need her help.

Michelle and María, with other institute facilitators, recognized that it was our work and responsibility to carve out a context not naively vacated by power issues but strategically infused by them. These spaces could not be "remedial" or supplementary, simply giving voice to those who have been oppressed. Nor could we simply encourage those with privilege to express guilt and responsibility and redeem themselves. Instead, we created a common project for analyzing the patterns of social injustice, generated with youth, sculpted from social history, participatory research, and the personal experiences of the young people present.

Interior Design: Creating the Counter Public Space

To understand the source of these young women's words and this *Echoes* space, we reach back in time. In the fall of 2001, a group of suburban school superintendents of desegregated districts gathered to discuss the disaggregated achievement gap provided by the states of New Jersey and New York. As is true nationally, in these desegregated districts, the test score gaps between Asian American, White American, African American, and Latino students were disturbing. Eager to understand the roots of and remedies for the gap, Superintendent Sherry King of Mamaroneck, New York, invited Michelle and colleagues from the Graduate Center of the City University of New York to join the research team. We agreed to create a multiyear participatory action research project with a broad range of students from suburban and urban schools.

Over the course of 2 years of participatory youth research, more than 100 students from urban and suburban high schools in New York and New Jersey joined researchers from the Graduate Center to study "youth perspectives on racial and class based (in)justice in schools and the nation." We worked in the schools long enough to help identify a core of youth drawn from all corners to serve as youth researchers—from special education, English-language learners, the Gay/Straight Alliances, discipline rooms, student councils, and Advanced Placement classes. We designed a multigenerational, multidistrict, urban-suburban database of contemporary educational opportunities and inequities analyzed through the lens of race, ethnicity, gender, (dis)ability, sexuality, and class (see Fine et al., 2005).

Students participated in a series of research camps, each held for 2 days at a time in community and/or university settings. Deconstructing who can do research, what constitutes research, and who benefits, the students were immersed in methods training and social justice theory. They read works by Patricia Hill Collins (1991), bell hooks (1984), Sandra Harding (1993), and others and learned about feminist and critical race theory, epistemology, ethics, and methodology. The students practiced conducting interviews, focus groups, and participant observations, designing surveys, and undertaking archival analyses.

At the first research camp we designed a survey to assess high school students' views of race and class (in)justice in schools and the nation. The youth researchers were given the "wrong draft" of the survey, and they dedicated the weekend to its revision, inserting cartoons, open-ended questions such as "What's the most powerful thing a teacher said to you?" and sensitive Likert scale items such as "Sometimes I think I'll never make it" or "I would like to be in advanced classes, but I don't think I'm smart enough." Over the next few months, we translated the survey into Spanish, French-Creole, and Braille and distributed it to 9th and 12th graders in 13 urban and suburban districts. At the second and third camp, another group of youth researchers from the same schools (with some overlap) analyzed the qualitative and quantitative data from 9,174 surveys, 24 focus groups, and 32 individual interviews with youth. Between the camps, teams of youth and adult researchers fed back their school-specific data to varied groups of faculty, students, and community members in the New York metropolitan area. Teams of youth researchers visited each other's schools, across four urban and suburban schools, to document the racialized impact of finance inequity and tracking on the structures, opportunities, social relations, and outcomes of public education. They presented their research findings to national conferences of educators, youth activists, community organizers, and racial justice advocates.[2]

Building on the central tenets of Participatory Action Research (PAR), the camps were organized around the following set of democratic beliefs:

each participant was understood to be a carrier of knowledge and history,

everyone held a sincere commitment to creating change for educational justice,

issues of power and difference were explicitly addressed and explored,

disagreements and disjunctures were excavated rather than smoothed
over,

individuals and the group were understood to be "under construction"
(i.e., opinions, ideas, and beliefs were expected to change and grow),
and

everyone was committed to a common goal of understanding,
researching, and presenting to varied audiences the history and contemporary politics of racial and class injustice in public education. ·

Most students received high school credit (when a course on participatory
research was offered in their schools), and 42 received college credit for
their research work.

In the summer of 2003, with the anniversary of the 1954 *Brown v. Board
of Education* decision approaching, we decided to launch into performance as public scholarship, and extend our Social Justice and Social
Research Camps into a Social Justice and the Arts Institute. We brought
together a diverse group of young people aged 13 to 21, with community
elders, social scientists, spoken word artists, dancers, choreographers, and
a video crew to collectively review data from the Educational Opportunity
Gap Project (Fine et al., 2005); to learn about the legal, social, and political
history of segregation and integration of public schools; and to create
Echoes, a performance of poetry and movement based on social justice
research—our contribution to the commemoratory conversation of the
50th anniversary of *Brown v. Board of Education of Topeka, Kansas,* the historic U.S. Supreme Court decision that declared segregation in public
schools unconstitutional.

The 13 youth researchers/performers were drawn from wealthy and economically depressed communities in New York City and the surrounding
suburbs, including those in northern New Jersey, representing the kind of
wisdom born in Advanced Placement classes and the kind born in special
education classrooms. We came together as Christians, Jews, Muslims, and
those without religious affiliation; with European, African, Caribbean,
Palestinian, Latino, and blended ancestries; some headed for the Ivy
League and others having spent time in juvenile facilities; some enjoying
two homes, and others having spent nights without one. We recruited a
group of youth interested (but not necessarily experienced) in writing,
performing, and/or social justice, intentionally diverse—by gender, race,
ethnicity, class, sexuality, (dis)ability, track/school level; by experiences
with racism, sexism, homophobia, school administrators, social service

agencies, "the law"; by (dis)comfort with their bodies, dance, poetry, groups. In doing so, we consciously crafted a radically inclusive research site that would function as a "contact zone," a messy social space where very differently situated people could work together across their own varying relationships to power and privilege (Pratt, 1992). To boost our collective knowledge we invited historians, community activists, lawyers, and writers[3] to speak with us over the course of the week about the history of race and class struggles in public education, the history of civil rights and the *Brown* decision, the fight for educational justice for students with disabilities, second language learners, and youth who are lesbian, gay, bisexual, or transgender. Emily tells us:

> Participating in something like *Echoes* and the Arts and Social Justice Institute was the first time where I had to work as closely and as intensely as I did with people who were so different from me. The project brought youth from very different racial, economic, academic, and social backgrounds into one space to be creative and to most importantly just be themselves. The comfort and safety that was established in the very beginning was instrumental in allowing for the work to get done and for the performance to be shaped and constructed.

Bearing Witness

Within the space of *Echoes,* all participants were recognized as holders of expert knowledge crucial to the collective project; in other words, expertise was distributed across youth and adults, as were needs, strengths, and responsibilities. Both theoretically and practically, we attempted to shift, in the language of Vijayandra Rao and Michael Walton (2004), from "equality of opportunity" to "equality of agency" and to strengthen what Arjun Appadurai (2004) has called the "capacity to aspire," which is inequitably distributed in the broader culture. Seasoned with a spirit of transgression, we worked to cultivate voices (and also the skills of listening), both individually and collectively, among those long oppressed and those long privileged, to help build "the sinews of aspiration as a cultural capacity" (Appadurai, 2004, p. 83) and the enactment of responsibility as a collective project. By weaving a stream of collective participation and engagement with issues typically represented as the problems of "poor people" or "people of color," we came to see these problems as historic and structural, and solutions as our collective responsibility.

"The imperative to tell—the vital urge not to forget—is driven by the imperative to transmit . . . to the 'awakening of others'" (Apfelbaum, 2001, p. 30). Inspired by the writings on counterstories by Erika Apfelbaum (2001), Sarah Carney (2001), and Anita Harris (2001), we encouraged the students to see patterns of historic inequity and to bear witness to the thick institutional, interpersonal, and embodied webs of injustice, ideologically normalized. In the spirit of bearing witness, Natasha chose to write a piece on the school-to-prison pipeline infiltrating poor African American neighborhoods. As Natasha explained:

> Writing "Rap Star" was a very interesting experience for me. My inspiration for the poem came from seeing a kid get arrested. This cop grabbed this African American kid saying to him "get in the car rap star." It hit me like a ton of bricks. Hearing the cop say that to this kid, made me think, damn is that all he really is to you—just a "rap star"? And then I thought to myself, you know what, that's probably what that kid thinks about himself too. So I wrote about it. Unfortunately it was not ready for the first performance of "Echoes" but after I received constructive criticism from the group and reworked it in the writing workshops, it made it into the final performance. I have been really surprised how it seems to hit home with very different audiences.

In her poem "Rap Star," Natasha Alexander writes:

> Simply being gifted
> Was your limitation
> Not encouraged to be a doctor or teacher
> Made to believe that
> Your only true place of success
> Is in being some sort of entertainer or athlete
> Talk in the staff meeting
> Not about your B+ paper
> But about how many yards you can throw a football
> Or your three point shot
> Or your beautiful tenor voice
> You're behind bars now
> Upon you those teachers look down

Because they say they put all their time into you
Your path is what you choose, right?
I guess they were never taught that teachers have a high calling
Oh Rap Star, the basement is just cold
No stage lights, hoes and cars
No buying rounds of drinks at bars
Just the silent memories of young men in this cell before you
Echo from window to door
You can feel it from ceiling to floor
You're dead to the core
You felt this before
About to be shipped off
Too far from the freedom
You were once used to
The liberty God gave you
The only real privilege you were born into
Gone, gone with the bang of a gavel
In a court room
Where Justice, who can't see
Points arms outstretched to sentence you
To life, to real life, to the rest of your life
To the life of so many other young men like you
Who share this same fate too.

People have had very strong reactions to my poem—they have told me it's "so beautiful," " so moving," "so powerful," which makes me wonder, how can we take this power and emotion and turn it into action? It's true that words are powerful, but they are not enough. My poem is really nothing in comparison to what needs to happen. After a recent performance, a reporter from a newspaper in Manila asked me to send him a copy of "Rap Star" because he thought the issues were relevant to young men in the Philippines—which made me think about young men of color all over the world and about the similarities of their experiences, the injustices they face . . . similar even to some ethnic White kids in the U.S., like some of the Bosnians and Albanians who go to my school. I just can't stop thinking that all this came from a poem that I wrote. Imagine what could come of a coalition of young people—not like the WMCA—but something like *Echoes*, something that gives us the space, resources and partners to build and realize our dreams—to fight for a better more equal world where being a rap star is just one of many careers, where visions of our future are more than entertainment and sports. I want to be an attorney, but I don't want to have to wait 'til I'm older to start fixing this mess we are in. I've already been to Albany, I have things to offer right now!

Writing from within the passionate concern of the bystander, Natasha uses her poem to draw attention to the relationship between the limited expectations placed on the lives of young African American men and the expanding prison industrial complex that appears to be anxiously awaiting the chance to poach these very same young men. As if echoing Apfelbaum, the French theorist of oppression and voice, Natasha epitomized our collective desire to bear witness, daring the audience to do the same.

Interrupting the Passive Revolution: Challenging the Science of Domination

The category of "passive revolution" is often used by Gramsci to qualify the most usual form of hegemony of the bourgeoisie involving a model of articulation whose aim is to neutralize the other social forces . . . enlarging the state whereby the interests of the dominant class are articulated with the needs, desires, interests of subordinated groups. . . . the objective of ideological struggle is not to reject the system and all its elements but to rearticulate it, to break it down to its basic elements and then to sift through past conceptions to see which ones, with some changes of content, can serve to express the new situation. (Mouffe, 1979, p. 192)

In the camps and at the Social Justice and the Arts Institute, young people were strategically engaged in the critical analysis of prevailing inequities and their ideological legitimacy. This work of analysis facilitated the production of their spoken word pieces and performances, what Chantal Mouffe and Antonio Gramsci (Mouffe, 1979) might call their "re-articulations" of social arrangements. We understood that in order to create a context in which young people could disarticulate prevailing ideologies, we needed radically distinct situated bodies in the same room, and that the youth would need tools for critically denaturalizing the science of social hierarchy and domination.

In one of the early research camps, Emily reviewed hundreds of qualitative responses to the question, "What do you believe are the causes of the achievement gap?" She discovered that many students responded with a powerful refrain of "Blacks are genetically inferior" or something similar. Pained and angered by the revelation that her peers really believed in genetic inferiority, she decided to write a poem that would challenge the science of genetic inferiority, the widely shared belief in a hierarchy of social categories, and the assumed homogeneity of each category. Speaking directly to the youth who filled out the survey, with words that transcend to others who never question their privilege, she wrote and performed her poem, titled "Focus/Refocus":

> You said some people are genetically less intelligent
> Whose genetics exactly are inferior?
> Whose genetics exactly are missing a few crossbars on the double helix?
> Whose genetics are you examining though your microscope?
> You don't need to specify
> Since it is misconceived that those people are usually the ones with the sun kissed skin
> The doorman who suffers through the 2-hour train ride from Queens
> The cleaning lady trying to hold down 2 jobs and a newborn at home
> The kid who plays his Slipknot CD too loud
> You wouldn't sit next to him anyway
> When you slide my culture under your power magnification you see me:
> A first generation college student
> Actress who will transcend the role of rape victim, maid, gossiping neighbor
> Poet whose grass roots are growing back in again
> Dancer with salsa in her hips and azucar in her blood
> Dreamer of Puerto Rican sunsets, Manhattan darkness, with a ocar on her Lower East Side
> Only it isn't your microscope
> It was passed on to you from your ancestral scientists
> Now it's your turn
> To look at everyone through the
> Antiquated lens

Only you don't turn it on yourself
Because you didn't inherit inferior DNA

Emily's richly layered poem simultaneously reiterates a series of feminist and antiracist challenges to science à la Sandra Harding (1993), Patricia Hill Collins (1991), and Gloria Anzaldúa (1987). She introduces the complexities of her multiple identities, linguistically and metaphorically braiding her Latina self into the text. Trumping the scientific microscope and the audience's gaze, she lifts the critical lens off of her body and her community and places it back onto elites. She uses her poem to insist that others think about privilege, responsibility, and science. In her abbreviated biography of growing up, she speaks through a discordant tongue about the privilege of her family and the structural deprivation of her public school education, jointly producing a sharp-edged blend of academic confidence and doubt. Emily explains:

Being a woman of color (although when you really think about it, all women are women of "color") there's already this sense of having to struggle that's built into the psyche virtually since birth. . . . There's this constant uphill battle that needs to be fought against stereotypes, prejudices and the faithlessness in our abilities. And some of those battles are definitely harder fought than others. In comparison to other stories I've heard, I was (and still am) pretty well off. Going to college was indeed possible for me but sometimes the decks are so stacked against us, the mere possibility seems to be well beyond our reach.

I never had to take care of younger siblings, because I am the youngest of two. And living in a home where both my parents worked decent-paying full-time jobs, money was not a negative issue. I went to school, helped out around the house, and did my homework. Mom was always around to cook dinner for us, and talk to me about how I was doing in school. Dad was always around if I ever needed things for school, and if I ever needed anything in general. They tried to lighten my burden as much as they could, because they wanted me to do well. They knew if I did well in junior high and high school that it could lead to bigger and better things. Which it did, since I'm now in my second year at Fordham University.

Now I did say that I didn't feel the overwhelming sense of doubt or constant fear of the future, but that doesn't mean that it never manifested in one form or another. As high school graduation neared in the spring and summer of 2003 the nervousness and anxiety reached an all-time high. I had already been part of the school finance equity research for a while, talking to different people and visiting different high schools. I was well aware of the discrepancies in funding for schools in the city and the true magnitude of the effect of those discrepancies. "AP," "honors classes," "Regents diploma" and the other jargon of well-funded high schools were not even remotely part of my vocabulary. The self-doubt crept in—I had to compete with these people in order to get into a good college? All my life I was told that I was one of the best. But now, I felt that even at my best I still wouldn't be good enough. Not when everyone else was packing more academic heat than I was.

Within the institute, an environment was created where adults and youth could reflect on our multiple identities and their varying relationships to privilege, injustice, and each other. As we read histories of oppression and resistance, reviewed our collective research, and scribbled the beginnings of our poetry, we dove deep within our multiple selves, reviewing each of our bodies as we hold and perform our many different identities, which are powerful in some spaces and less so in others. Throughout the week, we were able to call on different aspects of our identities to better understand the material, to move away from experiences that were too uncomfortable, or to make connections across seemingly different positions. While our collective work focused on questions of race, ethnicity, and class inside and beyond schools, the young women inserted questions of gendered violence, (dis)ability, language, bodies, science, danger and pleasure, oppression and privilege, the work of critical race and feminist analysis.

Interrogating Privilege

We elected to create a counter public space of young people that was neither simply a safe space for demographically similar peers to challenge offensive representations nor a precious, protected corner to critique stereotypes and the micro-aggressions of everyday life. While we have great respect for the need and life of such safe spaces, those in which historically oppressed groups gather to be free, safe, and challenging of dominant policies and practices (Weis & Fine, 2000), that was not our project this time. Instead, our goal was to bring very diverse young people into a space, filled with dynamics of privilege and power, and take up just those questions in our search for a project of collective struggle.

In contrast, then, to Michelle and others' chapter in the original volume of *Urban Girls* (Fine, Pastor, & McCormick, this volume), in the camps and at the institute, we created counter public spaces that depart in two specific ways. First, we built a community of difference by, in part, including privileged peers (Fine, Weis, & Powell, 1997). Second we sought to create a sacred space that would then launch us toward a more public theater of resistance for contesting structural injustices. A number of the youth performers, particularly White students from the suburbs, used the *Echoes* space to work through their own questions about privilege, in desegregated schools where they benefit enormously, if ambivalently (Burns, 2004), from the well-known (and equally well-silenced) racialized stratifications in their schools.

During the institute, Elinor Marboe, a White youth performer, wrote with wonder and rage about the racialized practices newly visible to her within her desegregated suburban high school in her poem "One Hand Clapping":

> Self-segregation in my public high school
> Different colored threads, on separate rolled spools.
> Is this a topic on which I can speak?
> Because my skin isn't brown
> versus Board.
> The Hispanic kids who sit in the Post Cafeteria—do I sit with them?
> Well, no.
> We get along. We get along well. One hand.
> One hand of the solution.
> But few kids have friends of other races.
> Where is that other hand?
> There was one black girl in my AP American history class.
> One day we read a poem comparing Booker T. to W.E.B.
> And we all stared at Alana
> waiting for her response.
> Then we realized we were staring,
> and slowly turned our heads, real casual,
> like nothing had happened.
> But it had.

> Kids are taught at my school that communities are divided by race
> This is the norm. This is acceptable.
> This blister of a problem, turning purply red and filling with fluid as
> we speak:
> My education, my school is shaped like a barbell,
> And I'm only at one end.

In the beginning of the week, Elinor was asking herself and others about whether or not silence is problematic. By Thursday she was clear that *not* speaking up against racially inequitable settings could not be justified as neutrality. In her performance, after speaking the words "slowly [we] turned our heads, real casual, like nothing had happened," she followed with a long pause, turned her head, and then, looking directly at the audience, said, "But it had." Elinor narrated, for White students and the audience, the damage wrought by refusing to speak out and turning away.

Kendra Urdang, another youth performer who is White and South African/Canadian, wrote and performed "Go Blue!"—a searing critique of the hypocrisy of her presumably desegregated suburban high school:

> And in the classrooms, the imbalance is subtle,
> undercurrents in hallways.
> AP classes on the top floor, special ed. in the basement.
> And although over half the faces in the yearbook
> are darker than mine,
> on the third floor, everyone looks like me.
> So it seems glass ceilings are often concrete.
> Although brown faces fill the hallways,
> our Principal doesn't know their names,
> they are just the free ticket to funding—
> And this is not their school.

In our work together, bodies and standpoints rooted in privilege sat side by side with bodies and standpoints rooted in historic oppression. Both brought into this space a set of perspectives that would be voiced, reworked, and blended, gently, deliberately, and intimately. As in a jazz performance, our struggle for justice brought our differences, discordances, and rough edges center stage. With no one person standing as the sole embodiment of either privilege or oppression, together we disarticulated the embodied workings, perversions, benefits, and assaults of social inequality. And only together could we rearticulate a vision of what a just world could be.

Counter Public Spaces for Contesting Social Injustice: Weapons of Mass Instruction, or the Sweet Energy of Collective Responsibility

> I remember at one point that everyone was really quiet and everyone was really thinking. I thought it was so cool to sit and hear the scratching of other pens and pencils besides my own. I thought that my pen was the only one moving to the rhythm of social justice. But now it's defiantly apparent that other pens and pencils are listening to the same beat. (Emily)

In this social historical moment, it is most discouraging to note that issues central to young people, particularly those articulated by the young women of *Echoes*—work, gendered violence, higher education, reproductive rights, racism, the prison industrial complex, apartheid schooling— reside in the margins (if at all) of most elected officials' political agendas. And yet we are reassured and energized by the knowledge that in spaces throughout the nation, in college campuses, suburban schools, jail cells, urban schools, and on the streets, young people are organizing. In the face of massive policy injustice, youth and adults are no longer simply passive or compliant. Working with activists, scholars, foundations, community-based organizations and progressive educators, youth are crafting participatory research projects and organizing projects that critically investigate the social policies that construct and constrict their lives, interrogating policies that ravage their communities and threaten their imaginations (Torre & Fine, 2005; Cahill, 2004; Kwon, 2004; Morrell, 2004). Across the country, in vibrant collectives dotting urban, suburban, and rural communities, we find youth researchers, both privileged and historically marginalized, bearing witness to the sacrifice and demanding radical reform.

Like wildfire, activist youth participation is captivating and life altering. It draws in young women and men who aspire to create a more just world, and it permanently changes the landscapes of their lives. Unequal systems and practices are no longer thought natural and unmovable. New growth is evidenced in rearticulations, critique, and action. Youth are "no longer able to see flat," to borrow the description of youth researcher Kouri

Martínez on the effect participatory action research had on her political standpoint. Engagement in democratic activist spaces nourishes critical worldviews and provokes a stance that not only asks questions but also assumes the right to participate in discovery and implementation.

Through our research with, and as, the young women of *Echoes,* we have come to understand this work, expanding spaces for critical engagement, intellectual exploration, creativity, and wonder, to be essential in our current political moment, one where preparing for high-stakes tests precludes curiosity and wonder, where library searches have become evidence of suspicion, and where social critique has become treason. Critical participatory research, launched in schools, communities, or prisons, around kitchen tables or in Girl Scout troops, provides a vital way of maintaining and resuscitating democracy, sustaining feminist and antiracist hope and possibility across generations.

The time is now. To be sure, the young women of *Echoes* have already entered into the debate. They are contesting, opposing, and redirecting visions for social and civic life—in essence, they have shown us what democracy looks like. And they insist, as Yasmine Blanding writes in her poem, "A Call to Action," to those "who have a chair in the meetings that are supposed to make a difference," that adults must join in the call to action:

> You must speak up for your words are arrested
> You must speak up for your words are congested
> You cannot afford to stop here!
> You are not given anymore than you can bear . . .
> Ah, if I could just share with you how much my generation has in store.
> I'm not talking about pushing others to the floor—
> . . . We have work to do, I encourage you to not die with your work balled up in your fist.
> Time is of Essence.

Discussion Questions

Reflecting on the experiences and analysis of the young women in the *Echoes* project, what ethical and methodological considerations might you make if you were to design an activist research project in your community?

1. What issues might young women in your community want to study?
2. What materials might you make available to deepen the historic and structural understandings of these issues?
3. How can differences among co-researchers facilitate learning? What needs to be in place in order for these differences to flourish, rather than being silenced or co-opted?
4. What would have to be in place if this were a coed group, and you wanted to keep issues of gender, race, ethnicity, and sexual power actively engaged?
5. Are some issues too provocative for schools to investigate? If so, how can young people interrogate the very issues that affect their lives so intimately?
6. How can community-based organizations work with schools and youth organizations to create activist projects?

NOTES

1. The authors wish to express their gratitude, admiration and respect to all the members and participants (in the widest sense) of the *Echoes* project. This chapter would not have been possible without our collective thoughts, outrage, work, sweat, tears and . . . hope.

2. Youth researchers took up (and published) research studies of finance inequity, tracking, community based organizing for quality education and the unprecedented success of the small schools movement. See http://www.thebrooklynrail.org/poetry/fa1102/moneyfornothing.html; http://www.rethinkingschools.org/archive/18_01/ineq181.shtml.

3. Guest educators included Robert Perry, Director of African American Studies, Saint Peter's College; James Campbell, Associate Professor of American Civilization, Africana Studies and History, Brown University; Tiffany Joseph, Brown University; Carol Tracy, Executive Director, Women's Law Project; Clare Tracy-Stickney, Assistant Principal, University City High School in Philadelphia; Lisette Nieves, Co-Founder, ATREVETE!; Marinieves Alba, Hip Hop LEADS Latino Youth Inc.; and Patricia J. Williams, James L. Dhor Professor of Law, Columbia Law School

REFERENCES

Anzaldúa, G. (1987). *Borderlands/La frontera: The new meztiza.* San Francisco: Aunt Lute Press.

Apfelbaum, E. (2001). The dread: An essay on communication across cultural boundaries. *International Journal of Critical Psychology, 4,* 19–34.

Appadurai, A. (2004). The capacity to aspire: Culture and the terms of recognition. In V. Rao & M. Walton (Eds.), *Culture and public action* (pp. 59–84). Stanford, CA: Stanford University Press.

Burns, A. (2004). The racing of capability and culpability in desegregated schools: Discourses of merit and responsibility. In M. Fine, L. Weis, L. Pruitt, & A. Burns (Eds.), *Off White. Readings in race, power and privilege* (pp. 373–394). New York: Routledge.

Cahill, C. (2004). Defying gravity? Raising consciousness through collective research. *Children's Geographies, 2,* 273–786.

Carney, S. (2001). Analyzing master narratives and counter-stories in legal settings: Cases of maternal failure to protect. *International Journal of Critical Psychology, 4,* 61–76.

Collins, P. H. (1991). *Black feminist thought: Knowledge, consciousness, and the politics of empowerment.* New York: Routledge.

Evans, S. M., & Boyte, H. C. (1992). *Free spaces: The sources of democratic change in America.* Chicago: University of Chicago Press.

Fine, M., Bloom, J., Burns, A., Chajet, L., Guishard, M., Payne, Y. A., et al. (2005). Dear Zora: A letter to Zora Neal Hurston fifty years after *Brown. Teachers College Record, 107,* 496–529.

Fine, M., Roberts, R. A., & Torre, M. E., with Bloom, J., Burns, A., Chajet, L., Guishard, M., & Payne, Y. A. (2004). *Echoes of Brown: Youth documenting and performing the legacy of* Brown v. Board of Education. New York: Teachers College Press.

Fine, M., Weis, L., & Powell, L. (1997). Communities of difference: A critical look at desegregated spaces created for and by youth. *Harvard Educational Review, 67,* 247–284.

Fraser, N. (1990). Rethinking the public sphere: A contribution to the critique of actually existing democracy. *Social Text, 25/26,* 56 80.

Harding, S. (1993). Rethinking standpoint epistemology: What is "strong objectivity"? In L. Alcoff & E. Potter (Eds.), *Feminist epistemologies* (pp. 49–82). New York: Routledge.

Harris, A. (2001). Dodging and weaving: Young women countering the stories of youth citizenship. *International Journal of Critical Psychology, 4,* 183–199.

Harris, A. (2004). *Future girl: Young women in the 21st century.* New York: Routledge.

hooks, b. (1984). *Feminist theory from margin to center.* Boston: South End Press.

Kwon, S. A. (2004, October). *Youth of color movement for juvenile justice.* Paper presented at the Youth, Communities, and Social Justice: Toward a National Strategy for Youth Development Conference, New York, New York.

Lesko, N. (2001). *Act your age: A cultural construction of adolescence.* New York: Taylor and Francis.

Morrell, E. (2004, October). *Youth-initiated research as a tool for advocacy and change in urban schools.* Paper presented at the Youth, Communities, and Social Justice: Toward a National Strategy for Youth Development Conference, New York, New York.

Mouffe, C. (1979). Hegemony and ideology in Gramsci. In C. Mouffe (Ed.), *Gramsci and Marxist theory* (p. 192). London: Routledge.

Pastor, J., McCormick, J., & Fine, M. (1996). Makin' homes: An urban girl thing. In B. Leadbeater & N. Way (Eds.), *Urban girls: Resisting stereotypes, creating identities* (pp. 15–34). New York: New York University Press.

Pratt, M. L. (1992). *Imperial eyes: Travel writing and transculturation.* New York: Routledge.

Rao, V., & Walton, M. (2004). *Culture and public action.* Stanford, CA: Stanford University Press.

Sen, A. (2004). How does culture matter? In V. Rao & M. Walton (Eds.), *Culture and public action* (pp. 37–58). Stanford, CA: Stanford University Press.

Smith, L. T. (1999). *Decolonizing methodologies: Research and indigenous peoples.* London: Zed Books.

Torre, M. E. (2005). The alchemy of integrated spaces: Youth participation in research collectives of difference. In L. Weis & M. Fine (Eds.), *Beyond silenced voices* (pp. 251–266). Albany: State University of New York Press.

Torre, M. E., & Fine, M. (2003). Youth researchers critically reframe questions of educational justice. *Evaluation Exchange, 9*(2), 6, 22.

Torre, M. E., & Fine, M. (2005). Participatory action research by youth: A national movement of research for action. In L. Sherrod, C. Flanagan, & R. Kassimir (Eds.), *Encyclopedia of youth activism* (pp. 456–462). Westport, CT: Greenwood.

Walkerdine, V., Lucey, H., & Melody, J. (2001). *Growing up girl.* Houndmills, England: Palgrave.

Weis, L., & Fine, M. (2000). *Construction sites: Spaces for urban youth to reimagine race, class, gender and sexuality.* New York: Teachers College Press.

Uncovering Truths, Recovering Lives
Lessons of Resistance in the Socialization of Black Girls

Janie Victoria Ward

For more than 10 years I have collected stories from parents of Black daughters and sons. Taken together, these stories provide a rich mosaic of ingenious resistance strategies that Black folks infuse into their daily routines of child rearing.

In 2000, I published *The Skin We're In: Teaching Our Children to Be Emotionally Strong, Socially Smart and Spiritually Connected,* based on research from a core set of qualitative interviews conducted in four cities in the United States. In this data set, which took place in the early and mid-1990s, about 70 African American parents of Black adolescents (though not necessarily in the same families) were individually interviewed in Boston, Massachusetts; Philadelphia, Pennsylvania; Raleigh, North Carolina; and Albuquerque, New Mexico. They were recruited through a number of formal and informal means, including recruitment letters sent to local Black churches, after-school programs, professional organizations (i.e., Jack and Jill, Black Women's Service Clubs), and word of mouth. The primary focus of the interviews centered on the questions, "Do you speak to your Black daughters/sons (or do your parents speak to you) about racial matters and why?" I asked parents (and adolescents) to talk about why and how these conversations take place in their families, and what was learned in these discussions. Interview topics included generational differences in perceptions of racial matters, racial identity, gender socialization, and race-related moral development. I interviewed each adult and teenager for 60 to 90 minutes. These interviews were audiotaped and later transcribed. A wide range of parenting experiences was represented in this group. Parents ranged from 35 years old to more than 65 years old at the time of interview. A few of the parents that I talked to were also grandparents, and some of the teenage women interviewed were also mothers themselves. Socioeconomically, they ranged from Aid to Families with Dependent Children (AFDC) recipients to high-salaried corporate executives. Parents' educational status was similarly diverse, ranging from high school dropouts to university doctorates.

In analyzing the interviews, I employed a grounded theory approach (Strauss & Corbin, 1998) in which I looked for trends and patterns in interviewee responses that I thought might contribute to an understanding of how parents of teenage children and teenagers themselves understand, enact, and communicate the experience of race-related socialization in African American families. Adopting an integrative approach, I sought to uncover the respondents' interpretations and understandings of racial socialization expressed in their own words and on their own terms, using a process of cross-participant analysis in which I compared participants' responses to reveal what I call *narratives of resistance.* These are a compilation of stories, directives, and pronouncements about the importance of resistance to the psychological and social well-being of Black children and youth.

Since the mid-1990s, I have continued to collect data from African American, Afro-Caribbean, and African girls. The young women I have taught, in my role as a college instructor, have contributed a variety of written materials to my studies of resistance, including autobiographical statements and essays and reports based on their own research findings exploring the topic of racial socialization in Black families (see Garrod, Ward, Robinson, & Kilkenny, 1999). More recently, I have been in conversation with Black girls (and other girls of color) in an urban, community-based girls sports program. These preadolescent and adolescent girls have broadened my understanding and appreciation of the constructive connections made between adults and girls that enable girls to interpret dominant, mainstream knowledge claims about race, gender, and social class and to challenge them when appropriate.

Raising Resisters: What Have We Learned?

In my 1996 chapter "Raising Resisters: The Role of Truth Telling in the Psychological Development of African American Girls," published in the first volume of *Urban Girls,* I provided examples illustrating the centrality of resistance in the psychological development of African American girls. Building on the work of social psychologists studying racial socialization in youth (e.g., Thornton, Chatters, Taylor, & Allen, 1990; Bowman & Howard, 1985; Branch & Newcomb, 1986; Marshall, 1995; Spencer, 1983; Spencer & Markstrom-Adams, 1990; Spencer, Swanson, & Glymph, 1997), I argued that the refusal to allow oneself to become stifled by victimization or to accept an ideology of victim blame requires the development of a critical perspective on the world, one that is informed by the particular knowledge gained from one's social and political position. Such knowledge mitigates self-abnegation, fosters self-esteem, and enables African Americans' resistance to oppression.

Not all resistance strategies adopted by African Americans are liberatory and psychologically healthy. Some strategies are what my colleague Tracy Robinson and I call *resistance for survival* (Robinson & Ward, 1991). These strategies tend to be transient, crisis-oriented, and short-term solutions that Black teenagers adopt in an effort to endure the stressful effects and consequences of their subordination. These survival strategies are often evoked in reaction to Black girls' sense that they are being attacked, demeaned, or psychically wounded and are evident in attitudes and behaviors that stem from anger, fear, or guilt. Although they may feel appropriate at the time, resistance strategies that are survival oriented are seldom in the Black child's long-term self-interest. Academic underachievement, Black-on-Black violence, the quick fixes of substance abuse, overeating, and irresponsible sexual behavior are examples of survival-oriented resistance strategies adopted by African American girls in this culture. While stressing the importance of talking with Black children about their racial realities, in "Raising Resisters" I made a distinction between the "tongues of fire truth-telling" and "resistance-building truth-telling" (1996). Tongues of fire truth telling is defined as the harsh tell-it-like-it-is negative critique of the world some Black mothers inflict on their daughters to unmask illusions and ostensibly build character and psychological strength. In contrast, resistance-building truth-telling strategies emphasize constructive, critical affirmation of the individual and the collective and encourage Black girls to think critically about their selves and their place in the world. Resistance-building truth telling can be employed to understand and address the escalating rates of violence in urban Black female populations. In other words, this form of truth telling can be used to help Black parents construct psychologically strong and socially smart resistance strategies for their daughters.

In contrast, Robinson and I posit that "resistance for liberation strategies" promote the search to discover people and activities in Black girls' environment that affirm and support that their belief in themselves is greater than anyone's disbelief. In other words, resistance for liberation is an oppositional lesson in self-determination. These strategies, which are drawn from knowledge produced within the consciousness of African Americans' victimization, hold the emancipatory interests of a subordinated people. As such, resistance for liberation provides the requisite perspective, vision, and ultimate wisdom Black folks need to live in ways that are self-defined, are in one's own best interest, and allow us to live out our full humanity.

The concept of resistance, which Pitt (1997) defines as "the refusal to accept the relevance of certain knowledge to oneself" (p. 129), was a recurring theme in my interviews with African American teens and parents. At the heart of this notion of resistance is a Black folks' truth: a particular and unique epistemological stance that has evolved over the centuries, which serves to interpret and, when necessary, challenge mainstream knowledge claims. Resistance is also the development of a critical consciousness that is invoked to counter the myriad distortions, mistruths, and misinformation perpetrated about the lives of Black women and men, their families, and communities. Black feminist bell hooks referred to this process as the development of an oppositional gaze (1992). According to Mansbridge and Morris (2001),

> Oppositional consciousness as we define it is an empowering mental state that prepares members of an oppressed group to act to undermine, reform, or overthrow a system of human domination. It is usually fueled by righteous anger over injustices done to the group and prompted by personal indignities and harms suffered through one's group membership. At a minimum, oppositional consciousness includes the four elements of identifying with members of a subordinate group, identifying injustices done to that group, opposing those injustices, and seeing the group as having a shared interest in ending or diminishing those injustices. (pp. 4–5)

The African Americans I interviewed indicated that the strength of the oppositional consciousness that they drew upon was forged in a common history of moral and political indignation at oppression. The lessons of resistance and authority passed down from parent to child are informed by the strength, power, and clarity gained from holding fast to a social and political perspective that allows a subjected people to know what the truth is. Knowing comes from being told the truth and learning how to interpret one's own experience, trust one's own voice, and give legitimacy to one's own perspective. Most important, being an effective resister demands that Black individuals be responsive to and responsible for this knowledge. In essence, resistance is a body of knowledge and requisite skills that can help Black children and youth read, interpret, and oppose racial bias and animosity, as well as affirm the self and one's cultural group.

Henri Giroux (1983) reminds us that not all oppositional behavior has "radical significance" or is rooted in a reaction to authority and domination. Resistance may be linked to interests that are race, gender, and class specific, but it is also true that acts of resistance may be little more than the unmindful, desperate behavior of subjugated individuals beaten down by the conditions of life. However, such survival-oriented resistance is often short sighted and ineffective for Black girls in the long run as it ultimately keeps them in a subordinate position. Healthy and effective resistance, on the other hand, prompts critical thinking because at its heart it contains a critique of domination and subordination (Giroux, 1983). Effective resistance strategies fortify girls from within by building upon and enhancing girls' psychological health and social strengths. Mindful of the role that sexism, racism, and social class bias continue to play in shaping our attitudes, beliefs, values, and behaviors, these strategies or systems of thinking and behaving in the face of oppression are designed in ways that are acutely attuned to the sociopolitical context of gender and race in America.

Janesia is one example of a Black girl who has developed and internalized a resistance repertoire to withstand the hardship of traveling an hour outside of her own community at 6:00 A.M. on dark and ice-cold mornings for hockey practice. She also stands up to the pressure of her Black peers who cannot understand why she joined a girls ice hockey team in the first place. Janesia explained:

> They were on my case for at least half of the season. They thought I was crazy, that hockey is a white boys sport—not even a white girls sport!—and they thought that there must be something wrong with me 'cause I like it. Like I'm lesbian or something. But then I thought about how I feel when I'm on the ice. It feels good. Real good. Yeah it's hard, and it's cold, and sometimes the whole team wants to be somewhere else. But I like hockey.

> And I'm good at it and it makes me feel good. And just because there aren't
> a lot of Black girls who do it doesn't mean no Black girls should do it. Tell
> me I can't do it 'cause I'm Black and a girl. You gotta be kidding!

Refusing to collaborate in her own victimization, Janesia will not allow others to define what kind of a Black girl she must be. Internalizing this type of resistance helps girls to withstand negative social influences; it requires a strong will and the ability to hold up under the kind of pressure exerted by people whose power you choose to question (Kohl, 1994, p. 23). Moreover, knowing that there will be times when they will have to resist pressure from others encourages and ultimately enables girls to take a stand for those things that promote persistence, positive self-validation, and resilience. The work of self-creation, with its salience in the adolescent years, necessitates that Black girls actively design and produce strategies of resistance that are appropriate to their life goals and demands.

Over the course of my interviews with Black adults who shared their narratives of resistance and talked about what they wish to teach their children, as well as with teenagers who talked about what they think their parents want them to know, I heard that resistance is about learning to stand up against those who dare to limit who or what you choose to be, and to stand up for what defines the best you can be. This is an internal resistance that has, at its best, the potential to motivate, energize, heal, and renew. For Black women, individually and collectively, cultivating effective resistance strategies has an element of transcendence and emancipatory possibilities, a fact that speaks both to its importance and, if we are not careful, to its potential for inadvertent misuse.

Child-Rearing Practices in The Skin We're In

Whatever generation gap there may be between baby boomers and the hip-hop generation disappears when it comes to being victimized by the limitations placed upon Black people due to race and gender. The responses from Black parents to questions about the messages they received from their own parents about race, and the messages they now deem essential to pass down to their own offspring, show that racism is still alive and well in nearly every American institution. Moreover, African Americans have learned all too well that "the isms travel in packs" (Jones & Shorter-Gooden, 2003, p. 37) and that interlocking biases and discrimination create inescapable traps for countless Black daughters (and sons) despite our best efforts. In my studies, Black mothers and fathers expressed fear about what can happen to a naive and unsuspecting Black child if she unquestioningly accepts the dominant cultural interpretation of her reality. There is a purposeful intent behind the child-rearing strategies of Black families who wish to raise emotionally strong, socially smart girls. The parents I interviewed for *The Skin We're In* unequivocally stated that it is the responsibility of the adults in the lives of Black girls to teach them how to resist in ways that are real, effective, and within their control (Ward, 2000).

Addressing racism and sexism in an open and forthright manner is essential to building psychological health in African American children. Parents are acutely aware of the reality of racism in their own lives, and say that they feel it is their responsibility to judiciously share their personal race-related experiences with their children. Healthy psychological resistance is fostered through a liberating truth telling that has a transformative quality. Both Black girls and Black parents find strength in the intergenerational perspective. I heard from several of the Black girls in my racial socialization study, as well as college students of African descent who contributed to the autobiographical reflections on growing up Black (see Garrod et al., 1999), that their parents' lives exemplify survival, growth, and resilience. According to these young Black women, knowledge of these characteristics has helped them discern their own personal and cultural strengths (Ward, 1996, 2000).

How Far Have We Come?

In both the popular press and the social science literature, Black girls are still described by a persistent pathologizing narrative of crisis. Despite the flurry of research activity from "the girls' movement" of the 1990s (what some call the decade of the girl) to the present, studies of Black girls (and other girls of color) are far fewer than those of their white counterparts. Studies that focus exclusively on Black girls, (as opposed to those in which the analysis of Black girls solely focuses on their comparison to White girls) also continue to be few in number despite the intense attention paid over the past 10 years to variability in the status and circumstances of girls in this culture. Indeed, attention has shifted to the plight of Black boys. As Dierdre Paul (2003) writes, "Blacks girls [have become] a footnote in the discourse on the endangered Black male" (p. 29). The prevailing concern for Black boys that now grips the social sciences and education is in response to frighteningly grim homicide, academic underachievement, and school failure rates. These statistics of Black boys' failure are contrasted with Black girls' successes. For example, Black girls have substantially lower dropout rates and higher college enrollment rates than Black boys (Cohen & Nee, 2000). However, it is not that Black girls are doing so much better, but that Black boys are simply doing much worse. Many of our Black girls are also still floundering and struggling to survive.

Welfare reform has pulled the rug out from under their families, forcing Black mothers into the workforce to hold down one, two, or three minimally paying jobs. Mothers have less time and energy for child rearing; daughters are frequently left to pick up the slack. Community-based programs that many Black families depend on have been eliminated. The schools that Black girls attend are reeling from the effects of No Child Left Behind and high-stakes testing, and resources are being funneled away from innovative curricula into basic skills. It is heartening that teen pregnancy rates are declining across the nation; however, the average age at first birth in 2000 for non-Hispanic Black women (and most Latinas) was 22.3 years (in contrast to 25.9 years for non-Hispanic White women), and the majority of these Black women are single at the time of first birth. Black female households without a spouse presently make up 39% of those living below the poverty line (CDC, 2002; U.S. Census, 2001). These social indicators remind us to stay vigilant and vocal about this population and to continue to sound the alarm about the perils of Black girls' adolescence without recognizing Black girls' inherent strengths. This ultimately undermines adults' recognition of the very skills that will enable Black girls to navigate this period with success (Ward & Benjamin, 2004).

In a discussion group with urban secondary school teachers, one white female teacher explained that she just cannot get that jazzed up about gender. She said she knew she should, being female and all, but it just does not excite her to work for social change. Shortly following her statement, which was not directly challenged by any of the other women present, another story was shared in the group that illustrated the importance of gender in their students' lives. Days earlier a poetry slam had taken place in the school's auditorium. A young Black student read a poem in which one Black woman was chastising another for dating a man who had callously mistreated and abused the speaker just a short time before. In the poem she anguished over why "sisters" can be so caring, so understanding, and so strong when it comes to helping one another pick up the pieces after a heart has been broken, yet that same woman will knowingly turn around and walk right back into a similar mess if the right man draws her in. As women, the poet explained, we have to love ourselves enough to make better decisions in our lives, and we must trust ourselves enough to believe the warnings we disclose. At the end of the poem the auditorium exploded in loud and raucous applause, especially from the young women present. It was, explained the teacher, a powerful moment, at least for the girls. Her female students stood together in solidarity, recognizing the vulnerabilities they share as women in the (dating) world. What was curious to me was the inability of the adult women teachers in the lives of these girls to see themselves connected in any way to the expressed concerns. Overlooking the insights and strengths inherent in Black and Latina girls' reflections upon their social world, these adult women miss an essential moment to connect meaningfully to the lives of these girls. Moreover, this lack of connection prevents women from being in the position to teach the requisite skills and offer the support that these girls need to effectively find their way.

Who Is There to Help?

Much of the work of adolescence for Black girls is to explore and integrate the multiple identities of race, class, and gender. To do this they look to their mothers, grandmothers, aunts, and other adult women for help in shaping the personal characteristics that support positive psychosocial development. In her study of family processes and child development, Shirley Hill (2002) found that "parents offer daughters a racialized gender socialization message that often seems contradictory"; they teach assertiveness yet also help daughters understand that they have to deal with the realities of White power and privilege. Black girls learn respect for authority (especially White), yet they also learn that they cannot afford to be submissive. Girls need to know when to stand up for themselves and when to fight back.

African American women tend to reject the traditional notions of womanhood, finding it necessary to redefine womanhood to more accurately reflect their own racial reality. Sociologist Patricia Hill Collins argues that Black women have always had to fashion an independent standpoint about the meaning of Black womanhood. Historically, Black women have used knowledge produced in Black communities based on African-derived conceptions of self and community, to resist the negative evaluations of who they are and what they are about (Collins, 1990). Some of the messages Black women pass on to their daughters help them identify and tap internal supports, strengths, knowledge, and fortitude, as well as external supports such as parents, teachers, and other trusted adults who will listen to them, encourage them, and remind them that they have what it takes to overcome the struggle. Black women's power lies in their ability to encourage their daughters to use their social knowledge to calculate their strengths and weaknesses and to deal with the limitations they face. For some Black women who are burdened by unrelenting racial and gender oppression, and overcome by chronic poverty and despair, the struggle to survive the exigencies of life disconnects them from the knowledge they need to foster their daughters' internal strengths and social competencies. However, the majority of Black mothers in my studies, those I talked to as well as the mothers mentioned by the Black girls and young women I interviewed or who shared their stories with me, acknowledge the enormous responsibility they hold and assert the right to redefine Black womanhood on their own terms. These women orient their daughters to the reality they must resist, living within a culture that perpetuates harmful biases and negatively constrains Black women's identities and opportunities. Recognition of this common cultural experience unites Black women and girls as partners in the same struggle.

Stepping Toward Healthy Resistance

Based on what I learned from the respondents in my studies, I have constructed a four-step model (Read it, Name it, Oppose it, Replace it) that is designed to help adults assist their children in developing critical thinking skills to effectively resist damaging racial and gendered realities. The model emphasizes the need for parents to foster girls' capacities to generate safe, creative, and effective internal (psychological) and external (social) strategies of resistance. Central to this process is the need for parents to listen to and learn from their daughters who are, in fact, crucial informants of their own cultural contexts (such as peer cultures, school cultures) and developmental needs.

If you ever wish to jump-start a conversation about youth culture, gender relations, race, and resistance, mention popular music videos produced for and consumed by American children and teens. Hip-hop music videos were frequently on the minds of the parents I interviewed, and they provide a rich forum for conversations about resistance. The concerns I heard again and again centered on the women in these videos. "Half-naked video hoochie mamas," as one mom put it, "gyrating to a seductive backbeat." These titillating images of Black women (and other women of color) are dished out for widespread consumption. Mothers who struggle to instill in their daughters the characteristics they would like them to possess—self-respect, respect for others, independence, and pride—feel undermined by these video messages. Anxieties surfaced frequently in our conversations about the extent to which Black girls internalize these narrow, objectifying stereotypes before they are old enough to resist their appeal. Although it might be futile for an adult to think that she can prevent children from watching the music videos that they and their friends enjoy, mothers say that their daughters must, at the very least, learn to bring a critical eye to the images they consume.

"Reading it" refers to analyzing a situation for the dynamics of race, gender, and class. Parents say that Black girls must develop a critical consciousness that allows them to ask the critical questions, challenge and test assumptions, and determine what is really going on. This requires that girls think carefully about what they see, hear, think, believe, and feel. Central to the process of reading situations and events is the ability to identify patterns, covert and overt, that show the routines and rituals of everyday racism and sexism. Reading it is about making connections, among what people say, do, believe, and feel. Racism and sexism evoke strong emotional responses, particularly in children and teens. These emotions are key survival signals in that they indicate something important is happening. It is essential to stay in touch with the feelings that surface. Do these images make girls feel sad? Mad? Hurt? Afraid? Despite the fact that these media images portray our nation's obsession with sex and materialism in (what some might argue) the worst of ways, Black mothers say that it is hard for their daughters to invoke a critique of music videos because it looks like the women are enjoying themselves. When adults help Black girls to read a situation, they give girls the skills to analyze whose interests are privileged, favored, and legitimized and whose are discounted, silenced, and ignored.

"Naming it" refers to the process of establishing criteria for determining if racism (or sexism) is, or is not, at play. After all, not everything is about race, and not everything that involves race is racist. However, if racism is involved, naming it becomes very important, to figure out socially smart strategies to oppose the injustices perceived.

Adults can help girls to identify and name the attitudes, behaviors, definitions, and assumptions that create barriers to healthy development. Naming it requires practical, accessible words whose meanings are shared and agreed upon by both adult and child. Most important, naming it is a powerful, sometimes painful process, especially for children and teens. It means bringing the existence of injustice and inequity into full consciousness, "telling it like it is." Black parents and teens work together to determine what constitutes racism and sexism and employ conceptual definitions that expose what they believe these words to mean. As video images multiply in number and show increasingly questionable taste, it becomes essential that girls, as consumers of these images, are given a way to determine for themselves what is going on. Girls need guidance, particularly from adult women, to identify the dynamics at play in what they are seeing. Lacking guidance, girls passively and uncritically consume the media products marketed to them, and, failing to see them as problematic, many lack the ability to resist these images. While many girls (and their mothers) may enjoy listening to the music, it is usually the lyrics of a song or the images that accompany the lyrics that the people I spoke to find objectionable. A first step toward helping girls to see and name the powerful forces at work in the videos calls for adults to attend closely to girls' emotional reactions to what they hear and see. For example, we can ask girls to share what they like or do not like about the videos. "How do you feel when you watch them? Do you feel embarrassed? Demeaned? Confused? Pissed off?" Why? By beginning with our feelings, we can then help girls to develop the cognitive processes needed to make sense of their emotional reactions. Frequently girls who claim to love the videos have a deep sense that something about them is not right. Helping girls to see and name what is not right calls on us to tap girls' moral sensibilities and explore the ways in which these images are perceived to be right or wrong, fair or caring. Sometimes girls "can't go there," but mom can, and adult women have a responsibility to share their concerns. We cannot assume that our girls know how or why we feel the way we do. Fortunately, assistance these days can be found in the form of newspapers, magazines, and other publications that address the media's role in crafting images for and of minority communities. One mom I spoke to explained that she learned the word *misogyny* in a magazine at the dentist's office, and that concept helped her understand more fully the fragmented ideas that had long been swirling around in her head.

An important element of helping girls to Read it and Name it involves providing girls with the tools needed to look for and identify patterns. We ask, "Where and from whom have you heard these ideas stated before? Where have you seen these and similar images like them in the past?" These questions help girls to make connections by searching for relationships between attitudes, behaviors, feelings, and ideas. I have found that upon reflecting on these images and what they may mean, Black girls often conclude that they are in the presence of something that is not quite right, and that the situation has powerful connections to how race and gender are stereotyped in this culture. It is in these moments of recognition that naming it becomes powerful, in telling Black girls that to uphold a sense of personal integrity, someone must respond.

"Opposing it" is about finding smart and effective ways for Black girls to respond to sexism. Opposing it means standing up to, fighting back, speaking up, and asserting moral authority in the face of injustice, intolerance, and ignorance. The resistance that Black girls employ (i.e., the calculated action steps that a girl might take in response to a situation that she feels is demeaning, constraining, and diminishing of her sense of self and her opportunities) requires an awareness of where I am now and where do I want to be in the future. These strategies must also be mindful of the consequences of missteps.

"Replacing it" (replenishing it) processes speak to what happens after the hard work of resistance. It takes tremendous fortitude to challenge self-defeating beliefs about who you are. It is hard work to be constantly on the lookout for and responsive to the negative feelings and faulty assumptions others may hold about you, or to the negative self-limiting attitudes girls may have internalized about themselves. In this step, replacing it refers to the process of replenishing the warrior spirit. Girls can substitute negative attitudes with positive self-images, cultural knowledge, pride, and self-respect.

Several years ago I visited a Black girls group in a neighborhood in Boston that was run by two charismatic Black women volunteers. The group met on Saturdays to discuss the hard work of growing up Black and female. From time to time guest speakers were invited to attend, sharing their own stories of trial and triumph, offering advice, and providing support. The program evaluations of this Black girls group consistently noted the excitement the girls felt in the presence of such a wide range of interesting, intelligent, committed Black women. Negative forces that these girls struggled against in their lives outside of the group were quickly dispelled during these Saturday meetings in the face of the racial pride, positive identity, and self-love that were central to the mission of the Black women assembled together.

Take Back the Music

The following letter was sent to *Essence* magazine, the most widely distributed fashion magazine marketed to Black women, by Moya Bailey, a campus activist who participated in a student protest against hip-hop artist Nelly (at Spelman College, a Black women's college in Atlanta, Georgia):

> Black women are often depicted as hypersexualized, and music videos exacerbate the problem and that becomes people's perception of Black women everywhere. I know people who've been on exchange programs to another country, say South Africa or Brazil, and they've had experiences in which people have approached them, thinking that they were prostitutes or that they were sexually open just because of the images that they have of American Black women. People don't have access to other images of us because videos are really what go out to the rest of the world. There aren't really pictures of us in school textbooks or things that counter the images that are seen in music videos. With White people, you have a wider range of depictions. You might have Roseanne, who represents a low-income White family, but then you also have Frasier and Friends, which represent wealthier White people; so there's a range. For Black women especially, there are not as many choices out there to counteract video images. I think it's deliberate. The media does an excellent job of keeping those more positive images about us away from people. (Byrd & Solomon, 2005)

Moya's campus activism at Spelman College in Atlanta is a graphic illustration of the Read it, Name it, Oppose it, and Replace it processes. Nelly was invited by a group of Black female undergraduates to attend a panel convened to discuss the images of Black women in music videos. The impact of these images had sparked an internal debate within the campus community for some time, and there was by no means consensus on this topic. Although Nelly declined the invitation, *Essence* magazine took up the cause and began the campaign, "Take Back the Music," continuing the debate in the magazine's pages. Moya's letter is an example of "Reading" the situation and "Naming" the dynamics she sees in play. Detecting racial stereotypes, understanding how these images shape perceptions of Black women, and the questions Moya raises about whose interests are served in this practice are important critical perspectives worthy of consideration by all Black girls.

Three examples of "Opposing it" are also evident in the letter from Moya. First there is Moya's individual action of writing a letter expressing her dismay about the images of Black women in music videos to a Black women's magazine. Second there is her activism, which involved organizing Black college women at Spelman to come together in discussion groups, panels, and campus rallies in order to raise consciousness about the issue with her peers. Finally, there are the efforts of *Essence* to use its considerable clout to enlighten its readers.

The last step, "Replacing it," can be found on the magazine's Web site (www.essence.com/essence/takebackthemusic/). In response to the outpouring of positive feedback that the publication received from its largely Black female readership, *Essence* began to provide lists of alternative hiphop music videos produced by artists who, the editors and magazine readers suggest, choose not to exploit and demean Black women. The individual efforts of women like Moya Bailey and other women of Spelman College became the adopted strategies of a larger collective movement of women dedicated to resisting those who see and treat us as worthless or expendable.

These examples are instructive to those who wish to inculcate (and critique) critical consciousness. They provide a catalyst for an intergenerational conversation about the ways in which images may directly or indirectly shape attitudes and perceptions far beyond anyone's control. They show girls how acts of empowerment can spring forth at both the individual and the collective levels, and that personal opposition can ignite the flames of a much larger social movement, when people work to make their perspectives known and their voices heard.

Conclusion

Liberatory truth telling in the context of adolescent development offers Black girls a corrective to the false, incomplete, and misunderstood interpretations of what it means to face life in the skin we're in. Talking to our girls about their racial and gendered realities is critical. Providing the support they need to read, name, effectively oppose, and ultimately replace the "injuries of the isms" requires adult participation and thoughtful and loving patience. These effective resistance strategies (truth-telling resistance) are not time bound or cast off at the end of adolescence. Indeed, Black parents say they are still called upon to resist and challenge oppression in their own personal and professional lives.

When we urge our daughters to define their own Blackness and refuse to buy into definitions of womanhood that do not adequately reflect Black women's racial reality, we sow the seeds of resistance. When we teach our daughters to resist the self-loathing that can arise when a girl compares her looks to a Eurocentric standard of beauty and feels she comes up short—we give roots to the warrior within. As we help our girls avoid the trap of seeking validation, approval, or sense of identity from a man, we give them the tools they need to become women who can appropriately and effectively rise above devaluation. We owe this to our girls. We owe it to ourselves.

Discussion Questions

1. How might we invoke a liberatory truth-telling strategy to help Black girls interrogate the limitations of emphasizing and embracing Black women's strengths?
2. Provide examples of ways in which we might identify and reframe unhealthy resistance strategies adopted by angry Black girls.

REFERENCES

Bowman, P., & Howard, C. (1985). Race-related socialization, motivation, and academic achievement: A study of Black youth in three-generation families. *Journal of the American Academy of Child Psychiatry, 24,* 132–141.

Branch, C., & Newcomb, N. (1986). Racial attitude development among young Black children as a function of parental attitudes: A longitudinal and cross-sectional study. *Child Development, 57,* 712–721.

Byrd, A., & Solomon, A. (2005, January). What's really going on: Entertainment insiders, thinkers and consumers candidly discuss hip-hop's outlook on Black women's sexuality. *Essence.*

CDC Media Relations. Press release, American women waiting to begin families. Retrieved December 11, 2002, from http://www.cdc.gov/od/oc/media/pressrel/r021211.htm

Cohen, C. J., & Nee, C. E. (2000). Educational attainment and sex differentials in African American communities. *American Behavioral Scientists, 11*(7), 1–39.

Collins, P. H. (1990). *Black feminist thought: Knowledge, consciousness, and the politics of empowerment.* Boston: Unwin Hyman.

Garrod, A., Ward, J. V., Robinson, T., & Kilkenny, R. (Eds.). (1999). *Souls looking back: Life stories of growing up Black.* New York: Routledge.

Giroux, H. A. (1983). *Theory and resistance in education: A pedagogy for the opposition.* Cambridge, MA: Bergin-Garvey.

Hill, S. A. (2002). Teaching and doing gender in African American families. *Sex Roles: A Journal of Research, 47,* 493–506.

hooks, b. (1992). *Black looks: Race and representation.* Boston: South End Press.

Jones, C., & Shorter-Gooden, K. (2003). *Shifting: The double lives of Black women in America.* New York: HarperCollins.

Kohl, H. (1994). *"I won't learn from you": And other thoughts on creative maladjustment.* New York: Norton.

Mansbridge, J., & Morris, A. (Eds.). (2001). *Oppositional consciousness: The subjective roots of social protest.* Chicago: University of Chicago Press.

Marshall, S. (1995). Ethnic socialization of African American children: Implications for parenting, identity development and academic development. *Journal of Youth and Adolescence, 24,* 377–396.

Paul, D. G. (2003). *Talkin' back: Raising and educating resilient Black girls.* Westport, CT: Praeger.

Pitt, A. (1997). Reading resistance analytically: On making the self in women's studies. In L. Roman & L. Eyre (Eds.), *Dangerous territories: Struggles for difference and equality in education* (pp. 127–142). New York: Routledge.

Robinson, T., & Ward, J. V. (1991) "A belief in self far greater than anyone's disbelief": Cultivating healthy resistance among African American female adolescents. In C. Gilligan, A. G. Rogers, & D. Tolman (Eds.), *Women, girls, and psychotherapy: Reframing resistance* (pp. 87–103). Binghamton, NY: Harrington Park Press.

Spencer, M. B. (1983). Children's cultural values and parental child-rearing strategies. *Developmental Review, 3,* 351–370.

Spencer, M. B., & Markstrom-Adams, C. (1990). Identity processes among racial and ethnic minority children in America. *Child Development, 61,* 290–310.

Spencer, M. B., Swanson, D. P., & Glymph, A. (1997). The prediction of parental psychological functioning: Influences of African American adolescent perceptions and experiences of context. In C. D. Ryff & M. M. Seltzer (Eds.), *The parental experience in midlife* (pp. 339–382). Chicago: University of Chicago Press.

Strauss, A., & Corbin, J. (1998). *Basics of qualitative research: Techniques and procedures for developing grounded theory* (2nd ed). Thousand Oaks, CA: Sage.

Thornton, M. C., Chatters, L. M., Taylor, R. J., & Allen, W. R. (1990). Sociodemographic and environmental correlates of racial socialization by Black parents. *Child Development, 61,* 401–409.

U.S. Census. (2001). Table 17: Poverty status of families in 1999 by type, race and Hispanic origin. March 2000. *Current Population Survey, March 2000: Racial statistics. Population Division.* http://www.census.gov/population/socdemo/race/Black/pp1-142/tab17.txt

Ward, J. V. (1996). Raising resisters: The role of truth telling in the psychological development of African American girls. In B. Leadbeater & N. Way (Eds.), *Urban girls: Resisting stereotypes, creating identities* (pp. 85–99). New York: New York University Press.

Ward, J. V. (2000). *The skin we're in: Teaching our children to be emotionally strong, socially smart and spiritually connected.* New York: Fireside/Free Press.

Ward, J. V., and Benjamin, B. (2004). Women, girls and the unfinished work of connection: A critical review of American Girls' Studies. In A. Harris (Ed.), *All about the girl: Power, culture and identity* (pp. 15–28). New York: Routledge.

What they're saying. *Essence.* Retrieved May 2006, from http://www.essence.com/essence/takebackthemusic/whattheyresaying.html

Part V

Claiming Sexuality in Relationships
Taking Stock and Gaining Control

"If You Let Me Play . . ."
Does High School Physical Activity Reduce Urban Young Adult Women's Sexual Risks?

Allison J. Tracy and Sumru Erkut

Sociohistorical Background

Glen Elder (1998) points out that "individual lives are influenced by their ever-changing historical context . . . [such] that changing lives alters developmental trajectories" (p. 1). The cultural shift toward greater gender equity represents a significant historical change that has the potential to alter the course of girls' development. One watershed event brought about by this cultural change is the 1972 federal legislation known as Title IX, which prohibits sex discrimination in any educational environment that receives federal support. Included in Title IX is a provision that entitles girls and women equal access to athletic facilities and funding. Although girls' participation rates, their athletic facilities, and funding for girls' sports are still far from achieving parity with those of boys (Women's Sports Foundation, 2002), the number of girls participating in sports has skyrocketed. In its report card for Title IX, published on the occasion of the 30th anniversary of the legislation, the Women's Sports Foundation (2002) reported an 847% increase in girls' participation in high school athletics from 1971, when girls made up 7% of varsity athletes, to the 2000–2001 academic year, when they made up 41.5% of varsity athletes.

The increase in women's and girls' sports participation is also integrally related to society-wide changes in gender roles. In the last quarter of the 20th century, more and more women and girls were engaging in recreational physical activities that a decade or two earlier had been considered gender inappropriate (Cahn, 1994; Connell, 1987, 1995; Desertrain & Weiss, 1988; Hargreaves, 1994; Kane, 1995; Messner, 1992).

These social and historical changes have affected the country as a whole, but the pace of social change can be uneven across subcultural niches (Rogers, 1995; Strang & Soule, 1998). As diffusion theory suggests, new ideas are spread unevenly across social groups. The uneven diffusion has two related consequences. The first is the initial relative absence of norms that support engagement. For example, an uneven diffusion of cultural attitudes toward girls' athleticism can manifest itself in differing degrees of *opportunities* and/or *encouragement* for girls' physical activities. In communities or cultural niches where new ideas about the appropriateness of sports for girls have not yet become the prevailing norm, girls who participate in sports can be considered tomboyish (Hasbrook, 1995), or norms persist that these girls ought to grow out of the desire to play sports by the time they attend high school. These communities may not provide adequate practice fields, equipment, or field time devoted to girls' sports teams. They may even limit the possibility of forming certain girls' teams (e.g., see Prine, 2001, for poor school districts that raise money for boys' sports but declare lack of funds to support girls' teams).

The second and related consequence of the uneven diffusion of ideas and new ways of doing things is the novelty effect: People who initially and readily adopt new ideas and practices tend to be different from late adopters. Early adopters tend to be more comfortable with change; they have greater self-confidence in their ability to succeed in novel endeavors; they are highly motivated and resourceful. When an activity is novel and lacking community endorsement, people who engage in it tend to be a selected group, whereas in communities where novel ideas and practices have become the norm, the selection factor ceases operating. Diffusion theory suggests that what is a norm in some communities may be a new practice in other communities.

Ideas and practices that originate in one sociocultural niche can be dispersed easily and quickly through global mass media, but their adoption is conditioned by several "boundaries." Race/ethnicity, region, and urbanization are three such boundaries that play a role in how widespread the adoption of a new practice will be. Different racial/ethnic groups tend to have values and practices not widely shared by other groups. Region also forms a boundary. Historically there has been a legacy of cultural differentiation both along North-South and East-West dimensions, generating different values and practices among contemporary American subcultures. Rural-urban differences, on the other hand, can be located within regions and include differences in population density, homogeneity, and availability of resources, as well as the complexity of social organization. Whether novel ideas or practices will be adopted across such boundaries depends in large part on the existence of compatible values along with resources to translate values into practice. In other words, existing values may make some ideas and practices easier or more difficult to disperse from the center to the periphery, and available resources or opportunities will facilitate the adoption of a novel idea or practice.

Dimensions of Social Diffusion

Norms governing girls' sexual activity, as well as the opportunities and support girls receive for being physically active, are largely conditioned by norms that define the adolescent female role. Gender roles vary by cultural contexts, which are defined, in part, by race/ethnicity and geographic location. We hypothesize that the relationship between physical activity and a girl's sexual behavior is moderated by the cultural context in which she lives. Racial/ethnic and geographic patterns governing gender roles affect girls' participation in sports and premarital sex.

Race and Ethnicity

Race and ethnicity appear to be one of the cultural dimensions along which there is uneven diffusion of attitudes favoring athleticism among girls and women because female gender roles vary across race and ethnicity. Hasbrook's 1995 ethnographic study of a mostly African American grade school in Milwaukee's inner city suggests that certain cultures (i.e., African American, Asian American) are less tolerant of girls who defy gender stereotypes than is white, middle-class society.

Further bearing out the consequences of uneven distribution of novel ideas across racial/ethnic boundaries due to differences in values and financial resources, in previous analyses we also found differences among Latino subgroups: Mexican American girls reported the highest rates of sports participation of these subgroups, and Cuban American girls reported the lowest rates (Erkut & Tracy, 2002). A multiracial ethnic study of physical activity by Eyler and her colleagues (2003) has found that a comparison of Latina, White, African American, and Native American women showed different personal attributes to be correlated with physical activity. For example, while regular attendance at religious services was associated with physical activity in some groups, among urban Latinas it had the opposite effect. The distinctive relationship between race/ethnicity and physical activity was further borne out by Eyler et al.'s finding that none of the environmental factors the researchers examined (e.g., availability of facilities, safety of facilities, other people exercising in the neighborhood) held across all the groups participating in the study. While a common set of environmental barriers may not be operating to suppress physical activity across racial and ethnic groups, more minority children than White children attend schools where physical activity is not a priority (Crespo, 2005).

Region

In the United States, geographic regions have their own history, social ecology, economy, and cultural values (see Plaut, Markus, & Lachman, 2002). These differences play a role in facilitating or hindering the diffusion of ideas. The historical resistance of the South to the northern ways continues to this day (Cohen, Nisbett, Bowdle, & Schwartz, 1996). New practices tend to originate in the West and are adopted in the East and Midwest, while parts of the South are not as open to ideas and practices that challenge the southern masculine ideal of upholding the "culture of honor" (Cohen, 1996; Nisbett, 1993).

The rationale for examining geographic region as a relevant social context also rests on previous research that has shown region to be a significant predictor of risky sexual activity rates. For example, Seidman, Mosher, and Aral's (1994) analysis of data from unmarried women aged 15 to 44 who participated in the National Survey of Family Growth Cycle IV showed that being born in the West or Midwest was among the risk factors for self-reports of having had multiple sexual partners in the last 3 months. Hanson, Morrison, and Ginsburg's (1989) analysis of the High School and Beyond data revealed that young men who lived in the South were more likely to have become a father before age 20 than were men who lived in other regions (after controlling for a number of relevant variables). Ku, Sonenstein, and Pleck (1992) showed in their study of a national sample of noninstitutionalized young men that male condom use differed by region. They found that the average use of condoms was highest in the Midwest but lowest in the Northeast and the West. Duncan and Hoffman (1990) found, using the Panel Study of Income Dynamics data, that regional control variables reduced the effect of AFDC benefits on out-of-wedlock births among African American teenage girls to small or insignificant levels, suggesting that regional differences played a significant role in rates of out-of-wedlock births.

An added source of complexity is the uneven distribution of racial and ethnic groups across geographic regions. While White and African American populations are relatively well distributed across regions, Latinos of Mexican origin tend to be concentrated in the South and West, Latinos of Cuban origin in the South (mostly Florida), and those of Caribbean origin (particularly Puerto Ricans) in the Northeast. American Asian populations have historically settled on the West Coast and have moved to other parts of the country in smaller numbers. More recent waves of refugees from Asia, however, have been located across the country.

In an earlier analysis of the Add Health data (Tracy & Erkut, 2003), we used multiple group discrete time survival and regression analyses to compare the effects of physical activity on sexual onset and sexual behavior, respectively.[1] In these analyses, we compared groups of White high school students and African American high school students from all four regions (Northeast, Midwest, South, and West), but limited the analyses of subgroups of Latinas to the regions where they are most heavily concentrated, yielding a total sample of 2,626 girls.

Among White girls in the West and Midwest and African American girls in the West, we found that the effect of being physically active (in both structured sports activities and unstructured physical leisure time activity) operated indirectly on sexual risk through delaying the onset of sexual activity. Among African Americans in the Midwest and Mexican American girls in the West, physical activity was associated with lower sexual risk once a girl had become sexually active. Conversely, physically active Cuban American girls in the South were *more* likely to report being sexually active and having had unprotected sex.

While most physically active girls delayed the onset of sexual activity or practiced safer sex once sexually active, the earlier onset of sexual activity among physically active girls of Cuban American origin in the South was unexpected. In this cultural niche, parents monitor girls to protect their virtue and place a low value on the importance of sports for girls. Once a girl breaks out of the protective circle by engaging in sports, the family may have less control over her activities, which can include sexual intercourse.

These results suggest that engaging in physical activity in high school *can be* associated with lower probabilities of engaging in risky sexual behaviors for some girls. However, the existence, strength, and direction of this relationship vary depending on the girls' racial/ethnic group and region of residence. Overall, although most of the statistically significant effects were "protective," either directly or indirectly or both, there was sufficient variability in effects by racial/ethnic group and region of residence to caution against generalizations. Due to the limitations of secondary data analysis, we cannot tell from these analyses why the relationship between physical and sexual activity varies across context, nor can we determine if these groups of girls engaged in the same types of physical activities. Still, the presence of contextual distinctions is compelling and warrants further study.

Urbanicity

Having examined race/ethnicity and region as important social contexts for influencing girls' physical activity, in this chapter we turned our attention to whether living in an urban context acts as an influential cultural context. For example, the rural-urban divide can be a barrier to the diffusion of ideas and information about the risks of unprotected sex. Urban and rural environments also encompass a wide array of factors that can be protective or risk factors for engaging in sexual activity with extremely high health risks (e.g., in the sex trade, or sex with drug users).

In some circles, an urban environment has come to be shorthand for poverty and an environment that poses many risks conducive to youth engaging in such risky behaviors as school dropout, substance use, precocious and unprotected sex, and crime. The assumption is that communities of color concentrated in the "inner city" live impoverished lives. However, relative to rural and suburban environments, cultural institutions and enriching opportunities may be more likely to be located in urban environments. Urban environments exhibit variations in income (very high and also very low), and in the quality of educational and recreational opportunities. Regarding health risks surrounding unprotected sexual activity, urban girls are likely to be at an advantage in terms of being better informed and having easier access to health care than their rural sisters. If one follows the logic of "idle hands are the devil's workshop," urban girls' opportunities to engage in positive activities can be protective of engaging in risky sexual behaviors.

In addition, urban girls may be more likely than rural girls to attend schools that have the resources to offer sports programs or intramural sports because urban schools tend to be larger. Thus, urban girls' physical activity may be more structured, rigorous, and time-consuming due to better access to organized school sports. Again, by the logic of "idle hands are the devil's workshop," rural girls who do not have access to school sports and other physical activity outlets may have more time for relationships with the opposite sex that can lead to intercourse at an early age.

On the other hand, not all influences that emanate from an urban environment are likely to be protective against engaging in risky sexual behaviors. While encompassing more diversity of opportunity, education, employment, and entertainment, urban environments also encompass opportunities for dangerous sexual relationships. These include a red-light district commonly found in any urban area, and the presence of people who lead dangerous lives who gravitate to the anonymity of urban environments. For these reasons, an urban environment may present more opportunities to engage in risky sexual behaviors than a rural area.

More than 30 years after passage of Title IX, White middle-class communities value and support girls' participation in physical activity and sports. They also have the financial means to provide the infrastructure to realize this value in community practices. Contemporary White, suburban communities are full of opportunities and facilities for girls' participation in a variety of sports, so much so that a girl in a middle-class suburban community might find it necessary to emphasize she is *not* interested in soccer in order to prevent her parents from signing her up for the local league. In contrast, in other communities, only those girls who display a keen interest in playing soccer and who are willing to take extra steps to find access to leagues get to play regularly because facilities are unequally distributed across the urban-suburban divide (Cradock et al., 2002). In many African American communities, there is a similar high value placed on girls' athleticism. In poorer African American communities, however, facilities and community resources for girls' participation in sports and physical activity are not widely available (Cradock et al., 2002), resulting in lower rates of sports participation among African American girls compared to White girls overall (Tracy & Erkut, 2002).

What needs to be examined is whether being physically active in high school will lead a young woman to connect with the protective elements in an urban environment or with the elements that promote risky sexual behaviors. In this chapter we extend our previous research to assess whether, and to which extent, physical activity in high school affects the likelihood of engaging in risky sexual behaviors in both rural and urban environments.

Our Current Research

We analyzed the relationship among physical activity, living in urban areas, and engaging in risky sexual behaviors using the Add Health data (Bearman, Jones, & Udry, 1997). The longitudinal analyses involved testing the long-term effects of high school physical activity on sexuality in young adulthood.[2] By young adulthood, sexuality becomes normative, and individuals form committed relationships. In other words, behaviors considered risky in adolescence (e.g., multiple accumulated partners, use of birth control) may no longer reflect sexual risk. Instead, we focus on three undesired sexual outcomes incurred by young adulthood: (a) having an unintended pregnancy, (b) being diagnosed with a sexually transmitted infection (STI), and (c) engaging in sexual behaviors associated with extremely high health risks—namely, involvement in the sex trade and/or having intercourse with a known intravenous drug user. We created a dummy-coded variable for each of the three sexual outcomes, using information from detailed sexual histories obtained in each wave and results from biological assays designed to detect the presence of an STI.

These data were collected using a clustered sampling design in which 80 high schools and 80 paired "feeder schools" (junior high schools that contributed students to the selected high schools) across the United States yielded a sample of approximately 90,000 adolescents in grades 7 to 12. These students were given a school-based survey in 1994–1995. From this group a random subsample of nearly 21,000 adolescents was selected for the longitudinal home-based portion of the survey, beginning several months after the in-school portion. The mean age of the adolescents at the first wave was 16.89 years ($SD = 1.09$). The second and third waves of the Add Health study were administered in 1996 and 2000–2001, respectively. Biological assays of STIs were available in the third wave of the Add Health data.

We used a number of exclusion criteria to define our analytic sample. Because potentially very different dynamics underlie physical activity and/or sexual behavior for certain groups of girls, we excluded disabled girls, girls with very low scores on a standardized vocabulary test (cutoff = 70, two standard deviations below the age-adjusted mean), girls who reported having had intercourse before age 12 (our proxy for defining childhood sexual abuse), and girls who reported being pregnant at either Wave 1

TABLE 12.1

Descriptive Statistics for the Model Variables Among Urban Respondents, by Race/Ethnicity

	Range	White (*n* = 917)	Black (*n* = 516)	Latina (*n* = 551)
Adolescence				
West	0,1	16%	13%	30%
Midwest	0,1	47%	35%	11%
South	0,1	19%	42%	42%
Northeast	0,1	18%	10%	17%
Social desirability	0–3	0.98 (0.71)	0.99 (0.68)	1.06 (0.72)
Neighborhood poverty	0–3	1.08 (0.96)	2.09 (0.98)	1.72 (1.03)
Mother's education	1–6	3.84 (1.21)	3.55 (1.14)	2.66 (1.36)
Two-parent household	0,1	53%	41%	46%
Physical activity	0–40	0.17 (0.09)	0.14 (0.08)	0.14 (0.08)
Young Adulthood				
Marital status	0,1	33%	20%	33%
Age	17–27	21.2 (1.56)	21.2 (1.62)	21.5 (1.64)
Unintended pregnancy	0,1	17%	32%	27%
High-risk sex	0,1	03%	03%	03%
STI	0,1	15%	35%	17%

or Wave 2 (because pregnancy may have affected their reported physical activity levels). Further, we excluded those lost to follow-up in Wave 3.

Since race/ethnicity was a key organizing variable in the analyses, we categorized respondents into mutually exclusive groups and assigned a single racial/ethnic category to each adolescent. Those who reported multiple racial/ethnic identifications were assigned a category based on the respondent's report of her best-fitting racial/ethnic category. We employed membership in racial/ethnic, regional, and urban/rural cultural niches as reported in high school.[3] Because too few respondents identified as solely or primarily Asian (*n* = 54) or Native American (*n* = 25), we did not include these groups in the analytic sample. The resulting racial/ethnic subsamples included 2,327 White (917 urban and 1,410 rural), 936 African Americans (576 urban and 360 rural), and 649 Latinas (551 urban and 98 rural).[4]

Using multiple group structural equation modeling, we modeled the direct and interaction effects of adolescent physical activity and urbanicity on the probability of each of the three undesired sexual outcomes—unintended pregnancy, diagnosis with an STI, or high-risk sex—by young adulthood. In these models, effects were estimated simultaneously for each of the racial/ethnic groups in the analysis sample.[5]

The descriptive statistics for analysis variables are given in Tables 12.1 and 12.2 for urban and rural girls, respectively. From these tables, we see

TABLE 12.2
Descriptive statistics for the model variables among rural respondents, by race/ethnicity.

	Range	White ($n = 1410$)	Black[a] ($n = 360$)	Latina ($n = 98$)
Adolescence				
West	0,1	11%	<01%	60%
Midwest	0,1	34%	<01%	06%
South	0,1	42%	99%	30%
Northeast	0,1	13%	<01%	04%
Social desirability	0–3	1.03 (0.71)	0.98 (0.75)	1.01 (0.66)
Neighborhood poverty	0–3	1.30 (0.92)	2.47 (0.72)	1.29 (1.18)
Mother's education	1–6	3.71 (1.17)	3.49 (1.19)	3.29 (1.39)
Two-parent household	0,1	69%	46%	51%
Physical activity	0–40	0.17 (0.09)	0.14 (0.08)	0.16 (0.08)
Young Adulthood				
Marital status	0,1	36%	22%	45%
Age	17–27	21.2 (1.52)	21.6 (1.57)	20.9 (1.73)
Unintended pregnancy	0,1	13%	26%	37%
High-risk sex	0,1	02%	03%	02%
STI	0,1	11%	35%	11%

[a] Because our sample of rural Black girls is sparse in regions outside of the South, estimates based on this group in our models should be interpreted as effects generalizable only to this region.

that there is very little variability in high-risk sex for any of the racial/ethnic groups in either urban or rural areas. Because of the effect of this homogeneity on the statistical power of tests among Black and Latina girls, who have smaller sample sizes—particularly in rural areas—we report the results of the models for the highest-risk outcome for White girls only. Variability for the remaining two sexual outcomes (STIs and unintended pregnancy) was sufficient for all groups except rural Latinas. Despite low statistical power, we chose to report the model results for rural Latinas in order to provide preliminary data for this understudied group. The key findings of the analysis are given in Table 12.3.

High-Risk Sex

The direct effect of physical activity was sizable and in the hypothesized direction for White girls (see Table 12.3). In addition, we had enough statistical power in the sample of White girls to test the statistical significance of the moderating effect of an urban context, which is shown in Figure 12.1. Inactivity is associated with predictions of a higher probability of high-risk sex, especially for White girls in urban areas. However, with moderate physical activity levels, the probability of high-risk sex was less than 3% for both urban and rural White girls.

Sexually Transmitted Infections

Earlier physical activity predicted lower levels of probability of being diagnosed with an STI only among *urban* White girls (Figure 12.2). The urban/rural differential effect was particularly evident among the least active girls: Whereas inactive girls in rural areas can be expected to have very low rates of STI diagnosis by young adulthood (approximately 8%), an astounding nearly one in four inactive urban girls are expected to be diagnosed with an STI (approximately 24%). Physical activity tempers urban girls' vulnerability, such that expected rates of STI diagnosis among the most athletic urban girls (approximately 7%) were as low as rates predicted for inactive rural girls.

Unintended Pregnancy

The analyses showed no significant effects of adolescent physical activity on experiencing an unintended pregnancy for any racial or ethnic group in either urban or rural areas, after controlling for marital status and other relevant demographic variables.

TABLE 12.3

Unstandardized Logistic Regression Coefficients and Their Standard Errors Estimated for the Effects of Physical Activity on the Probabilities of Sexual Risk in Young Adulthood, by Race/Ethnicity and Urbanicity

	Unintended Pregnancy	Diagnosed with an STD	Engaging in Very High-Risk Sex
URBAN			
White girls	-1.77 (1.30)	-3.70 (1.56)	-7.98 (3.64) [*]
Black girls	0.22 (1.67)	0.81 (1.93)	N/A [a]
Latina girls	-1.47 (1.68)	0.81 (1.90)	N/A [a]
RURAL			
White girls	-0.62 (1.22)	1.69 (1.40)	-9.34 (2.52) [***]
Black girls	-1.24 (2.19)	0.66 (2.80)	N/A [a]
Latina girls	-4.99 (3.65)	-1.11 (7.47)	N/A [a]

[*] $p < .05$, [**] $p < .01$, [***] $p < .001$.

a The occurrence of very high-risk sexual behaviors (prostitution and/or sex with an IV drug user) was too low among Black and Latina girls to estimate any regression effects. Therefore, the results of these models are not reported.

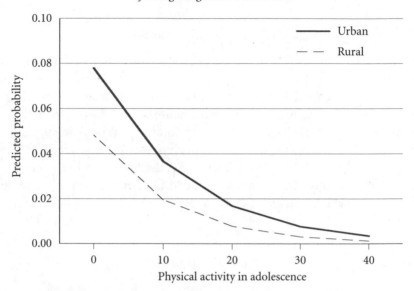

FIGURE 12.1

*Effect of Adolescent Physical Activity on the Probability
of Being Diagnosed with an STI*

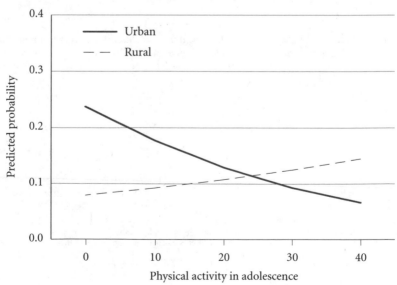

FIGURE 12.2

*Effect of Adolescent Physical Activity on the Probability
of Engaging in Very High-Risk Sex*

Conclusion

Evidence is accumulating that "if we let [them] play," girls may delay becoming sexually active and, when sexually active, may be less likely to engage in risky sexual behaviors. The effect of high school physical activity evident during high school extends to young adulthood and is detectable over and above the independent effects of relevant control variables. However, our research findings show that these effects depend on a young woman's race/ethnicity and on where she lives. In other words, the benefits of being physically active in high school, in lowering the likelihood of risky sexual behavior, extend to most but not all girls.

Diffusion theory suggests that the more diverse environment of urban centers combines both factors that protect young women from engaging in risky sexual behaviors and factors that increase that probability. This contrasts with the relatively greater homogeneity of rural areas. In urban areas, protective factors can be employment opportunities, a variety of recreational venues, and easier access to health care and information, while the risk factors include exposure to urban subcultures where risky sexual activity is more normative. Our findings suggest that having been physically active in high school makes young women less likely to fall under the influence of the factors that promote engaging in dangerous sexual relationships. We found that physically active White young adult women who live in urban environments are less likely than their rural sisters to engage in risky sexual behaviors, whereas physically inactive urban White young women are more likely than their rural sisters to engage in risky sexual behaviors. Greater understanding of the mechanisms connecting physical activity, race/ethnicity, urbanization, and sexual behavior is needed. Being physically active during high school may make a girl more aware of her body and decisions that affect her body. This awareness may be augmented by the employment and recreational opportunities, social supports, and health information and access that are more readily available in urban areas. Time in sports may also compete with time available for high-risk sexual relationships or dangerous sexual practices.

Limitations

Although our studies confirm the relation between being physically active in high school and exhibiting lower sexual risk behaviors, we recognize some important limitations of our results. Because these are secondary analyses of existing data, we were constrained by the parameters of this data set. For example, these studies do not address risky sexual behaviors beyond those that occur within the context of heterosexual intercourse. We also know nothing of these effects on cultural groups not included in our sample—Asians, Native Americans, and smaller groups of Latinas in each region. Filling these gaps in our collective knowledge will require the analysis of other data sets, either primary or secondary.

The analyses we reported here also do not address causal *mechanisms* underlying these relationships. It could be that the social and physical aspects of sports and exercise encourage a girl to modify her willingness to follow the gender and sexual scripts of her cultural niche, or it may be that both physical activity and sexual behaviors are influenced by variables not taken into account by our model. While our longitudinal models partially address the time-ordered condition required for causal inferences, we are still a long way from fully understanding the mechanisms by which physical and sexual activity are related in different sociocultural environments.

More research on mediators and moderators that operate in urban and rural environments is needed. We intend to make forays into deepening this understanding by modeling various social and psychological processes as mediators of the observed relationships. These explorations will be similarly constrained by the availability of good indicators of hypothesized mechanisms in the Add Health data set. In order to address this research question more adequately, extensive qualitative work is needed to augment quantitative findings in a mixed-model framework. We need to draw from the experiential knowledge of members of each cultural niche shown to be of particular interest in our models and of those in niches left out of our models.

Implications

This research suggests that strengthening high school girls' physical activity programs is important and that we should consider the cultural context in which girls play. Particularly for girls who come from highly sheltered backgrounds where girls' athletics is a new practice that is not highly valued, it may be important to inform the girls and their parents of the benefits of physical activity in terms of taking charge of one's body and physical and sexual health.

Participating in a school sport or becoming physically active through exercise appears to have long-term benefits for White girls from urban areas. Social supports and facilities that make it possible for these young women to take better care of their physical and sexual health need to be identified and implemented, as well as the functional equivalents of these supports and facilities for girls from other backgrounds. In that way, if we let her play, *any* girl can benefit from the protective effects of being physically active.

NOTES

Research reported here was funded by grant 1 R01 HD38530–01A1 from the National Institute of Child Health and Human Development. Ineke Ceder's expert editing is gratefully acknowledged.

This research uses data from Add Health, a program project designed by J. Richard Udry, Peter S. Bearman, and Kathleen Mullan Harris and funded by grant P01-HD31921 from the National Institute of Child Health and Human Development, with cooperative funding from 17 other agencies. Special acknowledgment is due Ronald R. Rindfuss and Barbara Entwisle for assistance in the original design. Persons interested in obtaining data files from Add Health should contact Add Health, Carolina Population Center, 123 W. Franklin Street, Chapel Hill, NC 27516–2524 (ww.cpc.unc.edu/addhealth/contract.html).

1. In the Add Health interview, respondents are given an explicit definition of sexual intercourse as a penis inserted into the vagina. This definition has made it difficult to ascertain the reporting of same-sex sexual relations that may or may not have involved using barrier methods of protection.

2. Physical activity was defined as the average frequency of physical activities reported at the first two waves of data collection, weighted by estimates of the intensity of the various activities. Intensity of physical activity was coded using the guidelines offered by the Department of Health and Human Services and the Centers for Disease Control and Prevention. These guidelines include lists of activities considered "moderate" (e.g., brisk walking, golf, softball) and those considered "vigorous" (e.g., jogging or running, aerobic dancing, soccer) These guidelines can be downloaded from the following Web site: www.cdc.gov/nccd-php/dnpa/physical/recommendations/index.htm.

3. We define *urban* as those living in census blocks containing 2,500 or more persons in 1990, an operationalization constructed by the creators of the Add Health Contextual database.

4. Although there were a large number of girls who could be identified under the umbrella term *Latina* (551 urban and 98 rural), this group was quite heteroge-

neous, made up of Mexican American, Puerto Rican American, Cuban American, Central American, and other Spanish-speaking groups. We know from our previous research that *rates* of adolescent girls' sports participation among different Latino groups vary widely (Erkut & Tracy, 2002). This variability requires caution in interpreting results pertaining to *relationships* among key variables in this mixed group.

5. We did not have the statistical power to also examine regional effects in conjunction with urbanicity and race/ethnicity. Instead, we modeled region as a control variable. Some of the control variables were based on information obtained in the first wave of data collection. These were geographic region of residence, adolescents' reports of mother's educational attainment (supplemented by the mother's own report, when available), adolescents' self-reports of residing in a two-parent household, and variables constructed from census block data (the proportion of households at or below the federal poverty line and urbanicity). We also controlled for marital status, social desirability, and the age of the respondent in Wave 3. Further details about the modeling specifications used in these analyses are available from the first author.

REFERENCES

Bearman, P. S., Jones, J., & Udry, J. R. (1997). *The National Longitudinal Study of Adolescent Health: Research design.* Retrieved December 12, 2005, from http://www.cpc.unc.edu/projects/addhealth/design

Cahn, S. K. (1994). *Coming on strong: Gender and sexuality in twentieth-century women's sport.* New York: Free Press.

Cohen, D. (1996). Law, social policy, and violence: The impact of regional cultures. *Journal of Personality and Social Psychology, 70,* 961–978.

Cohen, D., Nisbett, R. E., Bowdle, B. F., & Schwartz, N. (1996). Insult, aggression, and the southern culture of honor: An "Experimental Ethnography." *Journal of Personality and Social Psychology, 70,* 945–960.

Connell, R. W. (1987). *Gender and power: Society, the person and sexual politics.* Cambridge, England: Polity Press.

Connell, R. W. (1995). *Masculinities.* Berkeley: University of California Press.

Cradock, A., El Ayadi, A., Gortmaker, S., Hannon, C., Sobol, A., & Wiecha, J. (2002). *Play across Boston: Summary report.* Retrieved December 12, 2005, from http://www.sportinsociety.org/play_across_boston.pdf

Crespo, C. J. (2005). Physical activity in minority populations: Overcoming a public health challenge. *President's Council on Physical Fitness and Sports Research Digest, 6*(2), 1–6.

Desertrain, G. S., & Weiss, M. (1988). Being female and athletic: A cause for conflict? *Sex Roles, 18,* 567–582.

Duncan, G. J., & Hoffman, S. D. (1990). Welfare benefits, economic opportunities, and out-of-wedlock births among Black teenage girls. *Demography, 27,* 519–535.

Elder, G. H., Jr. (1998). The life course as developmental theory. *Child Development, 69,* 1–12.

Erkut, S., & Tracy, A. J. (2002). Predicting adolescent self-esteem from participation in school sports among Latino subgroups. *Hispanic Journal of Behavioral Sciences 24,* 409–429.

Eyler, A., Matson-Koffman, D., Young, D. R., Wilcox, S., Wilbur, J., Thompson, J. L., et al. (2003). Quantitative study of correlates of physical activity in women from diverse racial/ethnic groups. *American Journal of Preventive Medicine, 25*(3 Suppl. 1), 93–103.

Hanson, S. L., Morrison, D. R., & Ginsburg, A. L. (1989). The antecedents of teenage fatherhood. *Demography, 26,* 579–596.

Hargreaves, J. (1994). *Sporting females: Critical issues in the history and sociology of women's sports.* London: Routledge.

Hasbrook, C. A. (1995). *Gendering practices and first graders' bodies: Physicality, sexuality and bodily adornment in a minority inner-city school.* Cited in President's Council on Physical Fitness and Sport. (1997, May). *Physical activity and sport in the lives of girls: Physical and mental health dimensions from an interdisciplinary approach.* Washington, DC: Author.

Kane, M. J. (1995). Resistance/transformation of the oppositional binary: Exposing sport as a continuum. *Journal of Sport and Social Issues, 19,* 191–218.

Ku, L., Sonenstein, F. L., & Pleck, J. H. (1992). Patterns of HIV risk and preventive behaviors among teenage men in the U.S.A. *Public Health Reports, 107,* 131–138.

Messner, M. (1992). Boyhood, organized sports and the construction of masculinity. In M. A. Messner & D. F. Sabo (Eds.), *Sport, men, and the gender order* (pp. 19–29). Champaign, IL: Human Kinetics.

Nisbett, R. E. (1993). Violence and U.S. regional culture. *American Psychologist, 48,* 441–449.

Plaut, V. C., Markus, H. R., & Lachman, M. E. (2002). Place matters: Consensual features and regional variation in American well-being and self. *Journal of Personality and Social Psychology, 83,* 160–184.

Prine, C. (2001, May 23). Poor districts still find money for boys. Retrieved January 10, 2005, from http://www.pitssburghlive.com/x/tribune-review/specialreport/titleix/poordistricts.html

Rogers, E. M. (1995). *Diffusion in innovations* (4th ed.). New York: Free Press.

Seidman, S. N., Mosher, W. D., & Aral, S. O. (1994). Predictors of high-risk behavior in unmarried American women: Adolescent environment as risk factor. *Journal of Adolescent Health, 15,* 126–132.

Strang, D., & Soule, S. A. (1998). Diffusion in organizations and social movements: From hybrid corn to poison pills. *Annual Review of Sociology, 24,* 265–290.

Tracy, A. J., & Erkut, S. (2002). Gender and race patterns in the pathways from sports participation to self-esteem. *Sociological Perspectives, 45,* 445–466.

Tracy, A., & Erkut, S. (2003, April). *Physical activity and girls' risky behavior: The role of race/ethnicity and geography.* In S. Erkut (Chair), Adolescent Physical Activity and Sexual Behavior Symposium presented at the 2003 biennial meeting of the Society for Research in Child Development, Tampa, Florida.

Women's Sports Foundation. (2002). *Title IX at 30: Athletics receive C+.* Retrieved December 12, 2005, from http://www.womenssportsfoundation.org/binary-data/WSF_ARTICLE/pdf_file/902.pdf

Condom Use Among Sexually Active Latina Girls in Alternative High Schools

Jill Denner and Karin Coyle

I've only had two partners, and every time, the first couple times or whatever, I always use a condom because you want to protect yourself from STDs.

Estella

This study is guided by theoretical perspectives that situate sexual behavior within the context of personal, relational, and cultural factors. Theories that predict condom use in White and African American adolescents and adults focus primarily on individual-level factors and have not been tested specifically with sexually active Latina teens. We know a lot about what prevents girls from using condoms because most research has focused on the barriers to condom use. Studies suggest teens do not use condoms because they do not plan ahead or fear that others will think they are promiscuous if they carry them or know how to use them (Hillier, Harrison, & Warr, 1998; Tolman, 2002). However, many Latina girls like Estella do use condoms, and little is known about the factors that determine their use. This information is essential to strengthen interventions so they build on girls' strengths and strategies to promote safer sex, and avoid unplanned pregnancy and sexually transmitted infections.

To understand healthy decision making among Latinas, we expand on Ajzen's (1991) theory of planned behavior, a widely tested theory of sexual behavior. This theory suggests that intentions predict behavior, and that intentions are explained by attitudes toward the behavior, perceived norms about the behavior, and a sense of behavioral control. In other words, this theory predicts that girls would have greater intentions to use condoms if they had a positive attitude toward condoms, thought their friends were using them, and had the self-efficacy (perceived ability) to use them. Although this theory has explained intentions that are linked to condom use in youth, it does not address the contexts that support or undermine girls' strengths.

In this chapter, we examine condom decision making among a sub-group of Latina girls, those who attend community day schools, a type of alternative school. Most students in these schools have been removed from mainstream schools and come from families and neighborhoods that are marginalized from their communities (Figueira-McDonough, 1998; Loutzenheiser, 2002). According to the National Center for Education Statistics, in 2000 there were more than 600,000 students nationwide enrolled in public alternative schools or programs for at-risk students (Kleiner, Porch, & Farris, 2002). Alternative high schools serve students who do not progress academically in mainstream high schools, often due to issues such as disciplinary problems or chronic absenteeism. Some have described these students as "invisible" to the rest of society (Books, 1998). Because there is little research that focuses on Latinas in alternative schools, the following literature review focuses more broadly on Latinas.

Urban Latina Girls

According to the 2000 census, Latinos are now the largest minority group living in the United States (Guzmán, 2001). Two thirds of Latinos in the United States are of Mexican origin (Therrien & Ramirez, 2001); however, Latina girls are a heterogeneous group with a range of socioeconomic backgrounds and different histories in the United States. For example, some are from families that have lived in the Southwest since it was part of Mexico. Other families immigrated in order to find better economic and educational opportunities for their children (Suárez-Orozco & Suárez-Orozco, 2001). Although many were looking for better opportunities, some families were fleeing violence and corruption in their countries, and others came for professional promotions. Many urban families lived in a city in their home country, but there are also many who came from rural communities. Their children's experience in the United States depends on what researchers have called the social "capital" that parents and extended families bring from their country of origin (Portes & Rumbaut, 2001; Stanton-Salazar, 2001). Despite their growing numbers, there is still little research that focuses on the experiences of Latina girls, and even less that uses a strengths-based perspective (Denner & Guzmán, in press).

Latina Girls' Sexual Behavior: Risk and Protective Factors

Students in alternative schools are more likely to be sexually active than those in mainstream schools. Data from 9th to 12th grade students in a nationally representative sample from the Youth Risk Behavior Survey show that among Latinas, 46% were sexually active, 52% used a condom at last intercourse, and 7% reported at least one pregnancy (Grunbaum et al., 2004). In contrast, a national study of alternative school students that includes pregnant and parenting teens found that 82% of the Latina girls reported having had sex (Grunbaum et al., 1999). Condom use among Latinas has risen steadily over the past 10 years, and changes in contraceptive use vary depending on generational status and national origin. Among sexually experienced adolescents of Mexican origin, those born in the United States of immigrant parents were more likely to report using contraception than those born outside the United States (Brindis, Driscoll, Biggs, & Valderrama, 2002).

Condom use by Latina females is influenced by the nature of the relationship and by personal, cultural, and contextual factors. Among Latina adults, condoms are more likely to be used in the early part of a relationship or with new partners but are less likely to be used with someone who is considered a steady partner (Marín, Gómez, & Hearst, 1993). Among Latino college students, condom use at last intercourse was related to perceived partner approval (Jemmott, Jemmott, & Villarruel, 2002). Although fewer studies of partner characteristics have been conducted with Latina adolescents, one study found that girls gave different reasons for having sex with a steady partner (love) than with a nonsteady partner (pressure; Flores, Eyre, & Millstein, 1998). We expect that these different reasons for having sex will also result in different reasons for using condoms. In this study, we examine whether the relationship between intentions to use condoms and psychosocial factors is different for steady and nonsteady partners.

Sexual history also appears to play a role in whether girls have a sense of personal power and are therefore more likely to use condoms in their relationships. Hence, age at first intercourse may play a role. A study of African American and Latino adolescents found that being older at first intercourse increases the likelihood of using condoms (Smith, 1997). In addition, sexually active Latina adolescents are more likely to use birth control when they have had a previous pregnancy (Durant, Seymore, Pendergrast, & Beckman, 1990). On the other hand, Latina girls who reported that they were forced to do something sexual against their will were more likely to engage in sexual behavior that put them at risk for STIs and pregnancy (Marín & Arreola, 2000).

Studies of Latinos have found acculturation to be both a risk factor and a protective factor. Research on immigrant Latinos suggests that both physical and psychological health decline as youth assimilate to U.S. culture, resulting in more risky sexual behavior (Hernández & Charney, 1998). Communities that emphasize cultural factors, such as *familismo* (a strong connection to the family) and conservative norms about sexual behavior, can protect girls from risky sexual behavior (Denner, Kirby, Coyle, & Brindis, 2001; Villarruel, 1998). Another measure of cultural connections, speaking a language other than English, appears to protect early adolescents from engaging in sex (Santelli et al., 2004). However, these same norms can prevent sexually active teens from obtaining information about contraceptive use (Guzmán et al., 2003; Minnis & Padian, 2001). Several studies suggest that more acculturated teens initiate sex earlier and have more partners, but they are also more likely to use condoms (Ford & Norris, 1993; Kaplan, Erickson, & Juarez-Reyes, 2002). While Latino culture can motivate girls to delay sex, U.S. cultural values can legitimize the use of contraception among sexually active teens.

Beliefs about peer behavior play a role in Latina girls' beliefs about appropriate sexual and romantic behavior. For example, young adolescent Latina girls are more likely to engage in sexual behavior such as kissing when they believe their peers are sexually involved (Christopher, Johnson, & Roosa, 1993; Flores, Tschann, & Marín, 2002; O'Sullivan & Meyer-Bahlberg, 2003). Condom use is higher among African American and Hispanic youth who believe their peers are using condoms, a relationship that is particularly strong for girls (Norris & Ford, 1998).

In summary, condom use appears to be influenced by the characteristics of relationships, personal factors such as sexual history, level of acculturation to mainstream U.S. norms, sexual coercion, and perceived peer behavior. Nevertheless, little is known about the sexual behavior and contraceptive use of Latina girls who attend alternative schools who may be at

TABLE 13.1
Description of the Girls

Demographics	Percent
Born in the United States	86%
Language spoken at home	
Only English	22%
About half English and half another language	43%
Only a language other than English	10%
Grades last year	
Mostly As or As and Bs	13%
Mostly Bs or Bs and Cs	14%
Mostly Cs or Cs and Ds	31%
Mostly Ds or Ds and Fs	31%
Educational aspirations	
Not finish high school	4%
Graduate from high school	43%
Get an education beyond high school	49%
Family structure	
Live with mother	81%
Live with two or more parents or legal guardians	42%
Mother earned at least a high school diploma	65%
Family income	
Job or work	79%
Welfare	12%

particular risk for pregnancies and STIs. This chapter will provide some descriptive information about their behavior and intentions, test whether the theory of planned behavior can explain condom use intentions, and describe the factors that underlie their attitudes and condom efficacy. To that end, we address the following research questions:

1. What are the frequency and reasons for condom use among Latina alternative school students?
2. Does the theory of planned behavior explain Latina girls' intentions to use condoms at next sexual intercourse? Do the explanatory models vary by type of sexual partner (steady versus nonsteady)?
3. What factors predict condom attitudes and self-efficacy to use condoms?

Sample

Participants are a subset from a randomized controlled trial testing the efficacy of A114You! a school-based program designed to reduce teen pregnancy and HIV transmission (Coyle et al., in press). For the purposes of this analysis, we include data from the baseline surveys of 74 female students who indicated they think of themselves as "Hispanic or Latino," have had sex at least once, and are unmarried. The age of these 74 girls ranged from 14 to 18 years, with an average of 16 years. Basic demographics are shown in Table 13.1. Most of the girls were born in the United States, and most were bilingual (Spanish/English). The 72 participants who reported their grades last year had various levels of academic performance. Twelve percent were not in school the previous year. There was also a range of educational aspirations, and almost half expected to get an education beyond high school.

The larger study involved 24 community day schools located in four large urban counties in northern California. Thirteen schools were randomly assigned to receive the A114You! intervention; the remaining 11 schools served as comparison sites. In general, students are referred to the community day schools for severe discipline issues, substance use, and chronic absenteeism. The purpose of these schools is to help students make up lost credits so they can return to their mainstream schools or receive a GED. Students may spend from less than 1 month to more than 12 months in these schools, depending on their academic status. The evaluation compared students who received the intervention ($n = 597$) with those in a standard care control group ($n = 391$); the findings are reported in Coyle et al. (in press). Study schools included students in grades 9 to 12, and most were small (many were single classrooms). Students faced a range of challenges in their personal and academic lives, including learning disabilities, poverty, community and domestic violence, family drug abuse, and gang involvement.

Additional data were collected from a focus group about condom use from eight girls (four Latinas) who were enrolled at an alternative school. We present quotations from Latina girls who participated in this group.

Measures

Language at home was measured by one question. Responses were on a 5-point scale, ranging from 1 (*only English*) to 5 (*only my other language*).

Educational aspirations were measured by one question: "How far do you think you will go in school?" Responses were on a 4-point scale, ranging from 1 (*won't finish high school*) to 4 (*will graduate from college*).

Number of pregnancies was based on a single question: "How many times have you been pregnant?" Response options included 0 through 5 and *not sure*. The *not sure* responses were coded to *missing* for these analyses.

Forced sex was measured by one question: "Has someone ever forced you to have sex against your will?" Responses were either 1 (*yes*) or 0 (*no*).

Condom use was measured with one question: "During the past 3 months, how often did you use condoms when you had sex with . . . ?" Responses were separate for steady and nonsteady partners and ranged from 1 (*never*) to 4 (*always*), with the option to say they did not have sex with that type of partner in the last 3 months.

Contraceptive use at last intercourse was measured by one question "What did you or your partner use to prevent pregnancy the *last time* you had sex? Mark all that apply."

Reasons for no condom use were measured by one item: "Think of the times you did not use condoms. Which of the following were reasons for not using condoms? Mark a bubble for each reason." There were seven options, and a place for girls to write in a different reason.

Condom intentions were measured using one question: "The next time you have sex, how likely are you to use a condom?" This question was asked separately for steady and nonsteady partners. Response choices were on a 5-point scale ranging from 1 (*I'm sure we won't*) to 5 (*we definitely will*).

The *condom self-efficacy* scale includes 6 items that start with "How sure are you that you could . . . ?" The options are to buy or get condoms, have a condom with you when you need it, use a condom correctly, use a condom without ruining the mood, tell your partner that you want to use condoms when you have sex, and keep from having sex until your partner agrees to use a condom. The first 4 items were the same for steady and nonsteady partners, but for the last two, participants could give different responses for different types of partners. Responses were on a 4-point scale ranging from 1 (*I'm sure I could not*) to 4 (*I'm sure I could*). Alphas were good: for steady partner (.72) and nonsteady partner (.65). This scale was a modified version of Basen-Engquist et al. (1998).

Condom attitudes were measured using a 9-item scale that includes questions about personal attitudes toward condoms, including how the young women think their partner would react. Students responded to statements such as "Sex does not feel as good with a condom" and "Asking my partner to use condoms would be like saying 'I don't trust you.'"

Responses ranged from 1 (*strongly disagree*) to 5 (*strongly agree*), with high scores indicating more positive attitudes. The alpha for this scale was .79. Items come from Jemmott, Jemmott, and Hacker (1992).

Peer norms were measured by one item: "Of your friends who have had sex, how many of them use condoms most or all of the time?" Responses ranged from 1 (*none or almost none of them*) to 5 (*all or almost all of them*). This item comes from Coyle et al. (2001).

Steady partners were described as "people you go with" and *nonsteady* partners were described as "casual partners or people you've just met or picked up."

Data Analyses

The survey data were used to address the three research questions. Descriptive analyses, including percentages, means, and standard deviations, were used to describe the sample. T-tests were used to assess mean differences between those who did and did not use condoms at last intercourse. Finally, we used path analysis, which is a series of multiple regressions, to examine the links among the multiple variables.

Results

We first describe girls' reported sexual history and then report the findings for our research questions. The focus is on the survey data, but quotations from the focus group participants are inserted for illustration. Although participants were included in the study because they reported having sex at least once, only 66% reported having sex in the last 3 months. Multiple partners were not common: 11% of the respondents had more than one steady partner in the last 3 months, and 12% had more than one nonsteady partner. Five (7%) reported having sex with both males and females, and one person reported only sex with females. Age at first sex ranged from 10 to 17 years, with an average of 14 years. Twenty-six percent said they had been forced to have sex. One third (34%) reported they have gotten pregnant at least once, and 8% more than once. Alcohol use before sex varied, with 34% saying they never drank, 37% drank once in a while, 19% drank most of the time, and 8% always had alcohol before sex.

TABLE 13.2
Contraceptive Use at Last Intercourse

Contraceptive Method	Percent
Condoms	43%
No method	20%
Withdrawal	20%
Pills	11%
Depo-Provera	7%
Don't remember	4%

Question 1: What Does Condom Use Look Like in Latina Alternative School Students?

As shown in Table 13.2, condom use was the most popular form of contraception used at last intercourse (43%), but condoms were not used consistently. However, a total of 40% used either no contraception or the ineffective method of withdrawal. Relatively few (18%) reported using contraception that would be obtained through a clinic, such as birth control pills or Depo-Provera.

Several factors differentiated those who did from those who did not use condoms at last intercourse. Girls who reported using a condom also reported significantly higher levels of condom self-efficacy with both steady ($t[1,57] = -2.47, p < .05$) and nonsteady partners ($t[1,-2.69], p < .01$) than those who reported no condom use. Girls who reported using a condom at last intercourse also reported more positive attitudes toward condoms ($[t,1,52] = 2.04, p < .05$) and fewer previous pregnancies ($t[1,56] = 2.97, p < .01$). Past behavior predicted future intentions. Girls who reported using a condom at last intercourse were also significantly more likely to intend to use one at next intercourse with steady ($t[1.56] = -4.25, p < .001$) and nonsteady partners ($t[1,49] - 2.49, p < .05$).

"CONDOM USE DOESN'T DEPEND ON RACE OR ETHNICITY . . . IT DEPENDS ON IF YOU LIKE CONDOMS, OR IF YOU DON'T LIKE CONDOMS"

When participants reported that they had sex without using a condom in the last 3 months, they were asked to mark all the reasons for lack of use. As shown in Table 13.3, a summary of responses from 35 girls shows that their reasons for not using a condom included negative attitudes toward condoms and a lack of planning. One quarter of the participants reported that partner reluctance was one of the reasons.

TABLE 13.3
Reasons for No Condom Use in Last 3 Months

Reason	Percent
Sex doesn't feel as good with a condom	56%
I wasn't planning to have sex	46%
I didn't have a condom with me	40%
I didn't ask my partner to use one	38%
I was high on drugs and/or alcohol	28%
My partner didn't want to use one	26%

Of the 45 participants who reported currently having sex, the majority said that their partner uses a condom some or all of the time. Table 13.4 shows that only 11% reported that he refused to use them, but 18% said they did not know how he felt about condom use.

"GIRLS MAKE THE DECISION [TO USE CONDOMS] BECAUSE MALES DON'T REALLY CARE IF YOU HAVE A CONDOM OR NOT. . . . JUST AS LONG AS HE GETS TO HIT IT . . . HE DOESN'T GET PREGNANT"

As shown in Table 13.5, there was a range of condom use among the 49 girls who had sex with a steady partner in the last 3 months and the 22 who had sex with a nonsteady partner. Condom use appeared to be more consistent with nonsteady ($M = 3.27$, $SD = 1.12$) than steady partners ($M = 2.39$, $SD = 1.20$). Participants reported strong intentions to use a condom at next intercourse with both types of partners, but particularly with a nonsteady partner ($M = 4.57$, $SD = 1.02$) compared with steady ($M = 3.68$, $SD = 1.50$).

Question 2: Does the Theory of Planned Behavior Explain Latina Girls' Intentions to Use Condoms at Next Sexual Intercourse? How Does It Vary by Type of Partner?

The data suggest that the theory of planned behavior partially explained Latina girls' intentions to use condoms with both steady and nonsteady partners. A series of multiple regression analyses were run, and the standardized beta coefficients (path coefficients that measure the size of the effect) are reported in the two figures. Condom self-efficacy and attitude toward condoms were associated with intentions to use condoms the next time they have sex with a *steady* partner, but peer norms were not directly related. As shown in Figure 13.1, higher condom self-efficacy and more

TABLE 13.4
How Boyfriend Feels About Using Condoms with You

	Percent
Uses them every time we have sex	22%
Uses them some of the time	49%
Will not use them if asked	11%
Don't know	18%

TABLE 13.5
Condom Use and Intentions With Different Partners

	Steady Partners	Nonsteady Partners
Condom Use in Last 3 Months		
Never	33%	14%
Sometimes	22%	9%
Almost always	18%	14%
Always	27%	64%
Intention to Use Condoms		
Sure we won't	15%	4%
We probably won't	7%	2%
There is an even chance we will or won't	18%	4%
We probably will	12%	7%
We definitely will	45%	66%

positive attitudes toward condoms correlated with greater intentions to use a condom with a steady partner. Condom attitudes were also associated with condom intentions through their influence on self-efficacy: Those with more positive attitudes also had greater self-efficacy. Peer norms were not directly related to condom intentions, but they did correlate with condom self-efficacy and attitudes. In other words, those who reported that their friends always use a condom also reported more positive attitudes toward condoms and higher levels of condom self-efficacy with steady partners.

As shown in Figure 13.2, there was only partial support of the theory of planned behavior for intentions to use condoms the next time respondents have sex with a *nonsteady* partner. Condom self-efficacy with nonsteady partners was correlated with intentions. A more positive attitude toward condoms was associated with higher levels of condom self-efficacy, and those who reported more condom use by friends also reported more positive attitudes toward condoms. Neither condom attitudes nor peer norms were directly related to intentions to use a condom at next intercourse with a nonsteady partner.

FIGURE 13.1
Theory of Planned Behavior for Steady Partners

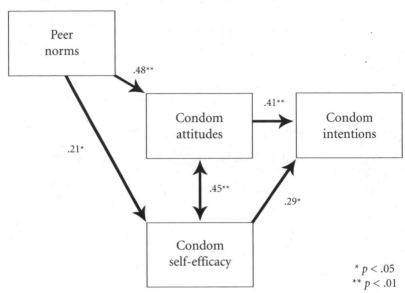

Question 3: What Factors Predict Attitudes, Norms,
and Perceived Control?

To better understand the contributions of condom attitudes, peer norms, and condom self-efficacy on girls' intentions to use condoms, we did a series of multiple regression analyses. Figure 13.3 shows the results of two separate analyses, one for steady and one for nonsteady partners. Condom self-efficacy was directly influenced by the number of pregnancies and age at first sex, but the relationship varied by partner type. Girls who report the highest levels of efficacy to use condoms with nonsteady partners were older at first intercourse. However, self-efficacy to use condoms with steady partners was mediated by the number of previous pregnancies. In other words, when girls were older at first sex, they had fewer pregnancies and higher levels of condom self-efficacy with steady partners. Age at first sex was related to language at home and history of forced sex; girls who spoke more Spanish at home delayed first intercourse longer, and those who reported no experience of forced sex also delayed their first sexual intercourse. Educational aspirations were not associated with age at first sex. The model did not explain the variance in either condom attitudes or peer norms.

FIGURE 13.2
Theory of Planned Behavior for Nonsteady Partners

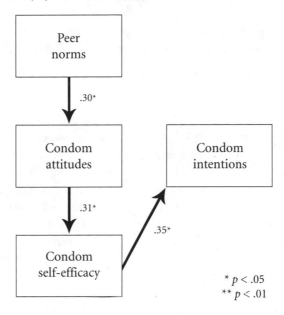

FIGURE 13.3
Factors That Explain Condom Self-Efficacy

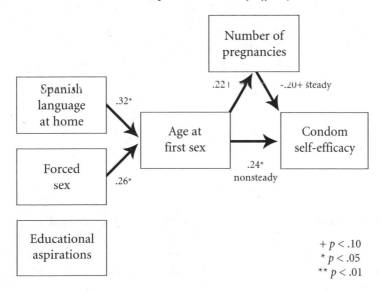

Discussion

Efforts to understand and promote condom use have focused primarily on the barriers to use, and many studies are limited by their focus on individual-level characteristics. The findings presented in this chapter fill a gap in our understanding of the broader contextual factors that result in condom use by an understudied sample of Latina girls, sexually active students enrolled in an alternative high school. In this sample, almost half of the sexually active teens use condoms, especially in the early stages of a relationship or with nonsteady partners. This is higher than the levels found in a national data set of alternative school students (males and females combined), where only 39% of Latino and Latina students used a condom at last intercourse (Grunbaum et al., 1999). The following discussion of these findings is organized to highlight the individual-level characteristics, as well as important aspects of the relationship and cultural influences on girls' condom use, condom intentions, and condom self-efficacy. These findings are interpreted in the context of gender and power theories.

At the individual level, several factors appear to play a role in condom use in this group of girls. First, a positive attitude toward condoms was related to greater intentions to use condoms the next time the girls have sex, a finding that is consistent with the theory of planned behavior and studies of other populations. Attitudes such as the belief that condoms reduce sexual pleasure have been described in studies of other populations (Jemmott & Jemmott, 1992). In addition, the Latina girls in this study indicated that their own lack of planning for sex and availability of condoms were also frequent reasons for lack of use. Contrary to our expectations and previous studies (Smith, 1997), educational aspirations were not associated with age at first sex or any of the psychosocial factors related to condom intentions. This might be due to the fact that it is a more distal factor that will likely have increasing influence as participants get older (Day, 1992).

Although the theory of planned behavior was partially supported, that theory does not help us explain the effects of sexual history, or variation in condom use across partner type. The theory of gender and power has been used to understand condom use among adult women in the context of their relationships (Wingood & DiClemente, 2000). In addition to the attitudes, norms, and perceived control described in the theory of planned behavior, this theory suggests that women must also feel a sense of sexual power, so that they can stand up to a partner who reacts with apathy, anger, or violence if asked to use a condom (Gómez & Marín, 1996). From this view, the context of the relationship is an important factor in determining condom use. Marín (2003) describes how marginalization (e.g., homophobia, poverty, and racism) and gender-based cultural factors (e.g., machismo and sexual silence) can increase HIV risk in the Latino community. Although traditional gender roles may limit a woman's sense of power to negotiate condom use, recent research suggests that Latino attitudes toward gender roles are changing toward more egalitarian norms (Denner & Dunbar, 2004; Harris & Firestone, 1998).

The factors that underlie condom self-efficacy in these girls show the important role of sexual history and suggest the long-term benefit of delaying first sex and avoiding pregnancy. The finding that being older at first intercourse is associated with increased condom efficacy and fewer pregnancies is consistent with other studies of Latino and Latina adolescents where those who initiated sex at an older age were more likely to use a condom regularly (Smith, 1997). Qualitative data are needed to explain whether delaying sex leads to more condom use, or whether an independent factor increases girls' sense of power to do both.

Those who reported partner reluctance as a reason for not using condoms and those who said they did not know how their boyfriend feels about condom use were a minority. Only one quarter said that partner resistance played a role in their lack of use, and when asked specifically about boyfriends, fewer (11%) said their boyfriend refuses to use condoms. The impact of power in a relationship was not a focus in the *A114You!* study; consequently, we lack more in-depth measures on this factor. Without other data, it is not possible to describe the extent to which power relations are a factor in condom use among these Latina girls. There is a clear need for research on the factors that explain girls' sense of personal power in different relationships to negotiate contraceptive use that will protect them from unwanted pregnancy or disease.

The finding that condoms were used more frequently with a nonsteady partner supports previous studies that Latinas are heeding prevention messages when they are not in a regular relationship (Marín et al., 1993). In addition, the majority said they definitely intend to use condoms the next time they have sex with a nonsteady partner. Although intentions to use condoms were higher with nonsteady partners, these intentions were not related to girls' attitudes toward condoms. Not liking condoms was more likely to undermine their use with a steady than a nonsteady partner. Thus, using condoms with a steady partner requires not only condom self-efficacy but possibly also beliefs that condoms will not diminish the romance or sexual pleasure or that they are still needed. While improving attitudes toward condoms may increase their use in steady relationships, they appear less likely to increase condom use outside of a steady relationship. These findings show the importance of tailoring risk-reduction messages to take into consideration how barriers and motivations for using condoms vary depending on the characteristics of the partners.

Cultural protective factors include social norms such as having peers who also use condoms and speaking primarily Spanish at home. Girls' perception of whether or not their friends use condoms played a role in their attitudes toward condom use and in their perceived efficacy to use condoms with steady partners. Research on younger Latinas suggests they are more comfortable talking about sex with friends than with parents or other adults (Guzmán, Arruda, & Feria, in press) and demonstrates the importance of peer norms (Norris & Ford, 1998). However, girls' beliefs about their friends' condom use were not directly associated with their intentions to use them with either steady or nonsteady partners in the study. Instead, the connection was indirect, through condom attitudes and self-efficacy. This finding suggests that peer norms may not be enough to change intentions directly, although they can have a powerful influence on individual-level factors that underlie intentions.

Language use is frequently used as a measure of connection to cultural values or acculturation. In this study, Spanish language use at home was associated with delayed first intercourse, which in turn was related to higher levels of perceived ability to negotiate condom use. Similarly, previous studies demonstrate the protective role that strong cultural traditions can play for reducing sexual risk behavior and Latina teen pregnancy (Denner et al., 2001; Hernández & Charney, 1998). Since mother-daughter relationships are central (Hurtado, 2003), and communication with mothers plays a critical role in Latinas' use of birth control (Guzmán et al., 2003), more information on how this subsample of Latinas talk with their mothers may reveal more about how this protective effect operates.

The girls in this sample who reported being forced to have sex were at considerably higher risk for STIs and unwanted pregnancy. For example, forced sex was also associated with sexual activity at a younger age. Earlier first sex was related to more pregnancies and lower levels of self-efficacy to negotiate condom use. Steet (1998) argues that studies of sexual behavior among alternative school girls must consider the role of oppression and abuse. This subgroup could clearly benefit from systems of support that build a sense of confidence and efficacy to negotiate condom use (see Banister & Leadbeater, this volume).

There are several limitations to this study. First, the sample size was small, which limited our analyses. Second, this is a secondary analysis of data from a larger study that was not precisely designed to understand condom use across partner types among Latinas. For example, no data were collected on factors that other studies have found to explain sexual risk behavior, including parent-child communication, religious identity, and access to condoms (Guzmán et al., 2003). In addition, marginalization (e.g., homophobia, poverty, and racism) and gender-based cultural factors (e.g., machismo and sexual silence) are important for understanding HIV risk in the Latino community (Marín, 2003).

In summary, the findings can be used to paint a picture of the risk factors and protective factors for condom use among sexually active Latinas who attend community alternative schools. Many of these girls use condoms, but their use varies by partner type. Building condom self-efficacy appears to be a promising strategy to increase condom use in this sample. Interventions with sexually active teens could benefit from more information about the factors that underlie condom use. While there is clearly a need for programs and services to increase the frequency and consistency of condom use among Latina girls from alternative schools, this study begins to offer an antidote to the negative media about this subgroup of girls.

Discussion Questions

1. Why does condom use vary depending on the partner? Consider both theories and the data described in this chapter.
2. To what extent might being Latina influence sexual behavior?

References

Ajzen, I. (1991). The theory of planned behavior. *Organizational Behavior and Human Decision Processes, 50*, 179–211.

Basen-Engquist, K., Masse, L., Coyle, K., Kirby, D., Parcel, G., Banspach, S., et al. (1998). Sexual risk behavior beliefs and self-efficacy scales. In C. M. Davis, W. L. Yarber, R. Bauserman, G. Schreer, & S. L. Davis (Eds.), *Handbook of sexuality-related measures* (pp. 541–544). Thousand Oaks, CA: Sage.

Books, S. (1998). *Invisible children in the society and its schools.* Mahwah, NJ: Erlbaum.

Brindis, C. D., Driscoll, A. K., Biggs, M. A., & Valderrama, L. T. (2002). *Fact sheet on Latino youth: Families.* University of California, San Francisco, Center for Reproductive Health Research and Policy, Department of Obstetrics, Gynecology and Reproductive Sciences and the Institute for Health Policy Studies.

Christopher, F. S., Johnson, D. C., & Roosa, M. W. (1993). Family, individual, and social correlates of early Hispanic adolescent sexual expression. *Journal of Sex Research, 30,* 54–61.

Coyle, K., Basen-Engquist, K., Kirby, D., Parcel, G., Banspach, S., Collins, J., et al. (2001). Safer choices: Reducing teen pregnancy, HIV, and STDs. *Public Health Reports, 116*(Suppl. 1), 82–93.

Coyle, K., Kirby, D., Robin, L., Banspach, S., Baumler, E., & Glassman, J. (in press). *A114You!* A randomized trial of an HIV, other STD, and pregnancy prevention intervention for alternative school students. *AIDS Education and Prevention.*

Day, R. D. (1992). The transition to first intercourse among racially and culturally diverse youth. *Journal of Marriage and the Family, 54,* 749–762.

Denner, J., & Dunbar, N. (2004). Negotiating femininity: Power and strategies of Mexican American girls. *Sex Roles, 50,* 301–314.

Denner, J., & Guzmán, B. (Eds.). (in press). *Latina girls: Voices of adolescent strength in the U.S.* New York: New York University Press.

Denner, J., Kirby, D., Coyle, K., & Brindis, C. (2001). The protective role of social capital and cultural norms in Latino communities: A study of adolescent births. *Hispanic Journal of Behavioral Sciences, 23,* 3–21.

Durant, R. H., Seymore, C., Pendergrast, R., & Beckman, R. (1990). Contraceptive behavior among sexually active Hispanic adolescents. *Journal of Adolescent Health Care, 11,* 490–496.

Figueira-McDonough, J. (1998). Environment and interpretation: Voices of young people in poor inner-city neighborhoods. *Youth and Society, 30,* 123–163.

Flores, E., Eyre, S. L., & Millstein, S. G. (1998). Sociocultural beliefs related to sex among Mexican American adolescents. *Hispanic Journal of Behavioral Sciences, 20,* 60–82.

Flores, E., Tschann, J. M., & Marín, B. V. (2002). Latina adolescents: Predicting intentions to have sex. *Adolescence, 37,* 659–679.

Ford, K., & Norris, A. E. (1993). Urban Hispanic adolescents and young adults: Relationship of acculturation to sexual behavior. *Journal of Sex Research, 30,* 316–323.

Gómez, C. A., & Marín, B. V. (1996). Gender, culture, and power: Barriers to HIV-prevention strategies for women. *Journal of Sex Research, 33,* 355–362.

Grunbaum, J. A,. Kann, L., Kinchen, S., Ross, J., Hawkins, J., Lawry, R., et al. (2004). Youth risk behavior surveillance, United States 2003. *Morbidity and Mortality Weekly Report, CDC Surveillance Summaries, 53*(SS02), 1–96.

Grunbaum, J. A., Kahn, L., Kinchen, S. A., Ross, J. G., Gowda, V. R., Collins, J. L., et al. (1999).Youth risk behavior surveillance—National Alternative High School Youth Risk Behavior Survey, United States, 1998. *Morbidity and Mortality Weekly Report, CDC Surveillance Summaries, 48*(SS07), 1–44.

Guzmán, B. (2001). *The Hispanic population: Census 2000 Brief.* Washington, DC: U.S. Census Bureau.

Guzmán, B. L., Arruda, E., & Feria, A. (in press). Los papas, la familia y la sexualidad. In J. Denner & B. Guzmán (Eds.), *Latina girls: Voices of adolescent strength in the U.S.* New York: New York University Press.

Guzmán, B. L., Schlehofer-Sutton, M. M., Villanueva, C. M., Dello Stritto, M. E., Casad, B. J., & Feria, A. et al. (2003). Let's talk about sex: How comfortable discussions about sex impact teen sexual behavior. *Journal of Health Communication, 8,* 583–598.

Harris, R. J., & Firestone, M. M. (1998). Changes in predictors of gender role ideologies among women: A multivariate analysis. *Sex Roles, 38,* 239–251.

Hernández, D., & Charney, E. (Eds.). (1998). *From generation to generation: The health and well-being of children of immigrant families.* Washington, DC: National Academy Press.

Hillier, L., Harrison, L., & Warr, D. (1998). When you carry condoms all the boys think you want it: Negotiating comparing discourses about safe sex. *Journal of Adolescence, 21,* 15–29.

Hurtado, A. (2003). *Voicing Chicana feminisms: Young women speak out on sexuality and identity.* New York: New York University Press.

Jemmott, J. B., Jemmott, L. S., & Hacker, C. I. (1992). Predicting intentions to use condoms among African-American adolescents: The theory of planned behavior as a model for HIV risk-associated behavior. *Ethnicity and Disease, 2,* 371–380.

Jemmott, L. S., & Jemmott, J. B. (1992). Increasing condom-use intention among sexually active inner-city black adolescent women. *Nursing Research, 41,* 273–279.

Jemmott, L. S., Jemmott, J. B., & Villarruel, A. M. (2002). Predicting intentions and condom use among Latino college students. *Journal of the Association of Nurses in AIDS Care, 13,* 59–69.

Kaplan, C. P., Erickson, P. I., & Juarez-Reyes, M. (2002). Acculturation, gender role orientation, and reproductive risk-taking among Latina adolescent family planning clients. *Journal of Adolescent Research, 17,* 103–121.

Kleiner, B., Porch, R., & Farris, E. (2002). *Public alternative schools and programs for students at risk of education failure: 2000–01* (2002–2004). U.S. Department of Education. Washington, DC: National Center for Education Statistics.

Loutzenheiser, L.W. (2002). Being seen and heard: Listening to young women in alternative schools. *Anthropology and Education Quarterly, 33,* 441–464.

Marín, B. V. (2003). HIV prevention in the Hispanic community: Sex, culture, and empowerment. *Journal of Transcultural Nursing, 14,* 186–192.

Marín, B. V., & Arreola, S. G. (2000). El impacto psicosocial del sexo forzado en estudiantes del octavo grado. [The psychosocial impact of forced sex on eighth-grade students]. *La Psicologia Social en Mexico, 8,* 829–835.

Marín, B. V., Gomez, C., & Hearst, N. (1993). Multiple heterosexual partners and condom use among Hispanics and non-Hispanic whites. *Family Planning Perspectives, 25,* 170–174.

Minnis, A. M., & Padian, N. S. (2001). Reproductive health differences among Latin American- and U.S.-born young women. *Journal of Urban Health, 78,* 627–637.

Norris, A. E., & Ford, K. (1998). Moderating influence of peer norms on gender differences in condom use. *Applied Developmental Psychology, 2,* 174–181.

O'Sullivan, L. F., & Meyer-Bahlberg, H. F. L. (2003). African American and Latina inner-city girls' reports of romantic and sexual development. *Journal of Social and Personal Relationships, 20,* 221–238.

Portes, A., & Rumbaut, R. G. (2001). *Legacies: The story of the second generation.* Berkeley: University of California Press.

Santelli, J. S., Kaiser, J., Hirsch, L., Radosh, A., Simkin, L., & Middlestadt, S. (2004). Initiation of sexual intercourse among middle school adolescents: The influence of psychosocial factors. *Journal of Adolescent Health, 34,* 200–208.

Smith, C. A. (1997). Factors associated with early sexual activity among urban adolescents. *Social Work, 42,* 334–346.

Stanton-Salazar, R. D. (2001). *Manufacturing hope and despair: The school and kin support networks of U.S.-Mexican youth.* New York: Teachers College Press.

Steet, L. (1998). Traditional stories of female students in an alternative school. In S. Books (Ed.), *Invisible children in the society and its schools* (pp. 111–120). Mahwah, NJ: Erlbaum.

Suárez-Orozco, C., & Suárez-Orozco, M. (2001). *Children of immigration.* Cambridge, MA: Harvard University Press.

Therrien, M., & Ramirez, R. R. (2001). The Hispanic population in the United States: March 2000. *Current Population Reports* (pp. 20–535). Washington, DC: U.S. Census Bureau.

Tolman, D. L. (2002). *Dilemmas of desire: Teenage girls talk about sexuality.* Cambridge, MA: Harvard University Press.

Villarruel, A. M. (1998). Cultural influences on the sexual attitudes, beliefs and norms of young Latina adolescents. *Journal of the Society of Pediatric Nurses, 3,* 69–81.

Wingood, G. M., & DiClemente, R. J. (2000). Application of the theory of gender and power to examine HIV-related exposures, risk factors, and effective interventions for women. *Health Education and Behavior, 27,* 539–565.

Girl-on-Girl Sexuality

Ritch C. Savin-Williams

First Same-Sex Encounter

Girls have sex with girls. Such encounters can be meaningful, trivial, plea-surable, shaming, intentional, and accidental. They are lustful and roman-tic, motivated by desire, by love, by curiosity, and by acceptance. Sex is with a childhood playmate, an adolescent friend, or a young adult roman-tic partner. It is with one other girl, with multiple girls, or with girls and boys. Yet these assertions are more speculative than empirically verified because investigators have generally ignored the same-sex experiences of girls. One alternative, to generalize from the far more studied sexual expe-riences of boys, would lead to misunderstanding about the same-sex expe-riences of girls. Among the questions addressed in this chapter are: Who are the same-sex partners of girls, and what is their relationship? What happens sexually, who initiates it, and who has an orgasm? Why this girl at this point of time? Is the sex wanted, pleasurable, or meaningful? Does it influence her sexual self-perceptions?

To answer these questions, I review findings provided by contempo-rary social and behavioral sciences and by the life stories of 78 young women I interviewed. Others (e.g., Tolman, 1996) have also listened to the sexual voices of female adolescents, but primarily from the girls' hetero-sexual perspective.

Research Design

Seventy-eight young women between the ages of 17 and 25 years (mean = 20.8 years) participated in a research project on the developmental life histories of sexual-minority young adults (for male findings, see Savin-Williams, 1998, 2004; for gender comparisons, see Savin-Williams & Diamond, 2000). All young women met the inclusion criterion of claiming physical or romantic interest in same-sex others. The young women were recruited through announcements in college classes on gender and sexuality, flyers to campus social and political organizations, postings on Internet list-servs for sexual-minority students on several college campuses, and referrals from other participants. To increase geographic diversity, a posting of the research was listed on several southern and eastern college campus list-servs. This multiple recruitment strategy drew participants along the spectrum of same-sex sexuality. For example, college courses on gender often draw students who tentatively recognize the complexity of their sexual attractions; campus political organizations, those who openly identify their same-sex sexuality.

To volunteer, women contacted the principal investigator by telephone or electronic mail. Special efforts were made to include young women who might not feel comfortable identifying as lesbian or bisexual by assuring them that such identifications were not necessary for participation and that the interviews were confidential and would be neither audio- nor videotaped. Due to the research design, response rate could not be calculated because it is unknown how many potential participants who met selection criteria did not volunteer for the study. However, 9% of women who originally made contact either did not return efforts to contact them or did not show up for the interviews. Due to human subject considerations, no attempt was made to contact these individuals or to discover reasons for their refusal to participate.

Procedures and Measures

The young women were interviewed in person or by telephone by the principal investigator (median time = 45 minutes) in a location chosen by youth that afforded privacy and confidentiality. The nature and aims of the research project were explained, questions were answered, and consent was secured in accordance with human subjects' stipulations. All participants understood in advance that the interviewer was a gay male researcher. Whether and how this fact affected responses is unknown; however, several women spontaneously offered at the close of the interview that it was a relief to talk about sexual matters with a perceived disinterested male. One young woman said, "If you were a woman, especially an attractive one, I'd be trying to impress you."

Initial questions ascertained the young women's age, ethnicity, hometown community size, and family social class (based on occupational status of parents). The remainder of the interview focused on developmental milestones, from earliest memories of same-sex attraction to current feelings about one's sexuality (Savin-Williams, 1998). For purposes of this project, only data concerning first same-sex contact were analyzed. Sex was defined as an act in which there was "genital contact on the part of either you, your partner, or both." Women could also use their own definition (e.g., intimate kissing). They were asked to describe in detail these encounters. From this information the following factors were assessed: age of partner, the partner's status (e.g., best friend, neighbor, cousin), how long the partner was known and what happened to the relationship after the encounter, what motivated the sex (e.g., love, lust, curiosity, peer pressure, drugs), who initiated the encounter, what activities occurred (e.g., kissing, fondling under clothes, mutual masturbation, fingering, oral activities), who had an orgasm, the effect of the sex on her sexual identity, and how the sexual encounter was evaluated (on a 7-point scale from "worst" to "best experience of my life").

The Young Women

The sample was composed of 78% White, 13% Asian/Pacific Islands, and 10% African American and Latino young women. Sixty-two percent were raised in small cities or suburbs and were middle-class to lower-middle-class in economic status. Geographically, 46% were raised in the Northeast, 24% in the South, 17% in the Midwest, 10% in the West, and 3% in other countries. All but 3% were or had been in college. In terms of their current sexuality, 35% identify as lesbian, 33% as bisexual, 13% as questioning, 10% as bi-lesbian, and 9% as unlabeled.

Girl-Girl Sexual Activities in Childhood

Based on intensive interviews with thousands of adult women, Alfred Kinsey and colleagues (1953) were the first to systematically document childhood girl-girl sexuality. They argued that girls are naturally sexual, and any reluctance girls might have to engage in same-sex activities is likely attributable to repressive feminine socialization that discourages or inhibits female sexuality. Despite these social prohibitions, many of the adult women reported that as children they had engaged in sexual activities with other girls as their principal source of erotic stimulation. Exhibitionism, genital examination, and manual manipulation of genitalia were most common; inserting objects/fingers in the vagina and mouth-genital contact were least common. Same-sex encounters peaked at age 9 and were as ubiquitous as heterosexual sex prior to age 13. By adolescence, one third of the women had had "homosexual" contact, but this proportion declined to 1 in 10 during late adolescence.

Same-sex encounters were experienced as pleasurable and as affording information about "private" body parts, masturbation, petting, sociosexual responses, and sexual techniques. Guilt was the downside for some girls, especially if they were reprimanded or punished by parents for their sexual explorations. Thus, Kinsey found little evidence for the traditional view of childhood sexual latency or arrest. Although pubertal increases in gonadal hormone levels corresponded to sharp increases in the *intensity* of self-reported sexual desires and activities among the girls, puberty was not an important developmental marker for the *onset* of sexual activities. As same-sex play declined during adolescence, the ratio of heterosexual sex play increased because, according to Kinsey, teens became heterosexually conditioned.

Several studies since Kinsey support the view that girls are sexual, if not always with other girls then certainly with themselves (Friedrich, Grambsch, Broughton, Kuiper, & Beilke, 1991; Larsson & Svedin, 2002). Nearly 80% of Swedish high school seniors reported that by age 12 they had engaged in autoerotic activities, slightly higher among girls from upper socioeconomic circumstances (Larsson & Svedin, 2002). Their favorite solitary sexual activities were looking at one's body in a mirror, exploring genitals, fondling, and viewing sexually explicit materials. Masturbation to orgasm increased from 7% from ages 6 to 10 years to 20% from ages 11 to 12 years. More than 90% felt good about these solitary sexual activities (excited, pleasant body sensations, silly/giggly, natural), although 24% also reported feeling guilty.

Among the young women I interviewed, 78% reported a same-sex encounter at an average age of 16.4 years (age range = 6–23 years old). The favorite time was freshman year of college (median age = 18). Only a small minority, 14%, reported they have only had sex with a female. Twelve percent ($n = 9$) reported *prepubertal* genital contact with another girl. The childhood partner was either a good or best friend whose sexuality was heterosexual or unknown ($n = 6$) or a cousin ($n = 3$). In all cases, sexual activity was motivated by curiosity or lust, was initiated by either girl, occurred before sex with boys, continued beyond the first time (in several cases for more than a year), never resulted in an orgasm, and consisted of kissing/fondling with genital contact or rubbing under clothes ($n - 4$) or mutual masturbation or fingering ($n = 5$). Sex took place within the context of normal child play—house, doctor, animal vet. After sex, the girls always remained friends, and all rated the sex as very good and pleasurable. One girl said the sexual activity pushed her in a heterosexual direction (because her mother found out and punished her), one said it caused her to think she might be gay, and seven said it had no impact on their eventual sexuality. Although they recognized their same-sex attraction and engaged in heterosexual activity earlier than other girls, their youthful sexuality did not result in an earlier age of labeling self, disclosure of this information to others, or involvement in a same-sex romantic relationship. They were no more likely than young women who had their first same-sex experience during adolescence or young adulthood to have subsequent same- or opposite-sex experiences or to label themselves as lesbian or bisexual. Three now identify as "not straight," two as lesbian, two as bisexual, and two as bi-lesbian.

Whether heterosexual girls also engage in these childhood same-sex play activities for the same reasons and with the same effect is unknown because the data have yet to be collected. Indeed, the "other girl" of the women I interviewed was in all but one situation perceived to be heterosexual, despite the fact that the sexual activities continued for many months. In retrospect, several of the girls speculated that they might have been more "into it" than their partners—but they were not absolutely certain of this.

Fan of Wonder Woman and *Playboy* centerfolds, interviewee Sybil exemplified common sexual behaviors between friends. Because her single mom was often at work and Sybil was able to have friends over, her first sexual experience was with her best friend, Ashley. As Sybil recalled:

> We were both 8 and it was penetration of each other with our fingers—this one, the big one. We had been best friends for several years and our play just naturally went this way. We didn't understand anything about sex or anything. I cared for her like I did for all my friends, but I did not love her in

any special way. It was play sex. Fondling and kissed a lot. We weren't lovers, just experimenters. Continued for 6 months until she told her aunt and then we had to give it up. Very little contact since. She is married with three children.

Sybil had sex with boys throughout her adolescence but no further sex with girls until college.

Another young woman, Valerie, recalled clear same-sex feelings during childhood—desiring her uncle's new wife, coloring only the girls in her coloring books, and wanting to nap beside other girls. She began her sexual career in the third grade with female cousins. She described it as follows:

> First sex stuff with cousins in my same age range. They'd initiate it. Three different ones. They're all heterosexual they say. Touching vaginas, kissing chests and breasts, holding, playing out boy/girl things. As we got older then we'd penetrate with fingers and she kissed my breasts. This was just for pleasure, just sex, nice, necessary. I've been masturbating since I was 9.

Most of the girls realized that no one should be told about their sexual activities because they would be punished. One girl who met her partner in parochial school said, "I'm not clear how it began but we had to stop after a year when our parents caught us and made us go to confessional." Valerie also did not tell her parents because she knew that she would get into trouble if "adults found out. Not a gay thing but because it was sex, not because it was gay."

Raised in an upper-middle-class home in Philadelphia, Alicia struggled with her feelings for her 7-year-old best friend. At first it was emotional, but it eventually became a physical attraction. Yet this was "wrong," but it felt so natural and good. Alicia explained:

> With the girl I told you about. We were playing house and pretending to have sex. So some rubbing our genitals together. Kissing, but could not do it on the lips. Genitalia touching, dry sex, rubbing. And with two other girls as well later on. Me always wanting more of it than them. I always ached to play these games but knew I shouldn't because they were wrong. Was this because of my emotional void? Something you can get from a girl you can't from a boy. Physical desire? Because it felt so good. To be different? I was always the rebel.

Although the traditional view may be true that most girls do not act on their sexual feelings until puberty, exceptions do occur. To adequately understand the intricate links between early sexual activities and later sexual development, more needs to be known about the genital activities of children—their contexts, meanings, and effects. These activities may be an altogether different phenomenon from adolescent sexual activity, with their own developmentally specific motives, qualities, and functions that correspond to a girl's social, cognitive, and biological maturation. Teenagers often distinguish "early sex when I was a kid" from their adolescent "real sex" experiences. Given the inherent difficulties in conducting sex research with children, it may be some time before answers are forthcoming. Although it is intuitive to believe that such behaviors are "rehearsals" for pubertal and postpubertal sexuality, no direct empirical data support this interpretation. Perhaps it is a test for whether they prefer boys or girls, or perhaps it is merely an opportunity for a fun time. Clearly, sexuality develops gradually over the course of childhood through a subtle and gradual intertwining of physical and social experiences. Once a girl is an adolescent, somewhat more is known about her sex life.

Girl-Girl Sexual Activities in Adolescence

In a Swedish study, nearly 70% of 11- to 12-year-old girls reported having a sexual experience with a girl (Larsson & Svedin, 2002). Of these, 40% had sex only with another girl and not with a boy. The female partner was nearly always a same-age friend. Although the behavioral and emotional data in this study were not separated by sex of partner, the sexual experiences of the early adolescent girls most often consisted of talking about sex, kissing and hugging, humping or pretending intercourse, and sex teasing (lifting skirts, using sex words, peeking in toilets). These were perceived to be natural, pleasant, and exciting encounters, although guilt was not an uncommon experience.

Not all same-sex-attracted young women, however, have sex with girls during childhood or adolescence. Reviewing the literature, Savin-Williams (2005) reported that the proportion of virgins—variously defined as not having "sex" with a same-sex partner—among girls who identify as lesbian or bisexual was slightly below 20%. If the criterion is applied to *nonidentified* same-sex-attracted girls, virginity approached 50% in an Internet survey (Kryzan, 1997). Reasons for not having sex with other girls span the same reasons heterosexuals give—physical and emotional immaturity, lack of opportunity, religion, social awkwardness, and personal values.

Most young women, even those with same-sex attraction, have their first sexual encounter with a boy, not a girl (D'Augelli & Hershberger, 1993; Hillier et al., 1998; Remafedi, Resnick, Blum, & Harris, 1992). Among the young women I interviewed, 62% first had sex with a male, 35% with a female, and 3% with no one. Indeed, in every study reviewed, only a small minority of gay-identified girls engaged solely in same-sex behavior, and some had a considerable amount of heterosexual sex (Savin-Williams, 2005). It is unknown what proportion of heterosexual and same-sex encounters represents experimentation, an expression of a sexual orientation, or another motivation (e.g., fun). For those who decide to engage in genital encounters with other girls, a wide range of ages is typical, although the average is several years after menarche.

Timing of the First Same-Sex Encounter

Considerable data indicate that the average age of first sex with a girl is 15 to 16 years and usually commences after first heterosexual sex (D'Augelli & Grossman, 2001; D'Augelli & Hershberger, 1993; Diamond, 1998; Faulkner & Cranston, 1998; Goode & Haber, 1977; Herdt & Boxer, 1993; Hillier et al., 1998; Kryzan, 1997; Remafedi et al., 1992; Rosario et al., 1996; Saewyc, Skay, Bearinger, Blum, & Resnick, 1998; Sears, 1991). The earliest average ages were recorded among urban samples. Rosario and colleagues (1996) reported an average of 14 years among young women recruited from a New York City recreational and social services agency. Typically, a girl had her first sexual experience with a boy and then crossed over to girls a year or so later.

Why should same-sex-attracted girls begin sex with a boy? Is it that boys are more readily available? Are girls less aware that their attraction to girls is sexual and not just "emotionally intimate"? Perhaps when the partner is a boy rather than a girl, a sexual encounter is simply more accessible because a boy is more willing to ask for sex or more willing to comply with her request. Another possibility is that a girl's willingness to have sex with a boy reflects the greater tendency for girls to be authentically attracted to *both* sexes (Baumeister, 2000; Diamond, 2003; Weinberg, Williams, & Pryor, 1994). Perhaps girls are more circumspect than boys regarding sexual activity, and thus sex is more likely to be postponed until a relationship develops. One study (Goode & Haber, 1977) suggested that it is the degree, proportion, and level of sex with women versus men that most clearly distinguishes same-sex from opposite-sex attracted college women. The former had sex with men but they had it less often, later, and enjoyed it less. As many had their most pleasurable orgasm with a woman as they did with a man.

It is also difficult to detect from these studies what it is that provokes one girl to engage in early same-sex encounters, even prior to menarche, whereas another becomes sexually involved only after all biological markers of pubescence are long past. In both very early and very late cases, psychosocial events likely take precedence over biological factors as motivating forces. It is the right alignment of congruent circumstances or "accidents." It is a willing cousin or friend sleeping over, a night when parents are out for dinner, a horny mood.

Whether more young women are having same-sex encounters or having them earlier than in previous generations is difficult to determine given the limited historic data. Girls seldom, however, chalk up extreme numbers of sexual partners. In the study by Rosario et al. (1996), the adolescent women averaged eight female and six male lifetime partners. However, they had far more sexual encounters with female (420) than male (103) partners. Young women might have forgone casual sexual relationships with girls, but they did not thus abstain from sexual contact. They maintained sexual relationships with their female sex partners for a long time.

The Same-Sex Partner

What is known about the same-sex partners of adolescent women is that they are usually a good friend, within a year or two in age, and that they remain friends after the sexual relationship ends (Larsson & Svedin, 2002; Rosario et al., 1996). Data from the 78 young women I interviewed confirmed these findings and provided additional information. The median age of first same-sex encounter was 16 for the young women and 19 for their first partner. Eighty-two percent of partners were within 2 years of the young women's age, and in only three cases were the partners more than 8 years older; in these situations the young women were involved in a romantic relationship with their partner. The first sexual encounter usually (61%) occurred within a romantic relationship, 18% were with a best or good heterosexual (or assumed heterosexual) friend, 16% were with a lesbian/bisexual friend, and 5% were with a cousin. In no situation did a young woman cease contact with her first partner after the initial sexual encounter. Contexts for meeting the first partner were everyday life—next door, school, a party. Not uncommonly, best friendships became eroticized, sometimes years after the pair first became friends. Only 11% of the young women had sex with their partner within a week of meeting; more often (66%) it was at least 6 months after meeting (38% after more than a year).

Stephanie's experience serves as an example of several of these trends. The summer before eighth grade, she was sent to summer camp. There she met Lolita, and they became inseparable. Two years later their platonic relationship became sexual. Stephanie recalled:

> She lived a little ways away and we were very emotionally close. I was totally thrilled to have a friend at school. We hung out a lot together. Lolita would sleep over a lot and one night she was talking about her boyfriend Juan and talking about sex. I was pretending to know more than I did. We had been very affectionate, like most girl friends. I asked her how he kissed her and so she kissed me like her Juan did. This was quite a shocker. From then on we kissed a lot when we got together, and began touching and caressing. To make it "okay," one of us would be Juan. Penetration with our fingers but never oral sex. She's straight as far as I know.
>
> Never talked about it. I can't tell what Lolita is but I was the only girl she did anything with. We never said we were lesbians. I kind of knew that it was not right but it felt okay. Mom caught us in bed and this was a big uproar. We had gotten together every day after school for 6 to 7 months but Mom made that more difficult.
>
> It was just a kid experience. Lots were having sex, only with guys, so having sex was not unusual. Mom never addressed that it was wrong for two girls to have sex but that sex was wrong.

What happens when two girls have sex is not well understood. Who would dare ask?

The Sex Act

Determining which adolescent girls have sex, at what age, and with how many partners depends in part on which behaviors are deemed "sexual."

Researchers usually assume some version of the generic question, "Have you had sexual intercourse with a male/female?" This is often asked without elaboration or probes, making it difficult for a respondent to know exactly which behaviors count (e.g., Remafedi et al., 1992). This matters because definitions of sex vary according to sexual identity status and sex of the young person.

In several studies, nearly all gay-identified young women considered oral-genital contact and use of sex accessories as sex, but somewhat less so hand-genital contact (80%) and oral-anal contact (70%). For some behaviors, especially oral and manual stimulation of genitals, women espoused more inclusive definitions than young men. Few women believed that orgasm was necessary for sex to happen (Mustanski, 2003; Rosario, Meyer-Bahlburg, Hunter, & Gwadz, 1999; Savin-Williams & Diamond, 2004). Responding to a sexual risk assessment questionnaire, on average young women had their first manual (hand-genital) contact with another female at age 13 but had their first oral contact at age 14 (Rotheram-Borus, Hunter, & Rosario, 1994).

Defining sex as any instance of genital contact (or their own definition), adolescent same-sex encounters among the interviewed young women was perceived to be initiated by the other woman (38%), mutual (31%), neither (15%), or themselves (15%). The young women often complained that opportunities for sex were tricky to arrange. "We had been dating for 7 months but we couldn't go further because her mother was a Southern Baptist and so we didn't get to see each other much." Orgasms were relatively rare, with 20% reporting one or both of them had one. The initial sex act consisted primarily of kissing and fondling genitals under clothing (66%), mutual masturbation or fingering (24%), and oral contact (10%). These proportions correspond to the most common sexual activities reported in a small study of college women in the 1970s (Goode & Haber, 1977): nude kissing and caressing without genital contact, manual genital contact, mutual pubic rubbing, and cunnilingus.

Growing up in a small central Florida town in a conservative Christian home, interviewee Barb found her true love during her missionary ninth-grade trip to Africa. She fell in love with her best friend, and their relationship, as described here by Barb, became sexualized, a natural outgrowth of their friendship:

> The first time was a gradual process. Neither of us had ever dated so we
> were very reserved sexually. She initiated the sex because I was uncertain. So

she went slow with me. I had been taught to be careful about sex, that it is very special and one should be sure. My parents thought I was too young for it.

I had kissed a girl before but that was not a girlfriend. We went underneath the clothes with some fondling. Again, very slowly. It is fuzzy and can't remember but was eventually mutual masturbation. Neither of us ever had an orgasm during the whole relationship. The sex was wonderful—it was what both of us needed at the time. Scary and exciting. I was hesitant because I didn't know what I was doing. I felt a lot more adult and sure of myself and my body. I had poor body image, like many girls. I was told I was fat and flat. Now I had someone to tell me I was gorgeous. We're still friends.

One point seldom addressed by researchers is whether the incidence, prevalence, or other developmental milestones vary depending on an adolescent's degree of same-sex sexuality. Does a girl totally committed to a same-sex sexuality have a particular sex act at a younger age than a girl only peripherally interested in sex with another girl? An Internet survey (Kryzan, 1997) suggested that the proportion of girls who engage in particular sex acts depends on the sexual identity of the respondent. Oral sex was the most common sexual activity among female pairs regardless of sexual identity, but lesbians (49%) were more likely than bisexuals (37%) and unsure women (14%) to give and receive oral sex from another female.

A more complete picture of same-sex behavior would emerge if researchers were to ask adolescent women specifically what they do when they have sex, whether they enjoyed it, and what motivated the sex.

Context, Motivation, and Evaluation of the Initial Same-Sex Encounter

Similar to what is known about heterosexual sexual activities, young women are most likely to engage in their first same-sex experience within the context of a friendship or a dating relationship (two thirds in one study; Herdt & Boxer, 1993). In a qualitative study of southern adolescents and young adults (Sears, 1991), young women tended to have stable same-sex relationships, had few sex partners, and attached emotional, romantic meaning to their relationships prior to sex. However, it is also true that some adolescent girls are okay with anonymous sex with girls. An Internet survey posed the question, "Would you likely have sex with someone you just met and would never see again?" (Kryzan, 1997). Nearly 4 in 10 young women replied in the affirmative when the someone was a female. Thus, although young women of all sexual orientations are likely to have and prefer sex within a known relationship, this is only a matter of degree. Some same-sex-attracted girls are similar to heterosexual girls in their preference for relationship sex, whereas others, similar to gay and hetero-sexual boys, enjoy anonymous sex (Herdt & Boxer, 1993; Peplau, Spalding, Conley, & Veniegas, 1999; Savin-Williams & Diamond, 2004; Tolman & Diamond, 2001).

Although many of the interviewed young women first had sex within the context of a loving relationship (53%) or a friendship (35%), several (7%) had their first sex with a casual female acquaintance. For the sample as a whole, the primary motivation for first sex was not love (22%) but lust (51%). The second most common motivator was curiosity (24%).

An additional question seldom asked of young women about their sexual experiences is simply whether it was good or bad. Not uncommonly for young women with same-sex desires, both gay and straight sexual experiences are satisfying. Sometimes this is only emotionally satisfying, sometimes only physically, but sometimes the sex is both emotionally and physically satisfying (Diamond, 1998, 2000). This characterization may also be true for the gay and straight sex of *heterosexual* youth, but these data have not been collected.

On a scale of 1 (*very bad*) to 5 (*very good*), on average, young gay Chicago women rated their first same-sex experience as 3.6 (Herdt & Boxer, 1993). Their first opposite-sex experience was 2.8, almost "average." In other surveys (Kryzan, 1997, 2000), more than half of same-sex-attracted young women evaluated their first sexual experience (partner's gender unstated) as positive. About one quarter believed it was negative. Bisexuals had the most positive first experience; questioning and unsure young adults, the least.

Among the young women I interviewed, few depicted their first sexual experience with another female as anything other than pleasurable (3% reported "neutral"). Typical was Ariel, who described it as the best sex of her life: "This was a revelation. Totally different than sex with a guy. Explosive! The best ever!"

One additional piece that is missing from the literature is an assessment of the meaning or impact of the sexual experience. For Ariel, "It affirmed what I was, and what I wanted was not relationships with boys."

The Impact of Same-Sex Activities

Although it is easy to assume that adolescent women who engage in same-sex contact are either experimenters who will eventually identify as heterosexual or gays who are expressing their gayness, contrary data (reviewed in Savin-Williams, 2005) caution against this simple conclusion.

> Not all same-sex-attracted girls are sexually active and are thus hetero-sexually and homosexually virgins.
> Some girls have only cross-orientation sex. That is, they are gay virgins but heterosexually experienced or heterosexually virgins but homo-sexually experienced.
> Most same-sex-attracted girls and an unknown number of heterosexual girls have sex with both girls and boys.
> Some girls, regardless of sexual orientation, have exclusive same- or opposite-sex encounters.

More than half (52%) of the young women I interviewed believed that their first sexual experience with a girl had no impact on their sexual self-perception. For the other half, the experience suggested to them that they might be gay (31%) or convinced them that they are gay (16%). Exemplifying the last group, one young woman attributed great meaning to the experience: "I knew then that's what I wanted. It helped me be more sure that this lesbian thing was not just a mental thing. It was a relief to have it sexualized."

Interviewee Rachel questioned her heterosexuality prior to her first sexual experience at age 12. After her first sexual/romantic experience with a girl several years older, she recognized that "there was no going back. I thought girls rocked but I never understood it as anything but that they were attractive." Thereafter she was willing to say to herself, "bisexual," without telling anyone else this fact—except those on the Internet chat room she frequented. As Rachel explained:

> The sex told me something. The whole sexual situation was slightly awkward but it did deliver a message to myself. I said to myself at this time that I must be gay but I avoided it altogether except from time to time when I thought about it. I just avoided labeling myself but after that disclosure then I was certain that I was bisexual. This was the beginning of my identity. So

now I knew that I had attractions to males and females at the same time. It
didn't make me less heterosexual, just bisexual.

The initial same-sex encounter seldom convinced the young women
that they are definitely lesbian or heterosexual. Stephanie's initiation into
girl-girl sex with her new friend Lolita continued her "seesawing" sexuality:

This was before I came out to myself. In my mind I would say I must be
bisexual and then other times I would deny it, that it meant nothing. I had
this political belief in sexual politics and all was okay. A very strong ally.
This sex thing raised possibilities, but I didn't think about it. This was just
one piece of the pie.

One girl thought her first infatuation would be a temporary aberration:
"I respected her and that she needed me was important. Did not think of
it in sexual terms. I always assumed that I would grow up and get married." Another rarely considered "about what it all meant. But I have to
admit that it did lead me to go to a library four towns over to look up
every homosexual book I could find. I must have known but never
allowed myself to think about it." Another realized that her friends would
not consider "just touching a boy's penis to be sex but to touch a girl
would be a lesbian thing to do."
   None claimed that sex with another female convinced her that she is
heterosexual, perhaps because the sex was so often agreeable. Nearly all
who first had sex with a girl during childhood, adolescence, or young
adulthood recognized that they had significant same-sex attraction prior
to the sexual encounter. Indeed, 78% identified as something other than
heterosexual prior to their first sex with a woman.

Conclusion

The literature reviewed in this chapter best illustrates what is *not yet
known* but *needs to be known* about same-sex sexuality among young
women (Savin-Williams & Diamond, 2004). The question for a young
woman as she sorts through her sexual encounters is whether they have
meaning about who she is. Clearly, if we want to understand same-sex sexuality, it would be beneficial to collect more data and to be more complex

in our research designs and interpretations. Same-sex sexuality is a matter of degree for many women, and the development of her sexuality is neither linear nor universal.

We must also listen to the new voices of young women as they tell us about their lives. Consider these comments by Susan:

> I'm in a physical/sexual sense 60% heterosexual and 40% gay. I find orgasm with a female harder, but it's a better experience overall. I find it harder to please a woman and this is bad for my ego. But is this because it means so much more? Or is it all in the plumbing involved? My sexual fantasies are often with a man but my romantic ones are with a woman, but I'm intimidated by heterosexual-type women.
>
> In the emotional realm I'm 30% heterosexual and 70% gay. I can't imagine spending my life with a guy! Sex wouldn't be enough. I want to take long trips with girls. I want to exchange lipstick colors and compare Hillary [Clinton] stories. Of course I'd like to grab her and make wild love!
>
> For me it's not a simple issue of the person regardless of their gender. I'm attracted to certain types of males, both the really femme girly boys and the really masculine studs who would just as soon spit in your face as fuck you, and the really feminine girls with powdered faces. The butch ones can be a Friday night fantasy.
>
> Don't think about writing down that I'm lesbian, or even bisexual. I hate both words! L-e-s-b-i-a-n is so political and what's with the bi in bisexual? Bi as in two or as in half? They're both so generational.

Few published investigations help us to understand her story.

References

Baumeister, R. F. (2000). Gender differences in erotic plasticity: The female sex drive as socially flexible and responsive. *Psychological Bulletin, 126,* 347–374.

D'Augelli, T. R., & Grossman, A. H. (2001, August). Sexual orientation victimization of lesbian, gay, and bisexual youths. Paper presented at the meeting of the American Psychological Association, San Francisco.

D'Augelli, A. R., & Hershberger, S. L. (1993). Lesbian, gay, and bisexual youth in community settings: Personal challenges and mental health problems. *American Journal of Community Psychology, 21,* 421–448.

Diamond, L. M. (1998). The development of sexual orientation among adolescent and young adult women. *Developmental Psychology, 34,* 1085–1095.

Diamond, L. M. (2000). Sexual identity, attractions, and behavior among young sexual-minority women over a two-year period. *Developmental Psychology, 36,* 241–250.

Diamond, L. M. (2003). What does sexual orientation orient? A biobehavioral model distinguishing romantic love and sexual desire. *Psychological Review,* 110, 173–192.

Faulkner, A. H., & Cranston, K. (1998). Correlates of same-sex sexual behavior in a random sample of Massachusetts high school students. *American Journal of Public Health, 88,* 262–266.

Friedrich, W. N., Grambsch, P., Broughton, D., Kuiper, J., & Beilke, R. L. (1991). Normative sexual behavior in children. *Pediatrics, 88,* 456–464.

Goode, E., & Haber, L. (1977). Sexual correlates of homosexual experience: An exploratory study of college women. *Journal of Sex Research, 13,* 12–21.

Herdt, G., & Boxer, A. M. (1993). *Children of horizons: How gay and lesbian teens are leading a new way out of the closet.* Boston: Beacon Press.

Hillier, L., Dempsey, D., Harrison, L., Beale, L. Matthews, L., & Rosenthal, D. (1998). *Writing themselves in: A national report on the sexuality, health and well-being of same-sex attracted young people* (Monograph series 7, Australian Research Centre in Sex, Health and Society, National Centre in HIV Social Research, La Trobe University). Carlton, Australia.

Kinsey, A. C., Pomeroy, W. B., Martin, C. E., & Gebhard, P. H. (1953). *Sexual behavior in the human female.* Philadelphia: Saunders.

Kryzan C. (1997). OutProud/Oasis Internet Survey of Queer and Questioning Youth. Sponsored by OutProud, the National Coalition for Gay, Lesbian, Bisexual and Transgender Youth and Oasis Magazine. Contact survey@out-proud.org.

Kryzan, C. (2000). OutProud/Oasis Internet Survey of Queer and Questioning Youth. Sponsored by OutProud, the National Coalition for Gay, Lesbian, Bisexual and Transgender Youth and *Oasis Magazine.* Contact survey@out-proud.org.

Larsson, I., & Svedin, C. G. (2002). Sexual experiences in childhood: Young adults' recollections. *Archives of Sexual Behavior, 31,* 263–273.

Mustanski, B. (2003). *Semantic heterogeneity in the definition of "having sex" for homosexuals.* Manuscript submitted for publication.

Peplau, L. A., Spalding, T. R., Conley, T. D., & Veniegas, R. C. (1999). The development of sexual orientation in women. *Annual Review of Sex Research, 10,* 70–99.

Remafedi, G., Resnick, M., Blum, R., & Harris, L. (1992). Demography of sexual orientation in adolescents. *Pediatrics, 89,* 714–721.

Rosario, M., Meyer-Bahlburg, H. F. L., Hunter, J., Exner, T. M. Gwadz, M., & Keller, A. M. (1996). The psychosexual development of urban lesbian, gay, and bisexual youths. *Journal of Sex Research, 33,* 113–126.

Rosario, M., Meyer-Bahlburg, H. F. L., Hunter, J., & Gwadz, M. (1999). Sexual risk behaviors of gay, lesbian, and bisexual youths in New York City: Prevalence and correlates. *AIDS Education and Prevention, 11,* 476–496.

Rotheram-Borus, M. J., Hunter, J., & Rosario, M. (1994). Suicidal behavior and gay-related stress among gay and bisexual male adolescents. *Journal of Adolescent Research, 9,* 498–508.

Saewyc, E. M., Skay, C. L., Bearinger, L. H., Blum, R. W., & Resnick, M. D. (1998). Demographics of sexual orientation among American Indian adolescents. *American Orthopsychiatric Association, 68,* 590–600.

Savin-Williams, R. C. (1998). *". . . and then I became gay." Young men's stories.* New York: Routledge.

Savin-Williams, R. C. (2004). Boy-on-boy sexuality. In N. Way & J. Y. Chu (Eds.), *Adolescent boys: Exploring diverse cultures of boyhood* (pp. 271–292). New York: New York University Press.

Savin-Williams, R. C. (2005). *The new gay teenager.* Cambridge, MA: Harvard University Press.

Savin-Williams, R. C., & Diamond, L. M. (2000). Sexual identity trajectories among sexual-minority youth: Gender comparisons. *Archives of Sexual Behavior, 29,* 419–440.

Savin-Williams, R. C., & Diamond, L. M. (2004). Sex. In R. M. Lerner & L. Steinberg (Eds.), *Handbook of adolescent psychology* (2nd ed., pp. 189–231). New York: Wiley.

Sears, J. T. (1991). *Growing up gay in the South: Race, gender, and journeys of the spirit.* Binghamton, NY: Harrington Park Press.

Tolman, D. L. (1996). Adolescent girls' sexuality: Debunking the myth of the urban girl. In B. Leadbeater & N. Way (Eds.), *Urban girls: Resisting stereotypes, creating identities* (pp. 255–271). New York: New York University Press.

Tolman, D. L., & Diamond, L. M. (2001). Desegregating sexuality research: Cultural and biological perspectives on gender and desire. *Annual Review of Sex Research, 12,* 33–74.

Weinberg, M. S., Williams, C. J., & Pryor, D. W. (1994). *Dual attraction: Understanding bisexuality.* New York: Oxford University Press.

Part VI

When Adversity Is Overwhelming—Then What?

Understanding Health Disparities Among Female Street Youth

Cecilia Benoit, Mikael Jansson, and Murray Anderson

Social science and media depictions of female youth who are found on our city streets typically focus on their health risk behaviors, including illicit drug use, unprotected sex, and involvement in prostitution. This risk-based perspective in Canada can be traced back to the release of the Badgley Report (Badgley, 1984). The report—named after Robin Badgley, the social scientist who chaired the commission responsible for it— marked the beginning of a new perspective on urban street youth. It moved away from the view that they were to blame for their plight (juvenile delinquents) and instead saw them as victims of others' wrongdoings (exploited youth).

Female youth are particularly vulnerable to physical and sexual exploitation. This is because once on the street, they come under the control of male recruiters who make the girls drug dependent and force them into trading sexual favors for money or in-kind goods (Badgley, 1984). According to Bagley and Young (1987), "the girl who finally tries prostitution is one who is already degraded and demoralized, in a state of psychological bondage, with grossly diminished self-confidence" (p. 23). Adults who exploit these female street youth take advantage of their feelings of disconnectedness and low self-esteem and isolation (Silbert & Pines, 1982), addiction to substances (Green & Goldberg, 1993), and complications related to fetal alcohol spectrum disorders (Government of British Columbia, 2005).

Yet many females who have been the victims of childhood physical and sexual abuse do not end up on the street; nor do all those who have been abused and end up on the street become involved in prostitution; and many of those who become involved in prostitution have no history of early abuse (Hagan & McCarthy, 1997). According to Canadian sociologist Deborah Brock (1998), the focus on this new "social problem" (youth physical and sexual exploitation) obscures other reasons that youth become street-involved in the first place. Such a one-dimensional focus also has the potential to stigmatize youth and deprive them of a sense of self, not associated with prostitution (Vanwesenbeeck, 1994). What may also be overlooked is an understanding of the more distal factors that are implicated in whether or not female youth leave home and live on the street or become involved in trading sex and other risk behaviors to survive (Link & Phelan, 1995; Williams, 2003)

Research Setting, Study Populations, and Ethical Considerations

Our main concern in this chapter is the females in the study Risky Business? focused on the impact of street involvement on the health and well-being of youth. We argue that female street youth deserve special attention due to the main focus in the research literature on the unique risks they face due to their gender. Nevertheless, as we have argued elsewhere (Jansson, Benoit, Hackler, & McCarthy, 2004; Jansson & Benoit, 2006), understanding the lives of male street youth is equally important and perhaps even more misunderstood and thus also warrants attention in its own right.

Our sample of female participants is drawn from the first wave of an ongoing longitudinal study of street youth interviewed in Victoria, British Columbia. Victoria, the capital of the province, is a midsize Canadian city of 310,000, located between the larger cities of Vancouver (population, 2 million) and Seattle (population, .5 million). Street youth—female and male are a social concern in all three West Coast cities. Because of the lack of a standard agreed-upon definition, street youth include not only youth who live mainly on the street but also "couch-surfers" who share shelter with intimate partners or friends, youth who are in and out of government care (also known as "systems youth"), and youth who frequent shelters for the homeless. The actual number of street youth is thus difficult to estimate with any rigor. Moreover, very few metropolitan areas have attempted to collect these kinds of data. In Seattle in the mid-1990s, 500 to

1,000 street youth between the ages of 12 and 24 slept on the street, or in temporary shelters; these estimates rise to as many as 2,000 if youth living in other unstable situations are included (Ensign & Bell, 2004). One study estimated that in 1990 there were 3,000 to 5,000 street youth in Toronto (Smart, Adlaf, Walsh, & Zdanowicz, 1992); another study estimated that 6,000 youth aged 15 to 24 stayed in various outreach facilities for street youth in Toronto in 1999 (Kraus, Eberle, & Serge, 2001). In Halifax, 300 youth used a youth drop-in center between April 1 and July 31 in 2000; in Ottawa, more than 500 youth sought help in emergency shelters in 2000 (Kraus, Eberle, & Serge, 2001). We found no estimates of street/homeless youth in Victoria, but, consistent with the estimates, there are likely between 250 and 300 street youth at any point in time between the ages of 14 and 24. We also could not find reliable estimates of street youth by gender. Most studies suggest that there are more males than females in this vulnerable population but that the percentage of females is growing (Kraus, Eberle, & Serge, 2001; Canadian Institute for Health Information [CIHI], 2005).

This study is part of a larger research initiative titled Healthy Youth in a Healthy Society, a university-community alliance for the prevention of child and youth injury. The research program is a multiyear initiative (2001–2006) that brings together an interdisciplinary group of university-based researchers and students with community groups, health policy makers, practitioners, and youth drawn from the local region (Leadbeater et al., 2006).

Due to particular characteristics of street youth, an assortment of sampling techniques was employed to reach participants. Staff at four community partner organizations that provide services to street youth helped to establish recruitment strategies. Their location in the inner city provided access to subgroups of marginalized youth who live part- or full-time on the street, thereby enhancing our sample's representativeness. We also recruited youth through contacts with the Ministry of Health Services of British Columbia and other frontline health and social services in the metropolitan area. In addition, we advertised the study at various locales where street youth are concentrated and employed a method referred to in the academic literature as "respondent-driven sampling" (Heckathorn, 1997). This technique is especially appropriate for recruiting hard-to-reach or hidden populations who are stigmatized by the wider society, when no sampling frames exist, and acknowledgment of belonging to the group is threatening. Participants served as "seeds" and were each given three recruitment coupons to hand to other youth whom they believed might come forward for an interview. This is based on the rationale that reclusive youth are more likely to respond to appeals from their similar-age peers who have already participated in the research project rather than from more privileged adults from either the university or community agencies (Ensign & Gittelsohn, 1998). A $20 honorarium was provided for the first interview, and participants received a $25 honorarium after completing subsequent interviews. The "seeds" were also paid a nominal honorarium of $10 for each peer who came forward to participate. Identified youth were asked to call a dedicated cell phone and anonymously answer a series of questions that assessed their age (they had to be 18 years or younger) and levels of involvement with the parent or guardian, the school system, the formal labor market activity, and the street-economy (e.g., panhandling, petty crime, selling drugs, and prostitution). We used a relatively conservative measure of street involvement (loose or no attachment to family and school, living on the street part- or full-time in the past month, and making part or all money for survival through street activities). We hoped to access those least connected to societal institutions, and most likely to be facing health challenges.

The sample included 104 youth ranging in age between 14 and 19 years at the time they entered the study. Just under half of these participants were female ($N = 50$). The street youth were interviewed twice in the first month and continue to be interviewed approximately every 2 months (for as long as they are willing to participate in the study). A relatively large number of research assistants have worked on this project over the years, including former street-involved youth who were in their middle to late twenties. They were identified by our community partners as promising researchers. Health and social service professionals and graduate students who showed an interest in working part-time on the study have also been recruited as interviewers. The research instrument includes closed- and open-ended questions, and the individual interviews range from 45 minutes to 2 hours, with the length depending primarily on the willingness of the youth to give thorough answers to the open-ended questions and the relevance of particular questions to their lives. For example, youth who have never worked for a salary or wage do not answer a lengthy set of questions about paid employment.

A number of ethical hurdles confronted us in launching the street youth study. Two issues were of paramount importance: how to balance mandatory reporting of designated individuals to the provincial authorities while obtaining informed consent, and how to overcome sample bias and at the same time maximize youth participants' anonymity and confidentiality while following them in the multiyear panel study. As discussed at length elsewhere (Jansson & Benoit, 2006), we were largely successful in overcoming these ethical challenges because of support from our university's Human Research Ethics Committee and guidance from an informed lawyer affiliated with the provincial Ministry of Children and Family Development. We maintained two databases to keep identifying information and responses to interview questions separate. This helped keep the participants' identities autonomous and their information confidential.

The chapter also draws upon data from a randomly selected sample of youth from the same geographic area. To attain the sample, in 2003 we randomly telephoned 9,500 households in the metropolitan area and asked if they had a youth aged 12 to 18 years living there. Of the households that had a youth, 82% of parents/guardians agreed for their youth to participate, and of those, 78% of the youth (664) agreed to participate. After attaining the consent of both the guardian/parent(s) and youth, face-to-face closed-ended interviews consisting of survey questions on a range of topics, including the assets and resources of youth, their families, and their communities, as well as individual, family, and community or cultural risks for injury, were conducted with the youth in their own homes. The youth received an honorarium of a $25 gift certificate for completing the research instrument. In 2005, the same 664 youth, now aged 14 to 20, were recontacted to participate in a second interview. Five hundred and eighty youth agreed to be reinterviewed, producing an 88% response rate for the second interview. The comparative data presented in the following are drawn from the Wave 2 interviews of female youth because of the closer proximity in their ages and the female street youth we surveyed.

In describing the results of this study, we present descriptive findings on selected self-reported health and health risk behaviors of both the female street youth and their counterparts in the random sample. This is followed by examination of the demographic profile of the two samples and a description of their family and school support systems.

Health Status

Self-Reported Health

While youth between the ages of 14 and 19 years generally enjoy healthy, disease-free lives compared with other Canadians (CIHI, 2005), the female street youth we interviewed shouldered a heavier health burden. None reported having tested positive for HIV-AIDS. Also, only 6% of our sample of street youth answered yes to ever having a sexually transmitted infection, compared with 8% of females in the random sample.

The self-reported psychological and physical health of our participants was more worrisome. Almost two thirds of the females in the street sample reported ever being depressed, more than half of them said that they experience flashbacks, just under half of them report having anxiety or panic attacks, and 14% had been treated for a mental illness. Forty-five percent of our female street sample had ever attempted suicide, and 37% had ever slashed/harmed themselves. While we did not ask exactly these same health questions of our random sample survey of female youth, 14% said yes to the question "Do you have a mental or emotional condition (depression, eating disorder, ADHD, learning disability, etc.)," and 23.4% said they ever attempted to harm themselves. These self-reported findings suggest that female street youth have more mental problems than young women in the general population.

Health Risk Behaviors

The female street youth in our study also reported comparatively high use of addictive substances: 74% take marijuana and 50% drink alcohol at least once a week, compared with 31.6% who drink alcohol and 19% who said they take marijuana at least once a week among the random sample of female youth. Even more disconcerting are the findings that in the last 2 months, 28% of female street youth reported taking cocaine or crack, 34% taking crystal methamphetamine (meth) or speed, and 12% using heroin, whereas in the last 12 months, only 10% of the random sample of female youth reporting taking cocaine or crack, 3% crystal methamphetamine or speed, and 0.5% heroin (see Table 15.1). In short, weekly use of alcohol and marijuana was a little more than twice as common for female street youth. They were also much more likely to take highly addictive substances than

TABLE 15.1
Alcohol and Drug Use

Substance	Street Youth	Random Sample of Youth
		Use at least once per week
Alcohol	74%	32%
Marijuana	50%	19%
	Ever used in last 2 months	Ever used in last 12 months
Heroin	12%	0.5%
Cocaine/crack	28%	10%
Crystal meth	34%	3% "Amphetamines"
	"Crystal Meth/Speed"	(diet pills, speed, crystal meth)

female youth in the random sample (keeping in mind that the time span used to record use is six times longer for the random sample, meaning that if the longer time span was used to record drug use by street youth, their rates would be higher). These high rates of drug and alcohol use by street youth are similar to findings of a recent provincial survey of male and female street youth (McCreary Centre Society, 2001, 2002).

The data presented here indicate female street youth have poor mental health and also are high consumers of addictive substances. In the following, we look beyond these health risk behaviors and investigate what social factors might help explain the health disparities among female street youth.

Health and the Social Environment

The Family Environment

Studies show that early life experiences determine opportunities, achievements, and overall health and well-being of adults. Compromised early childhood development can result in restricted brain development and reduced language development, and can increase illiteracy risks and poor physical and mental health throughout life. Children who grow up in poverty often have parents or guardians without advanced education or stable employment. These children are also more likely to have weak social ties with adults. Children of Aboriginal background or other non-White statuses are at greater risk of continued adversity in adolescence and adulthood, not least of all because of the discrimination and stigma they face (CIHI, 2005). Our data on some crucial social conditions give a picture of what life was like for the youth in our study before they became street entrenched.

Parental Educational Background

Parental or guardian education is closely related to the socioeconomic status of the household. Effective education gives individuals the requisite knowledge and skills to deal with daily problems and helps to provide a sense of mastery and control over life events and crucial turning points (Canadian Institute for Health Information [CIHI], 2004).

Educational achievement of the parent or guardian with whom our female participants lived the longest was low; 75% had finished high school, and 30% had no postsecondary education. Only 15% of them had completed college or university. By comparison, among the female youth in our random sample, almost 95% of parents or guardians had finished high school, and almost 50% had completed a college diploma or university degree.

Parents'/Guardians' Employment

Occupation/job of parents or guardians is also a key background factor shaping our female participants' life chances. Parents' or guardians' employment situation is closely tied to the socioeconomic status of the household, gives the individual and his or her family a sense of identity and purpose, and provides social contacts and opportunities. Anxiety and depression are common among financially unstable parents/guardians who do not have job security or who experience frequent unemployment, and these likely exacerbate the economic consequences of employment instability (Marmot & Wilkinson, 1999). We inquired about three aspects of parents' and guardians' labor force attachment and status: occupation, type of employment (e.g., part- or full-time), and frequency of unemployment. Occupational data indicate considerable diversity, with roughly equal proportions of parents or guardians employed in the professions, as skilled laborers, or in secretarial/administrative jobs. An additional 14% earned their income in unskilled manual labor, and 9 percent were self-employed. Two parents worked primarily in the illegal economy.

At the time of the interview, more than 80% of male parents or guardians and more than 50% of female ones worked full-time. Twenty-five percent of females worked part-time, and 20% worked occasionally or were never employed. Nine percent of males worked part-time, and about the same percentage worked either occasionally or was never employed. However, bouts of unemployment were also common while the youth were growing up. In fact, almost 45% of male parents or guardians and 70% of females were unemployed at least once, and almost 15% of males and 30% of females were usually or always unemployed. The data available for the random sample of female youth are less extensive but indicate greater labor market engagement of both male and female parents or guardians: when asked if their father or male guardian was currently working, 88% of the girls in the random sample said "yes" to full-time employment for their father or male guardian, and 9% said "yes" to part-time/seasonal/casual employment; the figures for the female parent or guardian were 61% and 22%, respectively.

In brief, what these data on parents' or guardians' educational attainment and labor force engagement tell us is that the female street youth in our sample come from social conditions of relative disadvantage.

FAMILIAL SOCIAL SUPPORT

Social support and healthy relations with parents or guardians can make a vital contribution to youth's health and well-being. Having someone to count on in a crisis, to confide in when you need advice, and to comfort you when you are feeling down is crucial to psychological and emotional health. Belonging to a caring family network makes youth feel good about themselves, loved, esteemed, and valued. These protective factors also help youth to develop healthy mutually supportive social relationships of their own (CIHI, 2004). Children and youth who experience frequent household change, stressful life events, domestic violence, social isolation, and abuse are also at greater risk of adversity in adulthood.

The females in our street youth study experienced considerable disruptions in their household situation before age 15. On average, they lived only 7 of their first 15 years in the family setting in which they were born. By their 15th birthday, only 10% of these youth were living where they were born. On average, they lived in three to four settings before they turned 15. As expected, the young women from families in which their biological parents or guardians lived in separate households spent most of their time with their mothers. One third of youth lived with their mother only or with the mother and an unrelated adult for their longest living situation; 22% of the youth had never lived with their biological father. One of our participants described her roller-coaster living situation: "The first 3 months that I was living here I was in a group home, I got kicked out of that, I got moved into a foster home, I got kicked outta that, I moved to [a youth shelter] and then to another foster home." Another respondent had this to say about her erratic living situation while growing up: "Ya, well, I was moving everywhere and I was getting shuffled from one place to the other and it was so hard to keep up." For another female youth, the structure of her household was so fragile and her parents around so infrequently that she felt all but abandoned: "Mmm [I had] sort of a difficult childhood because my mom was always working and my dad was in jail. So I pretty much had to take care of myself at home." In addition, 48% of the female street youth surveyed had also lived in government "care" at some point. For Aboriginal females, the figure was even higher: More than 50% of them had lived in care, either in a group or foster home or in another institution, for periods in their lives. The data available for the random sample of female youth tell a different story: 66% of them lived in only one family situation while growing up, 21% in two, with the remainder living in three or more situations.

We also investigated the quality of relationships our street youth sample had with the female and male parent or guardian with whom the youth lived for the longest time. On average, parents or guardians only "sometimes" cuddled these youth when they were hurt or feeling down, praised their achievements, or took them on outings. On the other hand, parental violence was surprisingly frequent, with 40% of the youth reporting that their parents or guardians "slapped, kicked, or hit them with a fist" sometimes, usually, or always. One respondent described her explosive relationship with her mother: "Up until I was eleven [and left home], I was in an abusive home, and my mother was very physically, verbally, mentally and emotionally abusive. . . . I look at my, my childhood, like it was scrambled like a fucking egg." Another respondent had this to say about how her father treated her when she was still residing at home:

> My dad was always like angry at me. [W]hen I got home from school, he'd just be like yelling at me about like nothing. . . . When my mom got home I'd like be locked in my room. [A]nd then when I was like ten or eleven I started fighting back. . . . [M]y parents split up because my mom saw that if it continued, um either my dad would be in jail, I would be dead, or I would be in jail.

Given the family context they were confronting on a daily basis, it makes sense that many of our participants saw themselves as better off living in a shelter or even on the street. They expressed agency by walking with their feet. As one of the girls put it: "For me [leaving home] was excellent. I mean, the place I came from everyone's always yelling and so stressed out and fighting and screaming and nothing was ever right. [I]t's just such a relief to be out of there." The data available for the random sample of female youth suggest a much more supportive environment while growing up: When asked if their "father belittles them," 81% said "no," and when asked if he "ignores them," 87% said "no." The responses regarding mothers or female guardians to these two questions were even higher: 91% and 94%, respectively.

The School Environment

SOCIAL SUPPORT FROM TEACHERS AND PEERS

Not being closely connected to the regular education system was also one of the criteria considered when screening youth for the interview. At the time of the first interview, only one quarter of girls said they were enrolled in the regular school system (secondary or high school), and almost half of these youth were enrolled part-time. By contrast, virtually all the girls in the random sample aged 18 or under were enrolled in school.

Another 25% of the female street youth were enrolled in other training programs, mainly part-time, in an alternative school setting. The overall education level achieved by these youth was low; only one had finished grade 12, and only 6 had completed a grade higher than grade 10. We anticipate that some of the female street youth will report to us in subsequent interviews that they have furthered their education. However, most will have a difficult time catching up to peers who did not have interrupted schooling. To better understand which factors were related to low levels of school attendance and dropping out of school, we asked how many days they skipped school during the last month that they attended, why they had not attended school, and what changes would increase the likelihood they would attend school in the future. The young women provided multiple reasons for not attending school. One reported serious academic problems that went unmet, saying: "I have a learning disability so not a lot of the teachers understand how they have to teach me. They just get frustrated and like yell at me and call me stupid." The turning point for other street girls was peer problems. As one noted: "I was that crazy chick in the corner in black that no one wanted to talk to. . . . Grade eight sucked, and I hated everybody in my grade, everybody my age." Others said economic issues influenced their decision to leave school. These girls made general comments, including that "being poor was hard," as well as more specific ones that highlight how shortages of money for transportation, food, or accommodation made it difficult or impossible to attend school.

Many of the girls were concerned about the consequences of having dropped out of school. Indeed, the vast majority said their incomplete education prevented them from getting their ideal job. As one of them stated: "I would like to get a degree in something and like actual work [and earn] like $114 dollars a week, you know. You can't even pick up garbage unless you have a college diploma." These young women also recognized the considerable obstacles to getting an education. Some aspired to acquire as much education as possible while they were still eligible for government assistance. Even paying for certificate courses within their reach was often a formidable barrier.

The Street Environment

The current living situation of the female street youth also showed considerable continuity with the social conditions of their early lives. Findings show that their place of residence was in constant flux. They often spent their nights outdoors or in crowded places without basic amenities, including access to a bed to sleep on, hot water to wash, and, of course, privacy. Here is how one of them described her current street situation:

> Ah, I'm staying here, there and everywhere. Sometimes I sleep in, like, alleys back behind buildings and sometimes in [the city park], and sometimes I get to stay at people's houses. It sucks to have to carry around a pillow and a blanket and a big backpack all the time. . . . Um, there's not really too many good things about it, besides, I guess you kinda just have the freedom to do whatever you want whenever you like.

Given that individuals were selected into the sample based in part on their weak relationship with a parent or guardian, it is not surprising that relatively few youth slept only in the home of their parent or guardian. Only 12 of the female youth in our study had slept "at home (with guardian)" in the last week, and only 16 in the last month. The variation in their sleeping places is very high: Half slept in more than one place in the week before the survey, 80% slept in two or more places in the previous month, and 40% had spent at least one night sleeping on the street. One of the young women explained: "I don't get proper sleep or being able to like, you know, clean yourself off and stuff. And, like, you can't get a job unless you have a house, and can't get a house unless you have a job, so it's like, to get a job you gotta clean yourself up and actually go out there!"

Our findings also show street-involved girls had tenuous connections to the formal labor market, if any at all. At the time of the initial interview, only five were working in a job that paid a salary or wage. All worked in minimum-wage jobs in the service or manual labor sector. Nevertheless, 70% had previously been employed, generally in the sales and service sector, with a concentration in restaurants and retail stores.

We also asked the participants how often they looked for employment. We defined looking for work as "filled out an application form, sent your resume, or asked a potential employer to give you a job that would pay you a salary or wage." About half of those currently not working, but who had worked previously, had looked for employment since finishing their last job. This is not always easy, as one respondent explained, "I've been getting my act together, I've been getting my ass out of the hole I dug myself, I've been looking for work."

As an indication of their resilience, our female street youth were generally hopeful that things would change for them in the future. When asked in an open-ended question how they felt about wage jobs and the kinds of jobs they would like to do in the future, many youth mentioned a desire to work in social service occupations that serve marginalized populations, particularly young people. Some participants, on the other hand, had indefinite ideas about the type of job they would like, and others said they could not really think about long-term employment at this time in their life because they had more immediate issues to worry about. As one young woman put it: "Not having a place that you can wake up to, get ready, and not being able to take a shower, be fully alert and awake, where if you don't eat properly, and you never sleep properly, you end up being, you go crazy. Like after a while it wears on you, with not having anything to do."

As a result of their tenuous attachments to the labor force, all the female street youth interviewed made some part or all of their living from other sources. In addition to asking a specific question about how much money they earned in the average week from jobs that paid them a salary or wage, we asked them to fill out a short table indicating how much money they received in the average week from various sources. The

TABLE 15.2
Average Weekly Income and Source of Money

Source of Money	Median	N
Selling drugs	$90	22
Friends	$20	21
Family members	$20	28
Panhandling	$50	28
Theft	$30	11
Selling sex	$900	4
Welfare	$100	9
Wage jobs	$60	5
Other	$25	11
Total	$115	50

sources they listed included panhandling, family members, theft, friends, welfare, selling sex or drugs, and "other" (Table 15.2).

Eighty percent of the female street youth received money from more than one source; however, their income was unrelated to the total number of jobs. Taking into account all sources, half of the youth received less than $115 per week. The two most lucrative sources of money were selling sex and drugs. Many also received money from friends and family members, but these sources provided only $20 in an average week. Nine youth were on some kind of social assistance that paid just over $100 per week. Social assistance was the only source of money that provided an income comparable to selling sex, selling drugs, and theft. All other single sources of income brought substantially less money to these youth.

Summary and Conclusion

The picture that emerges from these comparative findings of female street youth and counterparts in a random sample is that social factors play a significant role in their respective life chances. The health disparities faced by the female street youth are not easily explained by a single disadvantage; rather, it is the "clustering" of vulnerabilities than began in early childhood and extended to their transition to life on the street. Many of these young women had spent their childhood moving back and forth between different family situations, a pattern that continues to be reflected in the variation in their current sleeping situations. As children, many were left to their own devices as they tried to obtain basic necessities such as food and shelter. They currently generate most of their money in street activities, often illegal, which increased the likelihood of injury and other health problems. Although they hoped to find steady employment in the formal economy, most had limited success, in part because of their low level of educational achievement but also because of the instability in their living situations.

These findings are consistent with earlier research on street youth in Canada, the United States, and Europe (Hagan & McCarthy 1997; Ensign & Bell, 2004). Our findings point to the importance of parents' or guardians' socioeconomic status, including income and frequency of employment. When these childhood determinants are considered along with continuing weak social support in the family and school social environments, it is not surprising that most of the street girls were searching not for economic security but for emotional support.

Yet, while our female participants spoke about the lack of social support while growing up and about childhood neglect and mental and physical victimization by parents and guardians, they also described more positive interactions with their parents. These findings suggest more complicated family dynamics than is typically described in the literature and suggest that parenting often involves a mixture of positive and negative behaviors. Although most of the female street youth participating in the study valued an education and realized the negative consequences of dropping out of school, they did not have the personal, familial, and other resources necessary for academic success. Dropping out of school was a key factor in the pathway that led youth away from their families and to the street.

There are many challenges in research with hard-to-reach youth (Benoit, Jansson, & Miller, 2005). Limitations of our data on female street youth are that they are cross-sectional, collected in a single location, involve a small sample, and do not include information on several factors that we refrained from asking about in the first interview but did subsequently (e.g., childhood sexual abuse). A longitudinal study from several sites with a larger sample and a more detailed data collection instrument are needed for a detailed analysis of the causal forces that contribute to street involvement and participating in health compromising behaviors. What we do know with relative certainty is that an adequate understanding of street youth must be multicausal and include structural and mediating social influences; it must also resist stereotypes and pay attention to youth's personal experiences and perspectives. As one young woman without a home to call her own stated: "Most people think that all like street kids are just selfish little bastards, who left their house because they want to or whatever. It's not like that . . . [we] didn't just leave our houses because we wanted [or because] we were too selfish. . . . I hate how they look at us all."

As evident in this quotation, the systematic stigma that accompanies youth who become street involved is a topic that deserves discussion in its own right (Phelan, Link, Moore, & Stueve, 1997). The burden of stigma experienced by female street youth complicates matters even more when we attempt to untangle the social and individual factors determining their current situation—one in which they have no place that they can call home.

Discussion Questions

1   Explain why the health of the female street youth is as much a *social* as an individual issue.
2. What are some of the ways that the street girls showed their human agency in light of the adversities they face in life?

REFERENCES

Badgley, R. (1984). *Sexual Offenses Against Children: Report of the Committee on Sexual Offenses Against Children and Youths.* Ottawa: Canadian Government Publishing.

Bagley, C., & Young, L. (1987). Juvenile Prostitution and Child Sexual Abuse: A Controlled Study. *Canadian Journal of Community Mental Health, 6,* 5–25.

Benoit, C., Jansson, M., & Millar, A. (2005). Community-Academic Research on Hard-to-Reach Populations: Benefits and Challenges. *Qualitative Health Research 15,* 263–282.

Brock, D. (1998). *Making Work, Making Trouble: Prostitution as a Social Problem.* Toronto, Ontario, Canada: University of Toronto Press.

Canadian Institute for Health Information (CIHI). (2004). *Improving the Health of Canadians.* Ottawa, Ontario, Canada: Author.

Canadian Institute for Health Information (CIHI). (2005). *Improving the Health of Young Canadians.* Ottawa, Ontario, Canada: Author.

Ensign, J., & Bell, M. (2004). Illness Experiences of Homeless Youth. *Qualitative Health Research, 14,* 1239–1254.

Ensign, J., & Gittelsohn, J. (1998). Health and Access to Care: Perspectives of Homeless Youth in Baltimore City, U.S.A. *Social Science and Medicine, 47,* 12, 2087–2099.

Government of British Columbia. (2005). *Sexual Exploitation of Youth in British Columbia.* Victoria, BC: Assistant Deputy Minister's Committee on Prostitution and the Sexual Exploitation of Youth.

Government of Canada. (1985). *Criminal Code of Canada*. R. S. 1985, c. C-46, 213.1.

Green, S. T., & Goldberg, D. J. (1993). Female Street Worker-prostitutes in Glasgow: A Descriptive Study of Their Lifestyle. *AIDS Care 5*, 321–335.

Hagan, J., & McCarthy, B. (1997). *Mean Streets: Youth Crime and Homelessness*. London: Cambridge University Press.

Heckathorn, D. (1997). Respondent-Driven Sampling: A New Approach to the Study of Hidden Populations. *Social Problems, 44*, 174–199.

Jansson, M., & Benoit, C. (2006). Respect or Protect? Conducting Community-Academic Research with Street-Involved Youth. In B. Leadbeater, E. Banister, C. Benoit, M. Jansson, A. Marshall, & T. Riecken (Eds.), *Ethical Issues in Community-Based Research with Children, and Youth*. Toronto, Ontario, Canada: University of Toronto Press.

Jansson, M., Benoit, C., Hackler, J., & McCarthy, B. (2004). *Outcome Evaluation: Interim Report 2002*. Report prepared for the National Crime Prevention Centre, Justice Canada.

Kraus, D., Eberle, M., & Serge, L. (2001). *Environmental Scan on Youth Homelessness: Final Report*. Ottawa: Canada Mortgage and Housing Corporation.

Leadbeater, B. J., Banister, E., Benoit, C., Jansson, M., Marshall, A., & Riecken, T. (2006). *Ethical Issues in Community-Based Research with Children and Youth*. Toronto, Ontario, Canada: University of Toronto Press.

Link, B., & Phelan, J. (1995). Social Conditions as Fundamental Causes of Disease [Special issue]. *Journal of Health and Social Behavior*, 80–94.

Marmot, M., & Wilkinson, R. (1999). (Eds.). *Social Determinants of Health*. Oxford, England: Oxford University Press.

McCreary Centre Society. (2001). *No Place to Call Home: A Profile of Street Youth in British Columbia*. Burnaby, British Columbia: McCreary Centre Society.

McCreary Centre Society. (2002). *Between the Cracks: Homeless Youth in Vancouver*. Burnaby, British Columbia: McCreary Centre Society.

Phelan, J., Link, B., Moore, R., & Stueve, A. (1997). The Stigma of Homelessness: The Impact of the Label "Homeless" on Attitudes Toward Poor Persons. *Social Psychology Quarterly, 60*, 323–337.

Silbert, A., & Pines, M. (1982). Entrance Into Prostitution. *Youth and Society, 13*, 471–500.

Smart, R. ., Adlaf, E., Walsh, G., & Zdanowicz, Y. (1992). *Drifting and Doing: Changes in Drug Use Among Toronto Street Youth, 1990–1992*. Toronto: Addiction Research Foundation.

Vanwesenbeeck, I. (1994). *Prostitutes' Well-Being and Risk*. Amsterdam: VU Uitgeverij.

Williams, G. (2003). The Determinants of Health: Structure, Context and Agency. *Sociology of Health & Illness, 25*, 131–154.

Businesswomen in Urban Life

Carl S. Taylor, Pamela R. Smith, and Virgil A. Taylor

Establishing Relationships

The Urban Female Exploration Project that frames this ethnographic project set the stage for the establishment of effective, reliable, and honest communication between the researchers, the young women who participated, and other citizens and denizens of the community.

As in the ethnography of cultural anthropologist Margaret Mead, the principal investigator learned a great deal in this participant-observant project. The project is not the result of an impulse initiative or a sudden 5-year study that just arose; Taylor has strong ties to this community going back to the 1960's. Conversations, sharing of information, informal discussions, sharing of family issues, and assisting community members with problems all led to a determination that research and study of the ecological and cultural phenomena associated with this community were imperative. The trust that Taylor assumed not only as a scholar but also as a native son of this community required dedication to helping his old community and to seeing to it that this trust was also transferred to younger families and friends.

Two earlier projects documented in *Dangerous Society* (Taylor, 1990) and conducted over more than 20 years provide this project with a foundation and legacy of trust with youth and families involved in this study: the Neighborhood Youth Project a partnership with the now defunct community-based organization Operation Soul in 1975; and the Michigan Gang Research Project in 1985. These were longitudinal studies in which researchers observed gang members and non–gang members as they went about their daily lives. Critical observations were made of interactions between gang members, rivals, and enemies, as well as between non–gang members. The data gathered during these studies demonstrated the impact of gang behavior and activity along with other social conditions that affect all members of the community (Taylor, 1990).

Through the honest and caring concern demonstrated by members of the research field teams in the Neighborhood Youth Project, in Operation Soul, and in the Michigan Gang Research Project, the teams gained the reputation as trustworthy. The research group demonstrated their allegiance and commitment to the community and to the individuals participating in the study. Although the participants understood that the researchers were conducting these studies for academic purposes, they were also convinced that the field team members were not affiliated with any police or law enforcement agency or group and that their privacy would not be breached under any circumstances.

The field interviews for this chapter involved young women who had long-term relationships with field team members. In fact, relationships between the field team and a host of community members were established over a period of several years. In many instances, relationships existed years ago between parents and other relatives of the young women who we interviewed in this study. Participants in this study and other community members are accustomed to seeing field team members in their neighborhoods on a regular basis. Carl Taylor (principal investigator of the research group) lives within the community as an observer and has maintained communications with broad groups of people within the community for more than 30 years. His involvement with individuals from the community includes daily phone conversations with residents, town hall meetings, street corner chats, barber/beauty shop discussions, home visits, and detention facility visits.

Throughout the study period these informational meetings have been conducted frequently with participants. They are held in churches, recreational centers, basketball courts, schools, restaurants, social clubs, known hangouts, and public events. Discussions focused on current happenings such as shootings, government policies that affect community members, criminal acts that impact members of the community, and resources available to community members. These meetings and interactions recognize the humanity of the citizens of the community. Unfortunately, far too often members of distressed communities like the one in this research project are viewed as "less than human." To effectively communicate with this population, it has been crucial to "humanize" it, not only from an outsider's perspective but even from the perspective of each member within the community.

Many young people in this community have negative views of "institutions" because of strained relationships between institutions and either themselves or other family members. Entrance to this community was facilitated by an in-depth relationship established with Timothy Mitchell, a young man whom Dr. Taylor met more than 20 years ago. Initially a member of a group being studied, Mitchell, at age 17, joined the research team as an interviewer. Tim, or "Smut," as he was also known, had a well-established "street rep." He had been involved in gang activity, primarily as a member of a junior sect of one of the east side area gangs. However, Tim was also widely respected in the streets despite his young age. He was very street savvy and was known as cunning and capable of doing whatever was required to complete his designated determined task.

Initially, Tim was curious about, but also leery of, Taylor and this team of research associates who were so interested in his community. He was suspicious and doubted the sincerity of Taylor and the others. Gradually, he became more and more interested in what Taylor was up to. Eventually, this once disenchanted, mistrusting young man determined that the work being done by this group not only was valuable to his community but also was something he wanted to participate in. Tim became an amazingly important player in establishing Taylor and his team as the officially accepted outsider group in the street culture and street life of this community. Tim was the official envoy of the research team in the streets. Many of the most deadly and dangerous known street characters admired Tim and encouraged his pursuit of education and dedication to understanding and improving life in the "hood." At the time of his death in 1997, Tim had helped to establish an extensive network of reliable contacts and sources of information throughout the metropolitan Detroit area. It was, in large part, his connections with citizens from every walk of life throughout the community that led to the deep level of trust of Taylor and the research team in the streets and among the urban youth in this community.

In the book *Dangerous Society,* Taylor discusses the development of youth involved in gangs. *Dangerous Society* not only proved to be critically acclaimed, but gang members, street culture, and community leaders found that there was no hidden agenda in this work . Following up with *Girls, Gangs, Women, and Drugs,* again, the researchers kept their focus exclusively on the subject . At no time (just as with *Dangerous Society*) did the researcher betray the trust of participants. Although tension is part of fieldwork, both studies added to trust of community "folk" and continue to be part of the reason that the field team is able to move about the community with positive outcomes. Dr. Taylor and the team are involved as participant observers in a continuum: daily, weekly, monthly, and annually. We have "X" groups, similar to focus groups. Our meetings take place in the late hours of the night and in the early morning hours just before daybreak. It is not uncommon for Taylor to conduct meetings in unsafe places where prudence would generally dictate seeking safer accommodations. In order to stay abreast of street life, it is necessary to prove oneself not only "down" but also unafraid of the conditions and locations where the denizens of the culture go about their daily lives. The litmus test is making those who live there understand that living and surviving in this community is respected by the focus of our work. Our work, (understanding their lives) means that we cannot simply observe. We are relating to, interacting with, and caring about this community. Reciprocally, we demonstrate our commitment and investment, and each person we interact with gains a firm understanding that our goal is to bring something positive out of what they share and teach us in this unique environment.

At times we face problems and challenges, both major and minor, in conducting this study. It is not an easy task; our relationships are dependent on our personalities, as well as those of the individuals with whom we have interacted over two-plus decades. Our access to the young girls and women in this study is directly linked to what has taken place in days and years gone by. Recognizing the importance of the past and past relationships, we also know these only allow us to get in. To continue to be effective today, we must cultivate and nurture new relationships. These must also be based on a mindfulness of the ever-changing mores, rules, regulations, and values of street life and street culture.

Protecting the Identity of Urban Female Research Subjects

The urban centers where this work is conducted are part of what we have called the Third City. Mythical to most in America, the Third City is where the underground and underworld societies form another type of municipality, government, or perhaps nation. Marginal, and in some communities close to anarchy, street culture is the context for our understanding of urban females in 2006. We are hypercognizant of protecting our subjects' identities due to the ways of life in urban street culture. The young women in these interviews are taught from early ages not to discuss "their business." This fact alone underscores how very difficult it is to talk about issues in these communities. If it was not for our long-standing relationships over the years, we simply could not and would not have had access. It was also Tim's insistence that established the strict, hard-and-fast rule that demanded the use of nicknames and pseudonyms when referring to any individuals involved in any of our studies. Actual names were never used. Taylor, who had worked for years before enlisting Tim as a member of the research team, already knew of the dangers involving the use of names, as well as the critical importance of protecting sources. Researchers must also be aware that it is in their best interest to not make specific "discoveries" because doing so could make them culpable or endanger them. Knowing when it is important to "not know" is a survival skill that is often required when researching and studying the "hood."

Nicknames are used in all written or electronic documents, field notes, formal and informal writing, recorded or electronic correspondence, and other communications of any sort. This confidentiality policy also takes into consideration that new methods of gathering and documenting information are continuously being developed; thus, it purposely includes new and emerging technologies.

The most significant evidence of the honesty, sincerity, and truthfulness of the research project has been the success of the groups' ongoing publications, including all media reports. To date, nothing reported has in any way endangered or caused problems for research team members, associates, affiliates, or study participants. Taylor has always demanded that his oath to protect the privacy and confidentiality of any person involved in the research would never be breached or compromised. All team members stress to all subjects (ensuring that they clearly understand) that their accountings should not include any information that might be too revealing if reported in general. Participants are always advised that they are prohibited from sharing information with team members that might endanger or cause the indictment of either the team member or themselves. As Taylor insists, "If it is so serious, so bad, if it is something that could get you hurt, killed or locked up, then don't tell us. . . . I don't ever want to see harm come to you, or to have you coming back later and declaring that we are the snitches." Training for all team members repeatedly underscores that there is no professional immunity for social scientists and researchers.

All research participants and team members are identified by codes utilizing the alphabet, numeric coding, or generic formulas based on systems such as months of the year. An example of this system is as follows: Pamela Smith, a coauthor of this chapter, was assigned the letters AY, followed by a three-digit number code. Other methods utilized include the use of code names that were clearly not nicknames or names except to identify subjects for internal tracking purposes. Records are maintained temporarily, kept only long enough to provide support for final reporting. No information is ever kept beyond specified periods determined by Taylor at the onset of the research project. No identifying data or information is shared with any other party, organization, agency, group, or institution. In recognition of the potentially severe and damaging consequences associated with any breach of established protocols and confidentiality and privacy assurances, this project abides by three firm rules: no lists, "real" names, or use of any identifiable markers or traits in reporting (nicknames, tattoos, marks, scars, etc).

The effectiveness of this system is based both on understanding that breaches of protocols in conducting "street culture" research can result in very serious (sometimes deadly) outcomes and on trust among the researchers, participants, and other members of the community. Achieving and maintaining this delicate balance involves developing effective, healthy relationships not only with research participants but also with other community members, including civic leaders, police officers, club owners, clergy members, teachers, neighborhood groups, merchants, and gang members.

Uniqueness: *The Growth of the Urban Ecology of Detroit*

The uniqueness of the urban Detroit ecosystem is as a community whose historical foundation has mutated to the point that the social status, education, and economic standing of many of its citizens and denizens are homogeneous. This phenomenon is readily apparent for young women of color who live there. What it means to achieve an acceptable level of "status" in the community now appears to place value on obtaining, or at least creating, a perception that one has obtained material gains rather than on personal growth, "acceptable" moral values, or contributing to the community. Unlike any time in the history of urban America, particularly

Black urban America, today many young urban women aim to acquire wealth by any means at their disposal.

In 1905 the city of Detroit had an African American population of approximately 5,000 people, primarily relocated southerners, the descendants of slaves. In 1955, Detroit's Black population was approximately 16.2%. In 2005, Detroit had one of the largest African American populations of any city in the United States. Detroit also has the dubious distinction of being the poorest big city in America, one of the most violent cities in North America, one of the cities with the highest illiteracy rates—the list goes on. The State of Michigan also has the highest unemployment rate in the United States.

These alarming statistics have not ever been lost on the research team throughout the many years of studying the Detroit ecosystem. In Taylor's findings reported in *Girls, Gangs, Women, and Drugs* (1993), a very high concentration of single-headed families were led by females, and 80% of them live below the poverty level (p. 192). The plight of African American females suggests that this group might be predestined for ultimate failure. This is particularly troubling when one considers that the cornerstone for child development is typically the mother. A quotation from an unknown source further illuminates this dark and worrisome idea: "As go women in society, so goes society." Rev. Floyd David Smith, an adviser to the Michigan Gang Research Project, spoke of the odds against the young people (particularly women) in Detroit:

> It is a wonder that any of these children know anything positive when they are exposed daily to the very bottom of the barrel conditions. The question is not whether they are living but rather, aren't they, in all actuality, merely surviving? It does not seem that anyone recognizes the fact that girls, little girls, young and developing females, young women who are mothers, all females in these neighborhoods must fight daily just to try to make it through an amazing array of barriers and challenges . . . not to be successful, but rather just to be safe . . . to survive another day. . . . we are talking about such simple tasks as walking to the neighborhood store.

Years ago, middle-class and working-class families lived together. Oftentimes families lived in crowded residences so they could pool their resources to ensure that the children of the family would have a better future. Today more and more families are living together in crowded, cramped conditions but without the hope of promise for their children.

Today many poor, disenfranchised, disaffected, impoverished, and illiterate families are merely surviving, struggling in their neighborhoods, living within the Third City. Many young girls in the Third City have witnessed their mothers being abused, and many have suffered abuse themselves. Many routinely suffer domestic abuse, sexual abuse, mental abuse, and abuse of every kind.

In many homes within the Third City there is no father. The reasons for this are many and complex, and while there are those who would point to this single social issue as the cause of the "plight of the black community," absent fathers are but one of many social woes suffered by this community. This is not a race issue but more an issue of class within America today. The social ills that are the outcropping of extreme poverty, violence, and limited educational opportunities all contribute to an environment that is ripe for a young person to make very poor choices, choices that are far too readily available.

For many young people, both male and female, growing up in the urban community, there is little debate about which routes to take in order to survive. The street offers everything the young, adventurous, and developing mind believes it requires. For the young female the street lures her developing body, reinforcing the idea that by using her femininity and sexuality she can have everything she wants: appreciation, adoration, material gain, acceptance—it is all there for the taking if she just gives herself up to the streets. Today, the street is calling like never before. When all else fails, the institution of the streets—its craftiness, luring, and promising—tells the young girl to become a businessperson. Sell dope, sell your body, sell another person for money; become a pimp, a gangster, a thug; on the streets you can be what you want to be, even if just for a very short time.

The uniqueness of the Third City perhaps lies in how it has replaced the society that would not or could not let its denizens in. There are no citizens of the Third City because it is a culture devoid of members who want or need to ensure its survival. The Third City is not a community "of the people, by the people and for the people"; it is a community of "them that got to get their own," as the saying goes in the "hood." The Third City is a place where its denizens have created their own ecosystem, their own world. The very society that shunned and condemned them now chooses to ignore them, except when it is profitable: hip-hop, Black Entertainment Television, Music Television, *American Idol*–style "instant fame," rich thug celebrities, all mixed with street icons, little or no law, and pseudo-anarchy. Street culture rules Madison Avenue and Wall Street. Big business supports it because it sells. In the words of a hip-hop rhyme, "From the top to the bottom, from the bottom to the top!"

Sample

In the research we report on here, the interviewees were selected to illustrate the life studies of urban African American young women. Each one gives voice to a paradigm of African American female culture that needs to be explored in depth, in response to questions such as: How is she responding to the urban environment? How is she living? And how is she surviving? Studies framed in conventional ways often do not gather the whole picture; hence, we present their voices without interruption or theorizing.

The women in these interviews vary in their paths to success. Some are taking the road of street life; others are trying out the so-called legal path of obtaining an education, going on job interviews, or participating in training programs—the conventional roads to attempt to achieve the American Dream. Some are balancing the Third City "street culture" methodologies and practices with entrepreneurship in the "legit" world. For all of them, it is about resiliency, hard work, networking, and the indelible will to survive despite the odds.

Despite the negative die cast for them from the day of their birth, one unique factor that is proven time and again in this and other research studies is that many of these young women are determined to be successful and lead productive lives. Many times the challenge is to overcome all the odds in order to prove to themselves that it is possible to be successful without selling your soul. The young women in Detroit, like young people everywhere, want and need the same things as anyone else. Given the opportunity and the tools, they consistently show folks that it can happen.

Females, Gangsters, Thugs, and Pimps

The following interviews took place over the past 5 years in Detroit, Michigan. Five young women who are involved in street culture share their views on street life. Their ages range from 16 to 24 years old. Neither their real names nor their street nicknames are used, to shield them from problems that could arise from their participation. Included in the appendix to this chapter is a list of definitions to aid in understanding any unfamiliar terms.

Indigo Youngblood, 25 years old, mother of three, unmarried, former gang leader, one year of community college, just laid off from clerical job in a city agency, talks about her experiences in gang, street life, and motherhood. We asked her, "What is your take on females in gangs? Are there girl gangs in Detroit?"

Man, we talked about this before, yes, there are females in street life, that means gangsters, thugs, hoes, pimps, you got street life! Like I explained to Doc, those books wit your research peops saying lots of silly shit. I read some of that craziness, some bitch saying girls is this and that. Tell me something, how somebody that ain't never been here in the D, saying anything bout this? This is Detroit, they don't know us, they don't know shit, well, they talking to somebody, maybe its Five-o. . . . big nigga knows us, we got love for Doc, when it is bad, him and Timbo was there. I can't believe some that book shit people saying about fe-males, gangs? Wacked, lies, telling shit somebody is lying, why this, why why why? So, all them hating little fake bitches need to butt out! Lots of fake ass re-search-ers, nosey haters. How you gonna trust somebody saying shit comparing us to anythang, never met us, never talked? You don't know me? So for the last time Detroit got hard core gangsters that is females. Ain't bout one gang, we got 'em, but lots of fe-males got their own crew, lots of girls is hard, lots of gangsters, some lesbian pimping bitches, whatever fellas got, we got. Some fool saying that girls ain't in the mix? Or what about this shit, we ain't like fellas? Cuz they say we ain't around don't make it so. How you gonna say shit? They don't know us. . . . I'm always telling Doc, people, lots of white folks, some of them bougie blacks they don't want to be wit us, they hating, shit, it's all about us against them.

This interview takes place in a downtown hotel where all five females are having lunch with the interview team of one male and one female interviewer. The discussion at times becomes loud and profane. Trying to stay the course, Taylor has asked the young women to not speak loudly in a public place; this request is met with joking and rejection of the request. As Indigo responds:

What, speak quiet? Aight, listen if these people want it quiet better go home. . . . y'all want to hit about females in street life, gangs and shit? Well, it's loud sometimes, we ain't no bougie niggas, we street, I'm not some soft bitch, I will say it like I want when I want . . . what else you want? Remember, I went

to school, Doc got me and Shemeka in that college. . . . I went for one whole
year, got a certificate, that is how I got that job . . . Doc always talking about
getting an education. Aight, for what? Even when you got that so-called
bullshit job, they treat you bad. Looking at you wit their noses turned up
like we smell, paying you bullshit? So, you got yo education? No reason to
act like you all that . . . educated people wit degrees act like we stupid,
dumb, got no clue? If you try to be straight, you know like all them college
kids, get a degree, people think you soft.

Anyway, everybody always saying fucked up shit about the hood, or D,
talking bout we ain't got nothing . . . guess what college girls is the biggest
hoes! Anyway, street got bank shit, slinging dope pays, hootchie hoes get
paid. Monay, bank, college don't git no real monay jobs, nope, so I got laid-
off. That job was ok, but the black bitch my boss, hated that ho. Unemployment checks ain't shit . . . a girl needs some bank. Don't start that welfare
shit, I don't want no welfare, when we was young, well, my moms was
always gone, she loved the street life too . . . anyway me and my brothers
hated welfare cheese. I know how to hustle, I'm a hustler, gonna do whatever is making it happen, I'm a gangster, a hustler . . . I got kids, so fuck the
gang shit, bunch of niggas fighting over some little stupid shit like stealing
rims, selling trees, I can git more dun on my own, ok?

So gang life is not good for females?

Nobody cares about me, nobody cares about them, nobody gives a shit
about my kids. Gang life, what is gang life? (Laughing) Lookee, gangs is
gangs, I'm out here cuz I know how to make it happen. What you call gang
life is life. . . . This crew is good, but I'm older, need my own thang, if I need
these here bitches they is on . . . gangs, some good, some not, some girls run
with fellas, I done did it all. Best to do your thang, I like to make monay, it's
like that! Somebody always trying to git us to talk about the life. Guess
what? Talking bout yo business means you really not bout business. Why
would you tell anybody bout yo business or yo life? Lookee, girls can handle
business. . . . if you talking, folks think you ratting or working wit the law.

What can you say about your hustling?

Hustling is a job, street let you make monay if you know how . . . it's
rougher today, bet, lots of so-called goody girls, well like I dun said, you

might be surprised who is doing dope, selling their ass, and better, lots of goody people is smoking up some trees. I know lots of the same people who say I ain't shit is the same ones buying clothes, stolen clothes, televisions, trying to get me or the girls to help them shake a fake nigga. Hustling is what I do, hustling shows you who is on, hustling is the only way a black person is really going to make it today. Lookee here, ain't no good jobs, they want you to serve hamburgers, clean their houses, wash their cars, whatever is the worst job, cleaning shit is what all the Mexicano and niggas do, alght! (Pausing, while lighting a cigarette) White people think we, you know, us, the black people is the only people who are criminals . . . now that is just fucked up.

Are gangs, female gangs, different than male gangs? Are they organized?

Female gangs are different from males cuz females ain't showing off like fellas. My uncles and brothers are gangsters, some of them belong to gangs that got their shit on. . . . some guys get paid, they is real live gangsters, hardcore, niggahs be making it work . . . old school players. A few girls got their shit tight, running business like a true G . . . women know how to make things go smooth. Some guys think they running business, but it's some female behind the whole thang. Now, in Detroit, girls be working independent, self-governing, you know self-rule.

That is my thang, I'm a manager, working wit my old crew, best friends is in the Gucci Girls. Lots of times we work with our family, y'all call them a gang, whatever. . . . My younger brothers and sisters work together, my brothers is a stick-up crew. Younger sisters is this crew, they be having positions. Like my girl that just died, she was the contact for getting that dope sold to all the white boys over in Southfield, Warren, and up in Pontiac, Flint. So we work wit lots of different people, hustling means working wit different people that you can trust. Trust is hard in the streets, narcs is all over. Snitching is bad, a nigga will sell your ass out wit a quickness . . . don't go pass them niggas, my family, a few friends. When we started kicking it wit some other females some 'em be down wit the hook. Snitching is really messed up, another reason we trust Doc, you know lots of people is working for the po-lice. So you got to know your crew, best know who you dealing wit. The bottom line is this, females is gangsters, some in gangs, some in little almost gangs. Wo-men be gitting paid, females is thugs, females is in crews, fe-males are in charge of crews. Yes, some females is in big crews as part, members, others is groupies. Me? I'm an independent, a gangster, yea, I'm a mother (laughing), but I will do criminal thangs if I have to. Got no real job, ain't working no legitimate job, well, the street is always calling.

Urban Businesswomen

The following interviews are with three young women who are from the same neighborhood. Two of the women are cousins raised in the same household by their grandmother. Their names have been changed, as is the standard for all interviews. The subject is business, whether it relates to illicit narcotics commerce or legitimate commerce. These interviews were conducted over an period of 5 years. All interviews related to this segment are part of the ongoing Urban Female Exploration Project (UFEP) which was started in the fall of 1989 in Detroit, Michigan.

We have heard the word *business* over and over by many females in their descriptions of living in urban America. Some have claimed that they are businesswomen. Others have explained that selling illicit narcotics, prostitution, gambling is "business." The undercurrent is that for some there is no difference between illegal, criminal activities and legitimate business.

Micki, 23, described her work, giving insight into a view not heard often by the public. She explained her career goals, current job, and, most important, an insight into the diversity among urban females.

I'm a promoter, nothing illegal about my work. I promote parties, concerts, any event you want, I'm down. Hey, I don't do no freak parties, I mean real serious straight business, some males want to do freak shit, you know, butt naked sex parties, got no time for nasty ho business, still street. . . . I love to promote new rappers, working with their music, selling their CDs, helping bust out a new act. I worked with some dog ass fellas, don't get me wrong, lots of bitches is dogs, so I done seen it all. I learned this promoter shit from doing all the dog jobs, low paying ass, dog kinda business in record promotions, or helping sell some malt liquors, hardcore selling, but it is legal. Business, for me it's legitimate, straight up, legal. I know the other side, selling dope, being a thug, a gangster is not for this girl. That hard street gangsta life is too much. Promoting little parties, concerts, pushing CDs, selling clothes, I do it the old school way. See, it's hard work, it's straight, this is what I want to do . . . and I'm good at it. Street business ain't jest dope, almost everybody is trying to sell that shit, some fe-males think that is all there is in life, dope. Everything wit lots of girls is about getting paid, hooking up wit a baller. That is all you see, everybody is always chasing the ballers. Indigo is my cousin, she is built hard, I'm hard, street make you hard, we know about hustling. Hustling is what you got to do, that is all you can do . . . school didn't really mean that much, you had to understand that school is about getting ahead, Indigo, don't see no difference, mo? If it's about dope, selling ass, messing wit stolen shit, count me out. Too much John Law, business for me is doing it the old fashion way, legal. Well, nothing wrong wit having discounted shit (laughing) see something might be kind of illegal, but I'm talking bout not getting caught up wit that serious shit, anything wit gangstas smoking, beating down, all that serious regulating . . . count me out.

Lucy, 27, owns a beauty salon; she also is buying her home. Like Micki, Lucy considers herself a businesswoman, one who is not involved in any illegal commerce:

I get tired of everybody thinking we're all hoes, hootchies, or just plain ass gangsters. I pay taxes, been working all my life, hustling? Whatever, I know what is out here, yeah, I saved my money and got this here little shop. I'm raising my boy, he is a little cutie, I got him in a private school. His father is dead, so it's me, if a girl want to make it, she got to be strong, smart. Indigo knows, she out here, now I'm glad she is trying to do something else. Lots of girls working hard, but working the wrong way. Business? Street business means somebody is watching you. . . . niggahs is edging up on you all the time in the streets. Me? Got to do it straight up, I like dis here girl, Micki, it's hard out here, but if you in that shit, well, err, it's sure to be some killing. Not hearing that violent thing, no way. Business got to be legitimate, I'm going to Wayne County Community College, doing business, my one teacher is helping me a whole bunch.

See, street females know how to do things, shooting or killing somebody ain't the kind of skills I need . . . learning how to do a real business plan, ok? My mother was real young when she had me. I was raised by my grandparents, moms was still trying to figure it out, so my grandparents took me and my brother into their house. My grandmother is smart, she is a church woman, I know a lot of good things cuz of her. She and my grandfather were messed up when I got pregnant, see my grandfather was helping me with school. I made them a promise that I wouldn't do like my mother, get pregnant before finishing school, and get married first. Shit didn't work that way, my folks did not want me to associate with fellas like Melvin. I can't lie, he had bank, he was balling, I liked him cuz he was different from the gangsters on my block. He had style, quiet, we jest got along, he was really into me. He was changing, but like it goes, the street ain't seeing that.

It seems that you are on the successful path, how did you make it to this point?

With a little help from my family, everybody says shit about my man, but I learned to save money from my grandparents. I say one thing that matters, for me it was family and friends. My family, grandparents have always been there, even when I hooked up wit bad ass Melvin. Melvin, was my man, best friend, street businessman, but he helped me. Anyway, when I say help, that means more than money, in business you need advice. I got family, friends, and my teacher at school, that is what made me strong. Hey, Indigo has been my girl, her street sense is strong, so I can't front, she has always been my girl. It does matter, when she was out there real strong, super gangster, I wasn't feeling her, too dangerous. It wasn't that I was better than Indigo, use to see her with all the new styles, stupid rides, she was that girl. But, my grandmother hated the way Indigo momma let her run around wit her gangster family members. In a funny way, my grandparents gave us things so that we won't get caught up in that gangster life. Soon as I graduated I got a job, part-time at the mall, then I worked at the cleaners until they got beat down and sold their business. When some friends of my brothers said they could hook me up selling dope, that just wasn't hanging in our house. Plus, by that time, my moms had came on the scene, all into church, all into God. So, that meant more eyes watching me, hey, I smoked some, party some. Indigo, we use to see her out there in her new Vette, I wanted things like she had, but it had to wait. I did finish high school before having a baby, and Mel was going to marry me. Fellas like him, well, lots of street fellas believe in that shit, you know? M-O-B (money over bitches). So, first, I had to let him know, ain't no bitch here! He was into me, I was into him, lots of people say I liked him cuz of his money. Aight, he gave me money, but I was always like my grandmother said, "have your own, depend on yourself . . ."

I be lying if I didn't say he was real good to me, and when little Mel came along, well, he put up money real fast, hate he's gone. But, that what street life does, it kills.

At age 24, Indigo completed a training program for clerical skills; she graduated and took a job with the City of Detroit. She previously has had numerous contacts with both the juvenile and adult correctional systems. Part of her entering the training program was based on her probation. Responding to the same question about business, she is somewhat agitated by the question itself:

Business is business, everything is bullshit, it's all illegal if you let the book tell it. A-rabs sell cigarettes one at a time to poor ass niggahs in my hood, is that legal? Yeah, probably, even though they doing some wrong shit, but if you black, poor it's all about Po-Po put you in prison. I was a business fe-male, got me in big trouble, selling that dope is not legal so they say. . . . how come? If we suppose to be free in America, how come I can't sell dope? Dope is just another business, lots of fellas out there, they is businessmen. It's not fair, some shit is legal, and you know them crooked ass politicians is taking money for helping those al-coholic liquor stores that all them A-rabs own. Anyway, we have gambling parties, muthafuckas raid after hour joints, say they illegal, aight? Then they have lottery, seems like to me, it's only legal if you already got money, if you selling something that the white man says is legal it's ok, but when young bucks selling dope, guns, pussy it's illegal? They sell that yack, dope kills they say, well, so do lots of things, but is say-ing shit, hell, my old granddaddy died from drinking whiskey too much . . . nobody is arresting the whiskey makers? Hell, cigarettes, cigars all that shit is killing muthafuckas . . . eating all that fat food is killing lots of big fat greedy muthafuckas, shit ice cream is killing Fat Shemeka! (LAUGHING LOUDLY)

Well, you have a new job, working for the city, is this your first real legal job?

Naw, this is not the first legal job, I done worked before, it just means that street life pays right away, everyday, and no taxes. . . . I'm not like Micki, she wants to be some big Willie, she sees herself being a big time promoter. Me? The thing that made me try this besides the old ugly ass bitch judge, is my little girl. Street means shooting, gangster life is hard, never know when somebody is going to take your ass out. Don't want that for my little girl. I grew up in a gangster family, my moms was always on dope, so she didn't know what we were doing most times. I'm going to change, look at my girl Ms. Lucy with her salon, she is doing it . . . that is just the way the world is

... most of us fe-males in the streets. Street life is hard, gangsters don't want no job like the shit I'm doing, make more money in the streets, gangsters is about money. . . . They got gangsters in the government, they killing A-rabs for that oil, shit, lots of thugs work for the government. Business? All business is about that money, everybody wants bank money, business legal or illegal? What is business? Business means to me, one thing, business is about getting paid. Lucy got her hook-up, Micki is doing her thang, me, I'm a gangster on family leave, aight? I'm trying the legal way, but we all know, the best way is to take what you want. Ganking is the best way to get paid, if you want it, take it!

Conclusion

Traditional theories and perceptions are not enough to examine the total experience of the African American female living in urban America. The multiplicity of diversity warrants research to explore all avenues of the rich, multifaceted life experience of African American females. These women's lives are complex, not monolithic, and cannot be entirely understood through a single-lens viewpoint. There are several intertwining and interrelating systems of oppression, such as class, race, gender, and sexuality that should be examined intersectionally when documenting their position in society.

This is not our fathers' Oldsmobile. We must be able to translate, respect, and understand hip-hop, linking that understanding to street life and old-school Detroit, be-bop, Motown, the Nation of Islam, the Black church, the factory, the unions, Mayor Coleman A. Young, Councilwoman Erma Henderson, Mayor Kwame Kilpatrick, Congressman John Conyers, Congresswoman Carolyn Cheeks-Kilpatrick, and others. Our balance of Detroit is reflected in the historical accounting that sometimes is seen and viewed very differently from the perspectives of ethnic groups. There are many stories in this city; our focus in this particular study has been exclusively on African American females in one specific community.

It must be noted that there could and would be no studies of this kind without trust. All the work that we have conducted in Detroit is viewed as vital by the research teams and the community members that have chosen to participate in it. This study is based on a shared trust between the researchers and all the members of the community, whether they are part of the greater culture or what some might call the subculture—commonly known as street life.

The essence of how these young women live their lives touches upon their resilience. It is not necessarily considered by some of these young women as resilience; for some it is a matter of surviving in a tough environment. In this community there is an interaction of the working class, street culture, and youth. Isolation from mainstream support is more acute, since government has moved toward a policy of welfare reform. More than three quarters of this community is living in poverty. The state level of change in welfare not only has taken thousands off welfare programs but has replaced them with questionable alternatives. The message perceived by many families is that the state does not care about them.

Indigo talks about how she is willing to try the legal path. Yet, when the going gets tough, these women do not have the luxury of waiting for a new job policy in urban America. Indigo is in agreement with her cohorts that no one really cares what happens to Detroit. That perception may not be accurate to policy makers. Yet the state of the economy in Michigan cannot ignore the immediacy of a growing poverty. Jobs are scarce, and the thoughts of young women like Indigo are that it is up to them to make things work. Jobs are few, so it is not surprising to see how she interprets the necessity to make her own way. Yet some, like Micki, show how other young females see themselves working toward a more legitimate path. Micki—working a more friendly approach—is not willing to engage in what she thinks are dangerous working conditions. Her voice tells us that she does not agree with her friend Indigo about taking the same path to success. It is important to understand the challenges these young women face. But it would be an error to think that "one size fits all." Micki and the successful salon owner, Lucy, tell us that their views of life are very similar to the old work ethnic of traditional Black America.

Lucy's views of working have been influenced by what has diminished greatly in this community, a strong working class, including a class of teachers, lawyers, doctors, and other professionals. Lucy has knowledge, firsthand learning, and training from some older Black Americans, her grandparents. Topics such as legitimate work, savings accounts, and education have not been exclusively taught by Black professionals, Lucy's grandparents represent an education and guidance by working middle-class folk. Yet Indigo's plight is influenced by impressions of street-side society. Lucy lived under a strong guidance that seems to have left a lasting impression, lessons of living respectfully on a stable foundation. Some of these young women are considering the mixture of old-school tradition and street-side living of the Third City. The idea of living like an everyday traditional citizen is appealing to Indigo. She is ready for change, but is change really ready for her? When readers look at Indigo, they may see her willingness as an admission to a legitimate lifestyle. Yet her willingness is based on her survival; as she puts it, "I'm a gangster on family leave." What does that mean? It means that although she is becoming legitimate, her social and economic needs dictate her choices. Policy makers would do well to understand the common thread between these three women. The common factor is the desire to have an opportunity to succeed in life. Like Merton's (1938) theory of anomic society, Indigo represents those who want the America Dream but lack the resources to obtain it legally. While Micki and Lucy have found a safe passage, Indigo has created an alternative where she believes she is capable of both.

Resilience does not enter into what musical icon Stevie Wonder called "Living for the City." Here living life is not resilience; it is simply living and dying in the Third City.

Appendix

After-hours joints: Any place of business that is not open to the public during late night or early morning hours and is operating illegally, and is selling narcotics, alcohol, or sex to a select clientele. Some joints have gambling, sporting events such as boxing, or even car racing. Most after-hours places are like bars, sometimes called "blind pigs." Originally in the Black community a concept from the Deep South, these places are called "juke joints."

Aight: Slang for right, replacing the letter *r* with the letter *a* and pronounced as "ai-ght."

Baller: One who is involved in the street economy, living in the underworld, underground both socially and economically (which we call the Third City); can also mean a professional athlete within the urban culture, meaning football, basketball, or baseball, someone who has a generous income from either legal or illegal means. A baller is a compliment in street culture, even if someone like the president of the United States is called a baller. The terms means you are regarded as being "cool," a bit rogue. Drug dealers are big ballers, as is anyone in the street who is representing him- or herself as making money by hustling successfully.

Bank: Means money, not the traditional legal bank but anyone who has money or who stores or keeps large amounts of money. For example, "She got bank, she is rolling," means she has money and is doing well from something illegal perhaps.

Big Willie: Street term for anyone who is regarded as powerful, well-respected, or important.

Bougie: A declaration that a person is elitist, from the bourgeois class and an enemy to street folks. The general feeling is that Bougie folks put down everyday street folks as inferior.

Business: In this term it means all business is cool, good, this means illegal or legal. In the Third City illicit commerce is considered business, period. There is no such thing as illegal business within the thug-gangster frontier. Business is business, business can mean, and many times does mean, illicit activities, yet many in the Third City do not consider what they are doing as being wrong or illegal.

Crew: A group of men or women who are connected by either business or friendship. Sometimes labeled "gang," a crew is quite common in the urban landscape across the gender, class, and race identifications of youth and street culture.

Dope: Means something is good, for example, "he has a dope ride," meaning he has an attractive car; traditionally meaning narcotics of illegal source or means.

Freak: Anyone who is considered an extremist; applied to sexual, criminal, or violent behavior. For example, "He is a freak for beating women down."

Gucci Girls: A small, all-female gang on the east side of Detroit.

Ho: A loose woman, a whore; a ho in street language is a prostitute of low standard. Definitely a negative term; men also can be call hoes or ho's, but the term is used mainly to describe females.

Hood: The neighborhood in which one lives; it is the word for the symbolic meaning of homeland for inner-city life.

Hook: The police or anyone who is a member of the law enforcement community.

Hootchie: A derogatory term applied to a girl or woman, meaning that she is promiscuous, cheap, whorish.

Hustling: Means working in the streets doing various jobs that are not legal or sanctioned by the larger society. A good example of hustling is in the classic autobiography of Malcolm X in which he was a numbers runner (illegal gambling, like a bookie taking bets) and pimp. Hustling jobs vary from stealing clothes, called boosting, selling dope, which can be marijuana, cocaine, or crack, to selling sex for oneself or being the middle man, aka pimp.

In the mix: Means life as it relates to hustling, balling, and illegal commerce.

M-O-B: Taken from a popular rap tune, this misogynistic term means Money Over Bitches.

Narcs: Law enforcers, police who are working the narcotic units; can also mean anyone who is not police but who is assisting or informing on any illegal commerce to the authorities.

Nigga, niggah: In the street this word is common, not to be confused with the word *nigger.* It means anyone who is cool, like a respected comrade, a close associate, a title assigned not because of race exclusively. It is like a term of endearment, not a racial slur like the *nigger.*

Po-po: A general term for the police or any police agency; it is taken from either the Caribbean or South African slang for police.

Ratting: Sometimes called snitching; informing authorities of anything regarding urban life by someone in the know from within the urban setting to someone or somebody outside, mainly authority figures, officials, or law enforcement types.

Slinging: Used for the selling of dope, it means someone is distributing or selling something illegal. Sometimes it is referred to as "flipping." Thus, someone could be "slinging" or "flipping" stolen goods, selling illegal drugs.

Snitching: The act of talking, informing, or giving of information against someone who has been accused of a crime. The informer, who many times is from the area, neighborhood, or community where the crime has taken place, is considered a traitor, betraying those from their particular criminal group. Many times innocent folks do not speak up for fear of being sought out by the criminals. Snitching is considered a very serious violation within street culture.

Thug: Anyone who considers him- or herself an underdog or denizen in the underground-underworld societies of America. The origin of this word is from India, where it refers to a religious devotee who belongs to a secretive cult that practices a deadly art of strangulation against anyone deemed an enemy. Hip-hop icon Tupac Shakur, in the documentary *Tupac Resurrection,* declared that thug life was a lifestyle; being a thug was about being not a criminal but an underdog. This term is at the center of controversy within American culture.

Third City: The underground and underworld societies that form another type of municipality, government, or perhaps nation.

Trees: Means marijuana or smoking dope.

REFERENCES

Baulch, V. (2005). *Paradise Valley and Black Bottom.* Chapel Hill: University of North Carolina Press.

Merton, R. (1938). Social structure and anomie. *American Sociological Review, 3,* 672–682.

Taylor, C. S. (1990). *Dangerous society.* East Lansing: Michigan State University Press.

Taylor, C. S. (1993). *Girls, gangs, women, and drugs.* East Lansing: Michigan State University Press.

U.S. Census Bureau (1990). *Table 23. Michigan—race and Hispanic origin for selected large cities and other places: Earliest census to 1990.* Retrieved February 12, 2006, from http://www.census.gov/population/documentation/twps0076/MItab.xls

About the Contributors

Amy Alberts, M.A., Institute for Applied Research in Youth Development, Eliot-Pearson Department of Child Development, Tufts University, Medford, MA.

Natasha Alexander, Urban Academy High School, New York, NY.

Murray Anderson, M.A., Department of Sociology, University of Victoria, Victoria, British Columbia, Canada.

Elizabeth Banister, Ph.D., School of Nursing, University of Victoria, Victoria, British Columbia, Canada.

Cecilia Benoit, Ph.D., Department of Sociology, University of Victoria, Victoria, British Columbia, Canada.

Kristen Boelcke-Stennes, M.A., Institute of Child Development, University of Minnesota, Minneapolis, MN.

Ana Mari Cauce, Ph.D., Department of Psychology, University of Washington, Seattle, WA.

Elise D. Christiansen, Department of Counseling, Developmental, and Educational Psychology, Boston College, Chestnut Hill, MA.

Brianna Coffino, Institute of Child Development, University of Minnesota, Minneapolis, MN.

Catherine L. Costigan, Ph.D., Department of Psychology, University of Victoria, Victoria, British Columbia, Canada.

KARIN COYLE, Ph.D., Director of Research, ETR Associates, Scotts Valley, CA.

ANITA A. DAVIS, Ph.D., Department of Psychology, Rhodes College, Memphis, TN.

JILL DENNER, Ph.D., Department of Developmental Psychology, Teachers' College, Columbia University, New York, NY.

SUMRU ERKUT, Ph.D., Wellesley Centers for Women, Wellesley, MA.

KENYATTA ETCHISON, Social Development Research Group, University of Washington, Seattle, WA.

MICHELLE FINE, Ph.D., Department of Social/Personality Psychology, Graduate Center of the City University of New York, New York, NY.

YULIKA FORMAN, Ph.D., LMHC Institute for Applied Research in Youth Development, Eliot-Pearson Department of Child Development, Tufts University, Medford, MA.

EMILY GENAO, Fordham University, New York, NY.

MIKAEL JANSSON, Ph.D., Department of Sociology, University of Victoria, Victoria, British Columbia, Canada.

BONNIE J. LEADBEATER, Ph.D., Department of Psychology, University of Victoria, British Columbia, Canada.

CHALANE E. LECHUGA, M.S., Department of Sociology, University of New Mexico, Albuquerque, NM.

STACEY J. LEE, Ph.D., Educational Policy Studies, University of Wisconsin, Madison, WI.

RICHARD M. LERNER, Ph.D., Institute for Applied Research in Youth Development, Eliot-Pearson Department of Child Development, Tufts University, Medford, MA.

Nancy López, Ph.D., Department of Sociology, University of New Mexico, Albuquerque, NM.

Ann S. Masten, Ph.D. Institute of Child Development, University of Minnesota, Minneapolis, MN.

Jennifer McCormick, Ph.D., Graduate School of Education and Information Studies, University of California, Los Angeles, CA.

Jennifer Pastor, Ph.D., Department of Social and Personality Psychology, the Graduate Center of the City University of New York, New York, NY.

Erin Phelps, Ed.D., Institute for Applied Research in Youth Development, Eliot-Pearson Department of Child Development, Tufts University, Medford, MA.

Leslie R. Prescott, Rhodes College, Memphis, TN.

Jean E. Rhodes, Ph.D., Department of Psychology, University of Massachusetts, Boston, MA.

Ritch C. Savin-Williams, Professor and Chair, Department of Human Development, Cornell University, Ithaca, NY.

Anne Shaffer, Institute of Child Development, University of Minnesota, Minneapolis, MN.

Renée Spencer, School of Social Work, Boston University, Boston, MA.

Pamela R. Smith, MS, Department of Sociology, Michigan State University, East Lansing, MI.

Carl S. Taylor, Ph.D., Department of Sociology, Michigan State University, East Lansing, MI.

Jill McLean Taylor, Ed.D., Associate Professor, Departments of Women's Studies, and Education, Simmons College, Boston, MA.

VIRGIL A. TAYLOR, Project Manager, Michigan Gang Research Project, Detroit, MI.

MARÍA ELENA TORRE, Department of Social/Personality Psychology, Graduate Center of the City University of New York, New York, NY.

ALLISON J. TRACY, Ph.D., Wellesley Centers for Women, Wellesley, MA.

CARMEN N. VELORIA, Department of Language, Literacy and Culture, University of Massachusetts, Amherst, MA.

MARTINA C. VERBA, L.C.S.W., M.P.H., Kaiser Permanente, Redwood City, CA.

JANIE VICTORIA WARD, M.Ed., Ed.D., Africana Studies Department, Simmons College, Boston, MA.

NIOBE WAY, Ed.D., Department of Applied Psychology, School of Education, New York University, New York, NY.

Index

School-based community living rooms *(salas comunitarias)*

Interview frames, 170

Intimacy with others, basis of, 122

Inventory of Parent and Peer Attachment, 185

Issues Checklist, 183

Izumi, J., 124

Jarrett, R. L., 180

Jelicic, H., 27, 28, 29

Jemmott, J. B., 288

Jemmott, L. S., 288

Job competence, 59

Kett, Joseph, 5

Khmer girls, age at marriage, 212

Kilpatrick, Kwame, 354

King, P. E., 38, 43, 45

King, Sherry, 226

Kinsey, Alfred, 303–304

Ku, L., 266

Late adolescence, resilience during, 62

Latinas, 157–171, 281–297; acculturation, 284; affirmation of cultural values, 166; in alternative high schools, 281–297; Anglo identification with, 83; being yelled at/hit at home, 167–168, 171; condom use, 281–297; contraceptive use, 289t; Cuban American *(see* Cuban American girls); differences between ethnic groups, 165; Dominican *(see* Dominican girls); "double vision" of, 169; education, 107, 163–165; femininity, 163; graduation rates, 100–101; heterogeneity of, 282–283; high-risk sex, 271t, 272t; mentoring, 148; Mexican American *(see* Mexican American girls); mothers' experiences to, 165–167; occupational aspirations, 91, 109; pregnancy, 283; resistance by,

116; risk factors, 284; safe spaces, 97; school-based community living rooms *(salas comunitarias)*, 97; sexual activity, 284; sexuality, 82, 162–163; sexually transmitted infection (STI), 271t, 272t, 284; sports participation, 265–266, 277n4; stereotypes of, 105, 157, 162–163, 165; surveillance of, 162; unintended pregnancy, 271t, 272t

Latino families: "child-keeping," 144; extended kinship systems, 144; parental involvement in education, 107

Latino youth: condom use, 284; HIV risk, 297; occupational aspirations, 109; positive youth development (PYD) levels, 28

Leadbetter, B. J., 126

Lechuga, Chalane E., 101–102, 108, 162

Lerner, Richard M.: 4-H Study methodology, 27, 29, 31; Five Cs model, 25

Listening Guide, 161

Longitudinal studies. *See* 4-H Study of Positive Youth Development; Project Competence; Risky Business? study

López, Nancy, 101, 162, 170

Louie, V., 214

Low-income students, postsecondary education of, 159

Lykes, M. B., 78

MacQuarrie, B., 124

Maladjustment: conflict and, 189–190; risks of, 1, 4–6; self-worth and, 64–65; turnarounds, 65–66

Male violence/harassment in schools, 81–82, 90

Mansbridge, J., 246

Marboe, Elinor, 236–237

Marginalization, factors contributing to, 1

Marín, B. V., 295

Martínez, Kouri, 239–240